BREAKING RANKS IN THE MIDDLE™:

Strategies for Leading Middle Level Reform

With a foreword by
Theodore R. Sizer and
Deborah Meier

THE
EDUCATION
ALLIANCE
BROWN UNIVERSITY
PROVIDENCE, RI

NATIONAL ASSOCIATION
OF SECONDARY SCHOOL
PRINCIPALS
RESTON, VA

NATIONAL ASSOCIATION
OF SECONDARY SCHOOL
PRINCIPALS

1904 Association Drive
Reston, VA 20191-1537
www.principals.org

David Vodila, President
Joseph Militello, President-Elect
Gerald N. Tirozzi, Executive Director
Lenor G. Hersey, Deputy Executive Director
Rosa Aronson, Director of Advocacy and Strategic Alliances
Robert N. Farrace, Director of Publications
Richard Flanary, Director of Professional Development Services
John R. Nori, Director of Instructional Leadership Resources
Howard Wahlberg, Director of Marketing and Sales
James R. Rourke, Principal Author
David Fernandes, Production Manager

Editing and Design by EEI Communications
Cover design by Tanya Burke

ISBN 0-88210-366-0

Contents

Preface

In 2004, the National Association of Secondary School Principals published *Breaking Ranks II™: Strategies for Leading High School Reform*. NASSP offers this publication, *Breaking Ranks in the Middle:™ Strategies for Leading Middle Level Reform* as the missing link that will help middle level and high schools join forces and align efforts. The connections between this book and *Breaking Ranks II,* our high school field guide are obvious and purposeful. The message is clear, reforming high schools in isolation or working on middle level reform without attention to the secondary continuum will lead to future decades of chasing improvement with only pockets of accomplishment being realized.

For too long middle level schools and high schools have operated in separate spheres with minimal *institutional* effort to advance *secondary* school interests, the interests of students, and the interests of the nation. Some school leaders and some districts have attempted to look at education as a continuum, while others have been content to view the education of students as limited to the years when students grace their halls. Still fewer have focused their efforts specifically on the middle grades. As the authors of *Turning Points 2000* make clear, "If we can find the will to care about every young adolescent, in the 21st century we will move closer to realizing our cherished ideals of lasting, shared prosperity with equal opportunity for all." Middle level school leaders must accept the challenge to address all aspects of middle level education simultaneously.

To that end NASSP is proud to publish *Breaking Ranks in the Middle: Strategies for Leading Middle Level Reform*. It is designed to provide middle level principals and other school leaders with a field guide to school improvement. It purposefully avoids the question about grade configuration at the middle level and instead focuses on solid educational practices for young adolescents—no matter where they are being educated.

Breaking Ranks in the Middle is the most recent installment of NASSP's long-standing commitment to promote effective leadership in our nation's middle level schools. Much has been made in the popular press about the failures of middle grades education, yet we can point to successful middle level schools of success across the country. With the bulk of the responsibility for testing under NCLB resting at the middle grades, we have chosen to focus this guide on recommendations and strategies that principals have some degree of control over in reforming their schools. In addition we have included school profiles and vignettes that illustrate the concepts in the recommendations. Our hope is that the aligned practical strategies contained in *Breaking Ranks in the Middle* and *Breaking Ranks II* will help to join the two disparate entities of high school and middle level into one seamless track to student success.

Gerald N. Tirozzi, Ph.D.
Executive Director
NASSP

Foreword

In the "good old days," schooling rarely lasted beyond what we now refer to as the middle grades, and there are good reasons why. The onset of what we now call adolescence signaled adulthood, being out in the world, working in hard physical labor perhaps, and keeping company with the men and women these young people aspired to be. We have extended childhood, but we haven't figured out just what to do with it.

A small, specialized group of youngsters finds that the life of scholarly pursuits—solitary reading, poring over text, exploring the world of the mind in a passive manner—fits their temperaments, and they find success. But for the vast majority it's a misfit; for most, young adolescence is an age of sociability and activity, an age of exploration and risk-taking. Historically, it was the age when youngsters set to sea, joined their fathers and mothers in the mines and fields and factories, and underwent the rites of passage into adulthood. Hardly a past for which to be entirely nostalgic, but still, a past from which to learn; young people were doing meaningful work and making meaningful connections to their communities.

These days, the fatiguing and endless search for methods to motivate (through fear or reward) this age group for long enough to sit still and passively take in knowledge is well-intended but essentially counter-productive for all involved. One could put into a thimble all the stuff that sticks. The loss is enormous. We've badly used the energy, passion, adventurousness, romanticism and yearning to be grown-up that characterizes the age.

The reasons are not all malevolent, thoughtless, or unfair. In fact, much of what characterizes middle grades education grew from a desire to offer the vast masses the intellectual skills and knowledge that a favored elite alone possessed, that marked them as the rulers of the world. An attempt to achieve fairness helped lead us down a false path.

This book is about ways to stick to the vision of equality that led us to insist that youngsters stay in school until they are at least 16. It requires creating a setting much more compatible to the best the age itself has to offer us, rather than trying to stifle that vitality. If we don't stretch our aspirations for these young people in more imaginative ways, we will continue to pay the terrible price that now faces us: an age group truly being educated neither by their hard-working families nor their hard-working teachers, but by a voracious, well-funded advertising industry that forthrightly taps into their youthful energy in ways that are damaging to not only the kids themselves, but the larger society as well.

We need to use some of the same smarts as the media so well employs to recapture adolescents' energy for socially useful purposes. This book of ideas offers some critical directions, suggesting ways to create personalized education, connections and continuity from elementary school to high school, to family and community. Most of all, the strategies discussed in *Breaking Ranks in the Middle* and the schools featured here help principals create their schools as places of life, energy, engagement, and meaningful work for an age group ready to take on some of the challenges of adulthood with the spirit, passion, and energy unique to adolescents. It's a hard time, but a magical time, and middle grades education can be among the best years of schooling and growth. Here's how to make that happen.

Theodeore R. Sizer and Deborah Meier

Reflections on the Messages of
Breaking Ranks in the Middle

In this era of No Child Left Behind testing and standards, why should a school focus on relationships and connections first?

Because learning is ultimately about relationships—about making connections among people, places, resources, and ideas. If schools are to be centers of learning, they must be data-driven, student-focused places that help our young people know well their own strengths and achievement gaps, then go on to make clear connections between what they're learning in the classroom and how it links them with their own possibilities and the possibilities of the global economy. Our young people's ability to make connections will literally shape their places in the world and our country's position on the global stage.

I'd like to invite you and every middle and high school principal to take a trip with me to the elementary school down the street. Spend a day in kindergarten and first and second grade classrooms. Those classes will be bustling with activity. Students will be working together on teams to solve problems. They'll be in small groups talking about books. They'll be writing and illustrating their *own* books. They'll be using math skills to do everything from solving computer-based problems to cooking special treats to constructing intricate structures.

Ask any student what they're doing and why. If you listen carefully, they will tell you that they're learning to read and "do math" because they like to learn and it's fun. They'll tell you their teacher helps them to learn new things and to make connections between that learning. They'll hug their teacher. They'll probably hug your colleague, their principal. Urban...rural... suburban... the setting doesn't matter. The scene is more often than not the same—teachers and principals opening doors, nourishing dreams, and helping children make connections.

These connections and relationships are a significant reason our elementary students are high performers and score among the best in the world in reading and math. Unfortunately, the longer students are in our school systems, the farther down the global performance scale they slide. Why is this "slide" important? If each student is not able to reach his or her personal best, someone has failed. If large cohorts are not able to reach their best, then the failure goes beyond individuals—and the results will affect students' ability to share their ideas and talents in a global economy and the world.

Technology has "flattened" the world playing field, as Thomas L. Friedman makes clear in *The World Is Flat* (Farrar, Straus, and Giroux, 2005). We have passed through the industrial age dominated by the large companies of Western Europe and North America, through the information age, straight to the knowledge economy. Today, countries like India, China, and Romania...small businesses...and even individuals...are able to compete for global knowledge work right alongside the "big boys." Today, success is no longer dependent on your country or your company. Success in the flat, global world depends on how well you make connections among people, places, resources, and ideas across oceans and continents—and then how you use those relationships and connections to keep learning and building on what you know *today* to imagine what you could do *tomorrow*...and next year...and 10 years from now. Our young people's ability to make connections will literally shape their place on the global stage.

I asked you to take a trip with me to the elementary school down the street, because the students you have in your hallways today were recently in the kindergarten and first and second grade classes you just visited. Ask yourselves: Do the students now in your classrooms have the same excitement about learning, the same vision of education as the portal to the world that they once had? If not, how do we help those students regain the excitement and reclaim the vision?

I am heartened by what we see happening in our work in Ohio. School changes began with hope and optimism and excitement in the eyes of teachers and principals. As the adults have begun to feel more empowered to use their imaginations, students have begun to catch the spark. And it's contagious. While our efforts have been at the high school level, we see a need to keep the excitement about learning alive through the middle grades, where the sparks have sometimes been tamped out. Anyone interested in high school excellence must first be assured that there is elementary and middle level excellence.

How can elementary, middle, and high schools collaborate to accomplish this? In our work with Ohio schools, the ones that have proven successful are those that ensure that teachers emerge from their closed classrooms and work in teams to begin making connections among the knowledge and skills required in mathematics and English language arts, science and social studies. But the connections do not stop at the school door. Each school has implemented a rigorous, standards-based curriculum that reaches out into the community to help students regain the connections between the classroom and the future. Each school invites ideas and innovation from those whom the schools ultimately serve. The schools we work with are inspiring people—students, parents, business, and community—and getting them to ask "what if" questions. *They are using relationships and connections with students, parents, and community as the springboard for powerful academic achievement.*

I challenge the leaders of middle schools and high schools to take advantage of the aligned strategies and processes in *Breaking Ranks II* and *Breaking Ranks in the Middle.* Begin viewing your schools through the lens of a "flat world." Work together across the middle and high school grades. Reach out to elementary and higher education and the workplace. Build an educational experience that capitalizes on rigor *and* relevance, relationships *and* achievement to put our students—and us—in the global game.

Chad P. Wick
President and CEO
KnowledgeWorks Foundation

About the Foundation

KnowledgeWorks Foundation is Ohio's largest education philanthropy. Created in 1998, KnowledgeWorks is classified as an "operating foundation." That means we both award grants and receive funding that furthers our work. Our board and staff believe that education is the key to the success of individuals and society. We are dedicated to removing barriers to education for all individuals. To achieve that goal, we work to create partnerships that will produce measurably better educational results throughout the state. The foundation carefully focuses its limited human and financial resources on systemic initiatives in which there is a convergence of statewide attention to the problem and the will to effect real, lasting change. We believe that educational barriers can be eliminated by collaborating with those public and private entities across the state and the nation who share that goal.

KnowledgeWorks Foundation acts as a convener, a facilitator, a funder, and a technical assistance provider. Often, our focus on accountability offers "cover" for the innovators and reformers to give them time and space to achieve their goals. Acting in these roles, the foundation strengthens the independent, credible voice for education in Ohio; convenes education leaders around their priorities; facilitates stakeholder discussions with interests similar to ours; and defines and communicates the problem in a way that also advances reasonable solutions.

Acknowledgments

Many people and organizations deserve our thanks and acknowledgment for their efforts to ensure that *Breaking Ranks in the Middle* supports fundamental changes in middle level schools:

The Breaking Ranks in the Middle National Commission and its members for their thoughtful feedback on the drafts and for other contributions to the content that made the final product a useful tool for principals and their leadership teams.

- Gayle Andrews, Assistant Professor, University of Georgia

- Ray Burrola, Principal, Goddard High School

- Michael G. Curran, Jr., EdD, Associate Professor, Rider University

- August Frattali, Principal, Rachel Carson Middle School

- Tim Hadfield, Superintendent, Shelby County R-IV Schools

- John A. Harrison, President, Board of Directors, National Forum to Accelerate Middle Grades Reform

- Anthony Jackson, Executive Director, Asia Society International Studies Schools Network

- J. Howard Johnston, Professor, University of South Florida

- Deborah Kasak, Executive Director, National Forum to Accelerate Middle Grades Reform

- Tom Leyden, Director of Middle Level School Services, Texas Association of Secondary School Principals

- Michael D. Madison, Principal, Ann Arbor Open School @ Mack

- Kevin J. McHugh, EdD, Principal, Pennwood Middle School (National Middle Level Principal of the Year, 2002)

- Steven B. Mertens, Senior Research Scientist, University of Illinois

- Tom Rudin, VP, Government Relations and Development, College Board

- Clara Sale-Davis, Principal, Freeport Intermediate School

- Carol Tomlinson, Professor, University of Virginia

- Jerry Valentine, Professor and Director, Middle Level Leadership Center, University of Missouri-Columbia

- Ed Vittardi, Principal, Independence Middle School

- Karen E. Williams, Assistant Superintendent, Alhambra Elementary School District

- Ronald Williamson, Associate Professor of Leadership and Counseling, Eastern Michigan University

- Terry L. Wolfson, Principal, Hopkins West Junior High School

- Theodore R. Sizer and Deborah Meier for their work on the Foreword and their ongoing efforts to reform education for adolescents.

Thanks are due to the experts who contributed to our "Ask the Expert" and "Expert Essays" sections throughout the book, including the following:

- Donald C. Clark, Professor Emeritus, University of Arizona

- Sally N. Clark, Professor Emerita, University of Arizona

- Nancy Doda, Associate Professor, National-Louis University

- Dick Flanary, NASSP Director of Professional Development

- Vicki Petzko, Professor, University of Tennessee at Chattanooga

- Beverly Raimondo, Director, Center for Parent Leadership/Prichard Committee for Academic Excellence

- Pete Reed, NASSP Associate Director, Center for Principal Development

- Tom Rudin, VP, Government Relations and Development, College Board

- Carol Tomlinson, Professor, University of Virginia

- Karen Williams, Assistant Superintendent, Alhambra Elementary School District

- Ronald Williamson, Associate Professor, Eastern Michigan University

The many schools that have provided us with examples of practices to profile in *Breaking Ranks in the Middle,* including some we were not able to include but that greatly informed our work. Contributing schools include Alvarado Intermediate, Bowman Middle School, Casey Middle School, Cohoes Middle School, Cordova Middle School, Crabapple Middle School, Culver City Middle School, Erwine Middle School, Hopkins West Junior High School, Marsteller Middle School, Medea Creek Middle School, The Parker School, Port Chester Middle School, Rachel Carson Middle School, Saunders Middle School, and Thayer J. Hill Middle School. The efforts of four schools—Freeport Intermediate, Kennedy Middle School, Lehman Alternative Community School, and Upson-Lee Middle School—are profiled in greater detail. The principals, Clara Sale-Davis, Suzanne Smith, Joe Greenberg, and Patsy Dean, respectively, as well as members of their teams deserve our thanks for pulling these profiles together. Their experience, successes, and enduring challenges will inform implementation for other schools across the country. For more information about each of these schools, visit www.principals.org/brim.

- Sue Swaim, Executive Director, National Middle School Association, for her advice and support.

- NASSP staff members Rosa Aronson, Karen Danto, Catherine Gander, Jay Engeln, Bob Farrace, Dick Flanary, Jo Franklin, Carolyn Glascock, Lenor Hersey, Dianne Mero, Janice Ollarvia, Pete Reed, Judy Richardson, and Gerry Tirozzi for their tireless efforts to keep the project focused and on time.

- Kristin Nori for her elementary school perspective in the "Focus on Transition" journal and Anne Reed for her contribution, "Letter to the Principal," regarding differentiation.

- The Education Alliance at Brown University, and its Breaking Ranks in the Middle project team: Jill Davidson, Joe DiMartino, Sharon Lloyd Clark, Elaine Silva Mangiante, Naomi Sheffield, Patti Smith, and Denise Wolk.

- James R. Rourke, writer, consultant, former NASSP editor and program manager, and principal author of *Breaking Ranks II: Strategies for Leading High School Reform,* for his ability to compile and distill the thoughts of so many individuals and groups into a concise "field guide" for principals and leadership teams.

NASSP

The National Association of Secondary School Principals—the preeminent organization and the national voice for middle level and high school principals, assistant principals, and aspiring school leaders—provides its members with the professional resources to serve as visionary leaders. NASSP promotes the intellectual growth, academic achievement, character development, leadership development, and physical well-being of youth through its programs and student leadership services. NASSP sponsors the National Honor Society,™ the National Junior Honor Society,™ and the National Association of Student Councils.™

NASSP has found new ways to recognize excellence in middle level leadership and scholarship, most notably by honoring a middle level principal of the year in each state and a National Middle Level Principal of the Year.

Education Alliance at Brown University

For more than 25 years, the Education Alliance at Brown University has been a leading advocate for equity for public school students who are traditionally underserved. Since Ted Sizer joined the Education Department at Brown two decades ago, Brown has been recognized as a national leader in the move to create more personalized settings in secondary schools.

The Secondary School Redesign (SSR) program of the Education Alliance promotes a major overhaul of American secondary schools through personalization, collaborative leadership, instruction, and assessment. Their work builds on the research-based premise that student-centered learning contributes to high school students' academic success and social development. They have developed a variety of strategies to support student-centered learning as a norm in public high schools, helping secondary schools throughout the Northeast become more personalized in programs, support services, and intellectual achievement. Through such services as consulting, coaching, and professional development focused on school change and improvement, they help secondary schools form smaller, more personalized environments; create hands-on learning experiences that engage students in ways that are meaningful and relevant to them; and provide staff with professional development opportunities to meet the challenges faced in the classroom. Ongoing technical assistance and professional development are offered to secondary schools, districts, and states through on-site coaching workshops, academies, institutes, and networking opportunities for schools involved in the change process.

The Great Tug-of-War

"I could never teach kindergarteners," the college professor said half-jokingly, half-horrified to a few of the other educators during a roundtable discussion at the Education Continuum conference. "And I would never teach high school students," the third grade teacher chimed in.

A high school principal chuckled in response, "I doubt there's an incentive in the world that could get any of my teachers to tackle multiplication with your students—not to mention the eternal boy-girl giggling."

"So I wonder," ventured the note-taker, who happened to be a middle level principal, "if we can all imagine the consternation of a college's board of trustees if someone with experience and training as a kindergarten teacher was hired as the new history professor... or the consternation of third grade students if a high school chemistry teacher with a penchant for lecturing was hired to teach third grade math, why isn't there similar consternation when middle level students aren't exposed to professionals attuned to the students' unique intellectual, social, and developmental needs?"

From birth to death, human intellectual, developmental, and social needs change. At each stage, the tactics and strategies used to address those needs must also change. It has been said that a good teacher is a good teacher. That may be true, and over time it is conceivable that a college professor could become an outstanding kindergarten teacher and vice versa. But wouldn't it be more desirable to provide some of that training up front—before the professor started to lecture the six-year-olds that under Locke's social contract theory it is students' civic responsibility to keep their hands to themselves?

A great tug-of-war has existed for 40 years about how best to address the needs of students "in the middle"—the sixth, seventh, and eighth grades. Keep them with the elementary students? Put them in their own schools? Create 6–12 schools? Unfortunately, decisions about grade configuration often are based on district budgets rather than what is best for these students who are "stuck in the middle" between those who want to pull them toward high school and those who want to pull them back toward the elementary level. Even when districts have created separate middle schools, quite often these schools, and the strategies they use, are not designed to be *academically excellent, developmentally responsive,* or *socially equitable* (National Forum to Accelerate Middle Grades Reform).

Legitimate philosophical issues exist about grade configurations, and there is likely no one "right" answer that can be applied across the board regarding the appropriate configuration. Only one right answer can be universally applied: Regardless of grade configuration, policymakers, school boards, and superintendents must stop making decisions based primarily on budgets and the transportation schedule and instead create schools based on what is best for young adolescents—schools that address the intellectual and developmental needs of each student.

End the tug-of-war over these students and address their needs first! If communities begin to treat education as a continuum in which the needs of each student must be addressed, the potentially unsettling transitions from grade to grade and school to school will be far less traumatic for young adolescents and children as well as for those who guide their learning and development. In reality, aren't there academic, developmental, and social differences between first-graders and third-graders? Between 10th graders and 12th graders? Between college freshmen and the senior who is about to enter the working world? Don't we address each level differently? To further complicate the mix, aren't some first-graders more mature academically, developmentally, and socially than some third-graders? Perhaps a separate school for each student is in order?

If your school effectively addresses the academic and developmental needs of *each* student by creating small, personalized learning communities within the larger group, chances are that no one will care whether your campus is kindergarten through graduate school or 18 different schools—one for each grade from kindergarten through graduate school. Finding the right mix is up to each community. But as each community studies that mix, the goal should be to create schools that are academically excellent, developmentally responsive, and socially equitable for each student. *Breaking Ranks in the Middle* is a field guide to help school leaders and teams achieve that result.

Sweeping statements have been made about the academic mediocrity of schools teaching young adolescents. The bearers of this message have used it as an opportunity to lambaste "touchy-feely" middle level practices. Surely, some schools teaching young adolescents have neglected the critical "academically excellent" component of their mission. In the context of education, developmental appropriateness and social equity are meaningless without academic excellence. Schools that have helped middle level students feel welcome and respected have taken only the first step. True respect for the whole student requires that a school take the next step to challenge students academically and intellectually. To do anything less is neglecting student interest in intellectual development and the human desire to learn.

Yet, just as our college professor's lesson about Locke might not sink in for kindergarteners, how can academic excellence be achieved for any given age group if the instruction is not developmentally appropriate and informed by the social realities of our day? Why is it so difficult to imagine that each young adolescent has his or her own developmental assets that require curriculum, instruction, and assessment to be personalized for intellectual stimulation to occur? Circle-time sing-a-longs are rare in college, but does anyone contend that this technique can't be developmentally appropriate for kindergarteners learning their ABCs? Classroom lecture and animated debate are not the mainstays of the kindergarten classrooms, yet without these formats colleges would be very dull places. To learn is a choice each child must be encouraged to

Attributes of developmental responsiveness:

• Personalized environment that supports each student's intellectual, ethical, social, and physical development

• Adults and students grouped in small learning communities characterized by stable, close, and mutually respectful relationships

Source: Schools to Watch criteria

make—not once in his or her life but repeatedly throughout each day. If the curriculum or instruction or environment makes the student choose not to learn, academic excellence can never be attained.

From Middle Level to High School and Back Again

Personalizing the learning experience for each student was at the heart of *Breaking Ranks: Changing an American Institution,* published by NASSP with the support of the Carnegie Foundation for the Advancement of Teaching. Its debut in 1996 signaled the beginning of a new opportunity for high school principals and their school leadership teams to tackle the thorny issues involved in reform. The commission of principals, assistant principals, teachers, and students that developed the Breaking Ranks recommendations understood the importance of addressing the intellectual, developmental, and social needs of students to ensure student success and high achievement. Although the amalgamation of so many practitioners' perspectives may have been unique to *Breaking Ranks,* many of the recommendations evolved from the groundbreaking work of other practitioners and researchers who had tackled the topics individually or espoused various models of reform. **In fact, many of the recommendations mirrored activities that were taking place in schools serving middle level students. High school leaders were learning from their middle level peers.**

The Breaking Ranks in the Middle recommendations discussed throughout this book have been distilled from the original 1996 recommendations and the field guide for high school principals, *Breaking Ranks II,* and adapted to the middle level audience. Anyone familiar with the 1996 Breaking Ranks recommendations will see that little adaptation was necessary because of the close alignment of those recommendations with reforms already taking place at the middle level. The Breaking Ranks in the Middle recommendations are similarly aligned with various middle level reform efforts, including *Turning Points, Turning Points 2000,* NMSA's *This We Believe,* and "Schools to Watch" criteria. (The Middle Level Academic Rigor and Support Self-Assessment Tool is available at www.principals.org/brim.)

Breaking Ranks in the Middle is the most recent installment of NASSP's long-standing commitment to promote effective leadership in our nation's middle level schools. It draws on information and analysis presented in *Leadership for Highly Successful Middle Level Schools,* the recent iteration of NASSP's once-a-decade snapshot of the state of middle level education, which measures progress against similar large-scale studies conducted in 1965, 1983, and 1992.

Conscious of the need for middle level leaders to receive a single, authoritative message on improving middle level schools, NASSP seeks to align its agenda with that of other organizations by actively participating in the National Forum to Accelerate Middle Grades Reform and by seizing opportunities to continue the conversation in middle level education, for instance, by co-publishing *Turning Points 2000* and its study guide with Teachers College Press and NMSA.

The task of implementing the reforms called for in *Breaking Ranks in the Middle* clearly falls upon the shoulders of educators—teachers, para-educators, assistant principals, principals, the central office staff, and many others. Within the school building, the principal bears ultimate responsibility for schoolwide implementation. Inspired by principals' high level of interest in implementing a personalized environment conducive to learning and by the success of *Breaking Ranks II,* a field guide for high school principals interested in implementing Breaking Ranks–style reform,

NASSP decided to create a similar guide for principals and school teams serving young adolescents—students in the middle grades. *Breaking Ranks in the Middle* provides tools for and examples of ways middle level school principals can complete the unfinished business of creating academically excellent, developmentally appropriate, and socially equitable schools. *Breaking Ranks in the Middle* focuses on **the implementation of recommendations in which principals have a significant role** and offers strategies for school leadership teams to consider and adapt in accordance with local conditions and expectations. *Breaking Ranks, Breaking Ranks II,* and *Breaking Ranks in the Middle* all strive to make schools more student centered by personalizing programs, support services, and intellectual challenges for *all* students.

Why Reform Now?

Given the challenges of reform, why would a principal or school undertake Breaking Ranks–style reform? Generally, people make difficult changes because they are required to do so (mandate) or because they want to do so (enticement). That is no less true when it comes to implementing Breaking Ranks in the Middle reform.

- **The external accountability mandate:** Public schools in the United States are at a crossroads. Federal and state legislation have established benchmarks intended to improve achievement for all students—including those who in the past were accepted as part of the "normal" failure curve. Standardized testing will be one measure of whether or not the benchmarks have been met. In addition, an emphasis on raising achievement in subgroups of student populations, such as English language learners (ELLs) and special education students, will require a more comprehensive review of disaggregated data to ensure that all students are receiving the benefits of education. What will be judged is the percentage of students who meet the standard overall and within the subgroups, not—as has been the case—the average performance of the entire school. This mandate will not be met consistently by schools if current conditions persist. *Breaking Ranks* championed the cause of all students achieving at high levels; federal and state legislation will require it. Equity of participation, the status quo, must be forced aside as equity of outcomes comes to the fore. *Breaking Ranks in the Middle* provides strategies to help all students achieve at high levels.

- **The mandate for students to succeed in an increasingly global context:** Some research suggests that as students move from elementary to middle to high school, they become less able to compete favorably with their international counterparts. Each of our nation's schools must challenge each student in its classrooms if we are to provide an education that enables each student to succeed personally and professionally.

- **The enticement to foster each student's success:** Schools must be inviting places and, in some cases, must anchor community improvement efforts. If stu-

> "Providing high-quality education improves community life and social cohesion, attracts and retains families, helps develop a skilled workforce, fosters economic growth, attracts new jobs, and increases real estate values. City and school officials agree that the fortunes of our cities and our schools are closely linked."
>
> *Education Week* Commentary, Sept. 21, 2005, p. 38 (reporting results from a national survey of city officials and educators)

dents do not want to attend schools, then the environment, discipline issues, and violence all become problems—problems that disproportionately fall onto the shoulders of those students who need school the most: the underprivileged. For these and all students, we need to find ways to pull them into the schools, not turn them off to education. We need to ensure that students are not made to feel "stupid" in school and at the same time address the needs of average and advanced learners who become discouraged if they are not challenged. No student is interested in being thought of as stupid by a peer or a teacher, so the student becomes "bad" instead—after all, the student thinks, "It's cool to be bad; it's not cool to be stupid." Those students who are failing and think they cannot handle the challenges of school may feel academically inadequate or inferior. Schools must address this issue so students aren't getting the message "Hey, according to our assessment, you're stupid, kid—and, by the way, you are required to show up again tomorrow so you can be told that again." At the same time, schools must challenge advanced learners so they don't get the message "I know you weren't challenged yesterday or today, but according to the law you have to show up here again tomorrow. We're trying, but we have to get the other students up to standard first."

- **The professional educator's moral imperative enticement:** The final and most important reason each educator should want to take on Breaking Ranks in the Middle reform: To realize each educator's dream requires that each student's dream also be realized. Most principals and teachers took their first step down the path to educating the nation's children because they wanted to make a difference in the lives of individual students by helping them acquire a love of learning. Unfortunately, that dream is not being realized by all students. The promise of Breaking Ranks in the Middle reform is to promote a culture of continuous improvement to help each student become part of a community in which all students have the opportunity to achieve at high levels. In so doing, principals and teachers will make a deeper and more equitable difference in the lives of many more students and will reap the rewards of fostering student learning.

Many schools and the principals who lead them have been undertaking reforms to improve student achievement. Their success has shown policymakers that success on a grander scale is possible. Many schools, however, have failed to undertake reforms that have resulted in higher student achievement. Time is of the essence; federal and state benchmarks must be met, but, more important, each minute wasted means less time is spent addressing the needs of students who are not achieving at acceptable levels. Millions of young adolescents each year rely on principals and teachers to help them fulfill their dreams and show them how to embrace a lifelong love of learning. Failure in these, the most important of life's courses, is not acceptable.

If, after reading *Breaking Ranks in the Middle*, you see your work in the same light as before you read it, be assured that nothing of substance will change very much for very long. On the other hand, if you begin to see *yourself* differently in your work and in the way you help others see the wisdom of change, your school will change. Principals, in conjunction with their school leadership teams, teachers, and others, have the choice of either raising the white flag of surrender or aggressively beginning the conversations that will extricate them from adverse circumstances.

Adversity spawns discussion, discussion informs ideas, ideas **may** lead to change...the changing of an American institution. Begin the discussion today.

If, after reading Breaking Ranks in the Middle, you see your work in the same light as before reading it, be assured that nothing of substance will change very much for very long.

> "Sustainable transformations follow a predictable pattern of buildup and break-through. Like pushing on a giant, heavy flywheel, it takes a lot of effort to get the thing moving at all, but with persistent pushing in a consistent direction over a long period of time, the flywheel builds momentum, eventually hitting a point of breakthrough."
>
> Source: *Good to Great*, p. 186

How to Make the Most of This Guide

Breaking Ranks in the Middle should be used as a tool to help teachers and principals lead their school communities through a process of reform and improvement. Many different strategies and recommendations are proposed; they are intended to encourage conversation and action. Without that conversation, reform has little chance of success. Because of the guide's alignment with reforms proposed for high schools (as outlined in *Breaking Ranks II*), it creates an opportunity for districts and schools to implement vertical training programs.

Because principals and others may not be able to steal enough time to read this field guide in one sitting or as one integrated unit, its organization is especially important. *Breaking Ranks in the Middle* has been organized with a three-step progression in mind:

1. Realize that your school needs to change if it wants to serve each student.

2. Help others to see that need and collaboratively plan for change.

3. Implement the practices that support each student's improved performance.

Step 1: Realize the need. Schools are often told to change but are rarely asked whether they believe they need to change. In the chapter "Does Your School Need to Break Ranks?" you will be asked a series of questions—questions not often asked by schools—that will help you assess whether *your* school is doing all it can to address the academic and developmental needs of your students. Following those questions is a discussion of what a Breaking Ranks in the Middle school might look like. If you are not satisfied by your answers to the questions regarding how well you serve each student and would like to set your own vision for reaching each student, nine strategies are proposed to form the cornerstone of your efforts. The nine strategies are designed to help you capitalize on the interdependence of the 30 Breaking Ranks in the Middle recommendations and prepare you to implement them (i.e., if you adopt the cornerstone strategies, you will be well on your way to implementing the entire set of 30 recommendations). Because taking on more activities is simply not realistic for most schools without eliminating other practices, at the end of that chapter a panel of experts and practitioners identifies a host of practices that may help you free up time within existing constraints.

Step 2: Collaborate to plan for and implement change. Once you have answered the questions about your school, you may realize that your school must change. Fundamental to the success of making the necessary changes is providing a collaborative process in which others also see the need for, and participate in, implementing the changes. Chapter 2 may help you begin that discussion—it outlines the necessary steps to involve others in the change process through collaboration, review of data, and professional development. Skipping this step of the process may result in reforms that are either unsustainable or not well implemented.

Step 3: Promote improved student performance by providing opportunities for students to build relationships within the school and between themselves and what they learn. Chapters 3 and 4 discuss these relationships in detail, including the strategies and barriers to implementation of various practices.

How Are the Breaking Ranks in the Middle Recommendations Organized?

In developing *Breaking Ranks II* and *Breaking Ranks in the Middle*, the goal was to make the guides manageable, not overwhelming. For this guide, it was decided that the idea of 30 recommendations would be intimidating, so we gleaned cornerstone strategies from the recommendations. The guides could have simplified things by making *one* recommendation: Improve student performance. But that generic recommendation would not be very useful to the many educators who are already trying to accomplish that goal. Instead, we created a guide that includes more specifics rather than fewer. The cornerstone strategies provide a certain degree of specificity and, in turn, reference the recommendations, which provide a greater level of detail. Each recommendation includes practices to help implement it, the benefits of implementing the recommendation, challenges to discuss before implementation, and suggestions for measuring progress.

The 30 recommendations have been "clustered"; each has been assigned to one of these three chapters:

1. Chapter 2. Who Will Lead? Collaborative Leadership and Professional Learning Communities (p. 55)

2. Chapter 3. Personalizing Your School Environment (p. 127)

3. Chapter 4. Making Learning Personal: Curriculum, Instruction, and Assessment (p. 175)

For practitioners using this as a reference tool, the following may be helpful. If you are looking for

- The nine cornerstone strategies, see page 8.

- The 30 Breaking Ranks in the Middle recommendations, see page 23.

- Benefits, strategies, challenges, and progress measures for implementing the recommendations, see the figures in chapters 2, 3, and 4.

- Resources to support implementation of the strategies and recommendations, see page 259.

- Examples of specific schools that are implementing changes consistent with Breaking Ranks in the Middle, see the following:

  - Four extended profiles of school reform efforts are included, written from the principal's perspective (Kennedy, p. 31; Lehman, p. 107; Upson-Lee, p. 153; and Freeport, p. 219). Do not make the mistake of bypassing a profile because the demographics are not comparable to those of your school or because your situation is different. The profiled schools have been chosen on the basis of effective practices—many of which could be implemented in *any* school.

  - Following many of the recommendations, you will find "Recommendations in Practice." This section describes schools' implementation of Breaking Ranks in the Middle recommendations. Note that many schools other than those

If you are tempted to pick and choose a single strategy or section from the field guide or focus on one chapter that discusses a specific area of interest to you, remember that implementing one or two recommendations is merely tinkering around the edges of school reform and is therefore ill-advised.

profiled in this field guide have taken significant steps to change their approach to improving the performance of all students. The schools profiled, including several "Schools to Watch" honorees, are examples of schools that have made an effort to reach all students, some with greater success than others. Finally, as each of the schools in the extended profiles will attest, efforts are ongoing. Reaching the promise of a more student-centered school with more personalized programs, support services, and intellectual rigor remains a goal on the horizon.

If you are tempted to pick and choose a single strategy or section from the field guide or focus on one chapter that discusses a specific area of interest to you, remember that implementing one or two recommendations is merely tinkering around the edges of school reform and is therefore ill-advised. Substantive reform will only be successful and sustainable if it is continuous, involves an ongoing and rigorous analysis of the entire school's needs, and takes into account the interdependence of elements in a learning community. A best practice implemented in isolation may not be sustainable over time if it relies on other changes that are never implemented.

1 Does Your School Need to Break Ranks?

The real measure of performance...is how well your school is meeting the academic needs of each student within it. If 90% of your student population ensures that you are ahead of local, regional, state, and national benchmarks but the other 10% of the student population remains unchallenged, then it may be time for your school to break ranks—not only because the 10% are being ill-served, but because, more than likely, a large portion of the 90% could be performing at higher levels if your school knew the strengths and weaknesses of each student and tailored instruction accordingly.

—Breaking Ranks II

Asking the Right Questions

As a principal, teacher, or member of the leadership team, why would you be interested in breaking ranks from your school's current practices or breaking ranks from the schools in your area? If your school is featured in negative news stories or is performing below average on state or national assessments, you *may* see the obvious—a need to change. On the other hand, why make waves if your school is average or above average, stacks up well against the other schools in your area, and receives positive coverage from local media? In fact, you have proudly touted your achievements and even once boasted, "We have some of the best scores in the state; we'd be happy to compare ourselves to any school around." A school leader who rests on his or her laurels and doesn't try to improve is a failure for some students. An exemplary school leader is one who acknowledges strengths but knows that there is much more to accomplish.

Schools operating above certain benchmarks or schools that, *on average,* perform well enough to be highlighted in positive local news stories often don't have the "negative pressure incentive" to review how things could be better. In fact, these schools often are under pressure from the community to leave a good thing alone.

But what is this "good thing" that should be left alone? Are you properly measuring that good thing—whatever it may be? Is it a good thing for each student, or is it a good thing just for the average student (as if such a person actually existed)? Measures of low, average, and high performance can be useful for some comparative analyses and for setting benchmarks. While the results of your efforts can at times be

Posted throughout the school, the sentiment "Whatever It Takes" serves as a constant reminder of the incredible journey from being a low-performing, scholastically challenged school with no esprit de corps to becoming one of four schools in the nation chosen by the National Forum to Accelerate Middle Grades Reform.

(See Freeport profile on page 219.)

(See Freeport profile on page 219.)

Principal's Journal

We can't afford to be an "average" school. We're already good, but we aren't challenging each student well enough... reminds me of what Jim Collins says in "Good To Great:" Good is the enemy of great. We don't have great schools, principally because we have good schools....

measured by averages, the real measure of performance is how well your school is meeting the academic needs of *each* student. The most important part of any analysis is to ensure that the appropriate questions are being asked and answered—averages provide only one facet of any comprehensive analysis. To transform a school serving middle level students to the point at which it is academically excellent, developmentally responsive, and socially equitable for the benefit of each student requires more thorough introspection from the school community. This quest for internal accountability will aid any effort to meet external district, state, and federal accountability mandates such as those required under No Child Left Behind.

On the next page are questions that you as the principal, in conjunction with your school leadership team, may want to consider as you assess how well your school is meeting the needs of individual students. The questions are designed to address the individual rather than the "average"; however, if you are able to address the individual, chances are you will be pleasantly surprised by the "new average." If, after contemplating the answers to and implications of each question, your team decides that all the answers are satisfactory, perhaps you have already broken ranks from the pack and have created a school more personalized in programs, support services, and intellectual rigor. In the experience of principals undertaking reforms consistent with Breaking Ranks in the Middle recommendations, however, it is not possible to completely break ranks, **because breaking ranks is a process of continuous improvement.**

How Well Does Your School Serve Each Student?

1. Do you use data regularly to assess the effectiveness of your teams in developing differentiated lessons that meet academically rigorous standards, are consistently challenging, and are developmentally appropriate for each student?

2. Is each student achieving at a proficient or higher level of performance?

3. Does each of your students say he or she feels connected to or well-known by at least one adult in your building—an adult who knows the aspirations, strengths, and weaknesses of the student and uses the information to help the student become successful and personally challenged in all classes and student activities?

4. Is there adequate *scheduled* time each week for teachers to collaborate on planning instruction, reviewing student work, aligning instructional units with district and/or state standards, and encouraging interdisciplinary connections such as promoting literacy across the curriculum?

5. Do administrators participate in team planning time and work sessions on a regular basis?

6. Is each student regularly exposed to active inquiry and project-based instruction to ensure student engagement with essential knowledge, understanding, and skill?

(continued)

7. How many low-income and how many minority students are *identified and served* as gifted and talented in your school? Are *all* families encouraged to involve their children in challenging programs?

8. Is each of your sixth or seventh grade students and families introduced to programs or services to support college awareness, aspirations, and planning?

9. In addition to PTA and student council, how well does your school systematically extend opportunities to members of the community, especially the hard-to-reach parents, for input, feedback, and involvement in decision making regarding the academic, social, and co-curricular programs?

10. How would your teachers respond if you were to ask them whether they have been provided with the professional development *and* the time to

   - *collaboratively* and regularly (at least monthly) examine student data and plan for improved student performance?

   - *collaboratively* assess and plan for students' affective development?

   - *collaboratively* plan for the integration of curriculum?

11. Is each of your students involved in an ongoing effort (comprehensive multiyear program, class, advisory, etc.) that specifically promotes the development of the student's personal and social skills in the areas of effective communication, decision making, conflict resolution, self-awareness, personal safety, and stress management? Is each student assessed at different times on how effective these efforts have proven?

12. Do you know what percentage of each classroom's student assessments is authentic (e.g., portfolio reviews, student-led conferences, and/or exhibitions) versus more traditional assessments (standardized tests)?

13. Do you survey teachers as well as each student and family to discover whether the transition into and out of the middle level has been successful?

14. How many of your "graduates" need remedial help in high school and how many drop out of school by the end of the ninth grade? Has your district ever systematically interviewed them to discover why?

15. If you are a leader in a K–8, 6–12, or 7–12 school, are you satisfied with the steps your school has taken to ensure alignment of the academic, developmental, and social programs among the grades in your school for students in the 10–14 age range?

Adding an element of objectivity...

Were you able to

- answer each of the questions above?

- support the responses with data?

- share your responses with your leadership team, teachers, and families to affirm your assessment?

Note: A similar instrument is available at www.principals.org/brim. That instrument has been adapted and developed from the questions above for use in Breaking Ranks in the Middle training. If you decide to use this tool, keep in mind that your focus should be on *each* student. For example, if to the question "What percentage of your students feels connected to or well known by at least one adult in your school? you respond "95 percent," that means that each of your students is not being well served and you may never be able to move from being a good school to being a great school.

How Did You Do?

If everyone was satisfied with your responses, then perhaps your school has already made the change from good to great. However, if your leadership team's answers to this assessment indicate that there is room for improvement in your school, then you are likely in good company. Despite tremendous efforts and advances in meeting the needs of students in the middle level years, much work remains. A significant component of that work must be the creation of a vision of what *could be*. As you engage in many thoughtful conversations within your school and community to define and publicize that vision, keep in mind that your challenge is not educating students; rather, it is educating each student. At the heart of a family's vision, there has always been one constant—not the success of the amorphous "all students" but the success of "our son" or "our daughter." Your school's vision must take each family's vision to heart. Bringing that to reality will require a strategic plan for change—a plan that incorporates academic excellence, developmental responsiveness, and social equity at every opportunity. Remember, a vision will remain simply a vision unless your school is willing to embark on significant changes to bring it to life.

> Researchers from the Philadelphia Education Fund and Johns Hopkins University found that nearly 40 percent of the city's public school students who ultimately dropped out of high school could have been identified as being at risk as early as the sixth grade.
>
> *Source: Philadelphia Inquirer*

There is no template for what a Breaking Ranks school might look like, because school values differ from community to community. However, in the interest of beginning the conversation to define or modify your school's vision, the following fictional "Letter from the Principal" and its accompanying document attempt to paint a picture of what a school might begin to look like after implementing reforms consistent with *Breaking Ranks in the Middle*. The vision your community sets for your school may differ significantly from the one outlined. This document is designed to encourage your faculty and community to dream about what could be and to make sure that you are articulating a vision to existing and incoming students and families. The document is obviously not designed to be thrown on the copier and sent out to families with your signature at the bottom! When you do begin to articulate your school's vision, make certain that you help families understand the concepts entailed in the vision. If you believe, for example, that interdisciplinary teaming, heterogeneous grouping, and understanding learning styles and multiple intelligences are critical to how your team instructs and assesses, discuss with your team how you can creatively educate even the hardest-to-reach families about the terms and their implications.

Letter from the Principal

Dear Parent of an Aspiring Sixth-Grader:

Please read the document below, written by our Transition Team. It is based on our school's vision, which was developed in collaboration with parents, students, teachers, and others in the community. We hope it gives you an idea of the kind of atmosphere into which your child will be welcomed. I look forward to discussing it with you in greater detail at the upcoming open house.

Kindest Regards,

Principal, Breaking Ranks in the Middle School

Your Child's Future: Not a Roll of the Dice

Chance is not a game that should be played with any student's life—much less your child's. Rather than leave a student's school experience and the outcome of that experience to chance, we believe we have the obligation to understand a student's personal needs and to challenge him or her by meeting those needs **intellectually, socially,** and **personally.** We believe a high performing school is one that is academically excellent, developmentally responsive, and socially equitable. Some students have little problem finding a voice, while others struggle well into adulthood to find a productive voice. Both groups of students need help to appropriately develop that voice. By providing a variety of *structured* experiences in which students can be actively engaged, we believe we can address a student's need to achieve the following:

- Express personal perspectives
- Create individual and group identities
- Examine options and choose his or her own path
- Take risks and assess the effects
- Use his or her imagination
- Demonstrate mastery [Editor's note: e.g., mastery of essential knowledge, understanding, and skill][1]

Schools have been able to address **some** of these needs for **some** of their students since schooling began. We endeavor to fulfill **each** of those needs for **each** of our students.

How often is it that only a few students express themselves, although, in theory, everyone is permitted to speak? Does that mean others don't want to? Are afraid to? Some would say, "Part of growing up is finding the ability to express oneself, and if someone can't, then that's life." But what happens if one never learns that skill? Is that life? We don't think so. We will provide several arenas in which each student can express himself or herself in one-on-one and group settings—in each classroom, in our teams, through our **advisory** and **student activities programs,** and via student exhibitions and presentations.

(continued)

[1]Developmental assets noted by Clarke and Frazer (2003).

How often do students fall into the wrong cliques only because they want to belong to *something—anything*? Although we cannot dictate friendships, clearly we have an opportunity to provide groups (project groups, advisories, student activities, etc.) in which each student feels a sense of belonging and perhaps in which friendships will be fostered.

How often does *each* student have the opportunity to demonstrate **mastery of a subject,** a concept, an instrument, a sport? The "A" students, the lead in the play or the band, the star on the soccer team all have those opportunities—and they are well deserved. But are they being challenged at a level that is personally meaningful? And what about the students who haven't been working on a skill for as long or who try just as hard and don't quite make the cut? **We're not talking here about equality of rewards or giving everyone a star; rather, that each student should be encouraged to achieve a personal best and should receive recognition for it—individually and, if appropriate, in a group setting.** Our school has designed the practices to make this a reality in the classroom, in advisory settings, and through our student activities program. Students will be creating, developing, and publicly exhibiting projects that demonstrate their mastery of learning on a regular basis and will also be able to demonstrate their unique talents through a student activities program and a service-learning program tied directly to skills and knowledge needed to meet the larger learning goals for each student.

Our efforts to meet the needs of students are not made simply so that we can develop friendships with students and make them feel better about themselves. The business of education is about learning and achievement for each student. *We believe that without these personal connections and our understanding of the motivations, aspirations, and learning styles of each student, most students will never become engaged in their own learning and never really achieve to their potential.* The statistics about students who never make it past ninth grade tell only a small part of the tale. What about those students who leave eighth grade, never having been challenged, and then flounder in high school but still graduate? Or those students who are bored day in and day out? Or those top-notch students who could have been seriously challenged but instead are left to stare out the window and wait for the bell to ring while the teacher reviews materials the student has already mastered?

We need to reach each of these students on the first day, the first week, the first month, and throughout school. We can't wait until they leave us to say, "She has a lot of potential—I hope she has an opportunity to use it in high school." Our school will get to know the potential of each student through our **Personal Adult Advocate** program. Our emphasis on **decreasing the total number of students a teacher has** will allow teachers more time to confer with parents and mentors to personalize each student's educational experience and to be able to effectively advise a small group of students. Each advocate will work with students to develop and monitor individual **Personal Plans for Progress** that will detail the academic, social, and other aspirations and needs of students. The adult advocate will work with students, their parents, and their teachers to ensure that each student's potential is being realized in the classroom, on the field, in the community, and, most important, *in the mind of the student.*

Academic achievement in our school will be driven by students being engaged in classes and lessons designed by teams of teachers who integrate the curriculum and show connections in the curriculum. Students will be encouraged to write in *all* classes and to approach challenges from various perspectives, using their strengths

(continued)

and addressing their weaknesses. There will be no tracking of students. Instead, students will be grouped heterogeneously and will, when necessary, have multiple opportunities to redo their work until it meets established standards or to work at advanced levels of competency. The school will support personal drive and aspiration by providing a rigorous curriculum and service learning opportunities to all who are willing to take on the challenge. A measure of our success will be the level and intensity of questioning and listening by students and the teachers who are encouraging more questioning and listening. We invite you to see this intensity of interaction in the classroom whenever you have the opportunity.

Three years from now, when your child makes the transition to ninth grade, none of us—you the parents who will have supported, sacrificed, cajoled, and inspired your child, and we the teachers and administrators who have made our own sacrifices to make a difference in the lives of young people—as we stand together while your son or daughter says good-bye to the middle years, should have to wonder whether your child missed an opportunity to challenge himself or herself. At our school, neither teacher, nor parent, nor student ever need wonder. The work of each student and his or her portfolio will be one indicator that, at every step of the way, the student was challenged.

Compare the Vision to Your Own

Did the description of this fictional school make you think about something you might do differently in your school? Is your school already doing it all—perhaps even better than what is outlined? If so, congratulations! But don't celebrate too soon—remember, you weren't completely satisfied with your answers to the 15 questions about how well your school is serving each student.

What Should We Change First?

Let's assume that you are convinced that your school can do a better job of improving student performance. Let's further assume that the observations made thus far and your own experience have convinced you that improving student performance is inextricably tied to student engagement and that engagement for each student can be accomplished only through a more personalized academic and intellectual program. Finally, let's assume that you see a need for change in your school. Where do you begin? Which should you change first: School culture? School structures? Instruction?

Scholars, school leadership teams, and management experts have long struggled with this question, with few definitive answers. Without minimizing the importance of the debate, for the purposes of this field guide, suffice it to say that the three are highly interconnected, change is needed in all three areas, modifications to culture must occur before change truly becomes effective, and each school will approach the challenge from a different perspective depending on factors specific to the school's situation. Although the approach may vary from school to school, a number of common strategies have proven effective in supporting efforts to improve student performance.

Nine cornerstone strategies have been gleaned from the experiences of schools implementing strategies consistent with Breaking Ranks in the Middle recommendations. The strategies are designed to give your school possible "entry points" to pursue fundamental changes. Your school's priorities and stage of reform may require different entry points, or you may develop different strategies. The strategies are listed below. A more complete explanation of each is found beginning on p. 9.

A Vision for Improvement: Nine Cornerstone Strategies

1. Establish the academically rigorous essential learnings that a student is required to master in order to successfully make the transition to high school and align the curriculum and teaching strategies to realize that goal.

2. Create dynamic teacher teams that are afforded common planning time to help organize and improve the quality and quantity of interactions between teachers and students.

3. Provide structured planning time for teachers to align the curriculum across grades and schools and to map efforts that address the academic, developmental, social, and personal needs of students, especially at critical transition periods (e.g., elementary to middle grades, middle grades to high school).

4. Implement a comprehensive advisory or other program that ensures that each student has frequent and meaningful opportunities to meet with an adult to plan and assess the student's academic, personal, and social development.

5. Ensure that teachers assess the individual learning needs of students and tailor instructional strategies and multiple assessments accordingly.

6. Entrust teachers with the responsibility of implementing schedules that are flexible enough to accommodate teaching strategies consistent with the ways students learn most effectively and that allow for effective teacher teaming, common planning time, and other lesson planning.

7. Institute structural leadership systems that allow for substantive involvement in decision making by students, teachers, family members, and the community, and that support effective communication among these groups.

8. Align all programs and structures so that all social, economic, and racial/ethnic groups have open and equal access to challenging activities and learning.

9. Align the schoolwide comprehensive, ongoing professional development program and the Personal Learning Plans (PLPs) of staff members with the requisite knowledge of content, instructional strategies, and student developmental factors.

Together, these nine cornerstone strategies, if implemented effectively, will form the foundation for improving the performance of each student in your school. **The ninth strategy, regarding professional development, underpins all others—and in most cases is required for each of the other eight strategies to be adequately implemented.** Too often, professional development programs do not have a coherent or strategic purpose; instead, they relate to the interests of individual teachers. Placing professional development last in the list allows the reader to see what the focus of the professional development program must be: acquiring the skills, knowledge, and disposition to implement the eight previous strategies.

Let's take a closer look at the nine strategies to see how you can adopt them in your school.

Cornerstone Strategy #1

Establish the academically rigorous essential learnings that a student is required to master in order to successfully make the transition to high school and align the curriculum and teaching strategies to realize that goal.

Breaking Ranks in the Middle recommendations supporting this cornerstone strategy:

Rec. 19.   Each school will identify a set of essential learnings—in literature and language, writing, mathematics, social studies, science, and the arts—in which students must demonstrate achievement in order to advance to the next level (see p. 195).

Rec. 24.   Teachers will design high-quality work and teach in ways that engage students, cause them to persist, and, when the work is successfully completed, result in student satisfaction and acquisition of knowledge, critical-thinking and problem-solving skills, and other abilities (see p. 207).

Rec. 28.   Teachers will integrate assessment into instruction so that assessment is accomplished using a variety of methods that do not merely measure students but become part of the learning process (see p. 213).

Few undertakings require more leadership than the establishment of essential learnings. Politically sensitive, resource intensive, and emotionally draining, developing and implementing essential learnings is at the heart of education. School must be about intellectual development and what students learn—the relationship between students and ideas. What ideas? What content? What curriculum? To promote success for each student, each strategy, practice, and recommendation should be aligned with academic rigor or how it affects academic rigor. If your program is not rigorous for each student, the potential for the success of each student is diminished. Pursuing rigor requires you to devise a process to formulate essential learnings that take into account state standards and the standards set by individual disciplines and the school community. Almost all public schools now have state standards that dictate many curriculum decisions. Essential learnings… schools must know the state and district standards, study them, adopt them, and then enrich the list through the local filter.

Although state and district standards are often beyond your control, the process related to identifying the school community's essential learnings is not. Unfortunately, many schools believe that since the district and state have set standards, the schools do not need to engage in the conversation about essential learnings. The process related to identifying the school community's essential learnings might be similar to the one outlined in *Providing Focus and Direction Through Essential Learnings* (Westerberg & Webb, 1997).

Once a school has determined what it is that students should know, understand, and be able to demonstrate in order to advance to high school, the school can decide on the actions to take to ensure that students acquire the essential learnings. In other words, the school can begin with the end in mind and design backward from there. Actions to support adjusting the curriculum and teaching strategies to help students master the essential learnings might include the following:

■   Focus on mastery, not coverage; focus on what is learned, not simply what is taught. Use student exhibitions, portfolios, and capstone programs to demonstrate mastery and learning rather than focusing on seat time.

Principal's Journal

Essential learnings…
Tell us what
students should
know, understand,
and be able to do
(content); how well
students must do
these things
(performance); and
which instructional
techniques or
recommended
activities (curriculum)
should be used to
assist students in
accomplishing the
"what" and the
"how." Even though
the state and
district have
standards, we need
to put those
standards through
our local "filter" to
determine essential
learnings.

- Raise the level of academic rigor in all classes. (Go to www.principals.org/brim for a tool your team can use to assess perceptions about the level of rigor at your school.)
- If they exist at your school, open accelerated classes to all students and actively support the growth and success of each student in the class.
- Initiate interdisciplinary instruction, teaming, and an appropriate emphasis on real-world applications.
- Reorganize traditional departmental structures to integrate the school's curriculum to the extent necessary and emphasize depth over breadth of coverage.
- Teach academic vocabulary and numeracy in all content areas.
- Organize classes heterogeneously and provide high-level differentiated instruction to each student.
- Align student activities and service learning programs with essential learnings.

Cornerstone Strategy #2

Create dynamic teacher teams that are afforded common planning time to help organize and improve the quality and quantity of interactions between teachers and students.

Breaking Ranks in the Middle recommendations supporting this cornerstone strategy:

Rec. 4.   Teachers and teacher teams will provide the leadership essential to the success of reform and will collaborate with others in the educational community to redefine the role of the teacher and identify sources of support for that redefined role (see p. 90).

Rec. 10.   Schools will create small units in which anonymity is banished (see p. 139).

Rec. 11.   Each teacher involved in the instructional program on a full-time basis will be responsible for contact time with no more than 90 students, so that the teacher can give greater attention to the needs of every student (see p. 140).

Rec. 14.   Teachers and administrators will convey a sense of caring so that students know that teachers have a stake in student learning (see p. 145).

Rec. 21.   The school will reorganize the traditional department structure and foster the use of teacher teams provided with ample common planning time to integrate the school's curriculum to the extent possible and emphasize depth over breadth of coverage (see p. 201).

Actions to support this strategy include the following:

- Teachers engage in leadership professional development with a focus on facilitation/group process; data disaggregation and analysis; reform issues; best practices; and learning profiles (gender, culture, learning style, and intelligence preference).
- Cultivate leadership in teams beyond named team or department leaders.
- Teachers exercise the opportunity and authority to define their needs, identify problem areas, and find the resources and solutions to address the challenges.

- Teachers seek and use scheduled times to engage in common planning time for goal-setting, student work and data review, and formative and summative assessments by reducing workload (number of students, number of classes taught, etc.) and relieving duty assignments (e.g., students and parents serving as hall monitors).

- School leaders support teachers who want to work in new ways and look carefully at those who do not (either help them overcome their reluctance or find another situation or role that better meets their expectations and outlook).

- Form an interdisciplinary school team to coordinate learning goals across departments/teams and grades.

- Integrate discipline-specific staff into team structures to foster lesson plan sharing, interdisciplinary planning, and teaching that allows for the essential learnings to be taught across disciplines and through interdisciplinary projects.

- Allow time to create team-based integrated units.

- Ensure the integration of literacy across the content areas.

- Examine skills that are necessary across content areas and determine common benchmarks and strategies to use across the disciplines.

- Create student teams, match them with teacher teams, and keep them together all day.

- Create teacher teams that can effectively support differentiated instruction within each classroom.

- Provide time and support for peer observation and feedback so that teachers can learn from each other.

Cornerstone Strategy #3

Provide structured planning time for teachers to align the curriculum across grades and schools and to map efforts that address the academic, developmental, social, and personal needs of students, especially at critical transition periods (e.g., elementary to middle grades, middle grades to high school).

Breaking Ranks in the Middle recommendations supporting this cornerstone strategy:

Rec. 3.   Each school will regard itself as a community in which members of the staff collaborate to develop and implement the school's learning goals (see p. 89).

Rec. 12.   Each student will have a Personal Plan for Progress that will be reviewed often to ensure that the school takes individual needs into consideration and to allow students, within reasonable parameters, to design their own methods for learning in an effort to meet high standards (see p. 141).

Rec. 13.   Each student will have a Personal Adult Advocate to help him or her personalize the educational experience (see p. 142).

Rec. 18.   Schools, in conjunction with agencies in the community, will help coordinate the delivery of physical and mental health as well as social services (see p. 151).

Rec. 23. The school will promote service programs and student activities as integral to an education, providing opportunities for all students that support and extend academic learning (see p. 205).

Rec. 29. Recognizing that schooling is a continuum, educators must understand what is required of students at every stage and ensure a smooth transition academically and socially for each student from grade to grade and from level to level (see p. 215).

Actions to support this strategy include the following:

- Institute curriculum planning days to discuss data, goals, and strategies. Be sure to include special education, English as a second language (ESL), reading, and gifted education teachers.

- Encourage teams and/or departments to meet monthly to monitor goals

Cornerstone Strategy #4

Implement a comprehensive advisory or other program that ensures that each student has frequent and meaningful opportunities to meet with an adult to plan and assess the student's academic, personal, and social development.

Breaking Ranks in the Middle recommendations supporting this cornerstone strategy:

Rec. 12. Each student will have a Personal Plan for Progress that will be reviewed often to ensure that the school takes individual needs into consideration and to allow students, within reasonable parameters, to design their own methods for learning in an effort to meet high standards (see p. 141).

Rec. 13. Each student will have a Personal Adult Advocate to help him or her personalize the educational experience (see p. 142).

Rec. 16. The school will engage students' families as partners in the students' education (see p. 147).

Rec. 22. The content of the curriculum, where practical, will connect to real-life applications of knowledge and skills, and will extend beyond the school campus to help students link their education to the future and to the community (see p. 203).

Rec. 23. The school will promote service programs and student activities as integral to an education, providing opportunities for all students that support and extend academic learning (see p. 205).

Actions to support this strategy include the following:

- Institute a comprehensive transition program between the feeder schools and your school. This specialized program can be done in conjunction with the larger advisory program—or it can be a separate program—but it must provide an opportunity for an adult to get to know each student well so that the adult can regularly assess whether the academic and student activities programs are meeting the needs of the student.

- Establish developmental awareness resources for adult advocates/advisers, guidelines, and a proposed list of topics to be discussed in a small-group advisory setting or in an individual setting between an adviser or Personal Adult Advocate and an individual student.

- Create a structured program that allows each student to address issues of self-awareness, interpersonal skills, decision-making abilities, and personal safety skills.

- Provide opportunities for students to lead discussions about their own progress and their accomplishments in the advisory setting and in adviser/teacher/family progress checkups.

- Allocate resources and time for students to research and investigate high school opportunities and career choices.

- Require each student, in conjunction with his or her adviser *and* family, to prepare a Personal Plan for Progress (PPP) that might include the following:

  - Reflections on personal aspirations and an academic courses/student activities strategy that may lead to realization of those aspirations.

  - A review of the student's personal learning profile (gender, culture, learning style, and intelligence preference).

  - Areas of strength and areas for improvement (academically, developmentally, socially).

  - Specific products or portfolio items demonstrating accomplishments and progress in academic areas, student activities, sports, and school or community leadership. (See model PPP in Appendix 3.)

Many schools either have an advisory program or have tried one in the past. Often these programs have been little more than established "homeroom" time, opportunities to distribute paperwork, or time for school announcements. Effective, well-planned advisory programs can offer much more. In *Changing Systems to Personalize Learning: Discover the Power of Advisories* (Osofsky, Sinner, & Wolk, 2003), Clarke reviewed the research and found the following beneficial effects of an effective advisory program:

- Academic achievement was improved, failing grades were reduced, and test scores increased.

- 46 percent of teachers believed they influenced several of their advisees to improve their grades.

- Student attitudes improved significantly (75% by one measure).

- Student-teacher relations improved.

- Number of dropouts declined.

- Transition to high school was eased.

- Liaison for the parents was provided.

(See Appendix 1 for five key dimensions of an effective student advisory program.)

Ensure that teachers assess the individual learning needs of students and tailor instructional strategies and multiple assessments accordingly.

Breaking Ranks in the Middle recommendations supporting this cornerstone strategy:

Rec. 5. Every school will be a learning community in which professional development for teachers and the principal is guided by a Personal Learning Plan (PLP) that addresses the individual's learning and professional development needs as they relate to the academic achievement and developmental needs of students at the middle level. (see p. 94).

Rec. 6. The school community will promote policies and practices that recognize diversity in accord with the core values of a democratic and civil society and will offer substantive, ongoing professional development to help educators appreciate issues of diversity and expose students to a rich array of viewpoints, perspectives, and experiences (see p. 98).

Rec. 15. Each school will develop flexible scheduling and student grouping patterns to meet the individual needs of students and to ensure academic success (see p. 143).

Rec. 25. Teachers will know and be able to use a variety of strategies and settings that identify and accommodate individual learning needs and engage students (see p. 208).

Rec. 27. Teachers will be adept at acting as coaches and facilitators to promote more active involvement of students in their own learning (see p. 212).

Rec. 28. Teachers will integrate assessment into instruction so that assessment is accomplished using a variety of methods that do not merely measure students but become part of the learning process (see p. 213).

Rec. 30. Schools will develop a strategic plan to make technology integral to curriculum, instruction, and assessment, accommodating different learning needs and helping teachers individualize and improve the learning process (see p. 218).

Practices to support this strategy include the following:

■ Assess student readiness, interest, and learning profile (gender, culture, learning style, and intelligence preference).

■ Conduct inventories of instructional strategies through observations to discover whether or not teachers are using a variety of strategies. (See Instructional Practices Inventory, p 188.)

■ Engage teachers in in-depth discussions of the data and effective instructional strategies that promote student learning.

■ Allow students to construct knowledge. In an example in *Breaking Ranks,* teachers offer a list of key questions to guide this inquiry or provide students with the titles of books and articles that are pertinent to uncovering the knowledge. A student is then responsible "for unlocking the knowledge, analyzing it, synthesizing it, and presenting it as a body of material for which he or she has taken possession" ([*Breaking Ranks,* 1996, p, 62]).

- Provide development and teaming opportunities so that teachers learn how to incorporate seminars, inquiry-based learning, cooperative learning, debates, field experiences, independent study, laboratories, reflection, and project-based learning into the traditional repertoire of lectures and question-and-answer periods.

- Use preassessments, formative and summative standards-based assessments, rubrics, panel review, performance testing, or portfolio assessments.

- Investigate strategies to vigorously support the growth of students who struggle with school and consistently challenge students who are advanced in knowledge, understanding, and skill.

Many schools incorporate some of these practices to a limited extent, but how prevalent are they across the curriculum? How many teachers still rely on lecturing for every class? Do you have a way to assess how often teachers are using a variety of strategies? In what systematic ways does your school assess students' individual learning needs? These are just a few of the questions that should be addressed as you review the practices associated with this strategy—practices proven to increase students' level of engagement and improve academic achievement.[2]

In addition to learning being more memorable for students who are involved and engaged, the Education Alliance at Brown University has found that schools implementing this strategy have

- Fewer students dropping out.

- Improved class attendance rates.

- Fewer discipline referrals.

- Improved teacher attendance.

- Improved test scores.[3]

Cornerstone Strategy #6

Entrust teachers with the responsibility of implementing schedules that are flexible enough to accommodate teaching strategies consistent with the ways students learn most effectively and that allow for effective teacher teaming, common planning time, and other lesson planning.

Breaking Ranks in the Middle recommendations supporting this cornerstone strategy:

Rec. 3. Each school will regard itself as a community in which members of the staff collaborate to develop and implement the school's learning goals.

Rec. 4. Teachers and teacher teams will provide the leadership essential to the success of reform and will collaborate with others in the educational community to redefine the role of the teacher and identify sources of support for that redefined role.

Rec. 15. Each school will develop flexible scheduling and student grouping patterns to meet the individual needs of students and to ensure academic success.

Rec. 21. The school will reorganize the traditional department structure and foster the use of teacher teams provided with ample common planning time to integrate the school's curriculum to the extent possible and emphasize depth over breadth of coverage.

[2]Valerie E. Lee and Julia B. Smith's "High School Restructuring and Student Achievement" (as cited in Breaking Ranks: Changing an American Institution, 1996).

[3]Education Alliance at Brown University, Roundtable discussion of benefits, July 2003.

Does Your School Need to Break Ranks?

Rec. 26.   Each teacher will have a broad base of academic knowledge, with depth in at least one subject area.

Rec. 27.   Teachers will be adept at acting as coaches and facilitators to promote more active involvement of students in their own learning.

Rec. 28.   Teachers will integrate assessment into instruction so that assessment is accomplished using a variety of methods that do not merely measure students but become part of the learning process.

Actions to support this strategy include the following:

- Increase the time allowed for sustained learning by adjusting the length of class periods.

- Adjust the length of the school day.

- Adjust the length of the school year—trimesters or year-round school.

- Institute a.m/p.m. structures—mornings for class instruction, afternoons for work- and community-based learning, student activities, professional development, and integrated team planning.

- Integrate the curriculum to allow for more instructional time.

- Implement teacher and student teaming.

- Increase the frequency and improve the opportunities for common planning time for teachers.

- Take advantage of community-based learning opportunities aligned with essential learnings.

- Create small units to improve the quantity and quality of student–teacher interaction.

This strategy purposefully incorporates several concepts: flexible time, individual learning profiles (gender, culture, learning style, and intelligence preference), and preparation for implementing effective teaching strategies. Flexible scheduling should support instruction; it should not be a goal in and of itself. Implemented in isolation from other instructional changes, flexible schedules will simply permit teachers to teach the same way they always have *for longer periods.* Without preparing faculty for flexible scheduling and without a comprehensive understanding of the use of various strategies to accommodate individual learning styles and intelligence preferences, flexible scheduling will not achieve its intended results. Conversely, done properly, "flexible scheduling and faculty teamwork allow for a level of depth and an interdisciplinary approach that provides students with a much richer educational experience" (Fine & Somerville as cited in Cotton, 2004, p. 22). In general, flexible scheduling can also help teachers establish better relationships with students and lower the overall frenetic pace of the school. Students aren't racing from class to class (and don't need to be encouraged to do so, thereby eliminating opportunities for unnecessary confrontation), teachers have more than a three-minute time frame to switch their mindset from one class to the next, and roll call and other administrative tasks do not occupy such a high percentage of what should be learning time.

Institute structural leadership systems that allow for substantive involvement in decision making by students, teachers, family members, and the community and that support effective communication among these groups.

Breaking Ranks in the Middle recommendations supporting this cornerstone strategy:

Rec. 2. Each school will establish a site council and accord other meaningful roles in decision making to students, parents, and members of the staff to promote student learning and an atmosphere of participation, responsibility, and ownership.

Rec. 4. Teachers and teacher teams will provide the leadership essential to the success of reform and will collaborate with others in the educational community to redefine the role of the teacher and identify sources of support for that redefined role.

Rec. 7. Schools will build partnerships with institutions of higher education to provide teachers and administrators at both levels with ideas and opportunities to enhance the education, performance, and evaluation of educators.

Rec. 8. Schools will develop political and financial relationships with individuals, organizations, and businesses to support and supplement educational programs and policies.

Rec. 9. At least once every five years, each school will convene a broadly based external review panel to develop and deliver a public description of the school, a requirement that could be met in conjunction with the evaluations of state, regional, and other accrediting groups.

Rec. 29. Recognizing that schooling is a continuum, educators must understand what is required of students at every stage and ensure a smooth transition academically and socially for each student from grade to grade and from level to level.

Actions to support this strategy include the following:

■ Formalize participation of students, teachers, family, and community members in site-based decision-making teams, school leadership councils, strategic planning and school improvement teams, and so on.

■ Develop a program to support Personal Plans for Progress that allow students to plan their learning and the activities to support it.

■ Institute conferences in which the students lead the discussion (e.g., students would lead the discussion about strengths and areas of improvement in the parent/teacher/student conference).

■ Provide student government and other leadership forums with opportunities to be included in discussions of substantive issues.

■ Offer families significant opportunities to monitor student progress on a regular basis (i.e., report cards are not enough). Meet with families on weekends or at home, or accommodate work schedules in other ways.

Does Your School
Need to Break Ranks?

- Encourage family and community members to become involved in curriculum and fiscal conversations.

Schools should not underestimate the power that gaining the trust of families and parents can play in gaining the trust of students. Despite research indicating that students whose parents stay involved tend to fare better academically and socially than others, families become less and less involved as students progress from elementary to middle school to high school. This disconnect happens for any number of reasons but, as *Breaking Ranks* advises, commitment from both families and students is essential to improved student engagement:

> People more readily commit themselves to an institution that accords them a measure of influence over its operations. Students should know that things do not just happen to them; that they can act to affect outcomes (*Breaking Ranks,* 1996, p. 32).

Cornerstone Strategy #8

Align all programs and structures so that all social, economic, and racial/ethnic groups have open and equal access to challenging activities and learning.

Breaking Ranks in the Middle recommendations supporting this cornerstone strategy:

Rec. 12.   Each student will have a Personal Plan for Progress that will be reviewed often to ensure that the school takes individual needs into consideration and to allow students, within reasonable parameters, to design their own methods for learning in an effort to meet high standards.

Rec. 13.   Each student will have a Personal Adult Advocate to help him or her personalize the educational experience.

Rec. 17.   The school community, which cannot be values-neutral, will advocate and model a set of core values essential in a democratic and civil society.

Rec. 20.   Each school will present alternatives to tracking and ability grouping.

Rec. 22.   The content of the curriculum, where practical, will connect to real-life applications of knowledge and skills, and will extend beyond the school campus to help students link their education to the future and to the community.

Rec. 23.   The school will promote service programs and student activities as integral to an education, providing opportunities for all students that support and extend academic learning.

Rec. 25.   Teachers will know and be able to use a variety of strategies and settings that identify and accommodate individual learning needs and engage students.

Actions to support this strategy include the following:

- Construct teams with a range of expertise levels to encourage peer mentoring and ensure that a particular group of students does not get the uncertified, unqualified, or unprepared teachers.

- Review the composition of the student body. Document that minorities are proportionately represented in challenging classes and not disproportionately represented in less challenging classes or special education classes.

- Place your most qualified teachers to teach those in greatest need, so that these students do not fall farther and farther behind. (If you do not do this, by the time these students reach ninth grade the chances they will drop out are very high.)

- Ensure that each student has a Personal Plan for Progress (PPP) that the student, family, and adviser/teacher/counselor review regularly.

- Don't allow maturity levels to be the sole selector for class assignments. Intellectual development and maturity are not always in synch.

- Create a team to align the curriculum of "sending" schools with your own, communicate expectations for students, and collaborate with elementary grade teachers on teaching strategies that can lower the number of students who enter your school requiring remedial help to perform on grade level in reading and math and challenge the students who enter your school performing significantly above grade level in one or more areas. Create a similar team for "receiving" schools to test your school's ability to prepare students for challenging courses in high school.

- Develop students' ability to participate in and lead conversations focused on making diversity a valued part of the learning experience.

- Engage teachers in conversations about their assumptions/stereotypes.

Principles for Building an English Language Learner (ELL)–Responsive Learning Environment

School leaders, administrators, and educators recognize that educating ELLs is the responsibility of the entire school staff.

Educators recognize the heterogeneity of the student population that is collectively labeled as ELL and are able to vary their responses to the needs of different learners.

The school climate and general practice reinforce the principle that students' languages and cultures are resources for further learning.

There are strong and seamless links connecting home, school, and community.

ELLs have equitable access to all school resources and programs.

Teachers have high expectations for ELLs.

Teachers are properly prepared and willing to teach ELLs.

Language and literacy are infused throughout the educational process, including curriculum and instruction.

Assessment is authentic, credible to learners and instructors, and takes into account first- and second-language literacy development.

Source: Claiming Opportunities.

Cornerstone Strategy #9

Align the schoolwide comprehensive, ongoing professional development program and the Personal Learning Plans (PLPs) of staff members with the requisite knowledge of content, instructional strategies, and student developmental factors.

Principal's Journal
PLP vs. PPP

• PLPs (Personal Learning Plans) are for adults—faculty, administrators, staff, etc.

• PPPs (Personal Plans for Progress) are for students.

• Both PLPs and PPPs are designed to encourage the authors to look at their own learning needs, interests, strengths, and perceived weaknesses.

• Both should be reviewed and updated regularly.

Breaking Ranks in the Middle recommendations supporting this cornerstone strategy:

Rec. 5. Every school will be a learning community in which professional development for teachers and the principal is guided by a Personal Learning Plan that addresses the individual's learning and professional development needs as they relate to the academic achievement and developmental needs of students at the middle level.

Rec. 25. Teachers will know and be able to use a variety of strategies and settings that identify and accommodate individual learning needs and engage students.

Rec. 26. Each teacher will have a broad base of academic knowledge, with depth in at least one subject area.

Rec. 30. Schools will develop a strategic plan to make technology integral to curriculum, instruction, and assessment, accommodating different learning needs and helping teachers individualize and improve the learning process.

Actions to support this strategy include the following:

■ Align the schoolwide professional development program with the essential learnings, content and performance standards, and instructional strategies established in Cornerstone Strategy #1.

■ Ensure that each educator creates a PLP that addresses his or her continuous professional development. The plan should address knowledge and skills related to improved student learning and should be aligned with the school's essential learnings. Just as each student's PPP provides opportunities for the student to reflect on goals and progress toward reaching those goals, the PLP for each staff member should provide opportunities for formal, systematic reflection and self-appraisal. The plans should draw on

- Teachers' own professional reflections.

- Portfolios that teachers maintain of their teaching activities.

- Observations by supervisors and colleagues.

- Appraisals by students.

■ Institute a formal, comprehensive induction program for new teachers and experienced teachers who are new to the school.

■ Provide opportunities for teachers to teach colleagues what they have learned from various professional development seminars, conferences, and so on.

■ Develop a mentoring process.

■ Establish peer observation with feedback as a standard approach to identifying professional development needs and strategies.

- Ensure that professional development is continuous and that each development opportunity is reinforced with follow-up activities that include practice, performance, reflection, and feedback. (i.e., avoid "drive-by" professional development).

- Align the hiring process and subsequent professional development to ensure that the skills of new teachers can meet the challenges incumbent in instituting the Breaking Ranks in the Middle cornerstone strategies described in the last several pages.

Professional development is critical to the success of the other eight cornerstone strategies. Without proper planning and development, is it reasonable to think that a school could establish and implement essential learnings; create dynamic teams and improve the quality of interactions; align curriculum and facilitate smooth transitions for students; institute an effective advisory program; use a variety of instructional strategies and assessments; implement flexible schedules; increase the substantive involvement of families, students, and the community; and ensure equity?

The steps you can take as an effective leader to support a comprehensive, ongoing professional development program in the context of bringing about change in your school are discussed in greater detail in the next chapter.

Tying It All Together

The nine cornerstone strategies are an important beginning and provide a systematic approach to implementing most of the 30 Breaking Ranks in the Middle recommendations. Assigning the recommendations to three clusters as we have done may simplify discussion and digestion of the material; however, it is important to understand the interdependence of the recommendations. As *Breaking Ranks* reminds us,

> As a complex institution, [a school] comprises many interlocking parts. Alter one element and you affect others. Thus, the recommendations…are best viewed as a series of connected proposals that in many instances depend on implementation in one area for success in another…. Piecemeal change may lead to some positive results, but it is not apt to be as effective as efforts that reach into the various parts of the system, in other words, systemic reform. [Schools] need more than tinkering (p. 6).

As you begin to address challenges in your school, the interconnectedness of the recommendations will become clear. Figure 1.1 on page 28 portrays that interconnectedness graphically.

Breaking Ranks in the Middle Recommendations

Collaborative Leadership and Professional Learning Communities

1. The principal will provide leadership in the school community by building and maintaining a vision, direction, and focus for student learning.

2. Each school will establish a site council and accord other meaningful roles in decision making to students, parents, and members of the staff to promote student learning and an atmosphere of participation, responsibility, and ownership.

3. Each school will regard itself as a community in which members of the staff collaborate to develop and implement the school's learning goals.

4. Teachers and teacher teams will provide the leadership essential to the success of reform and will collaborate with others in the educational community to redefine the role of the teacher and identify sources of support for that redefined role.

5. Every school will be a learning community in which professional development for teachers and the principal is guided by a Personal Learning Plan that addresses the individual's learning and professional development needs as they relate to the academic achievement and developmental needs of students at the middle level.

6. The school community will promote policies and practices that recognize diversity in accord with the core values of a democratic and civil society and will offer substantive, ongoing professional development to help educators appreciate issues of diversity and expose students to a rich array of viewpoints, perspectives, and experiences.

7. Schools will build partnerships with institutions of higher education to provide teachers and administrators at both levels with ideas and opportunities to enhance the education, performance, and evaluation of educators.

8. Schools will develop political and financial relationships with individuals, organizations, and businesses to support and supplement educational programs and policies.

9. At least once every five years, each school will convene a broadly based external review panel to develop and deliver a public description of the school, a requirement that could be met in conjunction with the evaluations of state, regional, and other accrediting groups.

Personalization and the School Environment

10. Schools will create small units in which anonymity is banished.

11. Each teacher involved in the instructional program on a full-time basis will be responsible for contact time with no more than 90 students, so that the teacher can give greater attention to the needs of every student.

12. Each student will have a Personal Plan for Progress that will be reviewed often to ensure that the school takes individual needs into consideration and to allow students, within reasonable parameters, to design their own methods for learning in an effort to meet high standards.

13. Each student will have a Personal Adult Advocate to help him or her personalize the educational experience.

14. Teachers and administrators will convey a sense of caring so that students know that teachers have a stake in student learning.

15. Each school will develop flexible scheduling and student grouping patterns to meet the individual needs of students and to ensure academic success.

16. The school will engage students' families as partners in the students' education.

17. The school community, which cannot be values-neutral, will advocate and model a set of core values essential in a democratic and civil society.

18. Schools, in conjunction with agencies in the community, will help coordinate the delivery of physical and mental health as well as social services.

Curriculum, Instruction, and Assessment

19. Each school will identify a set of essential learnings—in literature and language, writing, mathematics, social studies, science, and the arts—in which students must demonstrate achievement in order to advance to the next level.

20. Each school will present alternatives to tracking and ability grouping.

21. The school will reorganize the traditional department structure and foster the use of teacher teams provided with ample common planning time to integrate the school's curriculum to the extent possible and emphasize depth over breadth of coverage.

22. The content of the curriculum, where practical, will connect to real-life applications of knowledge and skills, and will extend beyond the school campus to help students link their education to the future and to the community.

23. The school will promote service programs and student activities as integral to an education, providing opportunities for all students that support and extend academic learning.

24. Teachers will design high-quality work and teach in ways that engage students, cause them to persist, and, when the work is successfully completed, result in student satisfaction and acquisition of knowledge, critical-thinking and problem-solving skills, and other abilities.

25. Teachers will know and be able to use a variety of strategies and settings that identify and accommodate individual learning needs and engage students.

26. Each teacher will have a broad base of academic knowledge, with depth in at least one subject area.

27. Teachers will be adept at acting as coaches and facilitators to promote more active involvement of students in their own learning.

28. Teachers will integrate assessment into instruction so that assessment is accomplished using a variety of methods that do not merely measure students but become part of the learning process.

29. Recognizing that schooling is a continuum, educators must understand what is required of students at every stage and ensure a smooth transition academically and socially for each student from grade to grade and from level to level.

30. Schools will develop a strategic plan to make technology integral to curriculum, instruction, and assessment, accommodating different learning needs and helping teachers individualize and improve the learning process.

"We Can't Do Any More!"

On the preceding pages, we outlined a variety of steps your school should take to better address the needs of each student. It is likely impossible to implement these reforms without taking a serious look at your current practices and prioritizing the critical versus the important. You may find that some current practices could be handled more effectively or jettisoned altogether. Below, you will find a partial list of practices to review as you prioritize your efforts or seek to use existing time more effectively.

Practices to Creatively Use Existing Time

- Turn regularly scheduled faculty meetings into professional learning opportunities in which teachers study data, address challenges, design interventions, and then study best practices so they can effectively apply the interventions.

- Use a quality student information database that allows for efficient entry of student data. A database is particularly helpful for saving teacher time required to create various reports.

- Create a school lesson bank and organize it by subject, content, and team. With such a bank, for example, the English teacher can see how the math teacher in one team taught a lesson and build on or use that same approach/lesson. Even in schools where coordination among team members is strong, coordination across teams by content may not be so good. Stipulate that only high-quality lessons that have proven effective are added to the lesson bank.

- Hire substitutes for abbreviated time slots (an occasional day) to free up one or more teachers to coordinate or to meet as a group to design curriculum and instruction.

- Schedule regular early dismissal days so teachers can meet for professional development.

- Use parent volunteers, retired community participants, older students, or others to help with some forms of grading to relieve the teacher of those tasks.

- Investigate electronic phone messaging systems that contact parents with messages when students are absent or that ask parents to contact the teacher at a specific time to talk about a student.

- Encourage one member of each teaching team to manage and post information for teachers on the team. This will increase contact with parents and reduce the time needed by each teacher to produce copies and write specific information.

- Use parent volunteers, older students, and so on to produce manipulatives, copies, laminates, and other class materials.

- Implement a schoolwide discipline plan designed not only to be effective but to help teachers save time.

- Dedicate a one-hour after-school session each month to staff development. These sessions are most productive when an administrator or member of the teaching staff is the "expert" presenting the information. Allow teachers to suggest the areas of focus so they see the value in the use of their time and the resourcefulness of their colleagues.

- Use a substitute in a classroom one day a month and free a member of the staff to visit other classrooms in your school or district, or attend a local seminar. This teacher can then share the learning experience in the form of a "classroom spotlight" at the next general staff meeting.

- Invite the district instructional specialist to provide development in individual classrooms by team teaching or coaching.

Breaking Ranks in the Middle Recommendations

- Ask teachers to come in 30 minutes early on certain days to meet in their subject or grade-level teams. When the students arrive, the administrators can take them to the gym for a half-hour assembly (e.g., to honor student achievements). This gives the teachers an hour to study best practices, examine data, and create action plans.

- Hold an annual "Parent as Teacher Day," during which parents volunteer to teach in one of their children's classes for the entire day. (Some working moms and dads are given the time as a service day or volunteer time from their work place.) The lesson taught by the parent must be tied specifically to the subject area; in many cases, you will find parents who are practitioners in science, math, technology, or other related fields. While the parents are teaching, the faculty can meet as a whole, in teams, or by departments for in-depth training. Be sure to follow school and district guidelines regarding criminal history checks and other policies for volunteers.

- Use building or district administrators to cover classes so a teacher can meet with or observe a master teacher. You can also hire a substitute teacher to cover the classes of a novice teacher and master teacher. During the day the substitute will switch back and forth, covering the two teachers' classes, so the master teacher can observe the novice teacher teach, discuss the observation, have the novice teacher observe the master teacher teach, and have a final collegial discussion about areas of strength and those in need of improvement. This is an inexpensive way to give time for mentoring and collegial coaching. It is also nonthreatening, because it is tied to professional growth and development rather than to evaluation and appraisal.

- Create opportunities for central office staff to regularly substitute. For example, if six science teachers from two middle schools need to get together to work on differentiating science labs, six central office leaders could teach their classes on two successive Friday afternoons. It can be a very important experience for the administrators—and a huge sign of confidence, support, and investment in the eyes of the teachers.

- Provide mini-sessions with in-school experts during faculty meeting time (e.g., classroom management for new teachers, using technology to differentiate instruction).

- Allow teachers to apply in groups or teams of three to four for in-school grants that will give them released time to work on areas in which they want to develop additional understanding and skill. Hire substitutes to cover for the teachers one day every two weeks, generally for about two months, to give the teachers time to collaborate. The sessions should be supported by someone in the district who can guide the work of the teachers.

- Provide incentives for key teachers to work during the summer to develop curriculum that can be used by many other teachers at the same grade or subject level. District curriculum leaders should guide the sessions. The curriculum and supporting materials then become the focus of school and/or district staff development, so that a lot of time is saved by not having every teacher reinvent the wheel. The quality of the curriculum is also likely to be much more substantial. It is important to provide staff development in the appropriate use of the curriculum.

- Pay expert teachers during the summer to develop "curriculum tubs" that include well-developed concept-based lessons in key content areas. Place the materials in plastic tubs in a central location, so they can be checked out by any teacher who teaches those lessons. Each tub should contain key learning goals, alignment with standards, a thorough explanation of the lesson sequence, necessary preassessment and formative assessment materials, examples of how to differentiate the lesson for students whose assessment results indicate a need for support or extension, and materials a teacher would need to teach the lesson. Again, ensure that the teachers who create the materials have expert guidance from curriculum leaders in the district.

These lessons are a considerable time-saver for teachers. Be sure to provide a place for teachers who use the lessons to make suggestions for improving them.

■ Hire substitutes for a small group of teachers who are willing to be pioneers in differentiation (or any other topic), so that the teachers can have a one-day retreat early in the year. The retreat should be held away from the interruptions at school (possibly at someone's home) and district or school leaders should be present. Participants can share resources and discuss the need for and implications of differentiated instruction in their schools. Teachers should conclude the retreat by setting goals for themselves as individuals and as a group in becoming more confident practitioners of differentiation and supporting others in doing so. To support this effort, the group could include an agreement to meet one afternoon every other week for three months and one afternoon a week for the remainder of the year. The school should buy or have the cafeteria prepare a light meal for the teachers on retreat. If this is done well, the first group can become the catalyst for similar groups.

■ Hire or appoint a testing coordinator or data specialist to help disaggregate data and provide teacher leaders with vital information. The existence of a database alleviates the need for instructional staff to spend countless hours collecting and organizing data.

■ Start school late one day each month for students (e.g., Wednesday morning), and provide development during that time. If the lost minutes are an issue, extend the school day by one or two minutes.

■ Have the principal do lunch duty every day so teachers have free time to work with colleagues and/or students. Provide parent lunchroom monitors (paid or volunteer).

■ Convene two staff meetings per month: one for the principal; one for a team, grade-level, or curriculum meeting.

:■ Combine two monthly meetings into one longer session (e.g., 4:00–7:00 p.m.). Provide food. The staff may appreciate having one meeting instead of two, and you can get more accomplished during this longer time period.

■ Develop a master schedule that creates daily common planning time for teams and grade-level departments. This creates an additional 45 minutes per day or more of common planning time (above and beyond individual planning time) to discuss curricular and student issues.

■ Schedule elective lunch presentations that allow faculty to report on personal successes, progress in their graduate courses, successful methodologies incorporated in their classrooms, techniques for addressing parent and community issues, and so on.

[The practices in this list were compiled with contributions from Michael Curran, August Frattali, Tim Hadfield, Tom Leyden, Michael Madison, Carol Ann Tomlinson, Jerry Valentine, and Karen Williams.]

Figure 1.1. Nine Cornerstone Strategies

(Also available at www.principals.org/brim)

Category	Recommendation	Establish the academically rigorous essential learnings that a student is required to master in order to successfully make the transition to high school and align the curriculum and teaching strategies to realize that goal (see p. 9).	Create dynamic teacher teams that are afforded common planning time to help organize and improve the quality and quantity of interactions between teachers and students (see p. 10).	Provide structured planning time for teachers to align the curriculum across grades and schools and to map efforts that address the academic, developmental, social, and personal needs of students, especially at critical transition periods (e.g., elementary to middle grades, middle grades to high school) (see p. 11).	Implement a comprehensive advisory or other program that ensures that each student has frequent and meaningful opportunities to meet with an adult to plan and assess the student?s academic, personal, and social development (see p. 12).	Ensure that teachers assess the individual learning needs of students and tailor instructional strategies and multiple assessments accordingly (see p. 14).
Curriculum, Instruction, and Assessment	30 (p. 218)					X
	29 (p. 215)	X		X		
	28 (p. 213)					X
	27 (p. 212)					X
	26 (p. 211)					
	25 (p. 208)					X
	24 (p. 207)	X				
	23 (p. 205)			X	X	
	22 (p. 203)	X		X	X	
	21 (p. 201)	X	X			
	20 (p. 199)					
	19 (p. 195)	X				
Personalizing Your School Environment	18 (p. 151)			X		
	17 (p. 150)					
	16 (p. 147)				X	
	15 (p. 143)					X
	14 (p. 143)		X			
	13 (p. 142)			X	X	
	12 (p. 141)			X	X	
	11 (p. 140)		X			
	10 (p. 139)		X			
Collaborative Leadership and Professional Learning Communities	9 (p. 106)					
	8 (p. 103)					
	7 (p. 102)					
	6 (p. 98)					X
	5 (p. 94)					X
	4 (p. 90)		X			
	3 (p. 89)			X		
	2 (p. 88)					
	1 (p. 87)	X	X	X	X	X

Nine Cornerstone Strategies

Figure 1.1. Nine Cornerstone Strategies *continued*

Category	Recommendation	Entrust teachers with the responsibility of implementing schedules that are flexible enough to accommodate teaching strategies consistent with the ways students learn most effectively and that allow for effective teacher teaming, common planning time, and other lesson planning (see p. 15).	Institute structural leadership systems that allow for substantive involvement in decision making by students, teachers, family members, and the community, and that support effective communication among these groups (see p. 17).	Align all programs and structures so that all social, economic, and racial/ethnic groups have open and equal access to challenging activities and learning (see p. 18).	Align the schoolwide comprehensive, ongoing professional development program and the Personal Learning Plans (PLPs) of staff members with the requisite knowledge of content, instructional strategies, and student developmental factors (see p. 20).
Curriculum, Instruction, and Assessment	30 (p. 218)				X
	29 (p. 215)		X		
	28 (p. 213)	X			
	27 (p. 212)	X			
	26 (p. 211)	X			X
	25 (p. 208)			X	X
	24 (p. 207)				
	23 (p. 205)			X	
	22 (p. 203)			X	
	21 (p. 201)	X			
	20 (p. 199)			X	
	19 (p. 195)				
Personalization and the School Environment	18 (p. 151)				
	17 (p. 150)			X	
	16 (p. 147)				
	15 (p. 143)	X			
	14 (p. 143)				
	13 (p. 142)			X	
	12 (p. 141)			X	
	11 (p. 140)				
	10 (p. 139)				
Collaborative Leadership and Professional Learning Communities	9 (p. 106)		X		
	8 (p. 103)		X		
	7 (p. 102)		X		
	6 (p. 98)				
	5 (p. 94)				X
	4 (p. 90)	X	X		
	3 (p. 89)	X			
	2 (p. 88)		X		
	1 (p. 87)	X	X	X	X

Nine Cornerstone Strategies

In Their Own Words...

The following is the first of four school profiles. Each profile has been written from the personal perspective of the principal. The profiles are designed to show the comprehensive and interdependent nature of the reforms your school is being called upon to undertake. Although not all the changes each school has instituted will be appropriate for your school, the perspective of your colleagues should nevertheless be valuable and may form the basis of a discussion for your team. At the end of this profile, you will find a Q&A with the Principal followed by several questions to help lead your faculty or team through a discussion. For a protocol to help lead the text-based discussion, see Appendix 4.

It's Worked for 10 Years—Why Should I Change Now?
by Suzanne H. Smith

Only when we know where we are can we begin to determine where we need to go.

When I arrived at J. F. Kennedy Middle School in 1990, I had a pretty good idea of where we were. Turnover among school administrators was high; two principals had been assigned to the school in four years. I arrived at a site that was operating like a dysfunctional family, saddled with high rates of student suspension and expulsion, gang activity, low attendance rates, high tardy rates, high discipline referrals, no parent involvement, and staff dissension. Morale was low among staff members, who referred to the school as "the other junior high school across the tracks" of the El Centro School District. There was no time set aside for teachers to meet, plan, or collaborate—much less a desire or interest in doing so. Curriculum consistency was extremely limited, contributing to poor student performance; different textbooks were used in the same department and grade level. Low grades and low standardized test scores were the norm. Student scores on California's standardized test consistently ranked in the lowest quintile in both reading and mathematics. Special education students were grouped in pull-out programs; inclusion programs were not the norm—even students with stronger academic proficiency had little or no access to core classes. There was no advisory program or extended day program available to provide timely assistance to students in need. The only after-school "program" was detention.

The traditional row after row of desks was the norm and a do-not-speak-until-spoken-to attitude existed in many classrooms. Instructional strategies were very teacher centered, consisting primarily of lecture, drill, and practice with extremely limited use of technology to enhance student learning. The curriculum was textbook-driven and

School Profile 1
J.F. Kennedy Middle School   p. 31

School Profile 1
J. F. Kennedy Middle School

El Centro, CA

720 students

Grade span 6–8

68 percent limited English-speaking students

100 percent low socioeconomic

14 percent special education

For statistics, contacts, and other information about the school, go to www. principals.org/brim.

Practices to look for include:
- *use of data, vertical teaming, transition, common planning time, PLPs, and teacher portfolios*

strictly departmentalized. Curriculum integration, collaboration across disciplines, and communication left a lot to be desired.

Poor communication among the staff mirrored poor communication between home and school. No materials were available for parents who spoke a language other than English—this in a school in which the majority of parents are Spanish speakers—and communication with parents was limited by the teachers' inability to speak the parents' language. Parents were viewed as a relatively insignificant part of the teacher, parent, and student equation. Teachers made little effort to invite parents to become involved in the school—primarily because teachers simply didn't know how.

Why Change?

How can a leadership team begin to change a school in which a frequently heard sentiment was "I've used the same lesson plans for the last 10 years, and they've worked. Why should I change now?"

Unfortunately, the reality was that things weren't working. For many teachers, the daily goal was simply to keep the lid on an active volcano. Like a dysfunctional family, the formula was simple: If you do the same old things and ignore problems, maybe they'll just go away. Clearly there were problems, and everyone knew it. Though many viewed the problems as insurmountable, a few courageous teachers and I stepped forward to begin the process of change and reform.

Things have come a long way since those days. Kennedy Middle School now boasts attendance rates averaging 97 percent; since 1990, tardiness rates have dropped from a high of 45 per day to an average of 3 per day, suspensions have dropped by 50 percent, and office referrals have dropped by 55 percent. The staff works as a team—able to share values, beliefs, and vision, and with a desire to bring that vision to life. To increase student success, we have moved from a teacher-centered focus to a student-centered focus, all while moving toward site-based management. Parent involvement and participation is at 48 percent measured by involvement in parent trainings as well as attendance at Back-to-School night and at parent conferences.

The First Steps Toward Reform and Renewal

So how did we get from where we were to where we are? In education we are told *what* we need to do (improve student achievement), but often what is lacking is *how* to do it. Kennedy's success can be linked to a series of interconnected and overlapping steps toward improvement that our staff has undertaken. But something, someone, or some group had to drive that change.

As I reflect on the early years of my tenure at Kennedy, perseverance (some might call it stubbornness), drive, and possibly naivetè were my trademarks. It was difficult serving as the first female principal (and a non-Spanish-speaker as well) to lead a staff that had, for the most part, served in the educational system at least 10 years longer than I. With so many challenges, the question was where to begin. It was difficult to make changes, because the staff had "ruled" the campus for so long that any attempted change was perceived as an attack on their leadership. I quickly discovered that many had a direct line to Board of Education members, which caused the superintendent to question my decisions on a daily basis. The board actually hired an outside consultant during the spring of my second year to determine whether I was the problem. If the answer had been "yes," I would have been terminated. However, I believed in what I was doing and had no doubt what the outside consultant would find. In fact, the consultant reported that "the administration is to be commended for her commitment to the students. All feel that with some extra support from the District Office in reorganizing and/or improving the before-mentioned areas, the students could achieve their full potential." The board realized that I was not the problem but that a problem indeed existed and needed to be addressed. The slow and sometimes agonizing process of change could now begin.

Each night during that time I thought, "Why am I staying the course?" It would have been very easy to fall in line and just collect the paycheck. We could have simply maintained the status quo—with everyone apparently happy and no complaints to board members. But was it right? When I questioned myself, I always came back to the same answer: I was making decisions in the best interest of students—and that was the right thing. Students' needs had to remain first and foremost in my thoughts. I needed to identify the challenges to be addressed and then prioritize how to approach the necessary change. The challenges came in all four areas a principal might imagine: teachers, students, parents, and the curriculum. All four needed to be addressed at the same time, because one could not change without the others.

Modeling was and is the key. Doing what I said I was going to do and being honest, with no hidden agenda, was critical. Evaluating teachers fairly and honestly, showing them clearly what was expected for improvement and providing the support for that improvement set the stage for high expectations. Of course, along the way I had to accept the grievances and address differences in philosophy and attitude that sometimes translated into non-reelects, movement toward removal, or placing a teacher on administrative leave. It also meant long, long hours each night fighting the "paper war" of proper documentation.

A few teachers who were in agreement with my beliefs began to surface. I saw who the new leaders were going to be, supported their efforts, and placed them in charge of various committees. These appointments showed teachers what I valued. Staff members who had opposed what we were trying to do and who began to lose their self-perceived leadership roles either requested a transfer or decided to jump on board. After five years (and one teacher losing credentials, two put on administrative leave, four requesting a transfer, five non-reelections, the removal of a secretary, two depositions, and testimony before a judge), we were finally able to move forward with what mattered and why we were here: to educate students.

One necessary priority was to build trust among staff members—not from the top down, but by building collaborative relationships based on mutual dependence and support. I was earning the support of teachers, in part because I believed so strongly in shared leadership and decision making. It was critical to know when to "push" and when to "pull" staff, and when and how to plant the seeds so ideas for improvement and creation of programs were generated by staff.

After working together to identify problems at the site that we could control (and those we could not), teachers assumed leadership roles on newly formed committees for school improvement. Committees researched, presented findings to staff, asked for suggestions for improvement, planned, and monitored implementation of improvements, such as the creation of an advisory program, the design of a comprehensive discipline plan, and the inception of efforts to increase parent attendance at conferences. I knew that for solutions to really make a difference, they had to grow out of a collaborative approach to problem solving. Mandates from management might result in some change, but the change wouldn't be long lasting or meaningful. Everyone works more diligently if they are involved in creating the ideas. And, once involved, no one likes to fail. It was important during this time that I provide mini-

This had to be their idea, their way of problem solving, and I needed it to say "theirs," not mine. My job was to facilitate, provide some direction and ideas, accept their work, and offer praise for a job well done.

mal input, believing that teachers would make the necessary adjustments. This had to be their idea, their way of problem solving, and I needed it to say "theirs," not mine. My job was to facilitate, provide some direction and ideas, accept their work, and offer praise for a job well done.

As staff members became empowered, they realized the need to strengthen their classroom management skills; they also realized that with persistence, perseverance, and a clear vision, they could create classroom learning environments that were more favorable to learning and thus enhance student achievement. They began to look at the lack of student control as a *teacher* problem, not a *student* problem. As I often said, it's easy to kick a student out of class or school; it's difficult at times to keep them in. We began to understand that student failures were also our failures.

It was critical to listen to the underlying concerns of those who at first appeared to want to put their own needs above those of students or the team as a whole. It was important to draw from the teachers their frustrations and identify what they perceived as obstacles to student learning. As part of this effort, I asked teachers to list the items they believed we did not have control over. The list included undisciplined students, parents who do not care, poverty, non-English-speaking parents, limited resources, and kids not coming to school. Teachers were then asked what they thought was needed to solve each problem, and committees were formed to find solutions.

Use of Student and Schoolwide Data... from the Beginning

Let me repeat: Only when we know where we are can we begin to determine where we need to go.

Data analysis and goal-setting must go hand in hand. Proper data collection and analysis provide irrefutable evidence to support accountability and responsibility for student learning. Before my arrival, data collection was nonexistent, except for the results of the mandated California State standardized tests; these were received at the end of a school year—far too late to make adjustments for students. Even this information was not broken down by teacher, grade level, or department; it was simply placed in each student's folder. Without data, accountability becomes problematic or nonexistent.

I needed to know what was occurring (or not occurring) and be able to share the facts with the staff. With the help of the school secretary, I backtracked student information for the previous five years. By hand, we entered the information into a database—student by student, year by year. Our efforts included entering results of standardized tests in reading, language arts, and math; disaggregating performance and other data such as matched scores (cohorts), special education, migrant, and gender; creating graphs for each of these areas; and analyzing and graphing semester grades by department. In the areas of behavioral data, we completed the same process for attendance rates, tardy rates, suspension rates, expulsion rates, discipline referrals, teacher referrals, and so on. These data were compiled and the facts were shared with staff members during schoolwide presentations. After the initial introduction of the data, I informed the teachers that I would be breaking down the data by teacher to determine the impact each teacher was having on the population he or she served. I prepared the information and provided it to the teachers. It was an eye-opener for many and embarrassing for some, but the foundation was laid for the future. During teacher evaluations, I addressed the impact each teacher was having on student achievement in the "pupil progress" area. Teachers who were having a positive impact thanked me for acknowledging their hard work.

It's easy to kick a student out of class or school; it's difficult at times to keep them in. We began to understand that student failures were also our failures.

Today, I no longer break down the data for the teachers. Instead, they receive the schoolwide data, pull out their student data, analyze and interpret, reflect, and provide me with a written analysis of what they learned from the data. They write about their gains in student achievement, drops in student achievement, and their impact on various groups (e.g., ELLs, special education students, migrants). They analyze and target their areas of strength, identify areas for improvement, and provide "next steps." As one teacher said, "Having us pull out the data really made me look at each student. I had a much better handle on the situation and a better understanding of where my students were." Our use of data has allowed us to eliminate the excuses. We have moved beyond the principal providing the teachers with student data analysis; instead, I draw the analysis from the teachers and encourage them to tell me what they need to get the job done.

In moving toward high teacher accountability, it is difficult for teachers to be in denial or place blame on others if data are used fairly and appropriately. *Trust* in how the data are to be used is extremely important. You can only hold a teacher accountable for the time he or she has with the student—not what happened or did not happen in previous years. To be fair, one must measure where the students start at the beginning of the year and where they end up. For example, at the beginning of the year, a teacher is provided with student standardized test scores (and/or other measures). These data become the baseline. At the end of the school year, we review the data to determine the movement of students within a level or from one level to another. This review is one way to identify and target teacher and/or curriculum development and improvement while helping reinforce accountability for instruction. It is also a way to encourage teachers to let go of unproductive practices. Our use of data has evolved to include evaluating student achievement on multiple assessments, such as district writing and math assessments, quarterly tests in English language arts, math monthly tests, and semester grades. By measuring student progress throughout the year around established pacing guides, we are able to act immediately rather than wait until the end of the year. The use of data allows us to always ask, "Who is making it, who is not, and what are *we* going to do about it?"

In figure 1.2, 83 percent of Teacher A's students showed academic improvement, while 17 percent did not; 83 percent of the students either increased their math score but stayed in the same level or moved up an entire level or even two. The same movement occurred for Teachers B and C, but at different rates. Teachers D and E appear to have had a negative impact on student achievement: 63 percent and 79 percent of their students, respectively, dropped within a level or an entire level. These scores would be of great concern to the teacher as well as to the administration.

We share these data with the entire school. It is important for staff members to provide support to each other. It is equally important that teachers know who is having an impact on student achievement, so they know whom to observe, model, or go to for additional assistance, and who *may be* simply collecting a paycheck—and thus doing damage to students.

As data-driven decision making began to take hold at Kennedy, accountability and a sense of responsibility for student learning grew. Data truly began to drive the improvement process; all programs were monitored for their effectiveness, and adjustments were made as needed on an ongoing basis. Kennedy's data-driven approach eventually allowed the staff to track the growth and improvement of students and their rising scores. Planning and implementation were tied to California State Standards and the increased effectiveness of the entire school community. Not surprisingly, students

Not surprisingly, students responded positively to the increased level of specific feedback that teachers were able to provide.

responded positively to the increased level of specific feedback that teachers were able to provide. This clear picture of learning opened the doors for staff to work together even more closely to integrate various disciplines, thus increasing student achievement. Staff members also met by department at the beginning of the year to discuss school-wide achievement and target strengths and areas of weaknesses. Departments then presented the results of their findings to the entire staff.

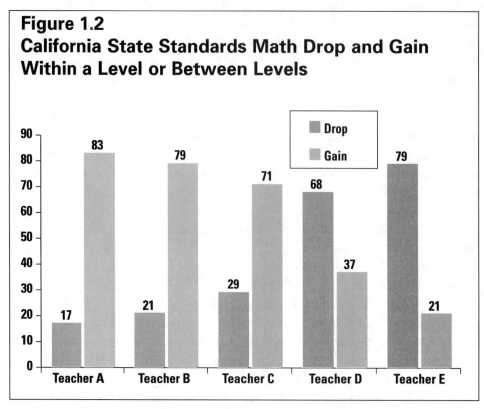

Figure 1.2
California State Standards Math Drop and Gain Within a Level or Between Levels

What do you measure and why? To determine the effectiveness of a program you must attach an assessment to it. At Kennedy, we measure all programs that are in place. Data are used to create seating charts for cooperative grouping; to build the master schedule; to determine which students would benefit from additional instructional time in math or language arts and which need to be in extended day support programs and/or Saturday school and summer institutes; and to target parents of struggling students for enrollment in parent training programs or for additional conferences.

We also used data to measure or review the following:

■ The impact of our parent training program on student achievement.

■ Grade point averages of students whose parents attended our "How to Help Your Child Succeed with Homework" compared with GPAs of students whose parents did not attend.

■ Achievement of students who attended an after-school writing program compared with the achievement of students who did not attend.

■ Review of our homework lunch program to see whether it increased the number of students doing their homework. (We found it had no impact on the number of students doing homework; however, it did lower discipline problems during lunch time.)

■ Interventions during the school day.

Student Use of Data

Students need to know how they are doing academically. Both schoolwide and individual data must be shared with students. At Kennedy, students use the data to set achievement goals. During the advisory period at the beginning of each school year, the teacher meets with each student to discuss various measures (e.g., state standardized scores, district assessments, GPA, behavioral data). Together, the teacher and student discuss strengths and challenges and set performance and behavioral goals and, if necessary, the additional support provided by the extended day program. It is critical that the goal be realistic, that the student knows that the goal is attainable if the student applies him- or herself, that progress toward meeting the goal is tracked and recognized, and that goal achievement is celebrated (e.g., at school assemblies, through an announcement by a teacher, through notes to students and their families). Students must know where they are so they can make a plan for where they want to be. To help students stay on top of where they are, advisory teachers review the grades their students have earned every six weeks. The advisory teacher provides counseling and guidance based on the grades.

Students must know where they are so they can make a plan for where they want to be.

Students and families are also kept abreast of how the school is doing overall. California provides each school with a target it must reach each year as measured by the California Standardized Testing and Reporting (CA STAR) test. A base is determined by the state. Figure 1.3 shows the progress Kennedy has made since the 2000 school year. The goal of the state is that all schools reach a score of 800. While we are not there yet, this chart shows the community, parents, students, and teachers the progress we are making.

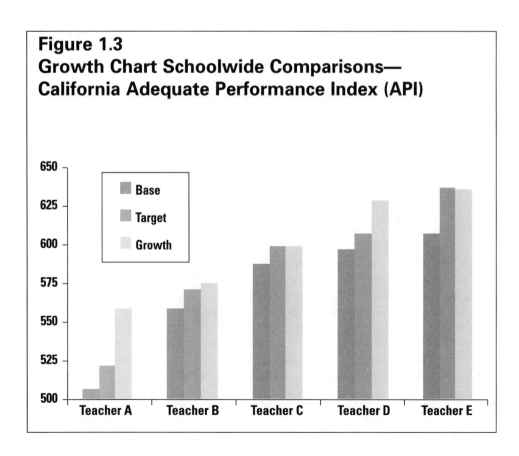

Figure 1.3
Growth Chart Schoolwide Comparisons—California Adequate Performance Index (API)

Teacher Use of Data

To facilitate schoolwide success, teachers need opportunities to learn and ask questions about data collection and reporting systems. Teachers need to use student data to differentiate instruction, to target struggling students, to heighten the level of student engagement, and to arrange cooperative grouping (e.g., setting up groups according to ability—a "low high" student with a "middle high" student, a "middle low" student with a "high low" student). It is critical for each teacher to clearly understand the impact he or she has on each student and the overall impact on student achievement. For us, this means ensuring that teachers have data to verify not only that student achievement is improving but how quickly it is improving and for which students, and which students need further assistance. Teachers gathered data about individual students—from test results, classroom and homework assignments, and so on—analyzed the data, and developed a plan for continuing to improve student achievement. (See figure 1.4.)

Teachers willingly provide the data broken down by student and class, because they know I would not ask them to do busywork. It did not take long for teachers to realize that change occurs more rapidly when collaboration exists among the staff. Teachers began to develop a common understanding of each student and to share techniques for working with each student. This collaboration allowed a teacher who may have given up on a student to realize that other teachers were successful in teaching that student; thus, the "unsuccessful" teacher was driven to redouble efforts and review his or her techniques for reaching that student.

Figure 1.4
Sample Student Placement Chart

(Based on California State Standards Levels of Achievement)

Far Below Basic (FBB) ≤ 256			Below Basic (BB) 257–299			Basic (B) 300–349			Proficient (P) 350–413			Advanced (A) ≥ 414		
0–85	86–170	171–256	257–270	271–284	285–299	300–316	317–333	334–349	350–370	371–391	392–413	414–488	489–565	566–643
student	student	student	student	student	student	student	student	student	student	student	student	student	student	student
student	student	student	student	student	student	student	student	student	student	student	student	student	student	student
student	student	student	student	student	student	student	student	student	student	student	student	student	student	student
student	student	student	student	student	student	student	student	student	student	student	student	student	student	student

Student lists are created placing students in one of five columns using the California State Standards Assessment levels. Each column is then broken down again into thirds by dividing the level span by three (the lowest scoring students in the first column). This is done for each student for each period taught by each teacher for each department. During department meetings, discussion centers around student achievement, student results on quarterly tests, district assessments, and so on. The teachers look for patterns and trends. If many of the Far Below Basic (FBB) students miss a particular math problem, the teachers look closely at student work and make the necessary adjustments in their lessons. Students who are falling behind are referred to an after-school program in an attempt to close the gap. Sometimes this means re-teaching, delivering the lesson in another way, or providing necessary background knowledge.

During grade-level meetings, sharing success stories and successful practices is more the norm. For example, if a student is doing poorly in social science but is successful with language arts, the language arts teacher might be able to share with the social science teacher insights about the student's learning style, differentiation techniques that have worked with the student, information about the home and parental involvement, and so on.

Evidence of Success: The vital role that data played—and continues to play—at Kennedy cannot be overemphasized. The data allowed a picture of what was really going on to finally become clear, encouraged the staff to accept that they were part of the achievement challenge, and, most important, allowed them to visualize how they could contribute to success. To help them see how they were contributing to that success, each teacher prepared a graph similar to the one in figure 1.5.

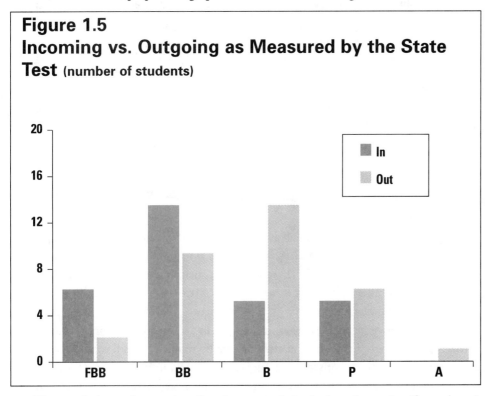

Figure 1.5
Incoming vs. Outgoing as Measured by the State Test (number of students)

The graph shows the *number* of students at each level when they arrive (first column) and then at the end of the year (second column) and reflects the number of students who moved upward or downward. Example: At the beginning of the year, six students were scoring at Far Below Basic (FBB); by the end of the year, however, all but two students moved up one level or more. This particular teacher had a positive impact on student achievement as measured by this assessment.

Similar charts were created by departments for each grade level. These data are shared openly. If the results are not as good as we hoped, at least we know where we are and recognize the need to develop strategies to ensure that we are not in the same

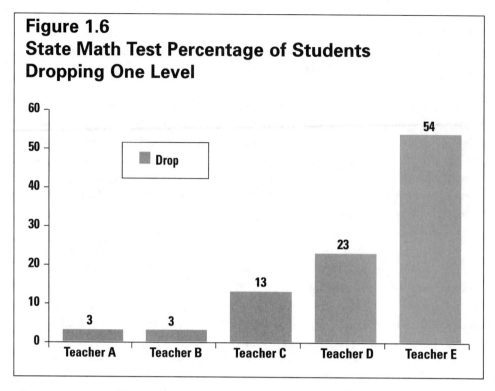

Figure 1.6
State Math Test Percentage of Students Dropping One Level

place next year. In figure 1.6, you can see that Teacher A and Teacher B lost ground with only a few students; however, Teachers C, D, and E lost ground with quite a few students.

Figure 1.7 shows the entire math department (all grades). It is amazing how the teachers whose students score above and below grade levels begin to talk. Teachers in the math department have taken the lead in observing one another and in lesson study and lesson adjustment. In some cases, there is healthy competition to see who will have the greatest impact on student achievement in math.

Principal Use of Data

At Kennedy, I use data to identify areas that require staff development schoolwide and for individual teachers. I hold teachers accountable for student progress and reflect this in their evaluation. Talk to the data, show the facts, help teachers identify areas for improvement, and then support staff development. At the department level, we look at the subgroups (clusters) and any consistently low scores, then the department targets that area for improvement. I also look at schoolwide data in a particular core area where scores are high. I then look at student data by teacher to see if some students in a given teacher's class are not scoring as high as students in other classes. This information is used to tailor development (e.g., content knowledge, instructional or classroom management techniques and strategies) for that teacher. We understand that our learning will never be over, yet we strive for perfection.

While *healthy* competition adds an interesting dynamic, it is the collaborative spirit that rules. Everyone is motivated to work together to be part of a constructive solution. Providing time for the staff to work side by side to remove obstacles and meet challenges head on has allowed the staff to become a true collegial team. New teachers who join Kennedy frequently remark about the unity that is so evident among the staff, the active engagement of students in learning, and the involvement of parents.

Figure 1.7
Impact on Student Achievement

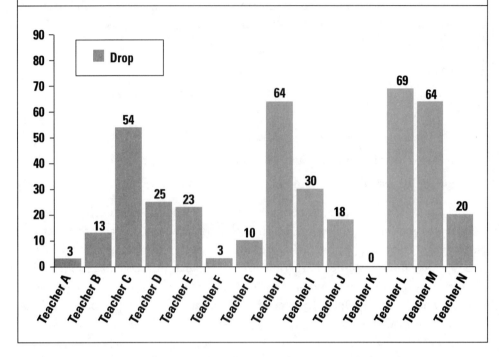

This collegiality has been established even without true interdisciplinary teams. Why don't we have these teams? We found it difficult to establish a true teaming situation because of credentialing issues and staffing based on FTEs (full-time equivalents) rather than the needs of the site. These and other constraints led us to team in other ways. [See Q&A with the Principal at the end of this profile.] In addition, we team in the sense that the curriculum is the same regardless of who is delivering it. For example, the math department lessons in sixth or seventh grade standards look the same in each room. What is different is the personality of the teacher.

Developing Professional Educators and Teachers as Leaders

Sometimes it is difficult to tell when things have changed appreciably, but I knew we had reached a certain benchmark of encouraging teacher leadership when all the math teachers and language arts teachers stepped forward to attend a 40-hour summer training in their subject area, even though they knew that—because of a lack of funding—they were not going to be paid for the training. When other teachers at this training, as well as their own association, told them they should not attend unless they received their hourly rate of pay, the response from the teachers was, "We are attending because we are Kennedy teachers." This statement will always ring in my ears and make me smile; it demonstrates the commitment, ownership, and passion of our teachers. Reform must begin with teachers before change will occur in student achievement. We must all realize that the finger points at the professionals for lack of student progress, not at parents and students. If students fail, it is our failure; if they succeed, teachers deserve praise.

Strategies to Encourage Dedication and Passion:
Time, Development, Alignment, Peer Coaching, Collaboration

Time! Time is our greatest enemy. As a leader of the school interested in encouraging ownership and buy-in, I wanted to be sure we built in time for teacher planning and collaboration, and for grade-level and department meetings.

Create Time

Teachers need time to

- make adjustments in pacing guides, target areas, student placement, lesson objectives, and so on;

- review data to identify areas of weakness and strength;

- talk about what is happening and what is not happening; and

- review goals and objectives and make progress toward meeting those goals.

To accomplish these tasks, our teachers are paid stipends to meet during the summer months and one hour is set aside each week during the school year for teacher planning and collaboration. Kennedy's team discovered that the most productive meetings were those scheduled during the regular workday, on weekends, and over the summer months—not at the end of the school day, when everyone is tired. Creating a master schedule with common department preparation periods was particularly helpful. The master schedule allows for preparation periods for both departments and core grade-level teams: English language arts, math, science, and social science. When teachers are given this time, they are able to meet as a department to discuss pacing guides, observe each other, study lessons, review assessments, and make adjustments in lessons on a daily basis, if needed. Release time also is provided for focused observations in areas identified as "in need of improvement."

We also chose to "create" time by protecting teacher instructional time with various strategies such as these:

- Adopting the 15-minute rule. No student is allowed to leave a classroom for any reason until after the first 15 minutes of class. This gives the student time to settle down; more important, the student will not miss the beginning of a lesson.

- Not interrupting classes with the intercom.

- Notifying teachers ahead of time if certain students are to report to the office.

Perhaps most important, time was provided to establish a leadership team and to carry out the team's work. The leadership team consists of five to eight teachers (volunteer and appointed, with representation from each grade level) and one or two administrators. The team

- looks at schoolwide academic and behavioral data for accomplishments and areas of concern;

- breaks into ad hoc committees to develop plans for improvement that are presented to the whole leadership team;

- helps present these plans to the entire staff for input and subsequent implementation; and

- monitors implementation and discussions that take place during morning in-service time and faculty meetings to determine the need for adjustments to the plan.

In addition to serving as the voice of the school and the ear to the staff, the team makes presentations to staff members on various topics, and attends and presents at conferences.

Staff Development

Every staff member must make a commitment to growth and continuous improvement. Information gathered in teacher portfolios should be used by *all* teachers for improvement. **Even the best teachers should be encouraged to stretch to increase their effectiveness.** Before the beginning of each school year at Kennedy, teachers reflect on what occurred the previous year. They set individual goals based on data, and staff development sessions are created around these goals. Each year, teachers submit their individual goals and analysis of the previous year to the principal.

New teachers, as well as teachers who are highly experienced, should have time to gain the knowledge and skills they need to be even more effective. When a new teacher arrives, I know I have to close the gap as quickly as possible between the new and veteran teachers regarding expectations and where we are in the change process. I assign each new teacher to a "buddy teacher"—a veteran who can to be a positive role model and provide support and guidance. Strong coaching relationships can be of great benefit to teachers and other staff members; good coaches provide key information and offer feedback as they monitor and observe teachers' progress.

To foster discussion of staff development, we gave each teacher a copy of *Classroom Instruction That Works* by Marzano, Pickering, and Pollock. Each teacher was placed on a team and assigned a section with the understanding that he or she would be the "expert" on that section and would explain it to the rest of the staff. Of the nine instructional strategies, we reached consensus on three areas that we would target to implement schoolwide: Note Taking and Summarizing, Graphic Organizers, and Questioning Techniques. During the first half of the year, staff brought ideas, shared techniques and examples, and discussed what was working and what wasn't with the entire staff during in-service time, preparation periods, and some faculty meetings. I also brought in an outside consultant to offer suggestions and provide support. We continue to focus on the three areas. When I'm observing classes or doing walkthroughs, I look for evidence of implementation. When I see no evidence, the teacher and I meet to discuss it further and to review expectations.

When we're looking at staff development opportunities, we encourage people within departments to attend as a team. Two things happen: Teachers get to know one another outside the school setting and all teachers receive the same information and can then discuss it more thoughtfully. In addition, we structure the agenda of our meetings around teacher-identified needs. At the beginning of each school year, we have a discussion about department and grade-level needs and then create agendas for meetings about those needs. To encourage accountability and active participation in the meetings, teachers respond to a reflection sheet and identify what was accomplished, what they contributed to the meeting, and what their next steps will be. The use of our teacher portfolios also helped to engage teachers in their own learning. As one teacher put it,

> Just when it seemed we were at our threshold as teachers, our principal dropped teacher portfolios in our laps. Little did I know it would make such a profound impact on my teaching strategies, my students' performance, teacher/administrator expectations, and understanding. It allowed for a nonthreatening way to evaluate myself as a teacher and understand how to look at my strengths and weaknesses.

The teacher portfolios created an awesome opportunity for teacher buy-in, accountability, feedback, and ultimately growth as teachers. It was an experience that all of us were leery of but it turned out to be a fantastic opportunity. It also allowed our principal to get a different perspective on our thoughts and feelings about teaching through insightful reflections. Through the reflections and discussions with my principal, I was able to plan and set out on a journey of focused lesson planning, better student understanding, and self-improvement. I learned to evaluate myself after teaching lessons and figure out where I, the teacher, needed to make changes and grow. I began to realize that it wasn't always the student who needed to change, but sometimes myself and how I taught the lesson. After three years of using the teacher portfolio, I have the awesome experience of looking back and seeing how far I have come, and, yes, how far I still have to go!

—Angela Maas, science teacher and lead team member.

"Owning" All Students: Feeder Pattern Articulation

As professionals interested in and responsible for the well-being of students and student learning, we need to look beyond the established boundaries of our schools. Students come to Kennedy from several feeder schools. Our focus has been on sharing curricula among fourth through sixth grade teachers. We first established a feeder lead team, consisting of representatives from each grade level and each school to work on the following:

- Building consistency up through the grades in communication with parents
- Homework issues
- Classroom expectations in the area of self-discipline
- Reporting student progress in a timely fashion
- Establishing parent conferences
- Providing information to parents in a similar fashion each time (so that parents aren't always trying to figure out new rules for communication)

We also recognized, of course, that we were dependent on the incoming feeder schools for student proficiency. Each year, the number of incoming students scoring in the lowest quintile was astounding. Much discussion occurred around this situation, and a plan to address it bloomed. I wrote a proposal to the superintendent asking for some financial support to pay teachers during the summer for a two-week project. With some district money and Kennedy footing part of the cost, we put the plan into action. The plan was to integrate technology into math lesson delivery, but our ulterior motive was to create "Kennedy teachers" in our feeder schools.

Fourth and fifth grade teachers who participated received a laptop computer and an hourly stipend. For the Kennedy team, I invited one seventh grade math teacher, a special education teacher, a sixth grade teacher who consistently demonstrated significant impact on student math achievement, and an eighth grade science teacher who had a master's degree in technology and knew which math standards could be supported in science class. This team created a two-week unit to develop proficiency in the creation of PowerPoint lessons around the California State Math Power Standards in grades four through six. Teams consisting of each of the grade levels from different schools were developed. This selection of teams was done deliberately to build trust and camaraderie for future vertical planning and collaboration.

The goal was to improve the content knowledge of elementary teachers in the area of math and, as a consequence, to improve student achievement and help students enter Kennedy closer to grade-level expectations. Last year was the first year students' scores did not dip between sixth and seventh grade. The feeder pattern teachers who participated in the two-week training continue to share ideas and have asked to meet quarterly for the upcoming school year. They want to focus on additional core areas and continue to perfect math. In addition to providing elementary teachers with feedback on their students' accomplishments in the sixth grade, our Kennedy trainers and the sixth grade Kennedy staff will be released to observe lesson delivery in the feeder pattern (and released time will be reciprocated). This plan allows for open discussion, support, guidance, suggestions for improvement, and, of course, the beginnings of lesson study. Significant additional benefits of the effort include teacher communication across school lines, teachers celebrating each other's successes, trust being built, teachers looking at problem areas, and teachers reviewing students' needs in vertical teams and owning these students, regardless of grade. They know all students belong to them. Vertical alignment can now be more easily addressed, and looping may be a potential next step.

The transition to high school, which happens to be in another district, is an area that still needs to be strengthened significantly. Currently, the high school provides Kennedy with student data only in the area of math. We need to know more about our students' success or lack of success, and we need to use this information to tailor adjustments. We have begun to expose students to the possibility of college—a critical step in middle school, especially for students whose parents may not have attended college. But we need to measure our success with the number of students who are positioned for college entrance and college success as well as the number of first-generation students who enter college.

Collaborate to Review Student Work

At Kennedy, we randomly gather student work and ask teachers for copies of assignments given to students. We mark the assignment by grade level and subject area, then ask the lead team to review the assignment to determine the lesson objective, the grade-level standard it addresses, and suggestions to bring it to grade level. Lesson after lesson, assignment after assignment is reviewed through staff presentations during planning and collaboration time. This is our way of ensuring that all lessons are directly related to grade-level standards. These presentations have offered safe ways for teachers to ask for and offer ideas for improvement. Because it is no longer just the principal pointing out areas in need of improvement, the strategy offers validation and/or different perspectives for the principal to consider. This approach can have significant benefits for individual teacher improvement efforts and may nudge people to improve or to move on. In addition to all the individual enhancements I have seen as a result of the presentations, one teacher came to the realization that he was no longer meeting student needs and turned in his resignation.

Peer Coaching

At Kennedy, substitutes are brought in to allow teachers to observe one another. To use this strategy effectively, the principal must calibrate what good teaching is. Brag about teacher accomplishments, and share examples in staff meetings of what you expect and how a teacher dealt effectively with a particular problem. Specifically identify teacher strengths in areas such as behavior management, classroom environment, and effective instructional strategies and techniques, and use these strengths as models for others. Let the teachers know what you'll be looking for during evaluations. To ensure that teachers know what I think good teaching looks like, I bring two or three teachers with me when I do observations. When I see powerful lesson delivery, I point it out. I ask them to look for the level of student engagement and the techniques the teacher was using to involve all students in the lesson.

I would ask them to focus on only one or two areas when we observed. I would say, for example, "Let's measure the level of questioning that is used by this teacher and determine whether the questions are at the knowledge, comprehension, application, synthesis, analysis, or evaluation level." This tally became useful information to the teacher working on more effective questioning techniques. I would choose a teacher to observe who was effective in these techniques, and let the teacher know we were coming and that we were going to focus specifically on questioning techniques, so the teacher could model them.

We also developed a form to help teachers more effectively observe peers (Appendix 5). As teachers (two to four at a time) observed each other, the form was completed separately by each observer. The forms were then given to the teacher and a discussion ensued. If the teacher was open to it, he or she could also request to be taped, and later review the tape privately or with colleagues. Observation is a powerful tool for teachers to provide feedback and offer suggestions for improvement. Teachers know that learning never ends, that even the best teacher can and should be stretched. At Kennedy, because individual teacher data are shared with all teachers and trust has been built to use the data productively, teachers are able to work together to improve achievement.

Peer coaching and observation have also helped to identify teacher needs, tailor professional development plans to address those needs, and develop a spirit of collaboration, which has led to the sharing of powerful, successful lesson plans.

> [The observation form] gave me a focus. At the end of all the observations, we were better prepared to discuss the good and bad qualities that we saw throughout the lessons. I also felt that the chart was less subjective. It was straight and to the point. I don't think that there is empty room for interpretations. No opinions, just facts....
> There has to be trust within the group. When I give my comments, both good and bad, I give them knowing that the teachers will not take them too personally. That they know that I'm trying to help them, not to throw mud on them.
>
> —Osvaldo Martinez, math teacher and lead team member.

Family Involvement

All the strategies described above were critical, yet the challenge remained: how to connect families with the school and encourage involvement of the entire school community. Parents are an integral part of student achievement. This was the last area we targeted, perhaps because it was the most difficult. (Also, I believed that I needed the house to be cleaner before I invited guests over.) Yet it proved to be one of the most rewarding. Although every school community is unique, most parents benefit from workshops, school-family sessions, and other opportunities to learn how to better communicate with teachers and others who are working with their children. Like parents in other communities that have many English language learners, Kennedy's parents want their children to have a good education, but language barriers can make participation more difficult. Parents must understand that their children have opportunities for higher education regardless of the parent's own level of education or language barriers.

Parent Classes

We instituted parent guidance classes. In the first year, more than 175 parents attended the six sessions of "How to Help Your Child Succeed with Homework" delivered in Spanish and English. Though parents of struggling students initially were the primary focus of outreach efforts, this focus expanded to all parents and to parents of fourth and fifth grade students enrolled in the three K–5 feeder schools. These parent classes have proven effective, as evidenced by student data. The semester GPAs of targeted students who scored below proficiency levels and attended the training with their parents significantly improved, as did the California State Standards Test results. Transportation to the sessions, childcare for younger siblings, materials, and homework supply kits (e.g., dictionary, thesaurus, pencils, ruler, stapler, compass, markers, three-hole punch, pens) were provided. A celebration was held at the end of each session, including recognition of parent participation. Initially, we provided a dinner in our cafeteria; however, because the parents wanted to express their gratitude for our efforts, the celebration has evolved into a potluck.

Family Nights

Teachers host content area (math, social science, science, English) Family Nights throughout the school year. Family Math Night was a "Probability Fair" with a focus on a sixth grade probability math standard. Students created a variety of math problems and displayed them on a threefold display board; parents walked around and participated in interactive hands-on problem solving. The student or group of students who created the problem challenged the parents and then showed them how to solve the problem—giving everyone an opportunity to see that learning can be fun and relevant to life. One parent wrote me complimenting a teacher for turning his child on to math—a child who formerly hated math, but now lists it as *the* favorite subject.

Provide parents with questions to ask teachers during parent conferences:

- What does GPA mean?
- Why is GPA important?
- What can I do at home to help my child with school?
- What additional assistance do you offer outside of the school day for my child?
- Will you provide me with a list of books by child should read?
- How much homework can I expect from your class?
- What is the best way for me to communicate with you?
- How will I be informed when my child falls below a C grade in your class?
- How much time should my child spend reading each night?

Other Strategies

- Invite parents to student-led demonstrations during Family Nights and ask parents to participate.
- Provide parent classes such as "How to Help Your Child Succeed in School" and "How to Gain Access to College."
- Provide classes for parents to learn to speak English. Pay a classified employee or computer teacher to run one of the software programs that help with language, or seek outside assistance.

- Hold classes for students—targeted interventions or enrichment—while parents attend evening events and training.

- Provide transportation for parents, feed them, and, of course, celebrate with them. Parents are willing to work with the school, but they often do not know what to do. Guide them.

- Provide parents with timely feedback on their child's progress and clarify what is expected of students. At Kennedy, this meant moving from a quarterly reporting system to a six-week progress report. In a previous position as a school counselor, I found myself counseling parents and students about grades (quarter failures) after the hole had been dug so deep it was almost impossible for the student to pass a class. When I shared my concern and experience with the Kennedy staff, they agreed that this was a problem. Everyone understood that more frequent progress reports meant more work for them; however, I promised that I would get the grades computerized (versus handwritten, as was the practice). A fair trade!

- Move parent conferences from late November to the first part of October, after the first six-week progress report. The information shared with parents at Kennedy includes the previous year's final grades, current state testing data, district writing and math assessments, current grades in each subject, behavior data, and attendance data. Parents meet with their child's advisory teacher, who reviews all the facts and provides suggestions on improvement and a schedule of after-school programs. If a child is failing a class, the parent is scheduled for a conference with the subject matter teacher. In addition, at the end of the first semester, conferences are held with all parents of students whose GPA falls below 2.0.

- Invite parents to roundtable discussions.

- Ensure that teachers and other staff make parents feel welcome at all times and provide information in the languages spoken in students' homes.

- Create a team of parents to become your voice—to lessen some of your load and to enable the school to reach more parents. There are always a few parents who will work closely with the school (e.g., School Site Council, parents of former students, former students who are now parents). Work with these parents. Ask them to walk with you through classes and talk to them about what is happening in the class. Let them know that the teacher is teaching grade-level standards, show them how well behaved the students are, and so on. Train these parents in what to look for and what to point out throughout the campus. Once you have these core parents, use them. Ask them to invite and guide two or three other parents on a tour. Empower that core, and let them know they are part of the team. This will assist in public relations. When these parents know what is going on behind the doors, they can stop many of the complaints about the school; they will proudly defend their school and talk from knowledge and experience. Let these parents speak to parents of incoming students, especially parents who may be afraid of the transition. Let these parents coach other parents to become involved. You will be surprised at how many problems, complaints, and meetings can be avoided when your parent team communicates with other parents first. Recognize these parents during open houses and at the eighth grade end-of-year ceremony, and acknowledge their contributions regularly in the school newsletter.

Words to the Wise

Frustration and excuses are often barriers to improvement. No one has all the answers, but if you don't try new things, it is a given that nothing will change except time. Through my years in administration, I have worked with and among many administrators, both middle management and upper management, who had difficulty making hard decisions, staying focused on the "plan," and following an unpopular course. A leader has to be a risk-taker, someone who is willing to try different things until the answer is found, and then tackle another obstacle and try different things until that answer is found, and so on—all the while being able to bring others along on the journey. Learning is never over, and the entire staff must realize there is always room for improvement.

The improvements in student achievement, student attitude, staff professionalism, and morale have been profound at Kennedy. The staff's willingness to pursue excellence has created a synergistic force that sustains change. The visible and the unseen, immeasurable events that occurred among staff members as they worked toward and through the process of change are reflected in the achievements of Kennedy students. A bond has been created that has united the staff in its quest toward success for every student—and it is that bond that makes me confident that improvement will be sustained as I move on to a superintendent position. The leadership that exists at the teacher level will ensure continued progress at Kennedy.

As you look at change and encourage teacher leadership in your own school, remember that you must earn respect, model the expected work ethic, say what you mean and mean what you say, never lie, build trust, and bring out the best in others. Remember to

- Be persistent, be patient, and persevere.

- Recognize positive improvement and change regardless of the increments.

- Refer to data (behavioral and academic) continually.

- Empower teachers; talk it and, more important, walk it!

- Maintain high accountability standards for administrators, teachers, students, and parents alike.

- Establish trust.

- Stay positive.

- Celebrate achievements.

- Listen, listen, and listen to parents, students, teachers, and community members.

If you do these things, you will create a team that has passion and a drive for excellence that cannot be stopped.

J. F. Kennedy Middle School has become a model for many school leaders and teams from the state and from across the nation who have traveled there to gain insight and network as they take their own paths to school improvement. Kennedy has been recognized as a Middle School Demonstration Site by the California State Department of Education Middle Grades Office in the areas of English language arts, math, and the use of student data. Recently, Kennedy has been recognized as a School to Watch by the National Forum to Accelerate Middle Grades Reform. Between 1998 and 2004, five Kennedy teachers were recognized as Teacher of the Year—three by the Association of California School Administrators (ACSA) and two by the California League of Middle Schools (CLMS). Suzanne Smith was named ACSA Region 9 Principal of the Year.

Frustration and excuses are often barriers to improvement. No one has all the answers, but if you don't try new things, it is a given that nothing will change except time.

School Profile 1
J.F. Kennedy Middle School

Q&A with the Principal
Suzanne H. Smith, J. F. Kennedy Middle School

Q: *Some readers may see your school as departmentalized. What specific practices were in place to support grade-level teams? Department teams? How were you able to afford common planning time for these teams?*

A: The initial pathway for improvement was through strengthening our departments. The grants that were awarded were in support of departmental staff development; thus, the focus on departments was heavy. We understood the need to look at the true meaning of the middle school concept, the need to look at grade-level teams, and the need to teach the whole child; however, so much change was needed that we had to start small. As departments' awareness grew (e.g., understanding what was expected of students at each grade level and above and below each grade level, creating pacing guides and assessments) they were also communicating with grade-level teams. To establish strong, dynamic departments, we created a master schedule that allowed departments to have common preparation periods. This change allowed departments time to meet each day to discuss, plan, observe, and so on. It was a conscious decision to move toward the departments first and the grade-level teams second. However, this does not mean we ignored the need for grade-level teams. Weekly in-service time was established on Mondays from 8:00 to 9:00 a.m., during which our grade-level teams planned thematic units, discussed lessons to support multiple disciplines, collaborated, and discussed curriculum and students. Teachers shared what was being covered in each department and identified common ground so they could support lesson objectives across various classes. For example, while the math department is delivering a unit on measurement, the science department could reinforce the concepts with a lesson on weight, mass, and so on. Teachers also focused on certain vocabulary words throughout the day, and the English and social science teachers coordinated so that a period in history was studied at the same time literature from that period was discussed.

Are department teams in place? Yes! Are grade-level teams in place? Yes! Strengthening each department was a necessary first step, but expansion into grade-level teams quickly followed. Can the master schedule support both department and grade-level teams? Yes; however, not in the same year. The teams can be adjusted depending on identified needs. If asked which is stronger, I would have to say the departments up and down each grade level, because more has been done with incoming and outgoing schools. Also, true teaming is difficult when some teachers have to teach two or three different grade levels in the same year.

Q: *How did these teams discuss individual students? How did they work to help students establish their own identities and help them become well-rounded students?*

A: Some Mondays are targeted just for discussion about individual student progress, attendance, and behavior. Since Kennedy has no counselor, teachers and administrators fill that role, looking at symptoms, changes in behavior, performance, and effort, and whether a student might be performing in one class but not doing homework/class work in another. What is changing, what is not changing, what needs to change? Who is having success with a particular student? Teachers share with each other, and then put into practice what appears to work, in order to better meet the students' needs.

Teachers are expected to contact parents when students are not performing up to expectation. These calls are for guidance, not just information sharing. In addition, all teachers make themselves available after school to provide additional support, whether it is for guidance or for academic support. Students are asked individually to report after school if the teacher thinks they did not grasp a concept. A teacher might ask a student to come after school just to talk if the teacher has seen a behavior change or other indication that something might be wrong. Students view this as an opportunity, not a punishment. Some teachers eat lunch in their rooms and allow students to sit down with them to talk or get assistance on a topic. We also have the standard advisory program that allows a small group of students to interact with one teacher and an Adopt-a-Student program for students who are experiencing difficulty outside the school setting. Our students know we are there to help. We treat each student the way we would like an adult/teacher to treat our child. Do we love our children and do we tell them that? Yes. Do we act like a parent or a grandparent? Yes. Do we use words that reflect caring and love? Yes.

Q: *Your school relies heavily on test data. What other ways does the school measure the quality of the curriculum and instruction?*

A: We are bound by No Child Left Behind and, in California, by the API (Academic Performance Index). The API has high accountability standards, so a lot of data are generated by this test. Do we use other assessments in a more timely fashion to prevent failure and lack of progress? Absolutely! District writing and math assessment tests are administered twice a year. Internal assessments are given every six weeks, with additional support provided after school or through Saturday school as needed. Before California mandated science and social science as part of the CST/STAR (California Standards Test/Standardized Testing and Reporting), the site used the Terra Nova test and a department-designed test at the end of the year to measure curriculum delivery. We know data are important and that it drives the curriculum, so the decision was made to require a test for all core areas, regardless of whether the state measured that area or not. We find that frequent monitoring of student progress allows us to discover the gaps in student learning and take action. Instead of waiting for the state results and reacting to them, we can target student learning gaps and work toward prevention.

Q: *In those subjects that do not have student standardized testing data, how did your team ensure the quality of the curriculum?*

A: Each teacher, by department, created a test using the "blueprints" and grade-level expectations (standards) as determined by the state. They continue to assess students based on the pacing guides, which indicate what a child should know and be able to do in each grade level and in order to advance. Assessment of students is not just to determine student progress, but also to determine fidelity of the curriculum and effective lesson delivery, to determine the individual teacher's impact on student achievement, to make adjustments in the creation of lessons and pacing guides, and to determine staff development that may be needed for teachers or departments.

Q: *What lessons can be learned by a good school that wants to be a great school?*

A: When you're working with a population that has many needs, communication among staff members is important. Walking in unison is paramount. There is so much more to teaching than just delivering the curriculum. To identify a "great" school, I would look past the "window dressing" for a belief that one can always get better, an understanding that perfection will never be reached, but we must keep reaching for it. I would look for the following:

1. What is the percentage of parents participating in schoolwide events (open house, Family Nights, parent-teacher conferences, assemblies, site visits)? What are the ethnic and socioeconomic breakdowns? Do they reflect the student body?

2. What is the school doing to reach parents who are not participating in such events? How does the school reach into the home?

3. How does the school know it is meeting the students' social and individual needs? How are the data used?

4. Does the school celebrate with the parents? What is being celebrated?

5. How do the teachers work together to help each other improve?

6. Do the teachers analyze their individual impact on student achievement and make adjustments?

7. Are teachers sharing lessons, discussing data, identifying evidence of success or lack of success, and using this evidence to make change?

8. How are teachers working together up and down the grades within the school?

9. How are teachers working together outside their school and with the feeder schools?

10. How are teachers looking at the standards, looking at how they spiral up the grades, and addressing the gaps between some grade levels?

11. Are teachers observing each other and providing input for improvement?

12. Are the expectations of the evaluator, teacher, and peer support calibrated? Does everyone have the same understanding of what is meant by "good teaching"?

13. How many students further their education? Are they successful when they leave the school? Is anyone being left behind?

14. Students who enter the world of work—are they able to hold a position?

15. Does the school have evidence that its data improve each year?

16. Is everyone—teachers and students—being "stretched" and showing improvement?

17. Do you know the difference between sustainability and one great year?

18. Is the school like an extended family? How do you know?

19. Do students trust adults? Do adults trust each other? How do you know?

Leading a Text-Based Discussion on This Profile (see protocol in Appendix 4)

■ How did the principal move staff from resistance to buy-in? To what purpose?

■ How can our school model the honest, "no hidden agendas" attitude that the author espouses?

■ What would it look like at our school?

■ What can we learn from how she used data to inform her decisions?

■ What methods did she use to promote learning communities? What professional development did these methods require?

■ What did you like most about the profile?

■ What did you like least about the profile?

■ What practices that you liked could be readily implemented in our school ?

■ In our school, do we have good models of high-quality instruction? How can we clarify expectations regarding instruction?

■ How do the roadblocks that the leadership team at the author's school faced compare with those at our school? Can we take any lessons away from how the team faced those challenges?

■ Have we fallen into the "We've been doing it for 10 years—why should we change now" trap? What practices can we take away from this profile to get us out of that trap?

■ Are all our decisions made in the best interests of students?

■ Reflect on the author's comment about individual classroom data: "We share this information with the entire school. It is important for staff members to provide support to each other. It is equally important that teachers know who is having an impact on student achievement, so they know whom to observe, model, or go to for additional assistance." What data would you use to facilitate modeling and observation at our school?

School Profile 1
J.F. Kennedy Middle School

Moving Forward

The strategies and practices offered in this profile offer some insights into how one school has tackled the use of data to improve student performance and encourage collaborative leadership. In the next chapter, you will find a plethora of suggestions to foster a culture of collaboration in your school. Keep the Kennedy profile in mind as you read the chapter—it may provide concrete examples of how the strategies and theories can be put into practice at your school. At the end of the chapter, you will find Breaking Ranks in the Middle recommendations that will further enhance your effort to turn theory into practice.

2 Who Will Lead? Collaborative Leadership and Professional Learning Communities

You've heard or read the following criticisms:

- "My daughter's school is too focused on the touchy-feely developmental issues at the expense of academics."

- "Our school changed its name from junior high to middle school, but it continued the same practices it has employed for the past 40 years, ignoring the developmental issues and personal changes students this age are going through."

- "Our district made decisions about middle level students based on budget and enrollment projections, not on what's best for students."

- "We had a great model in place, but the district cut it off before we could make it work."

At the middle level, the conversation about school reform has revolved around assertions that reforms are either focused too heavily on developmental factors at the expense of academic issues or are focused on academics without regard to developmental factors. Yet among the myriad reforms proposed, specifically those that the majority of researchers agree are effective, many are never implemented. Some reforms never gain traction; others are killed by boards of education, central offices, parent pressure, faculty opposition, principal reluctance, or inferior leadership.

What is your role in making Breaking Ranks in the Middle reform succeed where others have failed? *Create stakeholders in the process of reform by involving people in developing a plan, and be prepared at all stages to have the data to support your efforts.* Your school's plan should be values-driven and data-informed.

It is very difficult for a board or central office to oppose a reform if you supply before and after data that illustrate the specific benefits of the reform, publicly document the success of the efforts, and can make an effective case for its continuation. It is very difficult for parents to fight reform if you can demonstrate how a reform will benefit each student.

As you ask yourself how you can succeed with Breaking Ranks in the Middle reform where others have failed, remember that in many cases it was not a lack of effort that killed reforms. Perhaps it was a misunderstanding of how to implement change. Do not underestimate the importance of having a school leadership team that understands the change process, using data to justify the need for change, getting others involved in the process, and, finally, providing the necessary professional development to implement, assess, and sustain the change. Implementing Breaking Ranks in

Figure 2.1
How Principals See Themselves and How They Are Perceived by Parents and Teachers

	Percentage Saying "Excellent"		
	Principals	Teachers	Parents
Respecting the people in the school	78	36	34
Being approachable	71	39	34
Being a viable presence throughout the school	67	38	42
Supporting teachers in the school to be the best teachers they can be	65	33	28
Encouraging students to achieve	59	35	34
Being a good listener	53	30	27
Being an overall leader of the school	45	30	34
Providing opportunities for teachers' professional development	43	31	22

Source: Breaking Ranks II: Strategies for Leading High School Reform, Workshop Materials. Based on the Metropolitan Life Survey of the Teacher 2003: An Examination of School Leadership.

the Middle recommendations regarding personalization, curriculum, instruction, and assessment requires cultivating collaborative leadership to ensure that the school is fertile for change. But first, ask yourself what changes might be required in your own leadership style or what areas of your leadership might others perceive as needing attention. How you see yourself and how others see you may not synchronize as nicely as you would imagine. (See survey results in figure 2.1.)

The idea for comprehensive change may not begin in the principal's office, but it most assuredly can end there as a result of incomplete planning, failure to involve others, neglect, or failure to create conditions so that things can change. Creating those conditions is often the first challenge—and sometimes it must start with the principal's own thinking and interactions with people. Usually, when the status quo is found wanting, our initial impulse is to seek to change the world around us. From students to parents, to teachers, to school boards, to districts, to communities, to states, to the nation itself: "If only X were different—then everything would be fine." As you begin to think about change, remind yourself of these words in your interactions with others: "I cannot change you—I can only change how I respond to you."

A Tool for Leaders to Assess Their Own Developmental Needs
NASSP has developed a tool to help principals and other school leaders assess their own skills in 10 dimensions that have proved to contribute to effective leadership.

■   Setting instructional direction

- Teamwork

- Sensitivity

- Judgment

- Results orientation

- Organizational ability

- Oral communication

- Written communication

- Development of others

- Understanding personal strengths and weaknesses

Figure 2.2
Leadership Styles

Visionary change leaders view change as necessary and tend to be supportive of change efforts. However, visionary change leaders are often overly optimistic and tend to make global assertions about a change prior to a thorough analysis of all the possible effects.

Technocratic change leaders emphasize hard and quantifiable results while neglecting the concerns of the people who are affected by a change. The process and the concerns and emotions of those affected are viewed as barriers to be overcome in order to achieve a desired outcome. Short-term gains are accomplished at the expense of long-term resentment.

Sympathetic change leaders focus on the concerns of the people who are affected by a change, but they neglect the hard and quantifiable results. The concerns and emotions of people are viewed as the primary target of change intervention. As a result, change efforts often stall or move excessively slowly.

Source: Breaking Ranks Leadership (NASSP, 1998, p. 11).

The definition and a set of behavioral indicators for each skill dimension are included on an instrument available on the NASSP website at www.principals.org/brim. The purposes of this tool are to promote self-reflection on your own performance, provide feedback from colleagues, and present a comparison between how you see yourself as a leader and how others see you. Data from this process can inform planning for your professional growth.

Enabling others to shape and take ownership of a vision for change is fundamental to its success. Developing the skills necessary to facilitate change requires that the principal understand his or her own strengths and weaknesses and those of the leadership team, including the challenges associated with various leadership styles (see figure 2.2). Shortcomings are inherent in all three of the leadership styles—a synthesis of the styles will no doubt be required to successfully implement significant change. As you, the principal, begin to look closely at your own leadership style, and as your leadership team begins to discuss possible entry points for change and setting the conditions for change, do not underestimate the power that simply creating opportunities for conversation about change can have on the process.

Cultivating a Community of Collaboration

Comprehensive reform requires an extraordinary level of support from the community, the school board, the superintendent, families, teachers, and students—not only in

Figure 2.3
10 Assumptions About Change

1. **Do not assume** that your version of what the change should be is the one that should or could be implemented.

2. **Assume** that any significant innovation, if it is to result in change, requires individual implementers to clarify their own meaning.

3. **Assume** that conflict and disagreement are not only inevitable but fundamental to successful change. Smooth implementation is often a sign that not much is really changing.

4. **Assume** that people need pressure to change. It is helpful to express what you value in the form of standards of practice and expectations of accountability, but only if coupled with capacity-building and problem-solving opportunities.

5. **Assume** that effective change takes time. It is a process of "development in use."

6. **Do not** assume that the reason for lack of implementation is outright rejection of the values embodied in the change or hard-core resistance to all change.

7. **Do not** expect all or even most people or groups to change. Progress occurs when we take steps that increase the number of people affected.

8. **Assume** that you will need a plan. Evolutionary planning and problem-coping models based on knowledge of the change process are essential.

9. **Assume** that no amount of knowledge will ever make it totally clear what action should be taken.

10. **Assume** that changing the culture of institutions is the real agenda, not implementing single innovations.

Source: Adapted from Fullan, 2001.

Comprehensive reform requires an extraordinary level of support from the community, the school board, the superintendent, families, teachers, and students— not only in approval of the reforms but also in their implementation.

approval of the reforms but also in their implementation. Creating the right conditions for improvement will require significant planning and strong leadership. Properly cultivated teacher, family, and student leadership—all within the framework of a cohesive collaborative leadership plan embraced by the principal—will bring the implementation of Breaking Ranks in the Middle recommendations much closer to reality.

As important as bringing reform to reality, or perhaps more so, is the need for continuity and sustainability of the reform. Reform driven solely by the principal is not only less likely to succeed but also less likely to have long-term results.

Additional justification for principals to embrace collaborative leadership arises from continuity-of-leadership issues. Retirements in the profession and a dearth of people willing and able to take on the complex and demanding responsibilities of principalship have led to a shortage of highly qualified principals in some areas. This shortage, and various accountability adjustments, have increased the mobility of some principals and put additional strain on reforms that require continuity.

The four-step change process outlined in the succeeding pages should provide myriad opportunities to involve all stakeholders in your school in discussions about improving student performance. If you do not engage in these conversations and define a vision, the recommendations provided throughout this field guide may become merely a "To-Do List"—one that will never be done and may even prove counterproductive. Many of the charts, diagrams, worksheets, and supporting materials in this guide are intended to encourage conversations or to be used in text-based conversations. They are not prescriptive plans that must be followed to the letter. Indeed, your school may decide on a much more appropriate formula to improve student performance—but you may never know unless the conversations begin. As David Ferrero (2005) cautions:

> Explicit attention to what educators—and parents, students, and community members—believe about the purposes of school, the criteria for excellence, the practice of democratic citizenship, the knowledge that is most essential to effective reasoning, and other basic normative questions plays a crucial role in determining how research will be translated into practice….

> [I]f educators and reformers could become more self-aware and more articulate about their values and their philosophical underpinnings, they could defuse tensions among themselves and channel those values more productively into the creation of small, focused, effective schools.

A Sample Process: Five Steps to Change

Many schools have already begun the process of change; however, for those having difficulty with change, those considering change, or those looking to complement their own plans for change, the process outlined in the following pages (adapted from Gainey and Webb)[4] is designed to align with Breaking Ranks in the Middle change.

1. Establish the action planning team.

2. Use data to identify opportunities for improvement.

3. Assess conditions for change and develop the action plan.

4. Support the action plan with professional development.

5. Report the results.

Step 1: Establish the Action Planning Team

Whether a school uses an existing school improvement team to investigate a specific change or forms a new team for that purpose will depend on local circumstances. Regardless, successful implementation relies on substantive involvement by teachers and families in decision making, planning, and establishment and communication of expectations. In addition to achieving the stated goal of the planning team, the benefits of an effective team approach include the following:

- Forging a sense of community and shared commitment among teachers, contrasting with the culture of isolation and uncertainty often found in schools.

- Empowering teachers and establishing them as instructional leaders, so that they can stimulate change in multiple classrooms by serving as role models and mentors to other teachers in the building.

- Encouraging members of the team, including the principal, to develop personal relationships that would not be formed under other circumstances. Such relationships advance collaborative school cultures in which all members, including administrators, are supportive of each other (Maeroff, 1993; Painter & Valentine 1999) Source: NASSP (2000, p. 3).

Assuming that these teams are critical, and that a school does not currently have one established, how would a school select members for the team? Painter, Lucas, Wooderson, and Valentine (2000, p. 4) cited several options proposed by Maeroff (1993):

Principal's Journal

If you don't engage in these conversations and define a vision, the recommendations provided throughout this field guide may become merely a To-Do List—one that will never be done and may even prove counterproductive.

[4]The process outlined in the next several pages was originally a 10-step process. Several stages were combined for inclusion into this field guide.

> Teachers are typically expected to be involved to various degrees in their school's improvement processes; however, teachers are too often expected to implement plans they did not have any part in writing and may not even support or understand. The success of change initiatives lies in the meaningful involvement of teachers. If teachers are invited and even expected to be part of decision-making processes, they are more likely to be committed to successful implementation.
>
> *Source: Engaging Teachers in the School Improvement Process, Painter and Valentine, 1999, p. 3.*

- Teachers sign up for the team.

- Members are elected. [Editor's note: This option has its fair share of detractors and may be problematic in some instances.]

- The principal consults with other leaders in the school before designating members to fill the team.

- Members of an existing group, such as a faculty advisory council, become the team.

- Any combination of the above.

Specifically, they recommend the following (pp. 4–7):

1. Teams of four to six, including the principal (size can be adjusted to reflect faculty).

2. Include those who already serving in leadership roles or who have the greatest promise of becoming leaders.

3. All members of the faculty must understand the change processes and realize their potential roles in the process.

4. Members must serve out of conviction, not simply because they are asked, elected, or ordered to do so.

5. If a team is to be successful, change efforts "should begin, at least in part, with those most inclined toward and most sympathetic to breaking with the status quo" (Maeroff 1993, p. 41).

6. To help ensure faculty acceptance of the team, team membership should reflect the faculty as a whole.

   - Members' ranges of experience in teaching should be similar to the ranges of experience of the entire faculty.

   - Diversity of gender, race, and ethnicity should be considered.

   - Natural divisions in the school—grade levels, teams, subject areas, core and exploratory assignments—should be taken into account.

   - Special attention should be given to the cliques or subcultures that often exist in schools.

   - New members should be rotated periodically into the leadership team— both to invigorate it and to enhance support from the whole faculty.

7. Only faculty members who are apt to remain in the building for several years should serve on the school improvement team. Meaningful change takes years to accomplish.

> ## Characteristics to Look for in Potential Team Members
>
> - A commitment to growth and development
> - A reputation for innovation
> - An ability to make things happen
> - Evidence of energy and persistence
> - Demonstrated leadership ability
> - A willingness to work
> - Patience
> - The respect of the faculty
> - Small and large group communication skills.
>
> *Source: The Use of Teams in School Improvement Processes, Painter et al., 2000, p. 4.*

8. "The involvement of community members, nonteaching staff, and parents is important within school commmunities, but these stakeholders should not necessarily be members of school improvement teams." (Maeroff 1993). Members of the school improvement team are charged with engaging the rest of the faculty in change efforts—a difficult role if the team is composed of individuals who are not part of the teaching staff. The school improvement team is a working group, often meeting formally and informally during school hours, making it difficult for community members to be an integral part of the team.

9. Be wary of including only "yes" individuals or uncritical optimists. Healthy skepticism among team members can be productive. Team members who ask the tough questions and challenge processes can help a team to progress purposefully and thoughtfully.

10. The team should include a principal, but the principal should not assume the role of team leader. Each individual on the team should assume a liaison role; develop an awareness and expertise about a particular topic, such as school culture or teaching and learning; and share his or her expertise with members of the team and faculty.

Your individual situation will dictate the appropriate composition. For example, some will wonder where students or families or new teachers might fit into the team. Other schools may require some type of teacher union representation. In other situations, the school may feel it's important to have the principal be the team leader—though if you think this is the case in your school, consider this action's effect on the openness of conversations. Although the number of people involved on the team itself may be limited, a critical aspect of the team's charge is to involve others in the decision making. The level of involvement and the groups involved (families, teachers, students, the school board, the superintendent, the central office, community members, businesses) will be decided by your school's initiative(s). The process outlined is a framework that can be replicated or amended. Your action planning team may not be able—or best suited—to bring to fruition whole-school reform without the creation of other subteams to focus on issues such as guidance and advisement, curriculum, data, and assessment.

Teams must be provided with professional development in the areas to be discussed. In addition, to avoid some of the warning signs of teams in trouble (see Early

Warning Signs box above) be sure to incorporate team-building activities and establish effective dialogue practices in the team's process. It is advisable, however, to pursue team-building and dialogue exercises before the warning signs develop. Once you are satisfied that the team is up to the challenge, your next step is to use data and research to identify more substantively the opportunities for improvement. However, if a clear vision for the school has not been established, one of the first actions of the team (or perhaps the site council or other group) will be to define the purpose, future, and vision of the school. As Painter and Valentine remind us in *Engaging Teachers in the School Improvement Process* (1999, p. 6):

> [T]he foundation of the school improvement plan—the basis on which all decisions are made—is the list of shared values and beliefs....The development of values, beliefs, and mission statements is critical to subsequent pieces of the improvement process. These statements reflect what school members hold closest to their hearts and what they believe to be their purpose. These concepts feed into and guide the organization's vision, which provides a look at what the organization will be like in the future.

Step 2: Use Data to Identify Opportunities for Improvement

At this stage the team should outline the opportunity. Often, data will be the first indicator that there is a problem, but problems may be identified in other ways. Regardless of how it comes to your attention, after the problem is identified, data should be collected that will help the team understand it better and guide the necessary changes. Research should also be conducted on best practices and to see whether other schools have encountered similar challenges, the reforms they implemented, and the results. This research will inform your strategies and help to ensure that your expectations of outcomes are reasonable and that the strategies you choose are the best for the situation.

Gainey and Webb offer the following advice:

- Formulate a statement of what you hope to achieve. Describe the situation in the school environment that will be addressed by your efforts.

- If you are rectifying a problem, indicate what is wrong that will be addressed.

- If the intervention is seen as an opportunity to improve some aspect of the school operation, frame the opportunity in the form of questions.

- Develop an introductory statement and then list the questions that will be addressed in your action plan. State the problem or opportunity in one or two sentences. If you have trouble doing this, you may not have crystallized the focus of your efforts.

- Ask the team, Is this a serious problem? If so, are you likely to be able to do anything about it? If the answer to either question is "no," find another opportunity.

If a school cannot measure the effects of change, how does a school know the impact on students? How can a school justify its reform actions without the accompanying data? Underestimating the critical nature of data could dampen the prospects for success—even at a school with few *perceived* problems. As noted in *Using Data for School Improvement* (Greunert and Valentine, 1999), data serve critical functions in justifying and evaluating improvement initiatives:

> Data collected at the beginning of a school improvement initiative can serve as baseline information to assess progress toward the school's long-term goals. Periodic data thereafter provides insight on the realization of the goals established from the school's vision and as a formative assessment of continuous change within a school.

> Data are also essential to understand the disparity among current practice, current perceptions, and best practices. For many principals and teachers who believe their school is functioning flawlessly, data—particularly valid observation data—may challenge their convictions. Reflecting on the data may result in a number of different reactions. The most common initial reaction is denial: "I don't know who took these surveys, but they aren't talking about our school." Another reaction is resignation: "Yes, that's our school, but we don't need a survey to tell us how bad it is; we work here." (p. 1)

Deciding What Data to Collect

To help your team determine the appropriate data to collect, a conversation might begin by focusing on the following passage:

> Most schools have easy access to existing data such as student and staff attendance, discipline referrals, suspensions, participation in student activities, student grades, and student standardized achievement tests. However, most readily available data are ignored, and when they are used, they are often misused. For example, most schools review standardized achievement data annually. Some schools even analyze long-term patterns of achievement over several years. Such analyses tell very little about the true quality of the school. Is the school effectively meeting academic needs of all students? Do we know which segments of our student body we most effectively serve? Only by way of purposeful disaggregation of the data can we develop an understanding of our students' academic successes and failures. Analyses

by ethnicity, socio-economic status, gender, prior achievement, participation or non-participation in school-sponsored activities are some of the obvious and important ways to study achievement data. Disaggregated data analysis takes time, yet it is essential. (Quinn, Greunert, & Valentine, 1999, p. 3)

Go to www.principals.org/brim for a guide on the types of data to collect.

What Should the Team Do with the Data?

Summarizing the data, perhaps the most important element of data collection, is the team's next challenge. Parents, teachers, students, and others will want to know why an improvement team is proposing a change. A well-devised summary of the data will offer answers, begin to form the conceptual basis of the argument for developing an action plan, and convey an urgent belief that something has to be done. The summary's importance lies in its ability or inability to identify causes contributing to the problem—a step toward convincing the various stakeholders that change is necessary and that the causes may be addressed. Without this connection, "research and common sense tell us that data will not automatically motivate people to change what they are doing. Change begins with acceptance that there is a need to change. Data can serve as the basis for understanding and accepting that need." (Quinn et al., 1999, p. 2)

Your action planning team may have done all its homework up to this point, compiling the data and research to support change, but unless the team assesses how prepared the school is for the change, that homework may be all for naught. The next step is to assess the conditions for change.

Step 3: Assess Conditions for Change and Develop the Action Plan

Development and implementation of an action plan must take into account your school's "organizational readiness" for accepting the plan. *Breaking Ranks Leadership* (NASSP, 1998), a manual developed for a Breaking Ranks implementation training program, offers the following five areas of organizational culture (adapted from Dalziel & Schoonover, 1998) that must be considered when preparing any organization for change:

1. **An organization's previous experience in accepting change** is often the most accurate predictor of successful change implementation. Those who previously have had positive experiences with change are likely to have positive experiences with change in the future. Likewise, those who have had negative experiences with change are likely to have negative experiences in the future unless change leaders

   - gather all pertinent information regarding past changes;
   - spend extra time talking about the proposed change;
   - provide ongoing feedback;
   - arrange for an immediate positive outcome from the change; and
   - publicize successes.

2. **The clarity of expectations** regarding the impact and effects of a proposed change is a major consideration for change leaders. Change leaders need to scrutinize the varying expectations from diverse work groups and various levels of the organization to define and emphasize common interests.

3. **Leaders must also consider the origin of an idea or problem**, or where in the organization the idea for change originated. Consider the fundamental law of change: The greater the distance between those who define a change and those who have to live with its effects, the higher the probability that problems will develop.

4. **The support of district- and school-level management** is especially critical during the initial phases of change and remains an important consideration throughout the change process. In the most successful change efforts, top management is highly visible and actively participates throughout the entire project. In less successful projects, top management functions in a less visible role as a "provider of capital."

5. **The compatibility of a change with organizational goals** describes the degree of agreement between the proposed change and the current organizational situation. Whenever possible, changes should be integrated into the organization's overall goals and mission to facilitate the transition between old and new and start the change in an accepting environment.

In developing the action plans, teams must also address each of the following challenges (Gainey & Webb, 1998, pp. 2–3):

■ Resistance to change is consistently reinforced by the majority of people who tend to be satisfied with their school, although they generally concede that there may be some aspects of the school that can be improved.

■ A number of stakeholders, while not necessarily opposed to the plan, may be undecided regarding one or more components. Most of these individuals will be looking for reassurance that the proposed course of action will benefit all students.

■ Not only should you be prepared for opposition, you should not be surprised if some opposition comes from stakeholder groups who have traditionally been supporters.

■ Expect the degree of opposition to be positively correlated to the degree of change you hope to implement.

■ Anticipate where the opposition will come from and do not take for granted any one group as supporters.

■ Keep in mind the political reality…. Regardless of how sound a proposal might be from an educational perspective, it would take courage for policymakers to endorse an intervention that has strong opposition from key stakeholder groups.

The Action Plan

Given the wide variations in local circumstances and resources (fiscal, human capital, social capital, and time), it is impossible to provide a single comprehensive action plan for implementing the nine cornerstone strategies and the 30 Breaking Ranks in the Middle recommendations described in this field guide. A prepackaged plan would not be appropriate for all schools and the critical stage of getting others involved in developing a plan unique to an individual school would be forgotten. For similar reasons, your team should suppress the urge to have the team do all the planning—despite the team members' best intentions (Painter et al., 2000, p. 9). If your team includes others in the development of the plan and ties the strategies to the defined problem, the research, the data, and the specific circumstances of the school, the overall plan will be better defined and will more likely be defensible in the face of challenges.

Gainey and Webb (1998) cite several critical components to address in a successful plan:

- Describe in clear terms the expected benefits and how you will attempt to close the gap between what is and what the shared vision indicates should be.

- Provide milestones tied to the strategies.

- Develop indicators related to the quantitative or qualitative data that served as the basis for the intervention. Project incremental gains—immediate results are not realistic.

- Do not attempt to implement something beyond your team's scope of influence.

- Recognize that the time line will probably need to be revised.

- Indicate how others will be involved and how you will motivate and sustain the efforts of key stakeholders.

- Assess and address the influence of the following:

  - **Rules**—formal and informal policies, and contracts that will foster or impede implementation.

  - **Roles**—formal and informal leadership characteristics. Who makes things happen? Under what circumstances? Identify roadblocks or bottlenecks within the bureaucracy.

  - **Relationships**—Understand the potential for the various formal and informal relationships between individuals and groups to foster or impede your efforts.

  - **Responsibilities**—Existing rules may govern exactly how much responsibility you and your team will have and will be able to give to others.

- Monitor the plan regularly to help justify expenditure of resources and build momentum and participation; be prepared to respond to questions; modify the plan where necessary; and recognize and celebrate incremental successes as they occur.

Step 4: Support the Action Plan with Professional Development

To effectively implement and assess an action plan, principals, teachers, and other staff members require appropriate professional development. As important (and perhaps more so, given the breadth and depth of change called for in Breaking Ranks in the Middle) is developing a school community in which learning is not a *task for students* but rather a *goal for everyone*. The level of complexity in migrating from many traditional practices to those recommended in this field guide requires significant professional development. Follow-up, practice, opportunities to reflect, an assessment of how well the practice is implemented, and its effects on students are just some of the variables that should be included in a comprehensive professional development strategy. To adequately address comprehensive professional development, one must turn to the volumes of literature addressing the topic. For our purposes here, only the following aspects are covered as they relate to your leadership team's involvement in developing an action plan:

- Supporting a professional learning community.

- Standards and practices of professional development that may help your team prepare a comprehensive professional development strategy to implement your action plan.

- The need for each principal and staff member to have a Personal Learning Plan (PLP) that takes into account the skills and knowledge each staff member must acquire to implement the action plan. This plan will give every staff member an opportunity to critique his or her own skills in light of the overall action plan and seek development aligned with that plan. Without this self-critique and the review of the principal, it becomes very difficult for a school to implement a comprehensive plan for change.

Learning Communities

How effective have you—as a school, as a principal—been at establishing a community that respects learning for all: students, staff members, families, and community members? By reviewing activities associated with a healthy learning community (the highlighted column in figure 2.4), your team can better devise instruments to

- Evaluate whether teachers and other staff members are prepared to implement strategies in the action plan.

- Ascertain the type and level of professional development needed.

- Gauge progress toward establishing a community of learners in your school by establishing a baseline.

Use this tool to include the faculty and others in evaluating how your school is a learning community. Once identified, any weaknesses can be addressed in the comprehensive professional development plan and aligned with your strategies for change.

Align Comprehensive Professional Development Plan With Action Plan

Figure 2.5 provides a conceptual framework to guide your action planning team as it assesses the professional development required to support the strategies, processes, and programs detailed in your action plan. Your team should develop a similar chart outlining the content, objectives, activities, and evaluation of the professional development program.

As your team develops the action plan, it should ensure that the "activities" align with national standards. The National Staff Development Council (NSDC) provides such standards to ensure that quality professional development is tied to improving learning for all students. Several of those standards are highlighted in the box on the next page. Visit www.nsdc.org for a complete list of the standards as well as an assessment tool to help ascertain your school's level of adherence to the standards. Use the standards as a checklist against which to judge all professional development.

In addition, as you design your comprehensive professional development plan to align with Breaking Ranks in the Middle changes, an evaluative mechanism or instrument will need to be developed to ascertain whether or not the professional development provides the intended results. Developing the measures before offering the professional development is critical. Figure 2.6 provides questions and a sample grid to guide you in the evaluation process. *Making the connection between the need identified in the action plan and the need the professional development activity will address is essential to ensuring that development is tied to the goal of improved student performance.*

Figure 2.4
How Is My School a Learning Community?

On a scale of 1–5 (1 being the worst) I believe we do this…	Learning Community Activities	Direct Benefits
	Using shared planning to develop units, lessons, and activities.	Divides the labor; saves time because no one has to do it all; increases quantity and quality of ideas.
	Learning from one another by watching each other teach.	Provides concrete examples of effective practices; expands the observer's repertoire of skills; stimulates analytical thinking about teaching.
	Collectively studying student work to identify weaknesses and plan new ways to teach to those weaknesses.	Increases quantity and quality of insights into student performance; focuses efforts on the bottom line, which is student learning; increases professionalism and self-esteem of learning community members.
	Sharing articles and other professional resources for ideas and insights; conducting studies of books on teaching and learning.	Expands pool of ideas and resources available to members of the learning community.
	Talking with one another about what and how we teach and the results our teaching produces.	Decreases feelings of isolation; increases experimentation and analysis of teaching practices; increases confidence of teachers; provides teachers with greater access to a range of teaching styles, models, and philosophies; increases support of new teachers.
	Providing moral support, comradeship, and encouragement.	Enables teachers to stick with new practices through the rough early stages of learning to use new skills; decreases burnout and stress; increases team members' willingness to try new methods and share ideas and concerns with other members of the learning community.
	Jointly exploring a problem, including data collection and analysis; conducting action research.	Improves quality of insights and solutions; increases professionalism.
	Attending training together and helping each other implement the content of the training.	Helps learning community members get more out of training; enables them to go to one another with questions or to get clarification about what was presented during training.
	Participating in ongoing quality improvement activities.	Creates more efficient use of time; takes advantage of particular talents or interests of learning community members.
	Using collective decision making to reach decisions that produce collective action.	Improves quality of instruction, student performance, and school operations.
	Providing support for "help-seeking" as well as "help-giving."	Makes a strong statement of shared responsibility and commitment to one another's learning.
	Sharing the responsibility for making or collecting materials.	Helps learning community members feel secure in asking for help and advice; enables the giving of assistance and advice without establishing one-up/one-down relationships.

Source: Collins, D. (1998). Achieving your vision of professional development. Greensboro, NC: SERVE

Thus far, we have discussed professional development from the macro or school-wide perspective as it relates to bringing about changes consistent with Breaking Ranks in the Middle recommendations. Yet the impact must be made student by student, class by class—which requires a focus on individual teachers.

Figure 2.5
Overview of the Planning Process

Component	Primary Decisions	Sources of Information
Content	What knowledge, skills, strategies, and/or values and beliefs need to be studied?	■ Analysis of students' work or performance ■ Teacher self-assessment ■ School or district programs or practices ■ National standards (e.g., National Staff Development Council [NSDC])
Objectives	What will participants know and/or be able to do as a result of their participation in professional development activities? What is the desired impact on student learning?	■ Analysis of students' work or performance ■ Professional growth goal-setting ■ School or district programs or practices ■ National standards (e.g., NSDC)
Activities	What will participants do to achieve the identified objectives?	■ Five models of professional development (see p. 72) ■ National standards (e.g., NSDC)
Evaluation	How will the results of the professional activities be measured?	■ Changes in knowledge, beliefs, values, skills, or practices of participants ■ Changes in student achievement, behavior, or attitudes

Source: Collins, D. (1998). Reprinted with permission

Creating a Personal Learning Plan (Webb & Berkbuegler, 1998)

In the end, the effectiveness of a comprehensive professional development plan is 6measured by each staff member's awareness of the skills he or she needs to improve student performance—and in the staff member's ability to acquire those skills. If comprehensive reform is to be achieved, each person must reflect upon his or her development needs *as they relate to the action plan* and create and continually update a PLP consistent with the action plan. As Sparks and Hirsh (1997) remind us:

> Rather than basing the Personal Learning Plan solely on the teacher's perception about what he or she needs (e.g., to learn more about classroom management), the plan should consider what students need to know and be able to do and work backward to the knowledge, skills, and attitudes needed by the teacher if those student outcomes are to be realized. (p. 27)

Approaches to self-evaluation include the following:

■ Quantitative tools such as rating scales, checklists, and self-rating forms.

■ Videotapes of classroom performance, which allow "evaluatees to see themselves as others see them and reduce the subjectivity that is normally involved in evaluating one's own performance" (Webb & Norton, 1998, p. 390).

■ Portfolios.

Figure 2.6
Evaluating the Impact of Professional Development

Sample Grid
Key Questions to Guide the Evaluation of Professional Development Activities

Target or Group	What need will this activity address?	How was this need measured?	What change is this activity intended to produce?	How will this change be measured?
Teachers	Teachers need training and practice in strategies proven to be effective in improving reading achievement for at-risk students.	A survey was conducted in which teachers prioritized their professional development needs. Training and practice in reading strategies for at-risk students was the highest-rated need.	Teachers will be able to use the identified strategies with a high degree of effectiveness.	A large sample of teachers will be interviewed using the Levels of Use instrument from the Concerns-Based Adoption Model materials.
Students	Student achievement in reading among at-risk students has declined for three of the past four years.	A norm-referenced achievement test is given to all students each spring. Scores for at-risk students were broken out and analyzed to reveal this trend.	Reading achievement of at-risk students will improve.	The same norm-referenced test will continue to be given each spring and the results broken out to reveal the achievement for at-risk students as a subgroup.
Organization	The school needs to be responsive to the needs of all students.	Test scores of at-risk students declined, while scores of other groups improved or remained stable.	The school will improve its awareness of and responsiveness to the needs of all students.	Test scores will be disaggregated, and the performance of all subgroups will be identified and analyzed.

Source: Collins (1998). Reprinted with permission.

■ Peer-to-peer classroom observations; peer review of lesson plans, handouts, or worksheets; and student evaluations. Peers and students can provide valuable feedback. Research refutes the criticism that evaluations by students are nothing more than popularity contests, are grade dependent, or are of limited value because of the inexperience or immaturity of student evaluators (Follman, 1995). "Using student evaluations demonstrates to students that their opinions are valued and may encourage them to become more involved in the learning process" (Herbart, 1995).

The model in figure 2.7 provides a valuable tool to help teachers and principals in the process of self-assessment. Many of the nine cornerstone strategies and the 30 Breaking Ranks in the Middle recommendations outlined in chapter 1 could easily be adapted and plugged into the model—specifically in the top right box, "Ideal Teaching Practices."

Matching Type of Professional Development to the PLP
After reviewing professional needs, staff members must decide which of the five basic models of staff development (Hirsh, 1997, as cited by Webb & Berkbuegler, 1998)

Figure 2.7
Self-Assessment and a Self-Directed Change Model

Steps in Using Self-Assessment	Components of a Self-Directed Change Model
1. Identify practices to be studied. 2. Identify standards or criteria for judging targeted practices (these criteria describe ideal teaching practices). 3. Identify methods for collecting information about targeted practices. 4. Collect information. 5. Compare real practices with standards or criteria for ideal practices. 6. Identify priority areas for more in-depth study and professional growth. (What are the most significant differences between the real and the ideal?) 7. Identify the desired outcomes of the professional development activities. 8. Plan the professional development activities, including follow-up activities, that will address the targeted practices. 9. Implement the plan; assess and monitor its progress periodically. 10. Use feedback to determine the extent to which the professional development activities achieved the desired outcomes; continue or modify the activities as necessary or identify new practices for study.	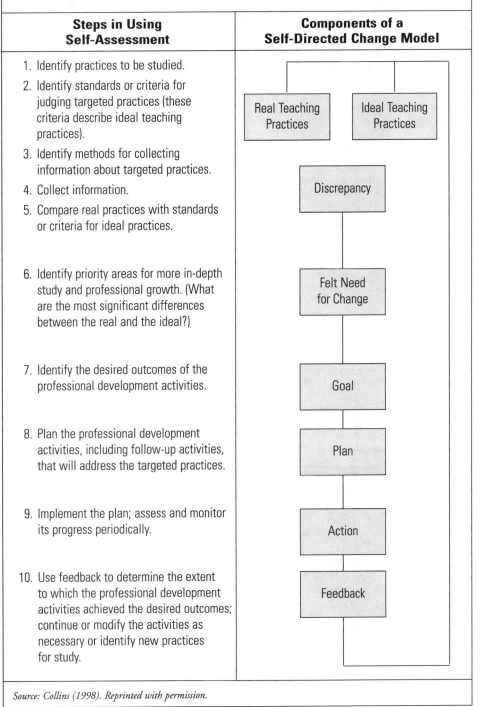

Source: Collins (1998). Reprinted with permission.

meet each need. The breadth of Breaking Ranks in the Middle reforms will require that several, if not all, models be pursued:

1. **Inquiry.** Teacher inquiry, be it a solitary activity or the collaborative project of a small or large group. It can be formal or informal and can take place in a classroom (action research), at a teacher center, or as a part of a formal educational program. As a result of engaging in the research process (defining a problem, reviewing the

Figure 2.8
Effectiveness Estimates for Five Models of Professional Development

Desired Outcome	Individually Guided	Observation/ Assessment	Development/ Improvement Process	Training	Inquiry
Mastery of simple, specific teaching skill	Medium: less efficient than other models	Highest: recommended components make it very effective	Low: better suited for broader outcomes	High: adding peer coaching can increase application to 80%	Medium: requires more time to plan than other models
Implementation of complex set of teaching strategies	High: adding peer coaching can increase application to 90%	Highest: more complex outcomes make follow-up important	Medium: less efficient than other models	Medium: harder to observe complex strategies	Medium: less efficient than other models
Gaining insight into how students learn	Highest: effective in testing hypotheses	Medium: less efficient than other models	Medium: less efficient than other models	Low: focuses on observing behavior of teachers, not students	Medium: includes professional reading, observation of students
Mastery of new classroom management skills	High: adding peer coaching can increase application to 90%	Highest: recommended components make it very effective	Low: better suited for broader outcomes	High: adding peer coaching can increase application to 90%	Medium: less efficient than other models
Implementation of new assessment procedures	High: effective but time-consuming	Highest: recommended components make it very effective	Medium: less efficient than other models	Medium: assessment procedures are not always observable	Medium: includes collaboration with others
Solving a complex problem dealing with improving student achievement	Highest: effective in solving complex problems, generates a great deal of learning	Low: better suited for supporting implementation than creating new knowledge	Medium: can be adapted to problem-solving tasks	Low: better suited for giving feedback than solving problems	High: flexibility allows activities to be designed specifically for this outcome
Acquiring group leadership skills/working as a team to solve problems	Medium: less efficient than other models	Low: better suited for supporting implementation than building leadership skills	Highest: leadership opportunities abound in this model	Low: less observable because skills are developed outside the classroom	Medium: allows group members to learn what they need, when they need to know it
Increasing knowledge of content or subject matter	Medium: less efficient than other models; focus is on creating new knowledge, not acquiring knowledge	High: effective in helping teachers acquire new knowledge, especially in applying it	Highest: important element is acquiring new knowledge to solve a problem or meet a specific need	Low: focuses on teacher's behavior, not content knowledge	Medium: include professional reading and contact with subject matter experts

Source: Collins (1998). Reprinted with permission.

professional literature, and collecting, analyzing, and interpreting data), teachers not only develop research skills and acquire knowledge but can use the results of the research to improve their own skills and improve practice schoolwide.

2. **Training programs.** In-service training historically has been the most common approach to professional development. Too often, it is of the "one-shot" mode, where some expert is brought in before the school year starts to give a one- or two-day workshop in which participants "sit and git." Typically, little or no follow-up or support for implementation is provided. However, if properly conducted, with a

clear set of learning objectives, training can be an effective process for improving skills and knowledge. A combination of components (exploration of theory, demonstration of a skill, practice of the skill, feedback on performance, and coaching in the workplace) are necessary. Research by Sparks and Loucks-Horsley (1989) also suggests that

- Training sessions should be spaced one or more weeks apart so that content can be "chunked" for improved comprehension and so teachers have opportunities for classroom practice.

- Teachers prefer their peers for trainers: When peers are trainers, teachers feel more comfortable exchanging ideas, play a more active role in workshops, and report that they receive more practical suggestions (p. 48).

3. **Involvement in a development/improvement project or process.** Teachers are commonly asked to engage in curriculum design, development, or revision, or to engage in systematic school improvement efforts aimed at improving the curriculum or classroom instruction. Participation in these projects may require the teacher to acquire specific knowledge and skills through reading, discussion, training, observation, or trial and error.

4. **Observation and assessment.** Research and the experience of hundreds of school districts support the fact that, when properly conducted, observations, including pre- and postconferences, can yield valuable and valid information about teacher performance. This model is based on the assumption that teachers will reflect on and analyze the feedback to improve instruction and student learning.

5. **Individually guided activities.** The teacher determines his or her staff development goals and selects the activities that will result in the achievement of the goals. The model assumes that teachers are in the best position to determine their own learning needs, are self-initiated, and will be most motivated when they select their own relevant learning activities. The types of activities teachers engage in (e.g., workshops or conferences, university courses, reading, action research) are determined by the teacher's preferred learning style.

As figure 2.8 demonstrates, each of the fives strategies has its advantages and disadvantages.

Different strategies and recommendations will require different models, but they all require continual revision of the PLP. The principal, the leadership team, and the action planning team must

- Clearly express a vision "with measurable objectives stated in terms of student outcomes."

- "Create an environment in which teachers will experiment, take risks, discuss their weaknesses, and share their successes and failures without feeling threatened."

- "Practice what they preach."

- "Provide the atmosphere, organization, and structure that allow teachers the freedom, time, and resources to explore and experiment" (Webb & Berkbuegler, 1998, p. 6).

Step 5: Report the Results

All too often, new programs are planned, announced with great fanfare and ceremony, and never implemented as intended or, if implemented, never evaluated…. They more or less seem to have a life of their own and continue to operate, whether effective or ineffective, until a new program comes along. (Gainey & Webb, 1998, p. 15)

Just as report cards for students are important for identifying areas of strength, weakness, and accomplishment, reporting the results of reform strategies should be given high priority. An effective report of the action plan and the results should be clear, concise, cogent, correct, and compelling enough that it will be read, yet detailed enough to indicate how the efforts support the improvement of student learning.

The report should include the following:

- An overview of the action plan.

- The methodology employed.

- The chronology of activities.

- The results of formative evaluation that occurred during the operational phase, describing what was accomplished, how it occurred, and who was involved, as well as any changes or modifications made as a result of monitoring the implementation.

- A discussion of the summative evaluation used to measure program effectiveness.

- A summary/conclusion that reports the effectiveness or ineffectiveness of the intervention, any constraints on the intervention, and limitations on the generalizability of the results.

- The implications for theory and practice.

This report can be shared in any number of ways with community, parent, and student organizations.

From a Five-Step Process to the Implementation of Specific Recommendations

The detail offered in the preceding pages about a sample process for change should serve as a guide to you when you implement the specific Breaking Ranks in the Middle recommendations discussed in the following pages. The first set of recommendations relate to establishing collaborative leadership and a learning community at your school.

Following is the first of several "Ask the Expert" selections in this field guide. These selections are designed to provide the reader with the insights of respected voices in the field of middle level education.

Ask the Experts

Q&A with Donald C. Clark, Professor Emeritus, University of Arizona, and Sally N. Clark, Professor Emerita, University of Arizona

Q: *What do you believe are the five or six most important indicators that a school and its leadership team have embraced collaborative leadership as a means to improve student success and achievement?*

A: Highly successful middle level schools that have embraced collaborative leadership to improve student success and achievement have the following:

- Principals who are highly committed to shared leadership and collaborative decision making that is focused on school mission, vision, curriculum and instruction, assessment, and professional development.

- A collaboratively developed and accepted set of values about young adolescent learners, student learning, and success.

- A strong community of learners in which students, teachers, administrators, parents, and community members collaborate to determine learning needs, develop appropriate learning strategies, and nurture student and adult learning.

- A culture built around strong relationships of cooperation, trust, respect, support, and appreciation.

- Organizational structures such as teams, advisory committees, school leadership councils, and ad hoc committees that provide multiple opportunities for frequent, regular, and meaningful participation in shared leadership and collaborative decision making.

- The time, resources, professional development, and support necessary to facilitate ongoing collaboration.

Q: *What is the biggest challenge to collaborative leadership in middle grade education? How would you address that challenge?*

A: The tradition of teacher isolation is the most formidable barrier to establishing collaborative environments. In these cultures of isolation, which are found in many schools, teachers often place high value on teacher autonomy and noninterference, and they use isolation to protect the time they believe they need to meet all the demands on them. When these cultural conditions exist, there are few opportunities for principals, teachers, parents, and community members to collaborate and share decision making about curriculum, instruction, and student learning and achievement.

To "reculture" a school to value shared leadership and collaborative decision making requires that principals and teachers ask hard questions about how their school is organized and why and how things work and do not work. Questions that might be used to initiate this inquiry into school purposes and organizational structures might include these:

- What does this school value?

- What are the cultural traditions of this school?

- What is the vision of this school?

- What organizational structures are found in this school and why?

- What curricular structures are found in our school?

- What instructional practices are prevalent in the classroom?

- How are we spending our time and resources?

In answering these questions, the focus must be kept on how what we do contributes to learning and success and what changes need to be made to enhance the learning of all people in the school. Teacher and principal inquiry into their schools leads to more collaborative cultures, which often serve as the basis for initiating teams, collaborative data analysis, task forces, and shared leadership and decision making.

Q: *Because trust is such an essential component of collaboration, what are five specific successful strategies or practices a principal can use to build trust with teachers and parents?*

A: Principals can build trust in their schools by using these strategies:

- Build strong, caring relationships. Principals who are successful at creating collaborative cultures build personal and professional relationships with their teachers. They know about their teachers' personal and professional lives, and they have empathy for the work they do and the lives they live.

- Listen and act. Principals who wish to build trust must be visible and available. They must be responsive to suggestions and, when necessary, take appropriate action.

- Make teachers, parents, and community members feel valued. Principals must recognize effort and success and celebrate accomplishments. Recognition is often the one thing that keeps people excited about their participation.

- Recognize that all teachers are capable of leadership. Principals who are successful at sharing leadership provide teachers with opportunities to exercise leadership and the necessary resources, time, and support to be successful.

- Engage teachers, parents, and community members in discussion, inquiry, and decision making. Principals who are successful collaborators involve all stakeholders in discussion and inquiry about major school issues and concerns, and trust them to do what's best for students.

Q: *For the principal who might feel threatened by collaborating rather than controlling, what advice would you give? What should be his or her first steps in appropriately sharing leadership?*

A: Principals must look at their own beliefs about and commitment to sharing power and decision making with teachers, parents, and community members. Successful collaboration is based on principals who are committed to sharing decision making, empowering others, creating supportive environments, facilitating broad involvement, and providing opportunities to acquire new knowledge and skills. Principals must believe in collaboration and must model shared decision making if it is to succeed in their schools.

As a first step, the principal should examine his or her own belief system regarding collaboration. Affirmative answers to the following questions would indicate a readiness to develop and support collaborative structures:

- Am I willing to share power?
- Am I willing to trust others to make informed decisions?
- Am I willing to engage in and support collaborative decision making?
- Am I willing to provide and engage in school-based professional development?
- Am I willing to mentor teachers, parents, and community members and provide them with opportunities and support to develop the skills necessary to be successful leaders?
- Am I willing to learn new skills and to reflect regularly on the effectiveness of my own leadership and collaborative efforts?

Ask the Experts:
Donald C. and Sally N. Clark

As a second step, the principal should establish small opportunities for shared leadership and collaborative decision making that are primarily focused on student learning. These opportunities might include the delegation of responsibility to a trusted teacher to provide leadership in addressing an important school issue (e.g., student activities, improving parent involvement, homework policy); appointing teachers, parents, and community members to ad hoc committees and asking them to provide information and recommendations; or establishing decision-making committees that are focused on a single issue (e.g., career day, interscholastic/intramural sports, exploratory curriculum, curriculum revision). Teacher teams also provide an excellent organizational structure on which to build shared leadership and decision making.

As principals and participants gain confidence and success in small collaborative projects, efforts can be expanded to include more and more of the school's stakeholders. Collaboration requires time to build relationships and trust, to develop confidence in the process, to gain experience and skills, and to become comfortable with new ways of doing things.

Q: *Does collaborative leadership apply to everything that happens in a school?*

A: In middle level schools that have a culture of collaboration, sharing leadership and decision making are the accepted norms of the school. Principals, teachers, parents, and community members value and trust each other and expect to be involved in school leadership and decision making. But while participation and involvement are expected, there is also an understanding that not every decision can or needs to be collaborative. Effective leadership is multidimensional, and there are times when even the most collaborative principals must act quickly and decisively. Because of the high level of trust, teachers, parents, and community members believe that the principal will involve the appropriate persons when making decisions. There is also an expectation that he or she will be true to the mission and vision of the school and act in the best interests of the students, teachers, parents, and community members.

Q: *When one thinks of collaborative leadership, administrators and teachers come to mind. What are some of the innovative and substantive ways in which you have seen other members of the school community involved in leadership and decision making?*

A: Parent/community member involvement is critical to collaborative school cultures, as it presents an opportunity for parents and community members to be heard, to learn about the school, to give input, and to be part of the decision-making process. To fulfill these important functions, involving parents and community members in leadership and decision making must include opportunities for participation in the daily life of the school; opportunities to learn about young adolescents, school organization, programs, curriculum, instruction, and assessment; and opportunities to share in the planning and decision making about school direction and programs. In highly successful schools, parents and community members have been involved in the following:

- Organization and coordination of parent enrichment seminars focused on middle school programs, young adolescent development, and helping your child be successful.

- Organization and coordination of parent/community members school volunteer programs.

- Organization and coordination of daily after-school enrichment programs for students, including tutorials, arts programs, athletic activities, and club programs.

- Organization and coordination of fundraising activities to benefit students, curriculum and instruction, and teacher professional development.

- Organization and coordination of student visits to and internship programs with local businesses and public agencies.

Q: *How does the presence of teams in a school help build a collaborative culture?*

A: In highly successful middle level schools, teaming structures play an important role in developing and sustaining collaborative relationships. Many teachers in these schools believe that teaming makes collaboration possible and that collaboration is responsible for building strong, positive relationships.

Teachers working together in teams are a powerful influence on curriculum, instruction, and school improvement. When it is supported by scheduled planning time, teaming provides teachers with opportunities to collaborate and reflect on curriculum standards, appropriate instruction, and student learning. It enables teachers to share and discuss data, participate in collaborative decision making, and take on additional leadership roles in the school.

Teaming, with its focus on learning, also facilitates a culture of learning in which a community of learners regularly engages in a variety of formal and informal continuous learning activities. The structure and processes of teaming allow teachers to build strong relationships of trust, to create cultures of collegiality and support, to exercise leadership, and to develop core values and beliefs that lead to successful student and adult learning.

The following are a few of the resources related to developing collaborative approaches recommended by our experts:

- Clark, S., & Clark, D. (2002). Collaborative decision making: A promising but underused strategy of middle school improvement. *Middle School Journal,* 33(4), 52–57.

- Clark, D. C., & Clark, S. N. (1996, March). Building collaborative environments for successful middle level school restructuring. *NASSP Bulletin,* 80(578), 1–16.

- Jackson, A., & Davis, G. (2000). *Turning points 2000: Educating adolescents in the 21st century.* New York: Teachers College Press.

- Lambert, L. (2003). *Leadership capacity for lasting school improvement.* Alexandria, VA: Association for Supervision and Curriculum Development.

- Valentine, J., Clark, D., Hackmann, D., & Petzko, V. (2004). *Leadership for highly successful middle level schools: vol. II: A national study of leadership in middle level schools.* Reston, VA: National Association of Secondary School Principals (chapters 4, 5, and 6).

- Wheelock, A. (1998). *Safe to be smart: Building a culture for standards-based reform in the middle grades.* Westerville, OH: National Middle School Association.

**Ask the Experts:
Donald C. and Sally N. Clark**

Ask the Experts

Q&A with Richard Flanary, Director, and Pete Reed, Associate Director, Professional Development Services, NASSP

Q: *What knowledge, skills, and attitudes are essential for all middle level faculty members? How can these be assessed and developed so that a school does not rely on "one-size-fits-all" professional development strategies?*

A: The Interstate New Teacher Assessment and Support Consortium (INTASC) standards establish a performance-based foundation that reflects the requisite knowledge, skills, and attitudes necessary for teachers starting their careers and thus serve as a solid foundation for effective performance for all teachers. The factor that keeps these standards from being a one-size-fits-all approach is the assessment of each teacher's performance against the standards.

1. Content pedagogy: The teacher understands the central concepts, tools of inquiry, and structures of the discipline he or she teaches and can create learning experiences that make these aspects of subject matter meaningful for students.

2. Student development: The teacher understands how children learn and develop, and can provide learning opportunities that support a child's intellectual, social, and personal development.

3. Diverse learners: The teacher understands how students differ in their approaches to learning and creates instructional opportunities that are adapted to diverse learners.

4. Multiple instructional strategies: The teacher understands and uses a variety of instructional strategies to encourage student development of critical thinking, problem solving, and performance skills.

5. Motivation and management: The teacher uses an understanding of individual and group motivation and behavior to create a learning environment that encourages positive social interaction, active engagement in learning, and self-motivation.

6. Communication and technology: The teacher uses knowledge of effective verbal, nonverbal, and media communication techniques to foster active inquiry, collaboration, and supportive interaction in the classroom.

7. Planning: The teacher plans instruction based on knowledge of subject matter, students, the community, and curriculum goals.

8. Assessment: The teacher understands and uses formal and informal assessment strategies to evaluate and ensure the continuous intellectual, social, and physical development of the learner.

9. Reflective practice/professional growth: The teacher is a reflective practitioner who continually evaluates the effects of his or her choices and actions on

others (students, parents, and other professionals in the learning community) and actively seeks out opportunities to grow professionally.

10. School and community involvement: The teacher fosters relationships with school colleagues, parents, and agencies in the larger community to support students' learning and well-being.

In addition to these "foundation" performance standards, experienced professionals should begin to demonstrate a higher level of performance as outlined by the five propositions from the National Board for Professional Teaching Standards. (Go to www.principals.org/brim for a more complete version of the performance indicators for each proposition.)

- Proposition #1: Teachers are committed to students and their learning:

  Teachers recognize individual differences in their students and adjust their practice accordingly.

  Teachers have an understanding of how students develop and learn.

  Teachers treat students equitably.

  Teachers' mission extends beyond developing the cognitive capacity of their students.

- Proposition #2: Teachers know the subjects they teach and how to teach those subjects to students:

  Teachers appreciate how knowledge in their subjects is created, organized, and linked to other disciplines.

  Teachers command specialized knowledge of how to convey a subject to students.

  Teachers generate multiple paths to knowledge.

- Proposition #3: Teachers are responsible for managing and monitoring student learning:

  Teachers call on multiple methods to meet their goals.

  Teachers orchestrate learning in group settings.

  Teachers place a premium on student engagement.

  Teachers regularly assess student progress.

  Teachers are mindful of their principal objectives.

- Proposition #4: Teachers think systematically about their practice and learn from experience:

  Teachers are continually making difficult choices that test their judgment.

  Teachers seek the advice of others and draw on education research and scholarship to improve their practice.

- Proposition #5: Teachers are members of learning communities:

  Teachers contribute to school effectiveness by collaborating with other professionals.

  Teachers work collaboratively with parents.

  Teachers take advantage of community resources.

However, in the final analysis, the formal knowledge teachers rely on accumulates and changes steadily, yet provides insufficient guidance for action in many situations. Teaching ultimately requires

- Sound judgment
- Ability to improvise
- Skills to converse about means and ends
- Human qualities that contribute to developing and maintaining positive relationships with others
- Expert knowledge and skill in at least one discipline
- Professional commitment
- Beliefs that direct use of knowledge and skills in the best interest of students

Q: *What are specific strategies to ensure that new teachers receive support from veteran teachers and the leadership team as it relates to professional development?*

A: An effective teacher induction model provides the kind of support new teachers need. An induction model provides systematic assistance rather than providing assistance after a teacher is in trouble. Abandoning the time-honored tradition of assigning the most difficult load to the least experienced teachers is also essential to ensuring the success of new teachers. The "trial by fire" initiation of new teachers contributes to the short-lived careers of many talented new teachers who are well prepared and have great potential.

Ask the Experts:
Richard Flanary and Pete Reed

Q: *What strategies can a principal employ to ensure that a teacher is getting the necessary help?*

A: An environment of open communication is the initial criterion for ensuring that teachers get the necessary help from the leadership team and from one another. The principal needs to establish an assistance and support network for both new and experienced teachers. This network can enable teachers to ask for technical assistance without fear of being regarded as incompetent and can support teachers in developing adaptive expertise to meet new challenges. Such a network requires the development of a culture of professional learning through collaboration and sharing. The principal must be seen as the principal learner in a school that has the culture of a learning organization. Even with a solid support network in place, there is no substitute for the principal's presence in the teaching and learning environment—the classroom—to ensure that internal accountability is in place for what is taught, how it is taught, and how well it is taught and learned.

Once you have assessed the conditions for change in your school, developed an action plan aligned with the nine cornerstone strategies or the Breaking Ranks in the Middle recommendations (depending on your school's stage of change), provided the proper professional development to implement the strategies, and implemented the action plan, you're finished, right? Not quite. Everyone wants to know whether the plan was successful—the good, the bad, the undecided. On to step 5.

Ask the Expert

**Q&A with Beverly N. Raimondo, Director,
Center for Parent Leadership/Prichard Committee for Academic Excellence**

Q: *What are the benefits that I, as principal, will get from involving parents in decision making?*

A: Parents will focus first and foremost on what is best for the children and how any decision will be good for children. That alone is leverage for principals as they work to improve achievement in schools by asking for curriculum or instructional changes, more challenging courses, more demanding schedules, and so on. By ensuring that parents have the information and data they need to ask good questions, make informed recommendations, and analyze needs, the principal develops an ally with a broader agenda. I watched a colleague do this while serving on a school-based decision-making council when her principal told her, "You make me do my job better."

Q: *What objective data highlight the benefits of involving parents meaningfully in decision making and education?*

A: See Anne Henderson and Karen Mapp's work, *A New Generation of Evidence of the Impact of School, Family, and Community Connections on Student Engagement,* Southwest Educational Development Laboratory (SEDL), 2002, for objective data. The work is available for free download at www.sedl.org/connections.

Ask the Expert:
Beverly N. Raimondo

Q: *What are the areas in which families must be engaged?*

A: In the middle grades, families must be engaged in monitoring their students' academic achievement, ensuring that they are taking high-level courses that prepare them for high school and college, questioning their students' placement, and understanding the importance of gatekeeper courses such as algebra and foreign languages. Because this is also such an important time for social and emotional development and peer pressure, families must know their children's friends, know how they are spending their time, and ensure they are involved in meaningful co-curricular activities. They must be clear with their children about their expectations of them, both academically and socially. Above all, they must be present; they must not disappear from the school even if their children tell them they don't want them there. There is too much evidence that children want their parents to be involved in their lives, even when they are sending a different message. Parents must continue to be parents and adults. At school, they simply need to be involved in different ways than they are at the elementary level.

The following are a few of the resources related to developing collaborative approaches recommended by our experts:

The Case for Parent Leadership, by Anne Henderson, et al., January 2004. Free download at www.centerforparentleadership.org.

Reaching Out: A K–8 Resource for Connecting Families and Schools, by Diane W. Kyle, Ellen McIntyre, et al., Corwin Press, Thousand Oaks, CA, 2002.

Breaking Ranks in the Middle Recommendations

Related to Collaborative Leadership and Professional Learning Communities

RECOMMENDATION 1: The principal will provide leadership in the school community by building and maintaining a **vision, direction, and focus for student learning**.

Strategies
- Administer NASSP 21st Century School Administrator Skills Inventory.
- Engage in reflective self-assessment of collaborative and facilitative skills.
- Review the comprehensive school improvement plan, vision, and mission on a regular basis with your site council and teacher leaders.
- Serve as an instructional leader who supports, encourages, and celebrates improved instruction that results in gains in student learning.
- Develop a relationship with an experienced mentor and regularly devote time to learn from him or her.
- Build sharing and support networks with colleagues and take advantage of resources offered by professional organizations such as NASSP.
- Stay abreast of district/state/federal mandates and align the school's vision accordingly.
- Communicate closely with stakeholders by way of community and parent forums, other communication, and surveys to identify community expectations of the school and keep people informed.
- Compare the school's curriculum map with those of feeder and receiving schools.

Benefits
- Provides the school community with clearly articulated purpose.
- Creates shared purpose and trust among administrators, teachers, and other members of the school community as they work as a team to improve learning:
  - Principal involves teachers in leadership roles under agreed-upon principles and standards.
  - Teachers develop leadership skills and gain respect for the demands of leadership.
  - Provides the common filter of "what is best for student learning" for every decision made at the school.
- Requires ongoing data-driven evaluation of how the current state of student learning compares with the established vision. As a consequence, the principal can target support and guidance to areas most in need.

Challenges
- Locating the appropriate person who has the time, willingness, skills, and commitment to serve as mentor.
- Allowing management demands on time to prevent purposeful and intentional activity that focuses on teaching and learning.
- Lacking adequate knowledge of diverse student needs, instructional strategies, or content required to support/guide instructional practices in each academic discipline.

Progress Measures
- Conduct and review results of teacher, parent, and community surveys regarding principal's leadership and ability to share responsibility with various groups.
- Articulate school vision through mission statement and assemble documents of support: strategic plan, meeting agendas, memoranda, and accreditation and staff development materials. Review documents (e.g., agenda for faculty meetings, staff development expenses, communication from the principal), and documents produced since the principal's appointment (e.g., accreditation materials, mission statement) to determine the degree to which the vision has been clearly articulated and consistently supported.
- Assess programs, practices, and budgets for relationship to student learning and achievement.

RECOMMENDATION 2: Each school will establish a **site council** and accord other meaningful roles in decision making to students, parents, and members of the staff to promote student learning and an atmosphere of participation, responsibility, and ownership.

Strategies

- Create bylaws and/or guidelines for establishment of the site council or design team:

- Include elected or volunteer parents, community members, and students, as well as members of the school administration, faculty, and staff on the school-based site council/design team.

- Within predetermined and agreed-upon parameters, give the site council/design team the power to make decisions.

- Train all members in group process and facilitation skills.

Benefits

- Ensures that the voices of all parts of the school community (students, staff, parents, community members) are heard and valued.

- Enlists all segments of the school community for accomplishment of schoolwide initiatives.

- Lays the foundation for a learning community in which the council/team has a stake in the educational process and is vested in helping to improve learning.

- Promotes development of group process skills that enhance the team's capacity to identify challenges and take appropriate and decisive action.

Challenges

- Developing a culture that supports the concept of a council so that its recommendations can be implemented.

- Gaining adequate participation from all groups, as well as maintaining interest and enthusiasm over time.

- Clarifying and revising existing authority and accountability structures.

- Providing design teams with skilled facilitation and training to foster a process in which the varied constituencies with potentially widely divergent agendas are able to discuss items thoughtfully and take action.

- Maintaining consistency of membership on the site council can become difficult if student, parent, or community members of the council believe that their opinions don't carry as much weight as those of the staff.

Progress Measures

- Document the establishment of a site council and other school advisory groups (design/action planning teams, task groups, special committees) through artifacts: letter of invitation, charge to the committee, initial agenda, and meeting notes/minutes.

- Advertise to all stakeholders, through published meeting minutes, agreed-upon benchmarks for site council and school advisory groups.

- Document and evaluate progress toward benchmarks through artifacts: meeting agendas and minutes, results of surveys/questionnaires, and advisory group actions and recommendations.

- Monitor student achievement data showing measurable and significant outcomes resulting from site council/design team recommendations or decisions.

- Assess the degree to which school advisory groups are active and engaged, and document the degree to which participation increases across the school community.

RECOMMENDATION 3: Each school will regard itself as a **community** in which members of the staff collaborate to develop and implement the school's learning goals.

Strategies

- Form an interdisciplinary school team to coordinate learning goals across departments/teams and grades.

- Create an advisory group, including representatives of elementary and high schools, to ensure articulation and planning across grade levels.

- Tie the learning goals to measurable benchmarks and encourage teams to regularly review disaggregated data.

- Model collaborative leadership as the means to maintain clarity of purpose and to establish and accomplish student improvement goals.

- Promote school spirit and a compelling sense of mission to attract all staff members to seek to be a respected part of a common, noble mission.

- Organize teams to define student learning goals in terms of higher order thinking.

Benefits

- Establishes realistic learning goals that fit local conditions and requirements.

- Empowers teachers and staff to take risks, try more creative forms of instruction, and become more responsive to student needs.

- Provides a framework to draw each member of the community into discussion with others—a prerequisite to establishing the culture of collaboration at the core of any successful community.

- Develops clarity of purpose, without which there is little coherence of effort and increased danger that people do whatever they want to do.

- Fosters an atmosphere of collegiality and respect in which ideas are shared respectfully—a model that can be replicated by students.

Challenges

- Covering state standards and district pacing guides often leaves little time for creative implementation of learning goals at individual schools and can lead to apathy.

- Respecting the work and suggestions of teams requires leadership and an understanding of your own strengths and weaknesses. In some cases, administrators give teams token responsibilities or ask them to revise a program or solve a problem…only to make their own decision in the end, a decision they had in mind from the beginning.

Progress Measures

- Verify the establishment of measurable learning goals and related student achievement outcomes across departments by publishing a list of interdisciplinary team members, meeting agendas and minutes, and a schoolwide learning goals document.

- Use student assessment data to document student achievement progress as related to instruction and disaggregate data to identify students to be targeted for additional individual and small-group work on specific areas of need.

- Administer surveys/questionnaires to evaluate the school community's understanding of and commitment to established learning goals and the extent to which the school climate is supportive.

- Employ analyses of student attendance, discipline, and test data to document decreases in behavior and absentee problems and increases in student achievement.

- Audit lesson plans and materials to evaluate links between ongoing assessment and instruction and to ascertain the extent to which differentiated strategies are used to address students' needs and strengths.

RECOMMENDATION 4: Teachers and teacher teams will provide the leadership essential to the success of reform and will collaborate with others in the educational community to redefine the role of the teacher and identify sources of support for that redefined role.

Strategies

Teachers will

- Engage in leadership professional development with a focus on facilitation/group process and teaming, data disaggregation and analysis, reform issues, best practices, and learning profiles (gender, culture, learning style, and intelligence preference).

- Go into the community and "court the support" of parents and community members by discussing how teachers and the community can work together for reform and increased achievement.

- Cultivate leadership in teams beyond named team or department leaders.

- Exercise the opportunity and authority to define their needs, identify problem areas, find the resources and solutions to address the challenges, and share the challenges/solutions with the site council.

- Develop new contract language that fosters the assumption of new leadership roles.

- Seek and use scheduled times to engage in common planning for goal-setting, student data review, and needs assessment; reducing workload (e.g., number of students, number of classes taught); relieving duty assignments (e.g., students and parents serving as hall monitors).

School leaders will support teachers who want to work in new ways and work with those who do not to overcome their reluctance or to find another situation or role that better meets their expectations and outlook.

Benefits

- Creates effective and sustainable schoolwide initiatives.

- Increases opportunities for community support for reform through communication with involved teachers who have regular contact with parents and other community members.

- Promotes professional development for teaming, which in turn nurtures a collaborative school environment.

- Engages teachers as professionals both in and out of the classroom.

Challenges

- Addressing existing accountability and department/department head structures that might be reluctant to give additional authority to staff members.

- Finding resources and time.

- Assessing the options under current contract language and proposing changes/solutions for the future.

- Overcoming old habits and fear of the new, as well as finding ways to encourage some reluctant teachers and administrators to step into new or redefined roles and see themselves in new ways.

Progress Measures

- Measure teachers' perception of shared ownership of policies, procedures, and programs through surveys/questionnaires or other measures.

- Document examples (anecdotal or objective) from each teacher of increased student engagement or performance resulting from specific instructional or assessment techniques learned through collaboration.

- Show evidence of each team's review of professional best practices literature and evaluation of its own effectiveness in this light by recording in the team notes professional best practices and other literature reviewed each week, the method by which the team evaluated its own effectiveness in this area, and what next steps are to be taken (if any).

Recommendations 1–4 in Practice

Alvarado Intermediate

Highlights of involving others in decision making include:

- Annual parent surveys.

- Student representatives sit on the school site council, the Parent Teacher Student Association (PTSA), and the district advisory council.

- The principal, vice principal, team leaders, and members of the leadership team meet weekly to discuss strategic planning. The team leaders and leadership team members serve as liaisons to inform and solicit input from the staff. The guidelines of the school leadership plan are published in booklets and provided to all staff members. The leadership team helps facilitate the implementation of new methodology and encourage staff buy-in. Leadership has evolved into a team of interactive school management groups such as the Student Achievement Council, Campus Management Team, Interdisciplinary Teams, Dens, Department Teams, and School Site Council, which promotes the free exchange of ideas. This dynamic structure nurtures a climate of intellectual development and a caring community of shared educational purpose. To acquaint new teachers with that spirit of caring, they are adopted by buddies. In addition, these teachers must take part in the district's three-year induction program, which introduces novice teachers to management techniques and instructional practices. Alvarado also works with colleges to prepare and mentor student teachers, many of whom are later hired by the school.

Bowman Middle School

The School-Based Improvement Committee consists of administrators, parents, teachers, community members, and business leaders who work together to develop school goals. The Bowman Leadership Team is composed of department chairs, academic team leaders, and counselors who study, discuss, and develop solutions for schoolwide issues. Parents are involved through the PTA; Padres Unidos, an organization developed to involve Hispanic families in the school; the Principal's Advisory Council, which consists of parent volunteers who focus on one major school issue a year; and the Mother/Daughter Program, in which girls and their mothers meet monthly to discuss school and life issues. Through our Campus Assessment Team and Special Education Admission, Review, and Dismissal (ARD) meetings, staff and families work together to make decisions for students. Students are also encouraged to be involved in decision making. The Bowman Leadership Club was established in partnership with the Plano Family YMCA to nurture leadership skills during weekly after-school meetings. In addition, the Bowman Peer Assistance Leadership class is made up of students selected to take part in a regularly scheduled class whose curriculum is designed to encourage students to become involved in their school.

Casey Middle School

- Master schedule is designed by anyone interested in volunteering.

- Executive Council—a group of teacher volunteers and the principal meet biweekly to decide issues of curriculum, instruction, and professional development for the school.

- The Site Leadership Team—the principal, assistant principal, and counselor—meet weekly to review student progress, events, and school climate.

- The staff created the Casey Student, a profile of what we expect and hope every student will do and be by the end of the eighth grade year

Crabapple Middle School

The school has a Leadership Team composed of representatives from every area in the building. The positions are filled annually from applications submitted by interested teachers. This team meets weekly to discuss school matters and is a decision-making body for the majority of issues directly affecting the classroom. The Leadership Team has participated in professional development activities focused on trust and consensus building and continues to engage in open dialogue as we study the leadership book *From Good to Great.* The team has taken a major role in determining the areas of emphasis for our district school improvement plan as well as planning and implementing strategies to meet those goals.

Hopkins West Junior High School
The school's improvement plan team is composed of students, staff, and parents. In addition,

- The junior high budget is developed by a group of staff, students, and parents.

- A committee of staff, students, and parents selects all individuals for building administrative positions.

- A committee of teachers, students, and parents recommended that all instructional staff members be expected to communicate biweekly with parents using either a website or a group e-mail communication system. The tactic has been put in place and is designed to allow parents to conduct an intelligent conversation with their children about what is occurring in the classroom.

Saunders Middle School

As a site-based managed school, Saunders ensures that all stakeholders have a voice. The Principal's Advisory Council is composed of teachers, parents, and students. The school plan is developed by this group with input from the community at large. A Town Meeting is held when the plan is in the last year of its cycle, and parents are asked to comment on which strategies have been successful and which have become standard operating procedure, and to suggest new strategies to address shortcomings in the current plan. The staff is asked to do the same. The student council representatives poll their classes and this information is also considered. The Advisory Council synthesizes the information, and the planning process moves into the drafting and approval mode. When all vested groups approve, the plan is submitted to the area associate superintendents for review before it goes to the school board for approval. Internally, department chairpersons meet regularly to share concerns and plan for the coming year. Teams meet with their concerns and suggestions as well. Departments meet and work together to analyze data and plan for improving student achievement. The vertically aligned curriculum in each of the core areas is posted in the hall for everyone to review. The administrative team meets regularly to discuss school issues and plan for coming events.

Thayer J. Hill Middle School

The school's efforts to involve others in decision making include the following. The administration works with the Student Council, the student faction of the PTSA, and student advisory councils to gain student input on school policy. In addition, two parent advisory councils meet on a monthly basis, and the school maintains 10 partnerships with local businesses and administers a mentoring program with the assistance of a local community social service agency.

**Breaking Ranks in the Middle
Recommendations**

RECOMMENDATION 5: Every school will be a learning community in which professional development for teachers and the principal is guided by a Personal Learning Plan that addresses the individual's learning and professional development needs as they relate to the academic achievement and developmental needs of students at the middle level.

Strategies

- Engage in practices that reinforce the notion of teachers as adult learners, such as the staff pursuing "action research" on a selected topic or reading and discussing selected books together.

- Institute a process that rigorously assesses (through reflection and feedback from a variety of external sources) the professional development needs of each staff member and ensures that development is tailored to those needs as well as the schoolwide student learning goals.

- Allocate time and resources to address individual professional development needs (some recommend allocating a certain percentage of overall staff development time for this).

- Adopt a collegial coaching, goal-setting, or mentoring program for teachers (e.g., College Board's SpringBoard), in which teachers develop skills in building robust PLPs.

- Provide new teachers with a mentor for at least the first year, and encourage all·teachers to be involved in a peer group that encourages skill development. Evaluation of programs by the groups and by the leadership team should be done at least annually.

- Provide resources to help families become familiar with educational practices and strategies.

Benefits

- Encourages staff members to reflect on individual strengths and weaknesses and prioritize professional development strategies and activities accordingly.

- Aligns staff development with the professional needs of teachers and the students they teach.

- Allows teacher teams and leadership teams to track the relative effectiveness of different types of development (e.g., seminars, workshops, in-classroom mentoring, peer coaching, other job-embedded approaches) in meeting school and student learning goals.

- Provides educators with opportunities to document the evolution of their own styles and to coach colleagues on effective strategies for professional growth.

Challenges

- Giving professional development the high priority that is required to accomplish this recommendation in light of the current time demands of professional staff.

- Motivating staff to address individual professional needs rather than engaging in safe, one-size-fits-all staff development activities.

- Addressing union contracts that specify professional development structures.

- Defining what is meant by "community" in this recommendation. Who will address the needs of those outside of the school? How?

Progress Measures

- Collect and review plans created by each staff member to support student achievement to ensure that each includes the following components: evidence of self-reflection, evidence of external feedback, and benchmarks for measurable professional growth.

- Devise and implement a system of review, revision, and evaluation of each staff member's plan for support of student achievement.

- Administer a survey or other measure to determine the level of satisfaction with professional development and personal goal-setting.

- Survey families to ascertain the level of awareness of best practices being used in the school and how those practices are used.

- Chart the progress of various schoolwide initiatives over time, using predetermined, objective measures (e.g., increasing percentages of teachers regularly using multiple instructional strategies in class).

- Prepare and execute an evaluation of teacher-mentor and peer group skill development programs to be conducted by individuals, groups, and the leadership team on an annual basis.

- Study specific outcomes (e.g., increased student engagement as a result of modifications to instructional style) that might be predicted from an initiative. If the outcome is realized, it may be an indicator of program effectiveness.

Recommendation 5 in Practice

Casey Middle School

Staff members collaborate in making decisions about rigorous curriculum, standards-based assessment practices, effective instructional methods, and evaluation of student work. They have opportunities to plan, select, and engage in professional development aligned with Colorado's content standards and have regular opportunities to work with their colleagues to deepen their knowledge and improve practice. They discuss student work as a means of enhancing their own practice, and teachers observe each other regularly. In addition:

- Teachers meet four days a week to plan with their grade-level or content-area colleagues (vertical and horizontal team plans).

- The Executive Council conducts a professional development needs survey at the beginning of the year and then designs professional development offerings during district professional development days and on staff meeting afternoons.

- Grade-level team leaders are being trained in professional learning communities and Critical Friends. As a result, protocols to discuss classroom observations and student work are being used this year, as are common assignments to better understand student learning.

- Title II money is available for extensive professional development to achieve goals.

- Common assignments help staff articulate and connect their curriculum, instruction, assessment, and expectations.

- Professional development is offered at a multitude of workshops, at our biweekly staff meetings, and on professional development days (six per year).

- Community members share their expertise in areas of interest/need (e.g., planning for differentiated instruction in a standards-based classroom).

Breaking Ranks in the Middle
Recommendations

Culver City Middle School

The growth and development patterns of young adolescents are a focus of the school's professional development. The district had an in-service for administrators presented by Clay Roberts relating to developmental responsiveness. The counselors serve as resources for staff and parents. Counselors are present at weekly team meetings and parent/team conferences, and provide information at parent nights relating to middle level development. Counselors administer surveys to students relating to individual learning styles and share this information with teachers, parents, and students during conferences. Counselors and designated teachers attend conferences relating to adolescent development and share the information with the staff. Last summer, administrators and teachers attended the National Conference on Differentiated Instruction. Session topics included the development of the adolescent brain, brain research relating to learning, building differentiated lessons, and implementing strategies for promoting social and academic development. Upon their return, these staff members became resources for their peers.

Crabapple Middle School

Teachers participate in Expeditionary Learning Outward Bound professional development, college courses, and local or district staff development. In 1999, the allocated remedial education allotment from the system was converted to the position of curriculum support teacher (CST). The CST is responsible for providing and/or coordinating local staff development opportunities. The CST also oversees all schoolwide testing as required by our school improvement plan, the district, or the state. Professional development offered can be divided into the following categories:

- Instructional strategies/differentiated instruction

- Technology

- Purpose and use of assessment/alternative assessment

- Expeditionary Learning Outward Bound

- Teaching in the block schedule

- Middle level learners

- Change theory/motivation

- Special education inclusion model

- Multicultural education

- Harry Wong—Effective Teaching

- Cooperative group instruction

- Writing across the curriculum

- New teacher support

- Learning styles/brain research

- Curriculum training based on system revisions

In addition, teachers have completed a three-day workshop on Learning-Focused Schools strategies. Teachers will review the types of extending and refining lessons that are taught for all essential concept objectives as identified in our prioritized curriculum. Teachers work together in developing unit maps for shared subjects and also plan assessment strategies as a team, by grade level or department.

Hopkins West Junior High School

Each staff member writes personal learner goals each year, and all professional development is aligned with the school's improvement plan, which focuses on literacy and equity. The Professional Development Committee, in collaboration with the tactic committees, team leaders, department chairs, and other district personnel, designs the opportunities to be offered each year. The following are other highlights:

- The National Urban Alliance literacy initiative is an interdistrict program that provides training in literacy strategies. The formal training is for two years; next year our third cohort group will participate. The training includes large-group sessions as well as work with a site consultant. Because each interdisciplinary team has at least one participant, peer training and coaching takes place at the team and department levels.

- Each school in the district is working with Glenn Singleton from the Pacific Education Group on equity. Each school establishes an equity team that receives formal training in large-group sessions. The equity team designs the professional development activities for the entire building staff. Currently, the work is focused on conversations about race; each person is required to evaluate his or her own beliefs and behaviors concerning race. Course curriculum includes a variety of readings addressing the achievement gap. Subsequent training will focus on strategies to improve instruction and reduce or eliminate the achievement gap, as well as ways to better engage and communicate with families of color.

- As part of our literacy tactic, for the past four years, the staff has participated in professional book clubs. We have read *Turning Points 2000* and Carol Ann Tomlinson's *Differentiating Instruction,* and viewed Glenn Singleton's tapes, *Closing the Achievement Gap.* This year, staff members participated in smaller groups: *Reading Don't Fix No Chevys, Bad Boys, Classroom Instruction That Works, Creating Culturally Responsive Classrooms,* and *The Other Side of the River, Why Are All the Black Kids Sitting Together in the Cafeteria.*

- For the 2005–06 school year, the National Urban Alliance cohorts and the Professional Development Committee have decided to incorporate a peer coaching model that will consist of small groups of instructors. At least two of the participants will have been trained in the National Urban Alliance (NUA) strategies.

Breaking Ranks in the Middle
Recommendations

RECOMMENDATION 6: The school community will promote policies and practices that recognize diversity in accord with the core values of a democratic and civil society and will offer substantive, ongoing professional development to help educators appreciate issues of diversity and expose students to a rich array of viewpoints, perspectives, and experiences.

Strategies

■ Provide professional development that equips all staff members to see diversity in its larger context as a *benefit* to the school in providing a variety of viewpoints, perspectives, experiences, and backgrounds.

■ Create a review process to make certain that curriculum is nonbiased, and create teacher training guides that promote diversity of opinion, expression, and background in each subject and classroom.

■ Ask cross-curriculum teams to develop civics, social studies, or history lessons that demonstrate how diversity of opinion is at the heart of our democracy and how, throughout our history, those opinions—informed by geography, country of origin, physical ability or disability, cultural and ethnic roots, and socioeconomic and other factors—have led to some of the most important developments in U.S. and world history.

■ Develop staff and student sensitivity to customs and traditions of members of the diverse groups in the school through professional development as well as various "noneducational" social events such as informational nights, inclusion of cultural "factoids" in newsletters, "distant land" game night, and so forth.

■ Differentiate instruction to address diversity in student learning and processing styles, and provide students with adult advocates/mentors to build relationships.

■ Recruit a staff diverse in its background, viewpoints, perspectives, and experiences.

■ Employ teaching styles and techniques that encourage student questioning and opinion sharing (e.g., the Socratic method).

Benefits

■ Exposes students and staff to viewpoints and perspectives they may not have otherwise considered.

■ Enriches the learning experience and curriculum by expanding horizons.

■ Creates a genuine multicultural community in which "otherness" is honored, not a detriment—a lesson that will stay with students throughout life.

■ Reinforces the idea that we are all different, and that each of us is valuable and has gifts to share. As those students who may have seen themselves as the only different ones begin to realize that the environment of the school encourages this individualism, they may become more engaged in learning.

Challenges

■ Confronting the potential biases (e.g., racial, ideological, political) of staff, students, texts, and the community.

■ Defining diversity to include all variations in human differences.

■ Locating appropriate materials and the resources to provide professional development.

■ Translating *sensitivity* to diversity into *respecting* and *valuing* diversity.

■ Addressing unfair biases toward segments of the population created by world affairs.

Progress Measures

■ Conduct frequent evaluations of staff development programs, curriculum, classroom activities, co-curricular activities programs, and other school activities to ensure that all promote and value diversity.

■ Document change in disciplinary incidents involving cross-cultural or "cross-population" violence or bullying.

■ Devise methods to solicit perceptions on the success of the diversity outreach in the school from representative students, especially in the areas of personal feelings, teacher actions and interactions, and effect on achievement and future plans (e.g., results of a survey might indicate increased effort by teachers to elicit student perspectives and opinions in class; a feeling of increased acceptance and self-confidence; greater interest in attending high school and college).

Recommendation 6 in Practice

Culver City Middle School

The school serves students who represent a range of backgrounds, cultures, religions, income levels, and learning styles. The school views this diversity as its greatest attribute, and diversity is celebrated throughout the school community. Racial incidents between students are minimal. The school provides strategies for being culturally responsive toward students in the classroom through the implementation of differentiated instruction and ways to build on students' strengths (scaffolding). Literature, articles, and learning materials are selected to reflect the diversity found in the student population. Field trips are planned to expose students to the diversity that is reflected across Los Angeles County. The students visit cultural centers, including the Museum of Tolerance, African American Museum, Olvera Street, and Little Tokyo in downtown Los Angeles. Students participate in multicultural events such as performances, concerts, and art exhibitions at local museums that reflect themes of diversity. Each grade-level coalition collaborates yearly to plan a multicultural festival with support from parents and communities. The school recognizes that its efforts to engage students must include actions that show how strongly diversity is valued in the community. Students develop high levels of self-efficacy, are proud of who they are, and are proud to be a part of the school. Programs to meet the needs of underrepresented groups have been very effective, as evidenced by assessments that show that the achievement gap at the school narrows each year. Extended learning time has been the most effective strategy for meeting the needs of underserved students. The school uses Title I funding to provide before- and after-school tutoring classes in math and language arts. Eighth grade students participate in the Algebra Institute two mornings a week. Students qualify for academic electives including math builders, literacy, and language arts skill builders based on academic performance. The AVID program is a year-long elective offering for seventh and eighth grade students, and part of the 10-week exploratory wheel for a third of the sixth and seventh grade students. AVID is geared toward meeting the needs of underrepresented students by improving study skills, promoting enrollment in high-level academic courses, and building college awareness. Students are also supported through tutoring offerings, homework clubs, and the Saturday Success Academy. The library is open for student use before and after school daily, and the computer lab is available for students who may not have Internet access at home. Parent classes have been held in the computer lab to increase access to technology for families of underrepresented students.

Breaking Ranks in the Middle Recommendations

Hopkins West Junior High School

Equity is a primary focus and is one of the two tactics identified in the school improvement plan. Highlights of the school's efforts include the following:

- To encourage more students of color and low-income students to participate in advanced placement (AP) courses at Hopkins High School, it was decided to implement the pre-AP program for all students (grades 7–9) in English, math, science, and social studies.

- The Autonomous Learner Model (gifted program) was expanded to include students of color who would not previously have been identified through traditional means.

- Get Connected is in its sixth year of existence and has been successful in closing the digital divide. Data gathered clearly indicate that students enrolled in the program improve their academic standing and increase their self-esteem.

- The Zoom summer program was intended to jump-start underachieving students. As a result of the program's success, last year it was expanded to include seventh into eighth grades and eighth into ninth grades.

- The School Success Program is designed to increase the number of low-income students and students of color who attend college. The program is geared to students who will be the first in their family to attend college.

- The National Urban Alliance literacy initiative is designed to create a critical mass of teachers who use literacy strategies and thinking maps in their instructional repertoire to help all students be successful.

Thayer J. Hill Middle School

The school's attempts to promote social equity include a Parent Diversity Committee that meets monthly to discuss social equity issues, to ensure that members of the school community are heard, and to plan information to share with teachers at faculty meetings and school improvement days; several diversity student forums and a parent roundtable; and staff development. The administration makes a conscious effort to hire staff that mirror the diversity of the student body; curricular differentiation continues to be a major staff development focus; the school has provided leadership to the district in revamping its strategic reading program for at-risk learners; a comprehensive mentor program is provided to selected students; and a homework club is provided four times a week to students who need after-school support. In addition, the school implements a comprehensive Positive Behavior Intervention System program through which specific social skill training programs have been developed for each grade level. Each grade level has a specific reward/incentive program, and the school reinforces students through daily positive referrals, a Student of the Week program, and a quarterly Hill Hero breakfast.

Rachel Carson Middle School

Highlights include the following:

- The College Partnership Program (CPP) is an academic and motivational support program designed to increase aspirations for secondary and postsecondary education. Five advocates (counselors and teachers) and 20–30 students are involved. Advocates monitor students' academic progress and provide academic and personal support. The program emphasizes the development of self-esteem, effective communication skills, study skills, and college and career exploration. Motivational speakers are invited to address the students. The group tours a university and a vocational school in the area. Community service projects, such as adopting elementary school reading buddies, are also under consideration.

- Mobile Team Challenge offers activities to students and staff such as icebreaking, team building, positive risk-taking, and problem solving. All students are involved in team-building activities on the first day of school to build relationships between students and staff. Social goals are emphasized during basic skill classes to learn cooperative problem-solving techniques.

■ A mentoring program is getting under way for ESOL students in conjunction with a local business partner, EDS. Students and mentors will be matched by gender and, if possible, by cultural background. The students and their mentors will e-mail each other monthly to discuss the following topics: (1) All About Me, (2) My Family, (3) My Former Country, (4) What Is Different about Living in the United States, and (5) What Is Hard for Me at School. At the end of the year, students will go to EDS offices, where they will shadow their mentors for two hours and then interact socially during lunch. The objectives of this program are (1) to provide ESOL students with an adult role model who is established in the American economic system and with whom they can relate by gender and culture; (2) to help ESOL students increase language competency; (3) to provide ESOL students with another adult in their lives who can explain the cultural and educational complexities of their new environment; and (4) to help ESOL students become more successful learners.

Breaking Ranks in the Middle
Recommendations

RECOMMENDATION 7: Schools will build partnerships with institutions of higher education to provide teachers and administrators at both levels with ideas and opportunities to enhance the education, performance, and evaluation of educators.

Strategies

- Develop formal partnerships with local higher education institutions (both in specific disciplines and with schools of education) in which

    - Teachers audit discipline-specific university classes and establish relationships with professors who are willing to share their subject-area expertise with teachers and students.

    - Teachers borrow software and other instructional support materials.

    - Teachers are informed of upcoming events, lectures, and projects that might be of interest to them and their students.

    - Undergraduates assist in classrooms before their formal practice teaching.

    - Teachers and administrators serve as "link-to-the-field" resources for teacher and principal preparation programs in schools of education by interacting with preservice students, proposing real-school dilemmas, and co-teaching classes with college personnel.

    - Professors in specific disciplines and schools of education guest-teach in the middle grades, gather case studies for use in their courses, and gain middle level practitioners' insights.

    - Your school and local colleges engage in open dialogue about how your school can better address current issues in instruction, assessment, learning styles, multiple intelligences, and other areas, and how schools of education can better prepare teachers and principals for the real classroom and the real school.

    - Members of the school community have access to the latest research, suggestions about current books for staff discussion, and a resource for faculty members doing action research.

    - Your school has preview of, and a better chance of hiring, the top talent from the prospective pool in teacher and administrator preparation programs.

    - Your school and the local colleges can seek and obtain grants for joint studies and putting research into practice.

    (Note: To sustain the support necessary to maintain the relationship, meticulously document the benefits of the partnership to both institutions: to the undergraduates who will see theory in practice and to your students and teachers who will benefit from extra classroom help as well as learning about current instructional and assessment techniques and theories.)

- Engage in initiatives in your state to align pre-K–16 curriculum and goals.

- Develop school-based master's programs or summer institutes in school improvement or other areas.

Benefits

- Opens the door to expert educational researchers who can help your teachers enhance their skills and take advantage of advances in knowledge about teaching and learning.

- Allows prospective teachers and faculty to translate abstract research into practice.

- Increases the responsiveness and currency of the offerings of higher education institutions by allowing them to routinely monitor and interact with "professionals in the trenches" and adjust their curriculum and techniques to the needs of middle level teachers and administrators. This should improve the institutions' marketability as well, because of the special attention they are devoting to the unique requirements of middle level educators.

- Improves teacher retention, especially for beginning teachers, by providing additional support and advice.

- Reinforces the idea that everyone in a learning community should be striving to learn. Students will appreciate teachers' modeling what they preach and will be exposed at an early age to the benefits of college.

- Aligning curriculum and goals to pre-K–16 initiatives can help with articulation across grades.

Challenges

- Creating partnerships between schools and colleges or universities that are geographically distant.

- Finding the time, money, and energy to pull programs together.

- Establishing a *formal* partnership with specific roles for all participants.

Progress Measures

- Establish and track explicit goals, responsibilities, and desired outcomes in the following areas: teacher satisfaction and retention, understanding of developmental issues for middle level students, teacher use of instructional strategies and assessments, student achievement, leadership development, and staff evaluation.

- Document and track the benefits to the higher education institution based on preestablished goals; for example, the number of their students and faculty who received practical and ongoing experience in a real classroom; the number of case studies and current classroom dilemmas based on your school that they were able to use in teacher prep classes; the number of their graduates who teach in your school; the number of your teachers who take classes at the institution; modifications to their own curriculum based on their experiences in your school; grant money for joint projects; and their ability to tout their special emphasis on middle level education research and practice as a result of involvement with your school.

RECOMMENDATION 8: Schools will develop political and financial relationships with individuals, organizations, and businesses to support and supplement educational programs and policies.

Strategies

Note: A How-To Guide for School/Business Partnerships and related worksheets are available on the NASSP website: www.principals.org/brim.

- Assess the needs of the school to determine the types of outside assistance required and appoint an individual either within the school or within the district to work with school leaders, teacher leaders, and community leaders to develop a strategic implementation and community outreach plan that *systematically* addresses those needs (*How-To Guide,* #1 and #12, and Matching Needs and Potential Resources worksheet).

- Develop a plan for staff members to strategically join and become active in community groups and civic organizations to build connections of support for school programs and changes being undertaken (*How-To Guide,* #1, #2, #4).

- Establish a community advisory board composed of parents, service organizations, and local business representatives to focus on school issues and to assess and access community resources and opportunities (*How-To Guide,* #6, #11, #15; Stop/Start/Continue worksheet; and Matching Needs and Potential Resources worksheet).

- Enlist the involvement of local businesses, community groups, retired businesspeople, and others in meeting the needs of the school by collaborating on projects; establishing a volunteer corps; providing internships, mentorships, tutoring programs, and other opportunities for students to learn outside the walls of the school; and helping to inform the larger community about the pressing needs as well as the successes and achievements of your school (*How-To Guide,* #5, #6, #7, #8, #11, #15; Stop/Start/Continue worksheet; and Matching Needs and Potential Resources worksheet).

- Develop and clearly articulate a public engagement strategy that includes teacher leaders and administrators (*How-To Guide,* #14, #15, #16).

- Inform local, state, and federal lawmakers about the unique developmental needs of middle level students and other middle level issues that have an impact on a large number of their constituents.

Benefits

- Provides community members with access to a first-hand look at the school that allows them to personally evaluate the needs of the school and develop supportive relationships with the school.

- Creates stronger relationships between the school and the community it serves.

- Opens avenues to financial, programmatic, talent, social services, and "moral support" resources for the school.

Challenges

- Helping others understand the goals and vision of the school, how community members can support that vision, and how the relationships can be mutually beneficial.

- Providing time and resources for staff to take on this work.

- Gaining time commitments from talented outsiders and ensuring that their time is not wasted.

- Taking care that funds raised through local businesses are used wisely so the relationship continues.

- Ensuring that partnership support does not drive educational decision making.

- Encouraging participation by varied segments of the community rather than just the traditionally influential.

Progress Measures

- Collect, analyze, and evaluate data regularly to determine accomplishments, strengths, and weaknesses of the partnership (*How-To Guide,* #18, and Alternative Assessment Instruments).

- Measure partnerships by how well they address the stated needs of the school and students as described in the needs assessment and strategic development plan—not by how many partnerships you have.

- Provide formal and informal evaluations based on predetermined, mutually agreed-upon benchmarks and expectations to the advisory council, volunteers in the school, business partners, and those offering internships to determine how they feel about their involvement with the school (e.g., satisfaction with communications, use of talents and time, involvement with increasing achievement and opportunity).

- Solicit endorsement of the strategic development plan by the advisory group and other community groups.

- Document benefits to be derived by both parties involved in each partnership and review on an annual basis.

Recommendations 7 and 8 in Practice

Cohoes Middle School

Over the past several years, the Capital Region of New York State has emphasized Tech-Valley initiatives, which focus on regional economic growth in technological sectors and the skills that are necessary for students to be successful in a technologically advanced workforce. Businesses in fields such as biotechnology, semiconductor research, and energy have become an integral part of the area. Acknowledging that technology will play an important role in preparing students for the workforce, in the spring of 2003, Cohoes Middle School (CMS) began a partnership with Rensselear Polytechnic Institute (RPI), one of the leading engineering schools in the country, to use technology in the classroom to support student achievement. The partnership is designed to provide the opportunity for teachers to learn and use pedagogical practices rooted in state-of-the-art technological applications and to allow RPI to pilot and implement programs it has been developing that use technology to enhance instruction in the areas of science and mathematics.

Initially, the school piloted an innovative eighth grade robotics program to address different student learning styles of at-risk subgroups by creating a hands-on, active learning environment. The success of the pilot program was evidence that this nontraditional approach to instruction would be of greater benefit if more students had access to the experience at an earlier age. The program has been fully implemented to include sixth-graders.

As a result of this partnership, technology is used directly in the classroom as opposed to in a separate computer lab or nonclassroom experience that is not rooted in instructional practice. Teachers can model technology's proper use and application in context, and students can incorporate it into the processes of authentic learning activities that build deeper understanding. In addition to robotics construction, programming, and use, students engage in various other technological activities, such as web quests, applying interactive media, and Internet research, which build both content and skill knowledge essential for technological literacy.

CMS and RPI continue to have a close partnership with regard to professional development for teachers. Beyond the formal in-service structure that the school has had with RPI, CMS supports consistent release time for teachers to participate in professional development activities. Biweekly staff development consisting of faculty meetings, department meetings, and team meetings focus specifically on training and enhancement in this area. Teachers plan together to ensure the successful implementation of practice, and monthly meetings at the RPI campus and at CMS ensure continued collaboration and professional growth. As teachers implement these activities directly in the classroom, faculty from RPI are participants, acting as mentors and co-teachers to support this pedagogical approach.

With the continuing curriculum revisions paralleling the recent changes in the state learning standards for mathematics, each strand now features the use of this type of technology as a performance of understanding. Students use robotics in "operationalizing" number sense, placing value, patterning, comparing/ordering decimals, time/distance relationship, explaining mathematical thinking and processes, supporting predictions using mathematical terminology, and many other areas.

The school's Summer Learning Academy, an enrichment program to sustain year-round learning for at-risk students, extends work in this area and trains additional staff in related concepts and applications. Teachers spend 40 hours over the summer working at RPI to develop new instructional practices, which can then be immediately applied in a classroom context.

The school's annual Student Exhibition has provided an opportunity to demonstrate and display the collaborative work that CMS students, CMS teachers, and staff at RPI have been doing in this area. The event not only includes peer-to-peer demonstrations but also involves parents and other members of the community.

This project's success and sustainability have been aided by public and private financial support from the Beaumont Foundation of America, the New York State Learning Technologies Grant, the Smarter Kids Foundation, and the Best Buy Teach-All Grant.

Bowman Middle School

With the help of tutors from the University of Texas at Dallas and Collin County Community College, students who failed the Texas math assessment can receive help during Math and Mentors class. This additional class is unique in that mentors are in the classroom the entire period and work with the students on guided practice after the lesson is taught. The students take this class in place of an elective.

Crabapple Middle School

During the past four years, the school has gone from one viable business partner to 11, with many other agencies supporting it in more informal ways. The partners support teacher recognition, student citizenship recognition, student achievement recognition, and volunteerism, and provide venues for students to perform. The following are other highlights:

- Community volunteers serve as mentors in our Mathletes Math Mentoring Program, which works with selected seventh grade students who are struggling in math.

- The ESOL program provides the school with the opportunity to reach out to a growing Spanish-speaking community.

- Teachers tutor each Thursday afternoon at STAR House, an after-school tutoring program for Spanish-speaking students conducted in the students' apartment complex. This link to the community has proven to be extremely beneficial for students. Members of the front office staff also work afternoons in the program and help to keep the lines of communication open between STAR House and the school.

- Through a collaborative effort with the local high school, the school offers a Saturday Scholars math tutoring program. High school students from service clubs spend 90 minutes each Saturday morning tutoring students who are struggling in math. The program served 40 students last year.

- A local business and community organization supports the school's tutoring program, in which eighth-graders who are proficient in math assist sixth grade students.

RECOMMENDATION 9: At least once every five years, each school will convene a broadly based external review panel to develop and deliver a public description of the school, a requirement that could be met in conjunction with the evaluations of state, regional, and other accrediting groups.

Strategies

- Ask members of the business council, higher education partners, parents, advocacy groups, community-based organizations, and others to contribute to the report by reviewing school practices with the help of some evaluative instrument such as a local/regional accreditation.

- Hire an outside evaluation firm to review the school and provide the report.

- Engage in school recognition programs at the national, state, and regional levels that require a thorough review of school policies, practices, programs, and progress in meeting student needs.

Benefits

- Provides independent assurances to parents (prospective and current), the community, and educators that the program of study is rigorous and the learning environment is healthy for all students.

- Demonstrates the school's openness to constructive critique and emphasizes that it has nothing to hide.

- Allows the school to benefit from the expertise of noneducators in such areas as program evaluation and oversight, process management, leadership development, management techniques, building effective teams, technology applications and systems, and so on. External evaluation helps with school improvement and reform efforts and allows outside experts to see firsthand the school's needs. This may lead them to volunteer or spearhead efforts to find necessary funding.

- Enables the school to offer a picture of its achievements and successes and to describe how challenges and efforts to improve student achievement are being addressed. This can provide a greater context within which other measures (e.g., annual yearly progress in testing as required by No Child Left Behind) make more sense.

Challenges

- Ensuring broad participation and unbiased cooperation so the report is honest and accurate, not just a reflection of what the school leadership wants to project as the school's image.

- Getting a reasonably priced review that is both expert and unbiased.

- Locating and using accreditation instruments for evaluations.

Progress Measures

- Document the following: List members of various groups who contributed to the project, describe the process used to employ an outside evaluation firm, describe the process used by the firm to solicit input, provide a copy of the evaluation instrument and the results.

- Commit to an honest and reflective report and issue the final report in a timely fashion.

- Create and execute plans for collaboration (with site council, teacher teams, and others) on a comprehensive school improvement plan, with measurable benchmarks to address areas of identified weakness. Review plan regularly.

In Their Own Words...

The following is the second of four school profiles. Each profile has been written from the personal perspective of the principal. The profiles are designed to show the comprehensive and interdependent nature of the reforms your school is being called upon to undertake. Although not all the changes each school has instituted will be appropriate for your school, the perspective of your colleagues should nevertheless be valuable and may form the basis of a discussion for your team. At the end of this profile, you will find a Q&A with the principal followed by several questions to help lead your faculty or team through a discussion. For a protocol to help lead the text-based discussion, see Appendix 4.

Making It Personal

by Joe Greenberg, Principal

With support from Dave Lehman, founding principal, and teachers Sarah Jane Bokaer, Rebecca Godin, and Steve Hoffman

Making It Personal by Valuing Their Time

I have heard the middle school grades aptly described as the turning point, when young people either see a future in this educational system of ours or merely begin to bide their time, essentially dropping out mentally until such time as they can do so physically. That is not to say that young people do not want to learn, as learning is actually quite inevitable. However, learning (in school) is a voluntary act. Even as an educator committed to the idea of school as a source of accessing the power of knowledge, I still regularly share with students what Mark Twain once warned: "Don't let school get in the way of your education."

Not too many years ago, I knew a young modern-day Huck Finn who personified for me Twain's sentiments about learning. Reuben had been home-schooled for most of his life; in fact, at age 11 or 12, when most of his peers were in middle school, he was serving as an apprentice baker with my father in our family's café in Maine. A few years passed before Reuben and I met up with one another again. He shared that he had enrolled in the local village school to see what it felt like to learn in that kind of environment. He admitted that the social pull was strong to be with friends, and school gave him more opportunities to interact with his peers. I should note that he was at this time about 15 and, in addition to attending school, was also very busily involved with running his own fishing and lobster boat. He was actually doing quite well for

School Profile 2
*Lehman Alternative
Community School*

Ithaca, NY

Grade span 6–12

266 students total (approximately 110 at the middle grades)

6 percent ESOL

17 percent special education

For statistics, contacts, and other information about the school, go to www.principals.org/brim.

**School Profile 2
Lehman Alternative Community School**

Practices to look for include:

- *Adult advocates*
- *Personal Plans for Progress for students*
- *Caring teachers*
- *Culminating project/exhibitions*
- *Integrated/interdisciplinary curriculum*
- *Community and exploratory learning*
- *Alternative assessment*
- *Flexible scheduling*

himself financially—although it required him to invest significant time and effort. His work ethic and persistence were virtues that were never in doubt. At the same time, he lacked patience for anything and anyone that failed to stimulate his curious mind. I recall during our conversation his deep sense of seriousness when he cited his primary area of frustration and dissatisfaction with his current school: "They don't understand how valuable my time is to me." For some this may sound like a silly comment to come out of a young person's mouth, but what he said and how he said it resonated with me then and continues to several years later. Reuben's story is an example of how our culture sends the message to young people that their time is not as valuable as our own, and when they express feelings that their time is being wasted, they are often not taken seriously or are ignored altogether.

Ensuring that all the students and staff members in school feel that their time is being spent well by engaging in personally meaningful and productive pursuits is among the most important priorities to which I, as a principal, dedicate myself. Trusting teachers and students to responsibly use their time is one of the most critical aspects of creating a healthy and trusting school community.

For the past 18 years, we have been a partner school of the Coalition of Essential Schools (CES). Informed by CES's Common Principles, LACS has developed a unique set of learning requirements (academic and beyond), and has sought new and alternative means of assessing and evaluating students' progress toward meeting those requirements, moving as far away as possible from the traditional "seat-time" credit system and the external standardized testing movement (in this case, the New York State Regents Exams). As a learning community, the educational aim of the school has always been to have the curricular emphasis philosophically oriented on "how to learn" rather than "what to learn."

We limit our student body to 265, with 110 at the middle level. This can make our admissions process gut wrenching. The only eligibility criterion to be considered for admission is that the student must legally reside within the district's 155-square-mile school zone. Admission decisions are made through a multipool lottery process, which is designed to honor the school's commitment to have the student population reflect the demographic composition of the community. We could enroll more students, but becoming an even slightly larger school would make us less, not more, in terms of what we value about fostering a safe and intimate community of learning.

Our current student population includes at-risk students from fractured and impoverished families, students from economically secure and intellectually rich households associated with Cornell University and Ithaca College, ESL students from refugee families, students with varying learning and emotional disabilities, and partially home-schooled students. Some families see LACS as a last hope for school success, while others are actively looking for a more progressive educational experience and a small-school alternative. Each of our grades has approximately 36 students. With some exceptions, our 25 teachers (a combination of full time and part time) offer both middle school and high school courses. The average tenure of most current staff members is 15 years. The hallmark of the staff is creativity and openness to experimenting with new ideas and approaches.

Joining the LACS community as principal at the start of the 2004–05 school year felt, in many ways, like a philosophical homecoming for me, and it has been extremely refreshing to be able to once again be part of a community whose educational values aim to cultivate an environment of teaching and learning built on trusting and respectful relationships that are personal and meaningful. From the time I first walked through the doors of LACS, I felt the resonating spirit of the school to be one that embraces Emerson's belief: "The secret of education lies in respecting the pupil."

While valuing time is essential, so, too, is establishing genuine trust. There is no question as to whom this school belongs, and with this sense of shared ownership comes the understood, and usually honored, expectation of shared responsibility and accountability concerning school issues. Subtle as it may be, the fact that students and staff are all on a first-name basis with one another adds to the sense that there exists a culture devoid of a hierarchal power structure; rather, it is a community of equal standing and mutual respect.

Making It Personal by Building Meaningful Relationships

Knowing students well is chief among the reasons we keep our school as small as we do. To be able to walk down our hallways and have teachers and students look at each other and honestly say, "Hey, not only do I see you, I know you" is really what makes us not just a school but a close-knit learning community. My general rule of thumb is that if I, as principal, cannot walk through the school and know the name and a few things about everybody I come across, the school is too big. Do I know everyone as well as I would like? No, but I am confident that every student in the school has at least one or two teachers who really know her or him on a personal level and can serve as an adult confidante and advocate. The sense of security and trust that is fostered is so great a determining factor in helping our students succeed that compromising on our school size is essentially nonnegotiable.

We do not make excuses for not offering the comprehensive array of courses, sections, and tracks that the bigger middle schools in our area provide. What we do, we do well, and even with our "less is more" approach, we have been able to creatively offer a rich and personalized experience for our students. A wonderful example of this occurs the week before school begins. Each of our new students is called by a current student in the school, personally welcomed into our learning community, and invited to a new-student orientation hosted and run by students. The day after the new student orientation, all students attend a full orientation, during which everyone participates in activities focused on team building and making the most of group dynamics. The day helps to remind all of us (teachers and students) how and why we are committed to the school's student-centered philosophy and to our alternative and progressive approach to learning. This orientation also allows new students to mingle with veteran students and get to know them. With our limited size, there is a smaller social pool to draw from when forging friendships, but it is surprising how well students socialize and engage each other in an inclusive, cross-age way, with less of a tendency for students to segregate themselves by age or break into social cliques.

We recognize that, especially for our sixth-graders, making the transition into middle school can be challenging. Most are going from being the oldest students in their elementary schools to being the youngest and, in our case, sharing a school with much older students. There are plans to reestablish a formal mentor program that would pair high school students with a sixth grade "buddy" during certain activities, to help support and guide the new student in the ways of the school. Older students still in the school who had a buddy when they joined the school as sixth-graders have indicated that they valued that mentor relationship. While bullying and harassment are not frequent concerns in the school, with students ranging in age from 11 to 18 years, the buddy program may also be a proactive measure to prevent intimidating behavior.

Making It Personal by Involving Parents/Caregivers

In helping students make the move to middle school, our important, but often overlooked, partners in the transition are the parents/caregivers. It sometimes seems that the older their children get, the less involved parents are in schools. This is unfortunate, as the adolescent years of middle school and high school are among the most tumultuous times of a person's life. I see us, as a school, needing to take much greater strides to encourage and include our students' families in the school community. Having said that, we do have a wonderful weekly school newsletter generated by parents (posted on a parent-created school community listserv), and the school also produces a monthly newsletter that is mailed to each family. We also have parents/caregivers working with some students and staff to revamp our web page to make it more appealing and useful for accessing information. In addition, parents/caregivers share their talents and interests with students by offering special workshops and projects that add to the learning choices available to students. Parents/caregivers also serve on our school's Site Council and on a school development and advisory board, which include staff, students, and community members.

I hope we will be able to reinvigorate our parents/caregivers group that used to meet regularly and that might help arrange lectures and workshops on various parenting issues. Offering parenting events and forums to many families would surely enhance the school's ability to get to know the parents/caregivers of the young people with whom we share a common interest and would allow parents to get to know each other a little more, too.

Making It Personal by Creating a Meaningful and Relevant Curriculum

While the school's curricular emphasis and focus are solidly oriented toward having process drive the content, this does not mean that teachers are not presenting key facts and information in their classes. However, we do veer toward offering middle school courses that are more focused on a specific topic as opposed to general survey classes, thereby allowing students and teachers to explore a particular genre of literature or a narrow era of history in depth. Learning how to be a student and an independent thinker who is able to apply creative problem solving and critical analysis skills is at the heart of what it means to prepare and educate students effectively for future learning, formalized or otherwise. The most *essential* ingredient in meeting any learning goal or standard for students is to cultivate their ability to know how to ask the right questions. Developing the ability to formulate and ask questions is the cornerstone of honing the basic skills of critical thinking and intellectual inquiry, which lead to enhanced creativity and empower students to become the problem solvers that our increasingly complex world requires. At its best, learning is a quest, and the similarity of the words "question" and "quest" should not be underemphasized or undervalued.

One initiative that the school developed as a way to make the sixth grade transition a smooth one was the creation of two integrated interdisciplinary extended-time courses for all sixth-graders in their first semester. Inquiry & Tools (I&T) is a science, math, and technology course, and People and Literature (PAL) is an English and social studies course. Our sixth-graders are divided into two groups; half take I&T first thing in the morning, the other half begin their day in PAL. Each class runs an hour and a half, and at mid-morning the two cohorts switch. Among other reasons, we began to offer these courses to provide a thoughtful transition into what can otherwise be an abrupt and uncomfortable change from the self-contained elementary school classroom. Offering these back-to-back integrated, inquiry-based courses also helps us show students the connections between academic disciplines in a way that is clear and meaningful, especially since many of the lessons and activities are hands-on and project based.

Several years ago, the sixth grade PAL and I&T curricula focused on the conceptualization of and planning for a new amphitheater for our campus. Students met with architects and structural engineers to learn the various options for and obstacles to building the theater, surveyed the entire school to determine the preferred site, and presented the whole school community with the pros and cons of various locations. Before long, the amphitheater project became a schoolwide initiative, and the pride in contributing in such a large and concrete way to their new school was magical for these sixth-graders. Today, the amphitheater is used throughout the year (weather permitting) for concerts, plays, and other special events sponsored by the school and by other community organizations.

We try to give our middle school students as much flexibility and latitude as possible in structuring their school day; obviously, in ways that are developmentally appropriate. Just as I encourage teachers to use their classrooms as laboratories for experimenting with different approaches to teaching, I also believe that students need to experiment with as many modes of thinking and learning as possible. After their first semester experience, when we limit to some extent the amount of choice students have over their morning schedules, our goal is to encourage students to choose from an array of teacher-offered courses and to guide them toward classes that address student-specific goals and learning needs.

Most of our teachers teach at both the middle and high school levels, so the entire school's schedule is generated in as collaborative a manner as possible. Again, the goal is to offer students choice and flexibility in selecting courses, projects, committees, and community-service/career explorations. Students may register for teacher-offered classes (which tend to be a mix of single courses with some extended-block interdisciplinary options) or they may opt for independent study with a teacher or a qualified community resource. For example, with oversight by an appropriate LACS teacher, a student who is passionate about ballet can take lessons outside of school and earn physical education or art credit for his or her involvement, if it is documented and evaluated by the professional instructor.

Although independent study is typically explored by high school students, it is an option for middle schoolers as well. Recently, we had a sixth-grader who was an avid horse and pony enthusiast. Her pony was going to foal, so she proposed doing an in-depth independent study with then-principal Dave Lehman. She spent a solid nine weeks studying the gestation and birthing process, with twice-a-week lunch meetings with Dr. Dave to monitor her progress. Sofi was present for the birth of the foal and then presented her independent study project to a small audience. I would like to encourage more students in our middle school to consider pursuing independent study, because I believe students are most successful when a school fosters in them the ability to set their own learning goals and allows them the freedom to pursue those goals in a personally meaningful way.

Before they are promoted to the high school, students must complete an independent study, which we call the Eighth Grade Challenge Project. Under the mentorship of a teacher or community member, these self-directed interdisciplinary projects are the most sustained and focused work many of our students have done—and the results are impressive. The projects range from building a solar-powered radio to writing a play to leading a social action initiative. Students present their Challenge Projects during a public exhibition followed by an end-of-middle-school promotion ceremony. During the ceremony, each graduate receives a personal tribute highlighting the student's accomplishments and contributions to the school during the middle school experience. It doesn't get much more personal than this, and it is clear that the teachers who speak on behalf of their students do so knowing them deeply and fondly.

Making It Personal by Allowing Experiences Outside the Classroom (Community Studies, Family Group, and Trips)

Before "graduating," middle school students also have a chance to explore personal interests outside of school through our community studies program. Students are required to spend at least one cycle (nine weeks) involved in a community service pursuit, as well as an additional cycle participating in a career exploration of their choice. Several years ago, the school created a community studies coordinator position, which has proven to be the key to the success and legitimacy of this requirement. Our coordinator has structured both the community service and career explorations in an extremely thoughtful and supportive way. He helps place students in their areas of interest and then follows up by visiting them at their site periodically to check in with them and their field mentors. Our coordinator has scheduled briefings with students at lunch or other times to see how things are going and goes over students' written reflections on their experience. Examples of student community service include volunteering at the local SPCA (the Society for the Prevention of Cruelty to Animals), visiting residents regularly at an area nursing home, participating in community cleanups, and mentoring in elementary schools. In the area of career exploration, students have been involved at radio stations, medical labs, glass-blowing shops, and more. As a result of the positive experience most of our students have had, many take on more service opportunities. LACS is frequently contacted by area organizations seeking civic-minded young people for community causes and events, because it is understood that we will likely have students who are willing to heed the call.

Another important personalizing feature of our school's curriculum is Family Group, an advisory system that consists of 12–14 students who meet twice a week for an entire period with an assigned teacher or someone else on the staff (custodian, secretary, or school nurse). Every adult in the building is involved in some way to support our Family Group advisory/advocacy system. Staff assigned to a Family Group help facilitate activities that foster positive group dynamics and team-building skills. Our middle school students are grouped heterogeneously with students in grades six through eight. The Family Group has proven to be a wonderful opportunity to foster social and character development, as well as introduce students to our approach to democratic school governance and shared decision making. Although we hold a weekly all-school meeting, Family Group tends to be a place where students, especially middle schoolers, feel the most comfortable sharing their views on a particular proposal that needs to be discussed and voted upon. This distinguishes Family Group from a traditional homeroom or more conventional advisory system. The name "Family Group" is important: We want each of our students to feel a sense of belonging in the school. This scheduled time at the start and end of each week serves as home base and a contact point with a trusted teacher-advisor and small group of peers.

Outside of the scheduled Family Group sessions, the group leader also offers one-on-one academic and social support for the students under his or her charge. Teachers who have a concern with a student or vice versa will share and consult with the Family Group leader, who will try to mediate a solution or common understanding. Family Group leaders serve as the liaisons between school and home and as advocates for students in times of emotional, behavioral, and academic concern. Students and their parents/caregivers meet at the start of the school year and again mid-year with their Family Group leader to develop and review personal learning goals, to construct a course schedule for the coming semester, and to review evaluations of progress in current classes. Often, Family Groups plan an overnight at school, get together for a night of bowling, or prepare meals for each other. Many Family Groups decide to work on a service project to help the community, and all Family Groups work to raise funds for two of our traditional personalizing events: the Fall Retreat and Spring Trips.

Within weeks after the start of the school year, LACS suspends classes for two full days to allow all the students and staff to attend a Fall Retreat that has playful bonding as its primary goal. For the past several years, we have traveled about 20 minutes or so to a rustic retreat center owned by Cornell University. There is a main lodge with a full working kitchen and dining room with stone fireplace. There is also a large open field. Students and staff participate in a variety of small-group activities, from woodcarving, guitar playing, and cider making to dancing, card games, volleyball, and rugby. It is spectacular to see how inclusive each of the activities becomes; for example, with 6th graders hopping on the backs of 12th graders for relay races. (For developmental and practical reasons, at the end of the first day the middle schoolers take buses back to the school; they return the next morning, following a special pancake breakfast prepared by the staff.) By the end of the second day, everyone is thoroughly exhausted, but the two days together away from the school achieves the goal of allowing time to form new relationships and galvanize existing ones.

For some students and staff, fundraising is a year-long occupation, especially if a spring trip abroad is in the works. In March and April, proposals for Trips Week are unfurled. These may include offerings that take students away from Ithaca—such as biking, canoeing, backpacking, or a community service trip to a Native American reservation school—or more local fare, such as glass blowing, a Habitat for Humanity project, filmmaking, or skateboarding. While fundraising initiatives are a schoolwide pursuit to help offset the cost of these trips, no student is ever prevented from participating in a trip because of financial constraints. Regardless of destination or actual purpose, the motivation behind breaking from the school-based learning model and venturing out and about with our students is to expose them to the world as their classroom and one another as their teachers. For some, it is the first and perhaps only time they will leave the country to explore a different culture and way of life. For others, the physical challenge and triumph are the best confidence builders imaginable. Nothing can erase the image I have of the beaming smile of one of our sixth-graders, diagnosed with autism, coming down our school's driveway on his bicycle into our parking lot alongside his dad, having completed a five-day, 275-mile bike trip. It was both exhilarating and moving to witness students, staff, and parents lining the path and showering this young man with loving applause and cheers. That's just one example of what these trips each spring mean to so many of our students—they are the culminating bonding experience of the year for many of our students.

Making It Personal by Cultivating a Trusting Culture of Choice and Voice

There's an old story about a reporter who interviews a very accomplished businessman about the secret of his success. When asked to what he attributes his climb to the top, the businessman replies, "Two words: good decisions." And how did he learn to make good decisions? "One word," says the businessman: "Experience." Following up, the reporter asks the businessman how he got most of his experience. With a slight pause, the businessman says, "Two words: bad decisions."

Like the businessman in the story, students at LACS are trusted to make decisions about their learning; some of the decisions will be good, and others not so good. Either way, students learn from the experience. First on the list of decisions students have to make: they must choose to enroll at LACS, as opposed to being assigned to attend. This is one of the distinct advantages we have as a school, which cannot be overemphasized. Having a school in which the presumption is that everyone involved is there of his or her own volition makes building a community much less challenging than in a setting in which students attend against their will. At LACS, everyone is assumed to be trustworthy; therefore, we try to have as few rules as possible. Of the rules we do have, students played a role in developing them and, therefore, understand and agree that they serve the collective good. More often than not, it is the exception that proves the rule that this trust is well placed. The following are a few examples of how this trusting environment looks at our school:

- There are no bells beginning and ending classes. The thought is that students need to hone the skill and discipline to regulate their own time and honor their commitments, including getting to their classes on time. Few, if any, will have bells determining when to begin and end their work tasks when they leave school for college or careers.

- Staff members are not assigned any supervisory duties during the day, such as bus or lunch duty. Everyone keeps an eye on one another, and students are just as apt as teachers to call other students on an unsafe or inappropriate action.

The commitment to providing students with choices stems from a desire to value their time and to trust them to use their time and the school's in a responsible way. One of the ways we try to offer choice at the middle level is to have the bulk of our middle school courses offered by semester, so the students are exposed to a wider topical array of classes rather than a small number of yearlong survey classes. For most, starting with some fresh classes in the middle of the year is helpful, especially for students who are losing steam with their first-semester routine. It also permits students to interact with a larger assortment of other students and teachers. With few exceptions, the bulk of our middle school classes are heterogeneously grouped with students in grades six through eight. We even have some middle schoolers opting to accelerate into some of our high school math, science, and foreign language courses, through which they can fulfill their middle school requirements while concurrently earning high school credits.

In another effort to offer choices for our students and additional ways to earn credits, we have created four "project splits" per week, two on Tuesday afternoons following lunch and two more Thursday morning before lunch. For this to work, we hold our regularly scheduled classes four days a week. We have found that the project time not only breaks up the normal academic monotony that can sometimes set in when students are following the same basic schedule every day but also provides a wonderful opportunity for students to get to know their teachers and one another outside an academic classroom setting. The list of projects offered is generated by teachers, other staff members, parents, and even students with a skill, talent, or interest that they feel they could share with others. What results is a fairly expansive assortment of offerings such as silk-screening, observing city court cases, a student-led project learning how to use the Linux operating system, and a parent-facilitated film-based discussion of Alfred Hitchcock films. For a student to ice skate with his or her math teacher for an hour and a half once a week or a Spanish teacher to help students create a music video adds a whole new dimension to the teacher-student relationship and often translates into a stronger bond in the classroom setting. Students who may not be too keen on a particular teacher often find that getting to know the person in a different setting allows them to reevaluate their impressions to the point that the students opt to sign up for a class with that very teacher the next semester. Project time also allows students to expand their social circle with other students in the school. Many of our projects are open to students in grades 6–12, so it is one way for the older students and younger students to interact.

In addition to their selected courses and projects, students choose to serve on a school committee that meets twice a week. Each committee is charged with some aspect of running the school. The committee structure is yet another example of creating flexibility within our school's weekly schedule to allow for more diverse learning opportunities. The important message is that we value our students' voice in school matters and appreciate interacting and sharing the responsibilities of the community outside a typical academic construct. Many of our committees—such as Ending Cycles of Oppression, Gay-Straight Alliance, Students for Social Responsibility, Eco-Action, Mediation, and Community Court—serve in the realm of student and social advocacy. The roles these committees take on include sponsoring multicultural events for students and "infusion" days that address any number of issues and "-isms." Other committees are more task-oriented, such as our Maintenance and Green-Thumb committees, which help with our building and grounds. Another set of committees—Agenda and Site-Based—focus on policies and procedures, and serve as facilitators of our school-based democratic governance system.

Active participation in school government is the expectation and the responsibility of everyone in the school. The school community meets weekly for all-school meetings to discuss student- and staff- generated proposals for new initiatives. Our all-school meetings are facilitated by students and run with a strict order that some find stifling, but it does seem to allow for decisions to actually get made (some more easily than others). We have a very comprehensive decision-making document, which is essentially our school's constitution or blueprint for school governance. The decision-making document was developed over the course of several years by a dedicated and focused team of students with the help of some staff. While we do have student representation on our district's school board, so far they are nonvoting delegates (a situation I would like to see changed). Students also serve on all interview committees when a staff position becomes available.

What's in a Name?
An Example of Practicing Democracy

It is only recently that our school has been called "Lehman" Alternative Community School. It was named in honor of Dave and Judy Lehman after Dave retired at the end of the 2004 school year as the only principal the school had known during its 30-year run. He was a trailblazing visionary and leader who was beloved by many for his deep respect for and unabashed celebration of students and teachers and their pursuit of learning, equaled only by his compassion for those who find school (and life) a struggle. Judy is still working at the school and continues to serve as one of the primary stewards of the school, as she knows intimately the challenges it has faced and overcome through the years. With a desire to honor his 30 years of dedicated service to the district and his commitment to the school, the superintendent and the school board decided to rename the school in honor of "Dr. Dave" and Judy.

No one objected to this well-deserved recognition of the Lehmans' contributions and legacy…except for me, the new principal. It wasn't that I had any desire to thwart the sincere intentions of the district's school board to commemorate Dave and Judy with the addition of "Lehman" to the official school name. But it seemed to me that, to truly honor them properly, the superintendent and school board should have navigated the same process that anyone else wanting to implement a change affecting the school community would be expected to go through. Given the school's commitment to a non-hierarchal culture and the fostering of democratic principles and full participatory decision making, the superintendent or school board representative could have presented a formal proposal at an all-school meeting, at which time the name change would have been discussed and likely voted upon. During the summer after I first began working as principal of the school, I had breakfast with the superintendent and explained why I thought it was necessary to bring the issue of the school's name change to the school community for discussion and vote. She smiled, let out a friendly sigh, and may have been reconsidering her recommendation to hire me.

True to my word, one of the first proposals I submitted to the school's Agenda Committee (responsible for facilitating our weekly all-school meetings) was to discuss the name change the school had experienced by the well-meaning school board. I added another item for staff and students to consider: whether we needed to retain the word "Alternative" in the name of the school. Although we refer to ourselves and are considered the alternative school in Ithaca's public school system, I don't particularly care for the term "alternative," as it is open to significant misinterpretations that cause confusion and assumptions that could be avoided by having that part of our school name changed. I pointed out that we are no more an alternative to the traditional middle school and high school than they are to us. While we approach teaching and learning from different perspectives and methodologies, the reality is that there is only one true alternative to education, and that is to have no education (and one could then extend the argument to include the important distinction between education and schooling).

The proposal opened up a fairly intense debate among the students and staff, with strong sentiments on both sides of the issue. My attempt at a concession was to consider renaming the school Lehman Community School, and adding the tag slogan: "Where the alternative goes without saying." While I was the one who put forth this particular issue, it is the right of anyone involved with the school to submit a proposal of any kind for consideration. Oftentimes, the wheels of democracy move quite slowly, regardless of one's position in the school; to date, the name of the school still remains somewhat in flux (so there is still an opportunity for you, the reader, to offer your two cents).

Making It Personal by Providing Authentic Assessments and Formative Evaluations for Students

At LACS, we believe that the only assessments that should be given are those that provide formative feedback to both the individual student and the teacher. In the absence of feedback, it is questionable how much actual learning can happen. It is feedback that drives new ideas and new avenues of thought toward improving one's teaching and learning. LACS teachers focus attention on developing authentic forms of student assessment (e.g., performance-based exhibitions and portfolios) that we believe demand problem-solving and critical-thinking skills. Many of these performance-based assessments require students to demonstrate and apply their skills and knowledge in a real-world situation. Often these demonstrations are evaluated not only by teachers but also by other experts in the community who can provide formative feedback to students on their work. Our approach to authentic assessment often takes learning beyond the bricks and mortar of the school by offering students opportunities to do work that is personally relevant and that allows them to make meaningful, positive contributions to their community.

Dynamic and successful alternative assessments are active and steadfastly student centered rather than engineered for teacher convenience, a neat grading grid, or a misleading box score representation in the newspaper (i.e., the state-mandated standardized test). LACS' middle school courses offer many opportunities for alternative assessment. Earlier, I mentioned the sixth grade I&T course and the amphitheater project. While the actual physical schematics of the structure were pursued in the integrated math-science-technology I&T class, in the sixth grade academic counterpart PAL course, students were reading and performing dramatic literature and plays, and studying the history of outdoor theater production from ancient Greece, Asia, and Elizabethan times. By assigning students to research, script, cast, rehearse, and then perform in original dramatic creations, our teachers developed an authentic performance-based assessment that could then be evaluated by a diverse audience on the basis of a rubric of targeted criteria of demonstrated skills and knowledge.

Medieval Studies is an interdisciplinary English and social studies course that has been extremely popular with our middle school students. One of the culminating performance-based assessments has students preparing a medieval feast and wearing costumes they have created, while playing the roles they have researched. Along with research papers, students rub medieval brasses and show their knowledge of heraldry by making shields using authentic elements. These demonstrations enhance students' abilities to answer essay questions and fuel their interest in learning time lines, geography, and history. In another example, to demonstrate their skills in critical thinking and understanding advertising and media manipulation, students in our Media and Critical Thinking course create and film their own commercials. They incorporate at least 13 propaganda techniques and perform the ads for other middle school classes. They produce print ads, news, and parodies, and make PowerPoint shows on gender bias in advertising to present to elementary school classes. After students master this type of performance-based assessment, written tests on naming and giving examples of various propaganda techniques seem easy. As a school, we have come to understand through intentional practice that standardized, multiple-choice tests are neither the best nor the most interesting way to assess critical-thinking skills.

With few exceptions, our middle school courses are designed around a scaffolding set of portfolio-oriented assignments; these assignments typically culminate in a final project or performance, and allow students to demonstrate their ability to integrate the medley of skills and knowledge from the class. Figuring Stuff Out is a semester-long, inquiry-based science course that has students assuming the role of scientists and inventors. Following several weeks of group instruction, demonstrations, and experiments, students are given the challenge of identifying an unmet social need or scientific issue and conducting a thorough study of the problem. Under tough peer and teacher review, the final assessment for this class requires students to present their research and any solution or invention they have to contribute to the scientific community. Examples include designing, building, and field-testing a white-wing glider as an assessment for an aeronautics class, and conducting compression and contortion tests on student-built bridges to determine their load-bearing capacity and to understand and explain the virtues or shortcomings of the structural design and the integrity of the construction. The latter undertaking requires a firm grasp of the core concepts of the technology class that is the source of the project, and allows the teacher to truly evaluate and provide constructive feedback.

Our students do not receive traditional letter or number grades as part of their school transcript. Although students and/or parents will sometimes ask to have a numerical or letter grade assigned, it is something we prefer not to do.

Instead, at the end of each cycle (equivalent to a quarter), every teacher prepares an individual written evaluation of a student's contributions and experience in each respective class. These qualitative narratives are written to the student and provide commentary on strengths the student displayed in areas such as class participation, completion of both short-term and long-term assignments, and performance on assessments. Often, specific references to actual work are included to provide anecdotal examples of the caliber of work produced. Teachers also provide feedback about areas of weakness where the student might need to focus attention to grow as a learner; for example, honoring deadlines, being open to divergent viewpoints, and revising work. Throughout the semester, before formal evaluations are written, the school has a "flag" system that keeps communication clear between school and home and can inform students and parents/caregivers of the problems in the class (e.g., missing assignments, skipped classes) or offer positive commentary (e.g., improved performance).

In addition to the teachers' evaluations, students are required to write a self-evaluation for each class, committee, and project they participated in and reflect on what they got out of the experience, what they are proud of, and whether they think they honored their responsibilities. Students are also given the opportunity to comment on the teacher's performance and the quality of the instruction or facilitation. As a school, we see real value in allowing students time to perform a careful analysis of their own work, thus learning what it means to be reflective self-assessors of quality. As students learn to apply their own defined standards of quality, they grow more confident and competent in evaluating their own work, which leads them to become more aware of how they learn and which should lead to better performance. Teachers tend to take this student feedback very seriously and use it to improve their approaches.

Working with other alternative schools around New York State, we have been successful in obtaining a standardized testing waiver for our high school program, but the waiver does not include lifting the battery of middle school tests. Although we object to the tests, our students have been doing quite well on them, but it is not without a cost. It is a clear breach of our philosophical belief that exploring topics in depth is more valuable than superficially surveying a breadth of material in order to prepare

LACS Middle School Requirements

The following guide serves as an overview of the minimum expectations for successful promotion to the high school. (Note: 1 cycle = 9 weeks)

A. Family Groups, Committees, All-School Meetings, Spring Trips

Attend, participate in, and pass three years of Family Group and committees of their choice.

B. Community Studies (2 cycles)

Complete at least two cycles of community studies: one cycle of community service and one cycle of career exploration.

C. Visual Art (4 cycles)

Complete at least four cycles of art, either through art classes or approved art projects.

D. Music/Theater (4 cycles)

Complete at least four cycles of music. Two cycles must be in a semester-long music class; the other two may be through music projects, music/theater productions, or approved private music classes/lessons.

E. Physical Education (12 cycles)

Complete a minimum of four cycles of physical education each of the three years of middle school, either through classes or approved PE projects. Students may also fulfill this requirement through approved participation in classes/fitness-related activities outside of LACS and/or through participation on an interscholastic sports team.

F. Foreign Language (minimum of 4 cycles; 3 years required for high school)

Complete at least one semester-long Introduction to Languages course in Spanish or French (students are encouraged to take both). Begin the three-year language sequence required for high school graduation: Beginning A, Beginning B, and Intermediate.

G. English (10 cycles)

Complete People and Literature, the first-semester interdisciplinary English/social studies course for sixth-graders. Successfully complete at least four additional middle school English courses.

H. Social Studies (10 cycles)

Complete at least five middle school social studies courses. Of the five, one will be the PAL English/social studies interdisciplinary course taken by sixth-graders in their first semester. Another course students should complete is Historical Researchers, a course for eighth-graders.

I. Science/Health (12 cycles)

Complete at least five middle school science courses and one middle school health course. Of the five science courses, one should be the interdisciplinary math/science course Inquiry & Technology that sixth-graders take their first semester. One should be a second-semester physical science course taken in eighth grade. Of the other three courses, one should be in life science and one other should be in physical science.

J. Mathematics (12 cycles)

Complete either of two sequences of semester-long middle school math courses, beginning with the interdisciplinary math/science course I&T that sixth-graders take their first semester.

(continued)

K. Technology (min. 3 cycles)
Complete at least three (3) cycles of technology (preferably some each year of middle school) through either courses or projects. Other projects such as Silk-screening, MS Photography, Set/Tech Design, R.I.B.S., etc. may also meet the technology requirement.

L. Computer Literacy
Complete at least the first of two (2) computer literacy courses (or their equivalent) required for graduation from LACS. *Keyboarding* and *Word Processing* is offered as a project the first three cycles each year, and is best taken in sixth or seventh grade. Middle school students may also take *Spreadsheet, Database, and Multimedia,* a semester-long course, in eighth grade when it is easier to schedule.

M. Eighth Grade Challenge Project
Work with a teacher/mentor to define an "individual project" that goes above and beyond the expectation for that course. Develop and create this project, and complete it over the course of the eighth grade year. Final Challenge projects will be on display at the Middle School Promotion in June.

2-Year Sequence (begin H.S. math in 8th grade)	3-Year Sequence (begin H.S. math in 9th grade)
6th Gr.: I&T, then Graphs & Statistics	**6th Gr.:** I&T, then Geom. or Ratios, Proportions, Percents
7th Gr.: Pre-Algebra, then Geometry 2	**7th Gr.:** Ratios, Proportions, Percents or Geom. 1, then Graphs & Stats
8th Gr.: Beginning Alg./Geometry (1st yr. H.S.)	**8th Gr.:** Pre-Algebra, then Geometry 2

students for an external exam. Having to give exams in our school and the requisite preparation for them have significantly compromised the way we approach our curriculum design. I don't like to admit it, but the tests have resulted in some significant changes to our program of studies and have severely limited access for students who are interested in pursuing studies in another (nonacademic) discipline. Art, music, and drama are prime examples of programs that have suffered because of the shifting emphasis on certain academic disciplines.

While NCLB is putting great pressure on schools to align standards and assessment measures in an attempt to ensure that all children are learning, it is frustrating that there is little or no questioning of the value or relevance of what they are learning. With less state testing required in our school, teachers would be able to focus attention on developing other educationally sound and authentic forms of student assessment that we believe get deeper into the higher order thinking skills that standardized tests are unable to effectively measure. In short, I agree with how Jonathan Kozol explained it at a conference a few years ago: "If you want elephants to grow, you don't weigh the elephants. You feed the elephants."

Making It Personal Through Collaboration
Practicing the art of inquiry allows teachers to truly create a student-centered learning experience. The teacher as facilitator and more experienced learner is what I have come to appreciate in those I view as the most effective in motivating their students to explore new and different areas of study. I have seen how inspiring and magical it is for young people to see their teacher so engrossed in learning. As I commented in a teacher evaluation: "[W]hen I see you in the classroom (or out of it, as is often the case), I view you not as a teacher, but as a fellow learner with your class. I think this is what makes you so popular and effective in your role. You seem to understand better than many

the value of young people seeing their teacher not as an authority and knower of all, but as an intellectually curious soul—a lifelong learner who is not only full of questions but possesses the desire and courage to explore them."

In the spirit of inquiry and teacher-as-learner, twice a month the whole staff engages in professional learning activities (PLAs). Teachers select a professional development focus to explore in depth with other colleagues who share a common professional goal or interest. Some examples include a book club that focuses on readings about issues such as understanding our most needy and at-risk students; exploring ways to ensure equitable learning opportunities and participation in school governance for students of color and others underrepresented in our democratic process; the impact of nutrition on students; and improving instruction by reviewing student work. Echoing the "respecting time" theme, I have received a lot of positive feedback on valuing staff members' need to have regularly scheduled time to pursue these topics for professional growth with other colleagues. One practice that was in place when I came on board and that I really like (although it would benefit from being better defined) is having teachers assigned to colleagues' classrooms to offer content area support. This practice improves overall instruction and specifically targets struggling students who benefit from the additional interaction with another teacher. As anyone who has taught knows, teaching can quite often be an isolating experience. Placing peers in the classroom at least one period of the day allows for feedback and support from a fellow teacher, and also for a sympathetic sounding board.

One of the first things I introduced in my first school year was a staff Listserv to which I would post a weekly "Faculty Forecaster" for colleagues to read and respond to about upcoming events or tasks, including the agenda for our biweekly staff meeting. Now that the staff only meets together as a whole twice a month, the listserv has proven invaluable for posting announcements or beginning or extending conversations on various issues or concerns. When we do meet as a full staff, there is time in the agenda for "milling," when teachers share updates on the progress of identified students; this often elicits feedback and suggestions from colleagues on a student of common concern/responsibility. Also, many staff meetings include time for members of departments to meet and discuss student issues and school initiatives. The school also provides time during the school day for teachers to interact both socially and professionally. Teachers are sometimes able to arrange to be free to meet during the nonacademic project times. Time is also allotted during the week for our curriculum coordinators to meet with one teacher representative from each department, the academic intervention support teacher, the librarian, and the principal. Also, our Support Team meets weekly to discuss student concerns (academic, emotional, etc.).

Before the start of the teachers' contractual school year, a weeklong August workshop is held with almost 100 percent voluntary participation by the staff. It is a time to reconnect and recommit to the values and beliefs of the school. We spend time that week on professional development work in an area of shared interest or commitment (e.g., equity, differentiated instruction, student advising) and task-oriented work such as assigning rooms for classes and scheduling conferences for students and their parents/caregivers. We also discuss and agree upon schoolwide goals. I ask that each member of the staff include at least one of the schoolwide goals into his or her individual goals for the year. Last year I had the staff share their goals with the group, which was helpful to all, especially to me, as I was just getting to know them. It turned out that many had similar goals and were able to plan to work in close collaboration to meet their shared goals. The staff seemed to like being able to share their goals.

Making It Personal by Cultivating Citizenship

We live in a time when the impersonality of large, bureaucratic schools—with their emphasis on compliance, control, and orderliness, and their preoccupation with testing and grades, competition, and individual success—has created a social structure within the schools that contributes to a sense of alienation, apathy, and isolation among the very students we are trying to prepare as democratic citizens. I see LACS as a school that is bucking this trend of merely preparing young people for their future, and instead making students feel that their lives have value in the present.

The LACS goal is that people feel they are trusted and empowered to be courageous, bold, and daring in supporting their own and others' attempts to explore ways of learning and doing things differently. I want those involved with the school to view it as a laboratory of ideas and initiatives. I remember talking to a longtime principal who said that the only thing of real importance that a principal can do is to create and manage culture. The culture at LACS works well because everyone is empowered to have a voice and, with it, the responsibility to share in making decisions and to be accountable for those decisions and actions. In many ways, the most vital part of our curriculum is the school itself. The opportunity to participate in the actual running of a school is perhaps the single most valuable learning experience we offer. To expect that on a daily basis we will see evidence of our students enthusiastically embracing and demonstrating their responsibility and commitment to the school's philosophy is perhaps unrealistic, but it makes it no less worthy a goal. In the end, there is no greater satisfaction than to witness the transformation of students who have literally grown up in our school, learning what it truly means to be a member of our small school community and what it takes and feels like to be a citizen of the world who is able to effect change and make a difference.

Q&A with the Principal
Joe Greenberg
Lehman Alternative Community School

Q: *One component of many successful middle level programs is the offering of vibrant exploratory courses. You say you do not make excuses for the fact that you do not offer the comprehensive array of courses. How do you provide the young adolescents in your building with an appropriate variety of learning experiences?*

A: Allowing students as much individual choice as possible in developing their own schedules is the most important way in which we as a school offer variety in the learning options available. While we are a relatively small school, we actually do offer our students a fairly impressive assortment of learning opportunities; in addition to the six regular courses that meet four days a week, students select up to four projects to participate in on Tuesday mornings and Thursday afternoons. Students are also able to pursue requirements by undertaking independent studies, engaging in community service and career exploration opportunities, and participating in school governance via our various committees. A typical student would be enrolled in six classes, four projects, and one committee, and would be assigned to a Family Group to meet with twice a week—giving him or her 12 different learning experiences during the week.

Q: *It's clear that you feel strongly that standardized testing has its deficiencies. For those who would argue that such testing provides a measure of accountability, how would you argue that you, as principal, ensure accountability for each teacher? For each student?*

A: While standardized testing may appear to provide a measure of accountability, I question that assumption. Often what is being measured is not what is intended or relevant, and sometimes what is being tested is simply how well students are able to take a test and how well a teacher is able to prepare students to learn how to take a test. As a principal, I am more interested in seeing students demonstrate their learning in an authentic fashion by applying whatever skills and knowledge are being assessed in a way that is real.

As for ensuring the accountability for a teacher, I feel that is done best by watching the teacher facilitate a class—ideally, in a situation where some form of project-based assessment is occurring. What I look for is a teacher who has given enough latitude in the assignment to allow students to make it their own while adhering to some criteria and standards.

The aspect I most take issue with regarding standardized testing is that, by design, the tests measure students against other students, which is harmful and inhibiting. I concede that the standardized test approach is often expedient and easier to administer, although these tests often have substantial costs associated with them, both in dollars and time beyond the actual tests themselves. To me, the stakes are too high to depend on one-shot high-stakes tests. Our students and their minds deserve to be treated with more respect than that.

Q: *Your school is not a typical middle school. What practices at your school could be modified and/or implemented in a typical middle school? What lessons could the average school learn from LACS?*

A: While it is true that we are different from many middle school programs, we have certain favorable conditions that are not available at many schools. First and foremost, we are a school of choice, so we can assume that everyone who enrolls at LACS is doing so because the student (and his or her family) appreciates what we have to offer and our approaches. That is a real luxury that cannot be emphasized enough. As far as replicating some of our existing practices into other schools, I would encourage moving away from numerical and letter grading and instead incorporating a narrative evaluation that offers personal commentary on the strengths and areas for growth of each student. I know how challenging it can be to change an established school culture, but establishing an environment in which students are given genuine choices in creating their schedules and are trusted to be involved in making important decisions democratically that affect them and their school experience is a critically important component that I would advocate for any school to incorporate.

Other suggestions would be to create some form of heterogeneously grouped advisory system that allow students to have one teacher advocate with whom they can spend time and build a small home base.

Q: *What are the greatest successes of the public goal-setting the staff at LACS has participated in recently?*

A: Somewhere in my professional travels I picked up a workshop activity for building consensus on how to prioritize a shared focus. The name a former colleague coined for the activity is "dotocracy." You post sheets of chart paper and ask staff to brainstorm a list of ideas or issues concerning or affecting the school. Once the list is generated and reviewed, each staff member is given three round sticker-dots to post next to the three ideas/issues that he or she feels are most important or interesting. (Use assorted colors if you want the staff to rank their three choices from most to least important.) When everyone has posted their stickers, it is usually clear that some areas of interest generate substantially more support than others. I ask that we agree to commit to working collectively on the three ideas/issues that receive the most votes. Also, I ask staff members to incorporate at least one of these in their individual annual goals. This gives us a unified purpose and a common commitment to some aspect of enhancing our school culture and our approach to teaching and learning.

For example, the staff decided to work together to make our Family Group advisory/advocacy system feel more substantive by agreeing on some norms of what we wanted to have that time be like for our students. One of the positive outcomes of working it through together was that we all agreed that every member of the staff needed to be involved, either as an actual Family Group leader or as an adjunct member supporting the leader. This was a huge shift in culture for the staff, but it sent a positive message to students that this aspect of our school is one that we value. We also agreed to try to expand the number of Family Groups so that we could lower the number of students in each group. Now we have slightly smaller groups (about 12, as opposed to 15 or 16) and two staff members assigned to each one, which has resulted in reducing the burden on the sole Family Group leader to do all the advising and family conferencing during scheduling and evaluation times. Not only does this new model feel more equitable, it has created a noticeable shift in attitude and culture during our Family Group meeting times.

Another example of shared goal-setting and prioritizing is the LACS staff's desire to focus on diversity in the school. A discussion of what we mean by diversity brought us to developing collaboratively a statement of our commitment to fostering a deeper level of understanding and support for diversity and how doing so strengthens us as a school community. We have formed task groups to focus on various aspects of diversity, including developing our curriculum with more emphasis on diversity issues.

Q: *How do you encourage teachers to use their classrooms as laboratories for experimenting with different approaches to teaching? What different approaches have been fostered as a result—and what successes have you seen as a result of this experimentation?*

A: We are an alternative school, so perhaps there is an assumption that teachers automatically have carte blanche to be experimental and different. While this is true to a point, it is still important for teachers to hear, and hear often, from me that I consider them trusted and respected colleagues. This goes for any school, whether it describes itself as alternative or not. With this trust has to be permission and encouragement to try new things and to teach in unconventional ways, if it inspires and connects with students in ways that elicit active participation in their learning.

When I meet with teachers, I often ask if they could teach any class, what it would be. When they tell me, I say, "Go for it," and ask what I can do to support them in making it happen. I really like to see teachers inspire each other by collaborating on an interdisciplinary course offering or developing a theme-based sequence of courses that allow students to pursue a focused semester of integrated study. For example, I have had teachers in art, science, and English develop a theme-based medley of courses around the natural elements of the Earth and approach them in an exciting way in each of these disciplines. This was not only motivating for students but also created some unique opportunities for connections that might not otherwise have been made.

Leading a Text-Based Discussion on This Profile (see protocol in Appendix 4)

- Some readers would say that the practices discussed here cannot be implemented in a traditional school. While wholesale implementation (if the reader found them all to be desirable) may not be possible, what practices could be implemented to a certain extent at our school?

- Did the sixth grade interdisciplinary classes (PAL—English and social studies focus; and I&T—science, math, and technology focus) as first semester requirements intrigue you? What would it take to implement courses like that in our school? How would they relate to standards?

- What would you see as the benefits of implementing a culminating (graduation) project at our school? What would be the challenges? Could we ensure that the benefits for students outweighed the challenges?

- Clearly, democratic governance at LACS is a priority. Is that a similar priority in our school? If not, in what ways do we provide students with a voice? What are specific challenges that may arise by giving students a voice? How can these challenges be overcome?

- What did you like most about the profile?

- What did you like least about the profile?

Moving Forward

The strategies and practices offered in this profile offer some insights into how one school has addressed personalization. In the next chapter, you will find suggestions to foster personalization in your school. Keep the LACS profile in mind as you read the chapter—it may provide concrete examples of how the strategies and theories can become practice at your school. At the end of the chapter, you will find Breaking Ranks in the Middle recommendations that will further enhance your effort to turn theory into practice.

3 Personalizing Your School Environment

On any given day, I think every adolescent is at risk in some way. How many schools approach such concerns with purposeful, planned, and progressive awareness building, and educational and intervention strategies?

—Marnik (1997) as cited in Promising Futures (Maine Commission on Secondary Education, 1998, p. 37)

Portrait of a Typical Middle School Student

Something buried deep within our genetic code must make us want to "paint" composite images. Demographers tell us what the "typical" American looks like and where he or she lives. Police sketch artists take the descriptions of many eyewitnesses and make a single composite image. As adults, we paint an image in our minds about the way things were… composites of our glorious youth, when things were so simple, when we were stars, when our biggest concern was getting a date, when there were no taxes, mortgages, orthodontist bills, or college tuitions to pay. Yes, your youth may have been glorious, but don't you remember that you were beat out for that soccer or orchestra or band leader position by your *former* friend? Don't you remember how ignorant you felt when you couldn't answer that one question in math class? Don't you remember the physical pain you felt when your first sweetheart dumped you?

Composites may be useful in some ways, but they also distort reality by focusing our gaze on one overly general and simplistic image. If we are not careful, the inherent diversity of the individuals or events that helped to build the composite image becomes less important than the composite itself.

Look down the hallway at your school. Do you see diversity in abundance? Look again, but this time pretend the diversity to which we refer does not include race, ethnicity, or gender. Do you still see diversity in abundance? Next, walk to the nearest classroom and sit in for a lesson. Do you see diversity in the level of student participation and engagement? Listen to the discussion. Do you hear diversity of opinion in abundance? Diversity is abundant because each student is an individual with different opinions, outlooks, histories, strengths, weaknesses, and needs. If you cannot see that diversity, or your schoolwide practices do not encourage and take advantage of that diversity, then perhaps it is time to adopt practices that cater to individual students rather than the "composite student." When you review the ways in which your school develops curriculum and how instruction is offered and assessment used, do you review them with your perception of the composite student in mind? Or do you try to create systems that will address the unique needs of each student and the thousands of permutations that could be added to the boxes in figure 3.1? Is it appropriate or even possible to use the same instructional or social skill–building techniques for each student?

Figure 3.1
Does Your School Address the Composite or the Individual?

Perception of the Composite Student	OR	Bob	Jamal	Cindy	Anna Maria
Hormonally imbalanced (does anything else matter?)		Puberty kicked in early for this 6'2" 6th grader with a mustache	8th grade's almost over and nary a whisker in sight for this 4'7" student	Rumored pregnant	Still plays with dolls
Athletically average		Trips going up the stairs	Sunday school little leaguer	Formerly a rising soccer star	Olympic gold medal winner
Average interest in school—mostly interested in friends and self		Turned off and looking forward to quitting school	Unrealized potential—does well enough to get by	Curious and enthusiastic learner	Likes to learn new things but sees no connection between school and life
Average parent involvement starting to wane		Parents want to help but don't know where to begin	Parents very involved in parent organization and in helping with homework	Parents' recent divorce leaves her in tears	Parents push so hard student says school and sports aren't fun anymore
Academically average		Unable to read the comics page	Reads the *Wall Street Journal*	Has trouble with whole numbers	Can solve geometry problems

Source: Adapted in part from From the Desk of the Middle School Principal, *by Kathleen Brown and Vincent Anfara, 2002, p. 132.*

Do you want to lead or teach in a school of composites or a school in which each student is personally challenged to develop intellectually, socially, ethically, and physically? If you believe that on any given day *every* adolescent is "at risk" in some way and that your school has the ability to help students address some risks, then you will prefer the second kind of school. But how does one create systems to ensure that each student is personally challenged? What does personalization mean? How can you personalize your school?

What Do We Mean by Personalization?

If high achievement for all students is the goal of reform, then a supportive environment for achievement must be established. Although some students might be able to make it through the middle level years *despite* the lack of personal connections, most students require a supportive environment—some more than others. Creating that environment is essential if a school is to bring learning to fruition for each student. In keeping with the sentiment implicit in the word, "personalization" can mean different things to different people, but most definitions converge on a few common principles associated with providing students with opportunities to develop a sense of belonging to the school, a sense of ownership over the direction of one's learning, and the ability to recognize options and make choices based on one's own experience and understanding of the options. The following is a working definition:

> Personalization: A learning process in which schools help students assess their own talents and aspirations, plan a pathway toward their own purposes, work cooperatively with others on challenging tasks, maintain a record of their explorations, and demonstrate their learning against clear standards in a wide variety of media, all with the close support of adult mentors and guides. (Clarke, 2003, p. 15)

To teach each student well requires that we know each student well.
—Ted Sizer

This chapter and its accompanying recommendations will focus on one facet of personalization: implementing structural and behavioral models to strengthen *relationships among people*—students, teachers, staff members, families, and the larger community. Chapter 4 addresses another facet of personalization: *relationships between students and ideas*—how the student interacts and directs his or her own learning with the oversight, coaching, and motivational strategies associated with student-centered curriculum, instruction, and assessment. Significant overlap exists between these two facets, providing further evidence of the need to review the Breaking Ranks in the Middle recommendations in their entirety, not as isolated pockets of "good ideas."

Personalizing Your School Environment

Practices Associated with Personalization and People

Many of the practices associated with personalization set the stage for learning. They are practices that address the school environment, climate, and culture, such as these:

- Creating structures so that students cannot remain anonymous.
- Establishing schedules and priorities that allow teachers to develop an appreciation for each student's abilities.
- Creating structures in which the aspirations, strengths, weaknesses, interests, and level of progress of each student are known well by at least one adult.
- Providing opportunities for students to learn about the values associated with life in a civil and democratic society, their responsibilities within that society, and how to exercise those values in the school.
- Offering parents, families, and community members opportunities for involvement in students' education.
- Ensuring that the physical and mental health needs of students are addressed.
- Providing students with opportunities to demonstrate their academic, athletic, musical, dramatic, and other accomplishments in a variety of ways.
- Offering opportunities to develop social, decision-making, and communication skills.

Implementing structural changes to foster these practices provides the "shell" in which productive interaction—relationships—can occur systematically.

> Young adolescents often place their social development needs above all else during these years. As life outside the home takes on greater importance, the school becomes the major structured arena for young adolescent social interaction. Middle level school programs, therefore, must afford students adequate opportunities for social interaction with peers and significant adults. If not, students find their own ways to fulfills those needs, including disrupting the classroom or skipping school.
>
> —*Achieving Excellence Through the Middle Level Curriculum, NASSP, 1993 (p. 10).*

Why Build Relationships?

The need to build relationships rests on the premise that many students require a supportive relationship with the school or with someone at the school who understands them personally. Critics may counter that schools are in the business of conveying knowledge, not catering to the personal needs of students. To help principals, teachers, and families understand why personalization is important and to prepare them for discussions of the broader issues of personalization, consider the following hypothetical question-and-answer discussion between a principal and a group of parents.

Q: *Why do we need to go to the trouble of "personalizing" our school? We're doing fine. It is rare that any student doesn't pass the state tests, and almost all our students go on to high school and most go to college.*

A: Yes, we are very pleased with our test scores and with the number of students who eventually finish high school. However, even though our test scores are excellent in comparison to most schools, on average 5 percent of our students will not complete high school in four years. For our school of 500, that means a lost opportunity for 25 students—statistically speaking, those 25 students can look forward to higher unemployment, lower compensation, and possibly jail time. Is there something we could have done to better prepare them for high school? Could we have reached these students? Maybe. Should we try? I believe we should.

Q: *C'mon—jail? Those are worst-case scenarios.*

A: You wouldn't be saying that if you were the parent of one of those 25 students. But what about those students who don't fall into the worst-case scenario? We've heard that a significant number of our students have had to take remedial courses in high school. They should not have to take courses to learn what they should have learned here. Yes, our averages are good, but our team believes we could do much better if we can get more students excited about learning. Our measure of success should be how well we are challenging each student—if the state test were to measure that, then fine. But if our students are passing the tests and still not being challenged academically, then we will have failed. Are we doing everything in our power to make sure that our high-performing students are not bored and in perpetual review mode? That our seemingly unmotivated students aren't just skating by, doing the minimum required? That our lower-performing students are not being turned off because of failure, real

> A significant adult who provides support and direction during difficult times is an important factor in helping students avoid academic failure and a variety of other problems. Among youth at risk from health or behavioral problems, family dysfunction, poverty, or other stresses, the most important school factor fostering resilience... may be the availability of at least one caring, responsible adult who can function as a mentor or role model.
>
> —*Turning Points 2000, p. 143.*

or perceived? These should be good enough reasons to personalize, but perhaps most compelling for me is Carmen—the eighth-grader who dropped out of school last year for "health reasons." As I'm sure you'll recall, we found out later that she had bulimia, which eventually killed her. Could we have reached her and referred her to professional help? We'll never know, because no one in the school knew this supposed "loner" well enough. How many students in this school do you think are on the brink of something tragic because of personal problems, an eating disorder, chemical dependency, or other harmful activity? Or are these just problems that we pass on to the high school—as long as they don't have an effect on our "averages"?

Q: *It sounds as though you want schools to fill the role of social services.*

A: No. Schools cannot be all things to all people. But we can do better. We have to remember the consequences of indifference to the personal needs and aspirations of students. Remember the effect Carmen's death had? Not only was her family devastated but so were many of the parents and students in our school community. Emotionally and academically, everything was put on hold. That's an extreme example, but similar tragedies happen more often than we'd like. Let's not forget the less cataclysmic events, the behavioral and discipline issues associated with students who are not fully engaged—those affect all students on a daily basis. Every student will be better off if we can reach each student.

Q: *But middle schools are already being accused of being too sensitive to the personal needs of students at the expense of academics. Will establishing these relationships lead to higher achievement?*

A: Yes. First we have to get all students to school. Research shows that personalized learning initiatives can increase attendance, decrease dropout rates, and decrease disruptive behavior. Next, we must engage them—know their interests and how each student learns. Adolescents are developing academically, socially, emotionally, and physically. Students will tune in or tune out based on how we engage them in each of those areas. These areas are not independent "silos" that can be filled when we see fit. Learning is not the highest of priorities when a student's parent loses a job or has health problems, or when there are stresses related to divorce, or when a student is homeless, or when a student doesn't get invited to a dance or party, or when a student did not make the cut for the band, the play, or the soccer team. *While differing in their level of importance to you or me, each of these is, at any given moment, potentially much more important to a student than learning is.* Our challenge is to ensure that the issue is appropriately confronted so that learning can again become a priority. A quick look at the potential items that interfere with learning leads me to guess that, on any given day, one-quarter of all students are somehow distracted from learning. In our school of 500, that's 125 students.

Q: *So you get the students to school and you're attempting to understand them. What is the tie to learning?*

A: There are many different "developmental assets" that determine the ways in which different students engage with learning, including

- Family support

- Parent involvement in school

- Positive peer influence

> Students need to make a strong connection to an adult they can see themselves becoming.
>
> —*author unknown*

- Time at home

- Bonding to school

- Personal power

- Sense of purpose (Scales and Leffert [1999], as cited by Clarke, 2003, p. 9)

Our job is to make sure we find the right entrée to get them personally engaged. We believe that the Breaking Ranks in the Middle strategies can accomplish that. Once we find that entrée, we are on our way to getting them interested and engaged in learning—and wanting to learn more. The handout I distributed a few moments ago (see figure 3.2) describes the characteristics of young adolescents. If schools are not prepared to take into account and address these characteristics, the environment of the school and the classroom will suffer, which will lead to decreased academic achievement.

How to Engage Students

What are the events and interactions that engage students during a typical school day? Researchers from the LAB (the Northeast and Islands Regional Educational Laboratory) at Brown University "shadowed" students at several different schools in a quest to answer that question. The researchers discovered six developmental needs of students (Clarke & Frazer, 2003):

- **Voice**—the need to express their personal perspective

Figure 3.2
Characteristics of Young Adolescents

SOCIAL

- Have a strong need to belong to a group
- Exhibit immature behavior because their social skills frequently lag behind their mental and physical maturity
- Are in search of self
- Desire recognition for their efforts and achievements
- Like fads
- Overreact to ridicule, embarrassment, and rejection
- Are socially vulnerable

EMOTIONAL

- Experience mood swings
- Need to release energy
- Seek to become increasingly independent
- Are increasingly concerned about peer acceptance
- Tend to be self-conscious
- Believe that personal problems, feelings, and experiences are unique to them
- Exhibit intense concern about physical growth and maturity

INTELLECTUAL

- Are in a transition period from concrete thinking to abstract thinking
- Are intensely curious and have a wide range of intellectual pursuits
- Prefer active over passive learning
- Respond positively to opportunities to participate in real-life situations
- Have a strong need of approval/may be easily discouraged
- Are inquisitive/often challenge authority

PHYSICAL

- Experience rapid, irregular growth
- Undergo bodily changes that may cause awkward, uncoordinated movements
- Have varying maturity rates
- Experience restlessness/fatigue
- Need daily physical activity
- Often lack physical fitness
- Have poor eating habits
- Develop sexual awareness

Source: National Forum to Accelerate Middle Grades Reform, www.mgforum.org.

- **Belonging**—the need to create individual and group identities
- **Choice**—the need to examine options and choose a path
- **Freedom**—the need to take risks and assess effects
- **Imagination**—the need to create a projected view of self
- **Success**—the need to demonstrate mastery

While the shadowed students were high school students, their needs were similar to those listed in the figure for young adolescents—though perhaps at differing levels.

How a school addresses each of these student needs will determine the outcomes of its personalization efforts. In the diagram in figure 3.3, the students' personal needs are on the left and school practices are on the right. If the school practices are in place to address the student needs, relationships can be formed (middle column).

Your school's practices may not be meeting student developmental needs if you see no signs of these relationships. In *Changing Systems to Personalize Learning* (Clarke, 2003), these relationships are discussed in detail:

Recognition: Personalized learning allows each student to earn recognition—largely from peers but also from teachers, parents, and school leaders. Earning recognition can happen only if each student has many chances in a school day to voice a personal perspective and assert a unique identity. Schools that personalize learning by expanding opportunities for recognition have to develop equitable processes that let many voices be heard and many kinds of success be celebrated. While most …schools prevent inequity by setting uniform expectations, those same practices prevent the majority of students from being recognized for their unique talents. For example, the honor roll, class rank, [sports] lineup, student government, and arts prize allocate recognition only to the few students ranked as the best in predetermined categories. The rest may receive very little recognition during a school day, often lapsing into passive disengagement that barely disguises their disappointment.… *Personalized learning depends on earning recognition under expectations designed to allow all to succeed.*

Acceptance: The shadowed students all exhibited delight when their learning became a vehicle for gaining wide acceptance in their school. The need of young adults to belong to a group where they can establish a personal identity has been well described.… For many [students], gaining acceptance within a group can be achieved only with a small group of four to five friends, who then form a self-protective compact or clique in the halls and cafeteria. Some cliques develop a tentative sense of belonging and earn small-scale acceptance by rebelling against the larger community—through drugs, violence, and habitual truancy. *Personalized learning depends on being able to gain acceptance within the whole school community for productive and distinctive achievements.*

Trust: The shadowed students wanted to be trusted to plan and carry out daily activities and direct their own learning. They wanted to exercise choice, examine their available options, and set their own path on a daily basis.… *Personalized learning depends on maintaining a wide range of opportunities for students to manage their own learning and direct their own lives.*

Respect: Engaged students in the shadowing study wanted freedom to take some risks on behalf of their aspirations, and the opportunity to earn respect from their

Figure 3.3 Interactions in Personalized Learning

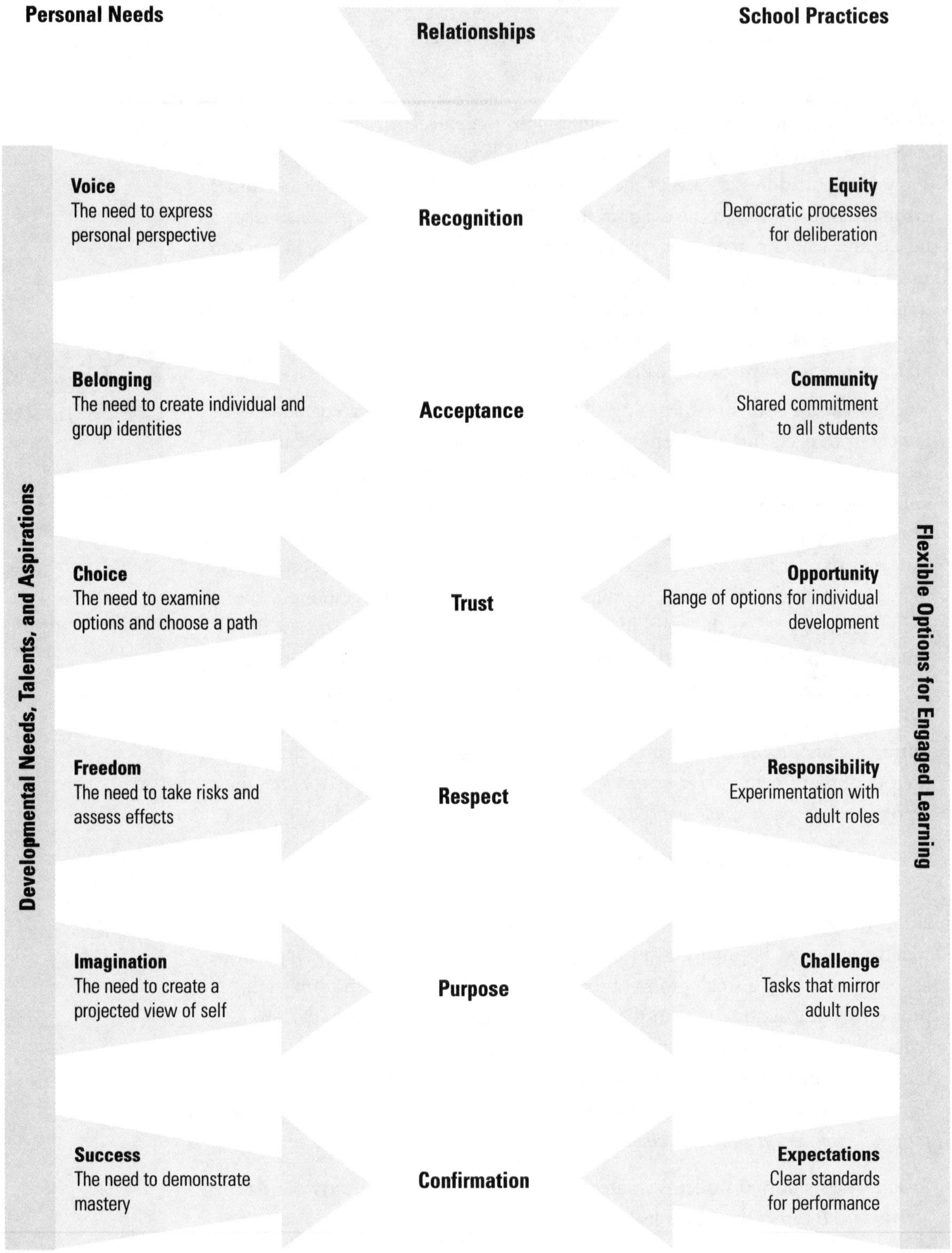

Personal Needs

Relationships

School Practices

Voice
The need to express
personal perspective

Recognition

Equity
Democratic processes
for deliberation

Belonging
The need to create individual and
group identities

Acceptance

Community
Shared commitment
to all students

Choice
The need to examine
options and choose a path

Trust

Opportunity
Range of options for individual
development

Freedom
The need to take risks and
assess effects

Respect

Responsibility
Experimentation with
adult roles

Imagination
The need to create a
projected view of self

Purpose

Challenge
Tasks that mirror
adult roles

Success
The need to demonstrate
mastery

Confirmation

Expectations
Clear standards
for performance

Developmental Needs, Talents, and Aspirations

Flexible Options for Engaged Learning

Personal Learning: Using information from the school experience to direct one's own life and to improve the life of the community

Source: Clarke & Frazer, 2003. Reprinted with permission.

peers and from adults in the school.... [School] tends to grant at least minimal respect, not for freely designed activities, but for compliance with existing rules and expectations. The student who says little in class but completes homework assignments regularly and prepares well for tests and quizzes earns the gratitude of teachers and administrators—and a modicum of respect. Students who press with questions, push their own perspective... earn disrespect. *Personalized learning allows students to earn respect from teachers and peers by asking their own questions and pursuing their own answers, even against the tide of opinion.*

Purpose: The engaged students in the shadowing study were confident that [school] offered a clear way for them to fulfill their own purposes by adhering to the school's declared purpose. They could use their daily work in classes, school activities, and community learning experiences to imagine themselves leading successful adult lives. In a subject-based curriculum, knowledge of facts and ideas is often represented without adult applications and without reference to the adult world, where knowledge truly makes a difference. Unless they are connected to problems and opportunities in the community at large, ...classes seem irrelevant and boring. *Personalized learning provides students with challenges that mirror the tasks and challenges of adult life.*

Confirmation: Engaged students in the study used their daily work to confirm their sense of progress toward personal goals. They needed to see small instances of success in order to understand that they were moving toward their longer-term goals. Being able to demonstrate mastery of skills or knowledge, particularly when their efforts could support others working on similar challenges, increased their confidence and often opened new avenues for exploration. ...[C]lasses in which students all seek the same "right answer" prevent students from recognizing how they can use knowledge to make a difference in their lives and the lives of others. *Personalized learning celebrates the unique achievements of individuals against broad standards shared by the whole community.*

What are the specific practices a school can institute to address the developmental needs of students so these relationships can become reality? Create small units through teaming, house, school-within-a-school, or advisory structures; decrease the total number of students for whom a teacher or a team of teachers has responsibility; implement Personal Plans for Progress (PPPs) for each student; provide a mentor or Personal Adult Advocate for each student; ensure that teachers and staff promote a sense of caring and concern for students; adopt flexible schedules; involve families; promote civic responsibility and core values; and help coordinate social services so that all students are prepared to learn. Each of these recommendations will help personalize your school. (See pp. 137–149 for the specific Breaking Ranks in the Middle recommendations related to personalization, as well as strategies for implementation, benefits, and challenges, and how to measure progress.)

In *Leadership for Highly Successful Middle Level Schools: A National Study of Leadership in Middle Level Schools* (Valentine et al., 2004), the authors describe strong support among highly successful schools for "five programmatic practices that are responsive to the developmental and instructional needs of young adolescents: interdisciplinary teaming, exploratory courses, adviser-advisee programs, cocurricular programs, and intramural activities." When compared with the national sample, principals of the highly successful schools were much more supportive of all five practices.

> [N]o school should exceed 600 students; ideally, a school should serve an even smaller number of young adolescents. The key principle is to create groupings of students and educators small enough to stimulate the development of close, supportive relationships. While not sufficient in themselves to create a learning community, such relationships are a necessary precondition.
>
> —*Turning Points 2000, p. 123.*

How to Assess Your School's Level of Personalization

The practices described above will help you create a more personalized environment for learning that begins to address the developmental needs of students. Systematic observation of relationships will provide your school with excellent insight into how well your school is able to personalize the school for students. Another rubric by which to judge your school's progress toward personalization was developed by the Northwest Regional Education Lab (NWREL) in conjunction with its smaller learning communities (SLC) work. (This effort is similar in purpose and function to teaming. If you do not have SLCs, read "SLC" in figure 3.4 as "team" or "school.")

This rubric will not only allow you to gauge your current level of personalization but can serve as a benchmark to illustrate progress as you strive to personalize your school. The following Breaking Ranks in the Middle recommendations are designed to build a culture and community dedicated to personalizing your school for the benefit of each student.

Once you have assessed your school's level of personalization, you can use these recommendations to address the weaknesses that your team has found.

Figure 3.4
Personalization

Key Element	Beginning SLC	Making Progress	Achieved
Connectedness	Students are not well known by their peers or their teachers within the SLC.	Students know the majority of their peers within their SLC; teachers know the names and abilities of all of their students.	Teachers and students know each other by name, and teachers are able to identify individual students' strengths and challenges.
Student involvement	No process is in place for students to play an active role within their SLCs.	Students may choose to play active roles within their SLCs and participate in SLC functions.	Students select specific roles within their SLCs and play an active role in governance.
Student involvement	Students are assigned to SLCs on the basis of individual academic performance and abilities.	SLCs are organized in heterogeneous groupings wherein individual needs are recognized and addressed.	SLCs are organized in heterogeneous groupings; teachers receive professional development to learn how to meet multiple needs of students with multiple abilities.
Student involvement	Students are not involved in activities beyond the classroom.	A majority of students participate in [student/co-curricular] activities beyond the classroom.	All students take advantage of opportunities to participate in [student/co-curricular] and SLC activities.
Teacher involvement	Teachers do not follow students for multiple years, and possess limited knowledge of students' personal lives. Teachers' primary contact with students is within the confines of the classroom.	Teachers follow students for multiple years and have a process in place to know many students on a personal level. Teachers have regular opportunities to interact with students through other intentional or ad hoc conferencing, e.g., advisories.	Teachers follow students for multiple years and know students' personal strengths, challenges, and goals. Teachers collaborate regularly with their team members and individual students to ensure academic and personal achievement for students.
Parent and community involvement	Parents and community members do not participate in academic/instructional support or governance, or activities within the SLC.	Some parents and community members participate in academic/instructional support or governance, or activities within the SLC.	The majority of parents and some community members participate in academic/instructional support or governance, and activities within the SLC.

Source: Cotton, 2004.

Breaking Ranks in the Middle Recommendations

Related to Personalizing Your School Environment

RECOMMENDATION 10: Schools will create small units in which anonymity is banished.

Strategies

- Establish schools-within-a-school or a smaller learning communities (SLC) model to organize large schools into smaller units.

- Establish a structure to ensure that every student in the building is known by at least one adult (see recommendation 13 for more information).

- Include special-needs students in SLC (i.e., do not isolate ELLs and others by placing them in one group).

- Employ looping to allow teams of students and adults to build relationships with each other over longer periods of time.

- Form workgroups inside classes (in all disciplines) in which small groups of students work together for extended periods (using the lab partner model).

- Include counselors, ESL, special education, and other specialists in the small units to ensure that all students are known and understood.

- Provide opportunities for adults to support each other in their efforts to ensure that all students are known, understood, and cared for.

Benefits

- Creates a support network for adolescents.

- Allows every student to be recognized and his or her progress monitored, enabling schools to devote more resources to those who need them most.

- Improves student discipline and the school climate.

- Diminishes alienation among students.

- Allows students to be known, understood, and recognized for their talents, not isolated because of their disabilities, language differences, or culture.

Challenges

- Growing student enrollment, overcrowding, and budget cutbacks.

- Overcoming parental objections.

- Training staff to take on new roles.

- Overcoming the perception that ELL and special needs students need to be isolated in order to "protect" them.

Progress Measures

- Keep an ongoing record to ensure that diversity remains stable in student, class, and team groups and that ELL and special-needs students are included in team, advisory, and SLC structures.

- Refer to disciplinary record and test result analyses (see recommendation 3) to document improved student achievement and behavior.

- Conduct periodic random checks by counselors to confirm that students are connected with a trusted adult.

RECOMMENDATION 11: Each teacher involved in the instructional program on a full-time basis will be responsible for **contact time with no more than 90 students** so that the teacher can give greater attention to the needs of every student.

Strategies

- Create teams of students/teachers with no more than 90 students per team. Schedule as close as possible to a ratio of 90:1 for core academic teachers.

- Prioritize staffing allocations among all positions to reduce student–teacher ratio.

- Consolidate nonteaching school positions in order to hire more teachers; seek outside funding for additional teachers; increase the size of noncore classes, if appropriate and possible.

- Encourage teachers to define their roles to include the modification of curriculum and instruction based on learner needs and the development of skills necessary to carry out those roles.

- Examine alternative scheduling strategies across the course of the school year, semester, quarter, and day.

- Devise a method of tracking individual and teacher-specific improved student achievement and critical-thinking/problem-solving skills that can be directly related to increased teacher-student contact.

Benefits

- Encourages teachers to develop closer relationships with individual students, creating a more personalized learning environment.

- Allows teacher teams to engage in various practices, such as reviewing student work, which will allow for closer monitoring of individual students and sharing information with one another.

- Decreases chance of students being neglected.

Challenges

- Addressing difficult choices on program size—could require cuts in programs that are important but less essential than others.

- Creating or finding the necessary space, because more classrooms or creative scheduling will likely be needed.

- Identifying methods of reducing ratios without additional money.

- Making structural changes to accommodate all learners.

Progress Measures

- Keep an ongoing record over time to ensure that teams remain stable with no more than 90 students.

- Track the extent to which individual student and (teacher-identified) whole-class achievement improves with a 90:1 student-teacher ratio, especially in the areas of critical-thinking and problem-solving skills. (This will be difficult to attribute to one criterion.)

- Track the extent to which disciplinary referrals increase/decrease with a 90:1 student-teacher ratio.

- Document the consolidation of nonteaching school positions in order to hire more teachers and the search for outside funding for additional teachers; then increase the size of nonacademic classes to free teacher time for core classes.

- Demonstrate that all professional development activities are geared toward helping teachers define their roles to include modification of curriculum and instruction based on learner need.

Recommendation 11 in Practice

Crabapple Middle School

The block schedule reduces the number of students with whom a teacher on a four-member team interacts daily from approximately 120–140 to approximately 80–96. This allows for greater interaction and the use of a variety of teaching strategies. Our teachers are organized into teams composed of two to four academic core teachers per team. A special education collaboration/inclusion teacher is present on most teams. One team is a looping team, moving along with students from sixth to seventh grade. Approximately 80 percent of the academic teachers hold a Middle Grades certificate; if new teachers do not hold this certificate, they enroll in the Nature and Needs of the Middle Grades Child class.

RECOMMENDATION 12: Each student will have a **Personal Plan for Progress (PPP)** that will be reviewed often to ensure that the school takes individual needs into consideration and to allow students, within reasonable parameters, to design their own methods for learning in an effort to meet high standards.

Strategies

- Establish an advisory that will allow advisors to help students create and review challenging PPPs (academically, socially, developmentally).

- Assign a group of students to each teacher, who will be responsible for monitoring and adjusting the PPPs for each of these students.

- Use student-led conferences to present the contents of the PPP to parents and others.

- Precede the PPP process with developmental guidance activities that provide students with an opportunity to articulate for themselves who they are—their skills, interests, passions, history, and so on.

- Include a variety of assessment data (e.g., interests, learning style, intelligence preference) in the development of the PPP.

- Define parameters for "student engagement" criteria and prepare an observation sheet for recording behaviors in class.

Benefits

- Increases student engagement, as students take responsibility for their own learning.

- Increases potential for improvement in academic achievement.

- Provides additional opportunities (e.g., through student-led conferences) for families to come into the school and actively participate in their children's education.

- Fosters ownership in learning, which becomes an asset to both the instructor and the instructed. A PPP shows the teacher and the student a common goal in their partnership for accomplishment.

Challenges

- Providing time, resources, and training for staff who are responsible for monitoring student progress.

- Developing appropriate means of assessing student progress.

- Resisting the temptation to "track" students in order to allow teachers to work with groups of students with similar PPPs.

- Creating plans that can inform meaningful classroom practice rather than becoming an impediment because of additional unproductive paperwork and meetings.

- Ensuring that a student's PPP is complementary to his or her Individual Education Plan (IEP).

Progress Measures

- Keep a record/list of PPPs created for each student; monitor the implementation of each PPP, including ensuring that a portfolio of the student's work is maintained through a checklist; and track student performance gains over time from student assessment records.

- Observe and document the degree of increased student engagement in individual learning.

- Evaluate the success of this activity by reviewing the PPPs, portfolios, and student performance results (including engagement) for each student, as well as the level of satisfaction with the PPPs (by teacher, student, and other resource personnel).

- Track student and family confidence in the process, the increased capacity of students to plot their own paths, and their understanding of options for the future (e.g., high school planning, college opportunities).

RECOMMENDATION 13: Each student will have a **Personal Adult Advocate** to help him or her personalize the educational experience.

Strategies

- Establish an advisory program that includes every student.

- Ensure that the advisory program supports the acquisition of the essential learnings established by the school.

- Provide staff with professional development on advocacy, and allow time for student/staff relationships to grow.

- Assign to each teacher and to other professionals a group of students for whom they will be advocates; recruit additional adult advocates from the community.

Benefits

- Encourages students to learn how to work together on intellectual tasks.

- Ensures that every student in the school knows and is known by an adult.

- Helps adults acquire a better feeling for what is going on in the lives of students.

- Decreases disciplinary problems.

- Provides students with an adult to turn to in times of need.

- Increases opportunities for students to receive extra help.

- Creates a more personalized learning community.

- Increases student engagement, which should lead to academic gains for all.

Challenges

- Scheduling a consistent time for advisory to meet while addressing other demands on staff time.

- Finding additional resources to vet and train outside mentors.

- Making sure that each child has an advocate who takes the assignment seriously and makes it meaningful for the student.

- Addressing the reluctance of some adults to face difficult personal issues encountered by students.

Progress Measures

- Measure the degree to which the advisory program includes every student, develops relationships between advisors/advisees, and offers adequate time to build relationships.

- Review student achievement and disciplinary data in light of this program.

- Document teacher contacts with the students for whom they are responsible through logs kept by each advisor.

- Conduct periodic, random checks with students by counselors to verify positive relationships with their advisors.

Recommendations 12 and 13 in Practice

Hopkins West Junior High School

All students, with the help of their advisors and parents, develop personal learner goals focusing on academic and social development. The process is developmental: Students in seventh grade learn how to become a successful middle level student; eighth grade students learn more about themselves as learners; and ninth-graders develop a transition plan for high school (9–12). The personal learning goals conferences are led by students. In addition, the school's offerings include the following:

- Each certified staff member serves as an advisor (groups of approximately 16) in daily advisory/check-in. The advisory groups are relationship based. The advisor serves as liaison between home and the team; advisors monitor academic, social, behavioral, and other developmental progress of students.

- Health classes teach all students refusal skills for chemical, alcohol, and sexual activity.

- At-risk students participate in a variety of peer support groups facilitated by counselors/social workers in areas such as grief, social/behavior development, Alateen, and sexuality.

- "Get Connected" provides computer and Internet access to low-income families. The computer serves as a tool to connect traditionally marginalized families with the school. Each student/family has a teacher mentor. Students and parents/guardians are required to complete a variety of assignments or contacts with the child's teachers.

- Twelve to 14 "Zoomers" (sixth into seventh grade) participate in a weeklong Minnesota Boundary Waters camping experience led by four teachers and two older student leaders. The intent of the program is to cement strong relationships with peers and adults and to provide adventure-based learning experiences to increase self-esteem.

Alvarado Intermediate

The school's daily homeroom guidance program curriculum offers lessons on character building, ethics, social responsibility, conflict resolution, and goal-setting. Investing time each day to build the whole child encourages a sense of security, helps students address issues, and builds a bond between the homeroom teacher and students. The school recently introduced the "Adopt-a-Student" mentoring program based on *40 Developmental Assets* by Mel Levine. Each member of the staff selects a low-performing student and informally reaches out to the student. The school also trains each certificated staff member to spot potential problems in adolescents.

Breaking Ranks in the Middle Recommendations

Casey Middle School

Students have many opportunities to find their voices—posing questions, reflecting on experiences, developing rubrics, and participating in decisions. These opportunities include the following:

- Student involvement in parent-teacher conferences, including student-led conferences.
- Student Council and leadership class.
- Promotion of pre-AP and critical-thinking strategies in every classroom.
- Three-day Outdoor Education trip for all students in the fall.
- Multiethnic Action Coalition (MAC), which celebrates and honors diversity, and teaches an anti-bullying curriculum to the school.
- Counseling groups in which students are encouraged to set high goals.
- Students choosing their own projects and designing their own games in electives based on the students' interests.
- Students choosing writing topics and genres of interest.
- An adult advocate and supporter in the school for every student.
- Staff members who do not use negative labels or discuss students in negative ways. Staff view the whole student, not just the problem. Teachers make special efforts for students who are shy, quiet, or troubled.
- Student focus groups that help adults understand what direction to take. (Examples of questions asked: What would make you feel more welcome? How could we improve our student satisfaction survey?)

Thayer J. Hill Middle School

In addition to advisory periods, the school schedules weekly Side-by-Side conferences with individual students. Four times a year, each student writes a reflection and the adult advocate responds to the student's ideas (the journal is maintained for the entire three years that a student is at the school, so the student can reflect on his or her growth). A wide variety of encore classes and student activities help students with identity development and competency building; the goal is to have each student participate in at least one activity.

Bowman Middle School

For 20 minutes each day, students take part in an advisory period that consists of a citizenship program (Heart of a Champion), tutorials, and sustained silent reading. Some students participate in the Safety Net program—specialized group counseling sessions conducted by an outside agency weekly for 10 weeks that focuses on anger management, conflict resolution, and decision making. Students are also mentored by volunteers from local businesses and through the Big Brother/Big Sister program. Grade-level counselors conduct classroom guidance sessions with students and sixth-graders receive three weeks of guidance on social skills awareness.

Saunders Middle School

A guidance counselor starts with a group of students as they make the transition from elementary school. This same counselor moves through the grade levels with these students until they transfer to the high school. This gives each student someone they can identify with during the entire stay at the middle school. This counselor is also the person who assists these students with their high school schedules. As the group moves on, the counselor moves back to the sixth grade and begins another cycle with the next group of students.

RECOMMENDATION 14: Teachers and administrators will convey a **sense of caring** so that students know that teachers have a stake in student learning.

Strategies

- Engage in teaming to foster teacher discussion of students' needs, progress, and plans.
- Practice dispensing discipline with dignity.
- Provide professional development on relationship building, components of personalized school culture, and practices that promote a sense of caring.
- Use data to determine additional support needed by individual students.
- Make the time and create opportunities for students to learn how to develop responsible relationships with each other.

Benefits

- Increases student feeling of being valued, which encourages students to take more responsibility for their learning.
- Decreases disciplinary problems.
- Supports emotional and intellectual development in students.
- Fills a void for some students.

Challenges

- Developing a school culture in which people are expected to care for one another.
- "Caring" can be misinterpreted—professional boundaries must be understood by all.
- Allocating resources and time may be difficult.
- Moving from teacher-centered to student-centered environments can prove difficult for some.

Progress Measures

- Conduct surveys of students, staff, and parents to determine views of the school's culture.
- Document and share staff practices of personalization that promote a sense of caring.

RECOMMENDATION 15: Each school will develop **flexible scheduling** and student grouping patterns to meet the individual needs of students and to ensure academic success.

Strategies

- Adjust the length of class periods to provide extended periods of time for core classes.
- Build in common planning time for instructional teams to work collaboratively.
- Consolidate noncore subjects to fewer days per week.
- Adjust the length of the school day; schedule extended days periodically.
- Dedicate a designated number of weeks as concentrated core curriculum weeks.
- Adjust the length of the school year: Go to a trimester or year-round school schedule.

Benefits

- Provides more time to devote to instruction in core subjects.
- Increases the quality and quantity of project-based instruction and creates more time for in-depth work, leading to greater student understanding of key concepts.
- Provides the time for students to do project-based and in-depth work.
- Offers a high degree of flexibility to a team of teachers when provided with a block of time.
- Leads to greater collaboration among teachers when common planning time is provided.
- Allows teachers to spend more time on classroom instruction and less on classroom management.
- Ensures that school isn't "run by the bell"—students and teachers have more time to devote to teaching and learning without predetermined periods of time being dictated by a master schedule.
- Helps families struggling with daycare issues when year-round schedules are implemented.

Challenges

- Deciding on program content can be very difficult, and making those choices can lead to friction.
- Handling issues related to autonomy over scheduling.
- Providing the necessary professional development for teachers to take advantage of the new time configurations.
- Scheduling the common planning time essential to the success of team/extended time teaching.
- Addressing transportation issues, bus schedules, athletic schedules, and so on.

Progress Measures

- Document the implementation of flexible scheduling, including lengthened periods for core classes and weeks dedicated to core curriculum, common planning for teaching teams, and adjusted length of school day and/or year.
- Show evidence that teacher teams are engaging in common planning time on a consistent basis (e.g., meeting minutes, reports, team planning products).
- Document any changes in the quality of instruction.

Recommendations 14 and 15 in Practice

Casey Middle School

At Casey, flexible scheduling enables students to engage in extended projects, hands-on experiences, and inquiry-based learning. The scheduling allows class time to be devoted to learning and applying knowledge or skills rather than classroom management and discipline. Students can have more time to learn the content, concepts, or skills if they need it. Highlights include the following:

■ A block schedule allows all students to engage in extended research-based projects and experiments in science, social studies, and electives.

■ Teachers, through more careful planning of instruction, have been working on providing more time for students to practice researching, writing, reading, or math in lieu of listening to teacher-talk.

■ Teachers have more time to discover what excites students and can use that knowledge to enhance standards-based learning. Specialized groups are arranged for students who need additional time in math, reading, or language arts.

■ Teachers use a wide variety of instructional strategies to foster curiosity, exploration, creativity, and the development of social skills.

■ Teachers use a wide range of technology and offer applied technology classes.

■ The schedule allows for writing and reading workshops in language arts classes.

■ There is zero tolerance for classroom disruption; students who disrupt class are sent immediately to the assistant principal.

■ Curriculum-based health classes are offered.

Hopkins West Junior High School

The school has an alternating day block schedule in which classes are 88 minutes long. The schedule offers teachers and students the opportunity to delve deeper into subject matter, participate in lab experiments, use literacy strategies, and engage in cooperative group learning. Other highlights include the following:

■ By intentionally clustering four to five gifted students in heterogeneously grouped English, social studies, and science classes, teachers are better able to differentiate their curriculum and instruction and to form flexible arrangements for cooperative learning groups.

■ Intervention Reading/Writing is a team-taught course in which two teachers loop a group of 15 students for two years. Part of the course curriculum is using Scholastic's Read 180, which effectively engages students by using technology to improve vocabulary and comprehension.

■ To ensure a systemic approach to writing in all school programs and more individualized instruction for students, the English Department pairs a writing instructor with teachers in the special education and ELL departments as well as in the alternative program.

■ The extended learning programs offered during the summer (Zoom, Step Up, Boost—one for each grade) offer a flexible schedule in which a team of three teachers works with 30 students in each grade using a literacy-based curriculum to teach reading, writing, math, and science.

Saunders Middle School

Teachers develop their schedules based on schoolwide parameters. They are given lunch schedules and encore class times. As a team, they determine their daily schedules. When adjustments are needed for special activities, testing, or celebrations, they adhere to the lunch/encore times but adjust the remainder of the day and send a copy of the revised schedule to the office. Teachers control their time.

Medea Creek Middle School

The master schedule embodies the school's philosophy of equity for and access to all—proof that one size does not fit all. Depending on grade level and subject areas, students are on a block or modified block schedule for core academic courses, with daily PE and electives. There is no tracking. "Inclusionary" defines the delivery of special education services, with a wide range and combination of approaches, including team teaching, pull-out and one-on-one assistance, instructional aides in the academic classes, special adaptations in the regular education classes and PE. ELL students with instructional aide support are immersed in language, reading, and the core curriculum.

RECOMMENDATION 16: The school will engage students' **families as partners** in the students' education.

Strategies

- Communicate positive news about students with their families through calls, e-mail, or notes from advisors.
- Include parents in development and assessment of their child's PPP.
- Invite families into the school to participate in student-led conferences.
- Schedule school events during a variety of work-friendly hours (e.g., evenings, weekends) to maximize family participation.
- Expand school newsletter content to include information about technology and other community resources available to families.
- Encourage family members to volunteer by developing a list of family member talents and skills and cross-checking it with a list of school needs.
- Embrace an understanding of family that includes the nontraditional family structures that exist in your school community and consistently use terminology that demonstrates that understanding.

Benefits

- Helps schools avail themselves of new and additional resources to support student success.
- Reduces parent/family isolation from the school.
- Increases student support during the time they are not in school.

Challenges

- Addressing the expressed interest of students to keep family members away from school involvement.
- Scheduling events so that families can attend may require overtime or trade-offs for staff.
- Getting family members to respond. Many may have had negative experiences when they were in school.
- Engaging families of immigrant children who may be afraid to participate because of their immigration status.
- Providing translation services for ELL families.

Progress Measures

- Document evidence of increased family contacts and participation of family in decisions about their child's school experiences.
- Demonstrate modifications of standard parent contact procedures to communicate with hard-to-contact parents/guardians.
- Record and compare the percentage of families attending school events and the percentage of parent volunteers active in the school community following increased contact with school personnel.
- Use a climate/culture survey to examine changes in mutual respect between the families and the school staff.

Recommendation 16 in Practice

Alvarado Intermediate School

Expectations for student achievement are communicated to parents through course descriptions, weekly progress reports for at-risk students, the Homework Hotline, parent information sessions, conferences, newsletters, the website, and other traditional routes.

Casey Middle School

Families are meaningfully involved in all aspects of the school:

- SIT—the School Improvement Team of parents and the principal meets monthly to monitor student achievement and well-being and help provide direction to the school.

- Casey Parent Group—meets monthly to focus on an education topic.

- All families are welcome to come to any meeting or be involved in any way; bilingual meetings and newsletters ensure communication and inclusiveness.

- PTA Adopt-a-Reader program matches enthusiastic parents and community members with struggling readers every week.

- Adopt-a-writer program meets in small groups to lead voluntary writers workshop groups outside of the classroom.

- Public Relations Task Force, including six parents and the district director of communications, prepared a PR plan for the year.

- Monthly bilingual parent meetings are held on parent-selected topics.

- Math Nights and Literacy Nights are held.

- The school offers adult education and recreation activities for families.

- ELL classes are offered in the evenings.

- The school has a staff member who serves as parent organizer to reach out to families.

- The school provides transportation, meals, childcare, and translation support so all families can attend school events.

- A PTA fall fundraiser dinner and silent auction brings the community together.

- AVID parent nights are held.

- School improvement team, PTA, and Casey Parent Group all meet on the same night, eat dinner together, and share agendas.

- A bilingual monthly newsletter is published.

- The bilingual community liaison as well as the counselor, interventionist, and school psychologist work diligently to help students and their families set and achieve goals.

Crabapple Middle School

Parents often serve as guest speakers in classrooms, volunteer in the media center and front office, chaperone fieldwork experiences and dances, assist with scoliosis screening, and serve on the local school advisory council. Other highlights include the following:

- The website provides up-to-date information for parents, including a curriculum link that hosts the unit plans for academic subjects by grade level. The goal is to provide parents and students with all the information they need for the students to be successful on all levels.

- The PTA focuses on parenting skills in the Love and Logic parenting program.

- Since moving to the block schedule in 1999, the school has hosted a Block Schedule Open House each year to offer parents an opportunity to visit and see a typical day on the block schedule. This has proven to be a very positive way for the parents to better understand the school's organizational structure.

- Each year the teachers hold numerous parent conferences. The school has conferences with more than 90 percent of the parents, either in person or via telephone at their request, during the annual fall conference period. Other conferences are held as requested by teachers or parents; conferences are required for students who are struggling academically at the end of first semester.

- As a part of the yearly transition program, the school hosts meetings for parents of rising sixth-graders to introduce them to the middle school program and programs for parents of eighth-graders to assist them in preparing for ninth grade placement.

Breaking Ranks in the Middle Recommendations

- The PTA offers Parent Life meetings throughout the school year on topics of interest for parents.

- The PTA also holds two meetings annually (fall and spring) in the county for parents participating in the voluntary Majority to Minority busing program. This is one way the school reaches out to parents who may not be able to come to evening programs.

Hopkins West Junior High School

The "Get Connected" program is intended to foster communication with families that traditionally would not be connected to the school. (By collaborating with a community-based program, families are able to use their state tax credit for education to participate in the program.) Other areas of family involvement include the following:

- The Hopkins School Success program to encourage preparation for college includes a parent component that helps families understand the process for what is hoped will be their child becoming the first generation to attend college.

- Math teachers conduct family math sessions.

- Monthly PIE (Parent Information Exchange) meetings are held to allow parents an opportunity to learn and share information on topics such as postsecondary planning, teenage sexual trends, chemical use among teens, and eating disorders.

- Parents coordinate and volunteer with each advisory group on the Eighth Grade Community Service Project.

Medea Creek Middle School

Mastery is the goal for all students. For example, in Humanities 6-7-8, standards are shared and sent home with each history and language arts unit. Ongoing communication with families on the achievement of standards takes the form of weekly notes home, frequent grade reports, e-mails and phone calls to parents, and parent conferences. Student self-assessment, with opportunities for two-way feedback from parents after major assessments, takes place in a number of ways. For example, students in all math and language arts classes set goals based on diagnostic tests that identify standards that have and have not been mastered, and these are sent home. Teachers' web pages also contain the standards each course is addressing. The sixth grade Friday notes sent to parents contain students' test scores, homework assignments, and upcoming lessons. The science classes follow a progression both in content and in the use of the scientific method. PE teachers have developed a rigorous curriculum containing flexible groupings. In math, students set individual goals and are offered a progression from sixth grade math to geometry. When asked, students overwhelmingly responded that they and their families have multiple sources for acquiring information and that the standards were made clear to them in most classes.

Saunders Middle School

Parents report that the dial-in homework hotline is an invaluable tool for them to help their child keep up with assignments. In addition, In Touch Online provides parents with Internet access to their child's grades on a daily basis. Teacher gradebooks are rolled into the In Touch system nightly. Parents get a password and can use it to check on grades, attendance, and student information. Students also access their grades, which gives them the opportunity to talk with a teacher and improve their performance.

RECOMMENDATION 17: The school community, which cannot be values-neutral, will advocate and model a set of core **values essential in a democratic and civil society.**

Strategies

- Establish structures and processes through which students participate in school decision making.

- Create a peer mediation program to involve students in fair and creative conflict resolution.

- Establish clear expectations, including rewards and consequences for compliance and noncompliance.

- Involve students in community-based projects and service learning projects.

- Provide opportunities for students to develop skills in decision making, critical thinking, and communication through advisory lessons, developmental guidance groups, and classroom activities.

Benefits

- Develops in students an understanding of citizenship values and responsibilities.

- Improves the learning climate, which should bring about greater student achievement.

Challenges

- Getting student buy-in; creating a climate of expectations that apply to all.

- Inspiring teachers to think of community-based or service learning projects and incorporate them in their curricula.

- Reinforcing school values at home.

- Answering skeptics who don't believe that schools should be teaching values.

Progress Measures

- Document evidence of both student and community engagement in formulating school vision, mission, and goals.

- Review discipline referral data to determine the effectiveness of student mediation.

- Show evidence of an increased number of students participating in student government and other school decision-making bodies, and in community involvement activities.

RECOMMENDATION 18: Schools, in conjunction with agencies in the community, will help coordinate the delivery of **physical and mental health as well as social services.**

Strategies

- Create and maintain a resource list of support agencies for use by all school staff members. Ensure that all understand how to appropriately refer students to agencies on the list for assistance.

- Establish relationships with community agencies.

- Invite local health centers to deliver programs that encourage students to take advantage of all health and social services available, and to deliver the services to students on campus.

Benefits

- Helps involve the community in the school.

- Supports teacher efforts to help students by providing links to professionals in mental health and social services.

- Decreases distractions from learning for students who might otherwise be preoccupied with health and other considerations.

- Enhances school climate of caring for student well-being.

- Improves attendance and may prevent early dropout.

- Helps families with heavy work schedules meet family needs more efficiently.

Challenges

- Developing a plan regarding confidentiality issues and permission/consent from families.

- Addressing language and cultural issues.

- Being sensitive to the social stigma attached to mental health and social services.

- Budgeting for increased costs of additional personnel and extended hours to build the operation.

- Dedicating staff to develop and maintain partnerships.

Progress Measures

- Use results of a climate survey to ascertain the degree of a sense of well-being among the students.

- Compile a list of students with physical and mental health concerns; provide increased services for these students and monitor absenteeism and performance over the school year.

- Track general student attendance, reporting statistics each quarter.

Recommendations 17 and 18 in Practice

Alvarado Intermediate

Each certificated staff member is trained to spot potential problems in adolescents, and students are informed of the wide range of services available. In addition, the Student Service Center is a safe haven and resource for students who need a trusted adult in whom to confide. The Center provides interventions and assistance to students and parents of students having difficulty in school. The following lend their expertise and contribute to an environment of student advocacy: school counselor, campus peace officer, guidance assistants and administrators, school nurse and health assistants (who are often called upon to support families who need special assistance), school psychologist, speech therapist, and resource teachers. In addition, Alvarado's community liaison helps economically disadvantaged families access resources such as clothing, school supplies, housing, transportation, meals, and medical, dental, and psychological services. Families benefit from support through counseling, bilingual parenting classes, local college outreach and recruitment, homeless-grant funds, and active parent associations.

In Their Own Words...

The following is the third of four school profiles. Each profile has been written from the personal perspective of the principal. The profiles are designed to show the comprehensive and interdependent nature of the reforms your school is being called upon to undertake. Although not all the changes each school has instituted will be appropriate for your school, the perspective of your colleagues should nevertheless be valuable and may form the basis of a discussion for your team. At the end of this profile, you will find a Q&A with the principal, followed by several questions to help lead your faculty or team through a discussion. For a protocol to help lead the text-based discussion, see Appendix 4.

Vision and Support Create a School to Watch

by Patsy Dean, Principal

School Profile 3

Upson-Lee Middle School

Thomaston, GA

1,258 students

Grade span 6–8

Less than 1 percent limited English speaking students

59 percent low socioeconomic

18 percent special education

For statistics, contacts, and other information about the school, go to www. principals.org/brim.

Practices to look for include

- *student-led conferences*
- *differentiated instruction*
- *teacher leadership*
- *collaboration to determine a vision*
- *integrating technology into instruction*
- *portfolios*
- *professional development and instructional coaches*

To be able to see progress, it is often necessary to look to the past. It is only through this perspective that we can see growth. Upson-Lee Middle School had been through five years of instability when I was appointed principal in 1997. The community had voted in 1992 to consolidate city and county school systems. The city system had a junior high school concept, and the county system, though designated a middle school, had only partially adapted to that concept. The physical merger into a middle school took place in 1994; in the next three years, three principals were appointed and then left. During those three years, the feelings of excitement and anticipation regarding the merger of two systems gave way to disillusionment and regret at the newly formed middle school. In short, I became the principal of a school in chaos. The staff as a whole had no common goals, no self-directed expectations, no structure, no firm educational concept, and, in truth, no voice. Students were performing below ability levels, were constantly fighting, and felt unsafe. Parents and community members viewed the school as too large, too unsafe, and too ill-equipped to offer quality education to our youth.

My first job was to connect the staff and the community to this new school and to the middle school concept. In an informal poll, teachers were asked their opinions on issues ranging from a master schedule to discipline policies. Random samplings of parents, students, and community members were surveyed concerning opinions of the educational program and other aspects of the school, and a suggestion box was established for these groups. That is not to say that I acted on every comment. A poll provides benefits beyond determining majority opinion; it also provides a quick snapshot of the people responding. From their responses, I understood where the parents, students, teachers, and community members were in their thinking and feelings about the school. From that, I determined how to approach the changes that had to occur. It was clear that morale, communication, safety, and public relations were the major problems that had to be addressed immediately in order to set the groundwork for the needed school improvement. Involving everyone in the improvement process and establishing clear lines of communication were my first two tasks. Team leader roles were expanded from that of liaison between administration and faculty to becoming part of a collaborative team, setting policies and procedures for the school to improve communication and morale. By the end of that first year, a steering committee had been formed, and we began research-driven improvement planning that would eventually lead to an exemplary school for all our students.

The focus that first year was on establishing the structure and management of the school; in fact, the structure set during that time remains in place now. The changes that led to a more effective and efficient day-to-day running of the school were not the difficult aspects of change. The really tough challenges of those first six years were the school reform changes dealing with improving student achievement. In fact, the majority of the staff welcomed the structure and much-improved communications. As we made the changes in the curriculum, instructional, and assessment programs, the culture of the school was reformed. The culture in our school today is such that high expectations are in place for all staff, students, and parents. Students' responsibility for their own learning and behavior has increased; parents are expected to be active partners in the day-to-day education of their children; professional learning is an integral part of every aspect of our improvement plan; and effective teaching is viewed by all of us as an evolutionary process of continuing growth. We are now a fully functioning learning community with a very tight-knit, supportive school family. Yet, this did not come easy. All of us increased the amount of time spent in planning and assessing. Furthermore, teachers gave up some autonomy and, for many, their comfort zone, to work and plan collaboratively. They had to learn to share materials and ideas; they had to learn to support and nurture not just their friends but all of their co-workers; and, they had to realize that only through targeted professional learning could we improve teaching and learning. As I discuss later in this essay, some could not adjust and left. But, rather than dwell on what we "gave up" to improve the school, I think we view it as what we "gave to" our students, school, and community and what has been given to us through this process. It really means a lot when you can look each day at what you are doing for the children who are our future and know that not only are you giving your best, but you have had a part in creating a place of learning where students can give their best.

By the spring of 1998, we had most of the procedures in place, had completed the first needs assessment, and were ready to begin the planning for school improvement. I knew going into the first steering retreat that the committee was strong in leadership but not in common vision. They lacked confidence in using their voice because they lacked experience with collaborative planning for school reform. Even though I had ideas for what would make our school better and what it needed to be, I wanted it to be a common vision, not something set by me. I wanted their voices first, because I knew that if I spoke initially of the vision I had, I would be setting the parameters. I wanted them to have this opportunity to ponder and reflect on what each one of them saw as the perfect school for our students. On the first day of the three-day retreat, I led the discussion by presenting "What are we doing right?" and "What are we doing wrong?" topics. I left the steering committee alone that afternoon so they could openly discuss what the vision should be for our school. Two hours later, when I returned, they had set a vision which was, in truth, more of the same. There was no real change of direction or focus. Why? They were concerned about money. They had been conditioned to restrict their goals because of lack of funding. I gave them a new assignment: Let me worry about the money, and you dream of the school you want to create.

We returned to school with that first school improvement plan and gave it to every staff member to review. We also left copies in the media center and issued an invitation to parents to come by the school to review it and make suggestions. Teachers who had never had a voice or a leadership role welcomed this new participation in the educational community. However, participation comes with a price: an increased workload. Having a voice also means doing one's part. The toughest initial challenge in our transition from a stagnant, low-nurturing environment to one where risk-takers were accepted, growth was expected, and students' needs came first was a confrontation with a basic human instinct: resistance to change. By the end of my third year as principal, more than 20 teachers had left Upson-Lee Middle School as a result of the changes— some complaining that the demands were too high, the work was too hard, or the expectations were unrealistic. School systems in small communities wrestle with political influence and interference, and complaints from staff members sometimes find a sympathetic ear among elected board members. A few of the disgruntled did speak to board members, but our board had (and still has) a firm belief in and commitment to improving student achievement. As principals, we understand that teacher turnover may be a partner to transition and that we must stand before the board and community and expect their trust in our leadership and decision-making ability. At ULMS, we received the support of our board and that of the community. We weathered the exodus and even welcomed the opportunity to find teachers who would embrace our commitment to doing the work. I know that my initial reputation was one of a hard-nosed, focused, driven, and relentless worker with unrealistic expectations for others to do the same—a principal who was hard to work for. Over time, the staff began to speak of me this way: "As long as you do your job, she cannot do enough for you and will take care of you. She will support you if she believes in your ability and efforts, even when it may put her at odds with the political realm." Also, they appreciated that, because of my leadership style and personality, I addressed individual behavior and did not make blanket criticisms and decrees to the entire staff because one or two individuals needed correction. My enthusiasm for education, my firm belief in the middle school concept, and my commitment to this school family led others to want to believe in what we could do if we all worked together with a common vision and took one well-planned step at a time.

A positive energy thrives at ULMS as a result of visionary and innovative leadership and teamwork, dedicated teachers, and students who benefit from the support of the staff and the community. "I am capable, I am important, and I influence what happens to me," is the creed repeated each day to guide staff and students as a learning community striving toward high academic achievement. Although ULMS serves more than 1,200 students, a close-knit, supportive atmosphere defines our school. An evaluator for the Lighthouse Schools to Watch award noted, "Everyone knows the expectations as they enter the building—students, staff, parents, community and school board members." There is a contextual message at ULMS that thinking is valued and that everyone must do his or her part. We have structured our school in a way that teachers are free to teach and plan. This means we have hired support personnel to do some of the noninstructional tasks that teachers were formerly performing, such as collecting monies, running copies, and designing schedules. Some of our most innovative and effective programs have begun with someone saying, "I know that this is probably impossible, but what if we…." We work hard to create an atmosphere that nurtures committed professionals who are risk-takers when it comes to meeting the needs of our students. We never let fear of failure or hard work stop us from doing what we feel is best for our students.

Results of Reform

Today's ULMS is far removed from the chaotic, floundering school of 1997. We have gone through many changes and wonderful experiences as we have become a model school with a focus on student-centered learning and teaching. ULMS is a nurturing environment for an adolescent; we serve the whole child by guiding students educationally, emotionally, and socially through the changes that naturally occur at this age. Successes are celebrated and used to encourage greater growth as we share with students, staff, parents, and the community. Our top priority is students, and every decision made hinges on the question, "What is best for the student?" The past eight years have brought dramatic and positive changes, as well as recognition and awards, to ULMS. Change at ULMS is still guided by research, data analysis, goal-setting, and a shared vision. Our goals have been achieved through strategic planning that has led to increased expectations of teachers and students, extensive and targeted professional development, student awareness of metacognition and motivation theory, a partnership with parents and community stakeholders, and implementation of innovative educational programs and methods. After receiving regional accreditation in 1998, we began a school improvement process that led to our designation as one of Georgia's eight Lighthouse Schools to Watch in 2005. In the summary report of the Lighthouse visiting team, it was noted that "the school's mission and its driving values are closely tied to academic achievement that is apparent in a climate of high expectations." This year, we were chosen as one of 14 Georgia schools (out of 60 nominated) to serve as a site for the Georgia Partnership for Excellence in Education's annual Bus Trip Across Georgia, which focused on schools that have built strong leadership capacity and made great strides in closing achievement gaps. Legislators, state and federal educators, and business/community members from across the state visited the classrooms of every teacher in the school. As I was working with the instructional coaches to determine which classes to send the guests into for their 20-minute visits, it struck me that as a result of our seven-year focus on effective teaching and our strategic support of new teachers, I could put any of the more than 70 teachers on the visitation schedule. That was a "wow" moment for me. I know my staff and will tell anyone how awesome they are with the teaching and care of our students. But the idea that I could send state department dignitaries and business members into the classrooms of novice teachers who had been teaching only six weeks was a wonderful revelation to me and a validation of how strong our instructional program had become.

In the current school year, we have again made a bold step toward enhancing education for every child by designating every class offered to sixth graders as "advanced." Again asking the question "What's best for the student," we decided that providing every child with the educational foundation to have a real choice regarding postsecondary education was the answer. That may seem obvious, but the truth in our community, and in many other communities, is that tracking students by ability was a long-standing tradition. Very few students of our community in any grade level choose a school option other than ULMS. As a result, our students come from widely varying socioeconomic backgrounds. As I reviewed the new Georgia Performance Standards, I realized that some of our students were not going to meet standards in math performance unless they had the opportunity to be in a learning environment in which their peers could help think through the problems and model learning. In discussing the issue with the math teachers, I proposed that we end our system of tracking students. We had made strides toward that goal previously, but this would be the final step. Language and literature teachers wanted to be a part of this plan (which still includes our gifted literature program). In June 2005, I attended the National Forum of Schools to Watch in Washington, D.C., and volunteered to participate in the topic discussion of tracking. I met an administrator who had ended the process and sought her advice, which was to strike the word "tracking" from our presentations and speak instead of creating enhanced educational opportunities for all students. In July 2005, during the parent orientation for incoming sixth graders, I announced that every sixth grader would be enrolled in advanced classes. Parents were encouraged to seek help for their children if they saw them struggle as a result of the higher demands in the classrooms. We would be prepared to help any students who fell behind. It is noteworthy that nearly four months into the school year, we've heard no complaints from parents or students. Our students are meeting these higher expectations, and so are our teachers. We have maintained our commitment to keep the academic rigor in the advanced classes in every academic area in sixth grade, and next year we will make the same transition in the seventh grade; then will complete the process with the eighth grade. We are excited that we are continuing to raise the bar, even a step ahead of state requirements. This is how it should be. Our educational goal is to give every student the opportunity to choose postsecondary education; to meet that goal, every student must be provided with high-level curriculum and instruction.

As part of our reform, we initially worked with Georgia's Quality Core Curriculum (QCC) as a guide for instruction. We are now phasing in Georgia Performance Standards that are a result of the response to an audit of the QCC done by Phi Delta Kappa three years ago. This stronger curriculum establishes the minimum standards and an alignment with state assessments. This year we are in year two of the implementation, with the new standards in all language and reading classes, in sixth grade math, and in sixth and seventh grade science. The performance standards include the content standard (the concept), suggested performance tasks, sample student work, and teacher commentary on the work. The state training included two of the works that we use as guides: Robert Marzano's materials and Grant Wiggins's and Jay McTighe's *Understanding by Design*. As has often been the case, we are integrating these changes fairly easily (as compared with schools that were not familiar with the current research). To explain how we got to this point, I have outlined our first initiatives, the strategies we used to reach those first goals, and the impact of reaching those and other goals. There is no way to include all our initiatives; therefore, I am detailing our most successful initiatives, as well as some of our most current. Included in these are technology integration, assessment, professional learning, curriculum design and instructional practices, and supplementary programs.

Technology Integration

Our first school improvement plan included a technology goal that focused on improving teacher and student competency in technology. In 1998, we had one computer in each classroom, 30 typewriters in the keyboarding classroom, no computer labs, and no networking. Since then, we have evolved to a fully networked school, with a ratio of one computer for every two students and an almost frightening reliance on e-mail and other communication programs. Every academic classroom is equipped with wall-mounted electronic ACTIVboards, ceiling-mounted multimedia projectors, document cameras, surround sound, DVD/VCR combination players, wireless keyboards, remote presenters, and integrated cable television. This level of technology does not come cheaply. Overcoming the challenge of initial technology expense and continuous upgrade costs led us to seek grant funding, system and community support, some creative budgeting, and a strategic plan for replacing outdated hardware. Going from "target-assisted" Title I to "schoolwide" in 1998 created greater flexibility in spending and allowed us to spend the money on all students. This is how we began to build the technology program that now exists to enhance the learning of our students. We have written and received three technology grants from the state in the past eight years for a total of approximately $250,000. Initially, some of the state's lottery funds were earmarked for technology, and we benefited greatly from that money. Our community is very supportive of the educational programs and passed a special local-option sales tax three years ago that funded the multimedia classrooms in all our schools. Other funding came from community grants such as Community Enterprises, Inc. (a local philanthropic foundation) and various company grants.

Advancing the level of technology use brought another challenge in those early years. In order to allow teachers to focus on planning and teaching—a major priority of mine—we needed to take the pressure off the teachers to keep up with the rapidly advancing world of technology. This problem was solved by hiring an instructional technology coordinator (ITC), whose original role was to assist our teachers in identifying the appropriate software, become an expert in the use of the software, and then teach our educational staff and students to use it. Since that time, this position has grown to include continually evaluating the effective integration of many forms of technology into the classroom curriculum using observation and surveys and coordinating professional development accordingly. Staff development needs were also determined using the LoTI (Levels of Technology Implementation) instrument. Additionally, a modified version of the LoTI instrument was created for use by the ITC while observing the integration of technology in individual teachers' classrooms. The purpose of these observations was not to evaluate teachers but rather to identify strengths and weaknesses in order to improve overall teacher effectiveness. Further support was provided by hiring a fulltime technology specialist (a position that was later funded by the state for all school systems) to help with troubleshooting hardware and software problems so that teachers could deliver instruction as planned.

Technology use is now woven into the fabric of our instruction. In an effort to increase our emphasis on 21st century learning skills, we strive to create an environment that fosters that learning. We have consistently found that teachers are using technology to challenge students in higher order thinking skills and to engage students as active learners. Students are taught to use 21st century tools and to be lifelong learners. As outlined in "A Report and Mile Guide for 21st Century Skills" by the Partnership for 21st Century Skills, we teach students to use the tools they will use in the everyday world. Science classes participate annually in the JASON Project, an online connection to the expert in the field. We designed one of our supplementary math programs around Smartmath (iLearnMath) software, which is a web-based math curriculum. Math teachers can easily pull a chart or pie graph to the ACTIVboard screen and engage students in the creation of a data chart. Social studies teachers often use video streaming and flip charts that include interactive maps to enhance their lessons. In language classes, the ACTIVboards and document cameras allow students to compare their own work with high-quality writing examples, and to edit their work and other samples. We are currently implementing wireless math classes in the sixth grade and equipping each classroom with 28 laptops as part of a state 1:1 wireless initiative for which we received grant funding.

In addition to these initiatives, we took the following action steps over the past eight years to help us reach the technology goal of improved teacher and student competency in technology that was contained in our first school improvement plan:

- Creation of four networked computer labs with various hardware and software. These labs are available on a first-come, first-served basis for use by teachers and students to complete project-based learning activities.

- Design and implementation of two technology connections classes: (1) a semester-long computer skills class that all students must take in which they learn keyboarding, Microsoft Word, Access, and Excel; and (2) a technology lab in which students study other applications of technology such as robotics, graphic design, electronics, digital imaging, and multimedia.

- Creation of Web Design Clubs in which students learn how to create web pages.

- Training of students in various software programs, including Inspiration, Perfect Copy, the Microsoft Office Suite (including PowerPoint), TI-84 Calculator, Smart-Math, PrimeTime Math, and Brainchild.

- Full staff training in In-Tech and, more recently, ACTIVboard use. Training is followed up with mini-training sessions before and after school, during teacher planning periods, and during faculty meetings.

- Enhanced student presentation skills through use of interactive electronic white boards.

- Training of students and parents on the use of the Internet for researching.

- Creation of multimedia presentations to demonstrate knowledge gained in academic areas.

- Creation of student projects for entry into the school Media Festival.

- Delivery of distance learning opportunities with the Georgia Marine Extension Service, Zoo Atlanta, and Fernbank Science Center.

- Participation in hands-on learning activities such as the JASON Project and Quest Expeditions, which expose students to real-life learning situations.

We have evolved into a highly technological school, as evidenced by the students' abilities to work independently on classroom assignments, projects, and presentations. Our students are now very savvy with computer use and even some basic troubleshooting.

We learned quickly that we needed to add a focus on the effective, seamless integration of technology into the instruction. We conducted a needs assessment of professional learning, facility needs, and software and hardware needs, and created a strategic three-year plan to reach our goal. We decided to send five teachers to a state educational technology training center (Macon ETTC) to be trained as a redelivery team for a 50-hour instructional technology integration class to be taught at our school to all staff members. Within two years, the initial staff was trained and new staff members were trained as they were hired. This method of redelivery allowed us the flexibility to tailor the training to the unique needs of our individual teachers. Having the training on site also encouraged a close relationship between our teachers and the instructional technology coordinator, as lessons integrating technology were planned and delivered. Our teachers and students are so adept in the use of technology as a teaching tool that we were selected by Macon State College from 24 systems to send a team of students to Capitol Tech Day to showcase technology for our legislators. Our students were so impressive using the ACTIVboard that legislators and state education leaders were calling others to come see what they could do.

Assessment Practices

We have grown immensely in our use of data analysis to improve teaching and student achievement. We evaluate all facets of student performance using test scores and system, school, and individual student data. We are using data more and more in our program evaluation and in planning programs for students and teachers. For example, by using a spreadsheet of individual data (special education designation, co-curricular participation, previous program participation, etc.) and cumulative test scores on each student, we can determine which remediation/acceleration program a student needs each year. I analyze each individual test score for any student who has failed or nearly failed any portion of the state criterion-referenced test in fourth grade through seventh grade and review other pertinent information in order to personalize the learning opportunities for every student. In previous years, we trained parents to interpret test and performance data. In a pilot project this year, we are training the students in all grades to interpret their own data and further training sixth grade students to share the data with their parents in student-led conferences. As with other initiatives that we have implemented, the student-led conference initiative will be implemented over a three-year period as we train each incoming sixth grade class.

We learned quickly to use data analysis and opinion surveys to assess our progress on each improvement initiative. Each year, we begin the steering committee retreat by looking at what's working, what's not working, and what we can do to make this more effective. There are times when we set an initiative aside, but very seldom. Most of the time, we tweak our plan until it works, remaining focused on research-proven strategies that fit and meet the needs of our students. Initially, we used the National Study of School Evaluation guides and some self-made surveys. Now, through our research and growth, we use our data analysis, our knowledge of the initiatives and our students, and less formal program evaluations to guide us.

The changes in evaluation and assessment of student learning were slower to move forward than other assessment initiatives, partly because I understood how territorial teachers felt about these topics. I decided the best way to approach this "sacred cow" was to move the staff forward first through research and study, so they would be willing participants in the initiative. I had to tame my own impatient nature in this process. As an added challenge, professional learning requirements and opportunities had been limited at ULMS to only the state-required 10 hours every five years, which weren't necessarily specific to teaching assignments. This had to change in order to move the school improvement process toward more effective teaching. I had been in a class during my specialist program that focused on the current brain-compatible learning and teaching strategies and knew that this information would begin the discussion and information-seeking that was needed for teachers to evaluate their assessment practices. Working with our regional education service agency (RESA) staff, a two-year professional learning program that focused on brain-compatible learning strategies, multiple intelligences, and emotional intelligence was established for ULMS educators. I never mentioned evaluation and assessment but instead talked about improving teaching and learning. I also never mentioned that the training was mandatory but simply said, "This is a class that we will all take sometime in the next two years." Out of this first professional learning initiative grew the changes we made in evaluation of students. We established homework guidelines and a standard weighted grading chart for each academic area, so that we had more consistency across the school in how students were evaluated. The teachers were ready for this change, because they had participated in the professional learning, and while I set standards and percentage ranges, they had a voice in the specific ranges for their subject area.

Granted, many of us still are not in favor of the current number grading system, but we have decided to approach a fairer system through changes in our assessment practices. As all of us went through a study of Robert Marzano's *Classroom Instruction That Works* to improve instructional practices, more and more of the staff began to see the need to discuss how we were assessing our students' learning and how we were using those assessments to inform our teaching. Through experiences and training with GLISI (Georgia Leadership Initiative for School Improvement) and ASCD, we have expanded our knowledge and expectation for changing our practices. This year, we are studying Anne Davies's book, *Making Classroom Assessment Work.* All staff may not be ready for this next step forward, but there are enough teacher leaders at ULMS who are ready that this will be an easy and successful transition.

Some people would argue that assessment and evaluation for student learning should be the first major initiative in a school's transition from ineffective to effective, but this approach has worked for us because teachers became educated about the need for change rather than being handed a decree from the administration. Evaluation and assessment are among the most sensitive issues in an environment in which teachers have traditionally been given total control. I truly believe that part of turning around the morale and direction of our school required all staff to become active learners of current research and evaluators of their own practices. In turn, we created an environment in which teachers model effective change processes for students as they set high goals, reach those goals, and are proud of their accomplishments.

Better Teaching Leads to Increased Learning

The higher expectations for the students required a higher level of effort and performance from the teachers. The initiatives in our improvement plan are used annually to help determine staff development needs and direction. We began with the brain-compatible strategy training noted above, but that truly was just the beginning. You may wonder, "How did she influence all of the teachers to participate in this level of training that continues to this day?" Well, I have found that the best way to approach an initiative that has to occur is to simply assume that everyone will see the need and participate. The culture at ULMS is such that teachers now expect the professional learning support that will help them implement an initiative.

Teachers at ULMS annually participate in an average of 75 hours of targeted professional development including, but not limited to, the following:

- In-Tech: A state training initiative for integrating technology seamlessly into instruction.

- Reading Renaissance: A three-day training and follow-up on reading strategies for the adolescent. All staff participated.

- Reading and Writing in the Middle Grades: A 50-hour class that the state required at one time. Thirty of our teachers completed this class.

- Test data analysis: Delivered by RESA personnel and designed to train teachers in the training of parents to interpret student performance data. We are expanding this training to include training students to interpret and follow their longitudinal performance data by subject and domain (objective). Students will keep these data sheets along with individual goals for improvement in the portfolios that they keep in each academic area.

- Learning-focused schools and Robert Marzano's *Classroom Instruction That Works:* Current analysis of mega-research done on effective teaching and learning. Our staff has completed more than 100 hours of training in each of these.

- Collaborative training: Any teacher involved in a co-teaching model for inclusion of special education students in the regular environment is trained in effective strategies.

- JASON Project: A science/social studies program that connects students to professionals in the field during projects.

- Learning-focused strategies workshops: These are designed to review relevant research as teachers design units. Some of these are summer classes and others are held on release days during the school year.

- Differentiation training: ASCD tapes on Instructional Strategies for the Differentiated Classroom were used last summer as a support for all sixth grade teachers and all science and social studies teachers as we implemented advanced classes for all in those areas.

- Georgia Performance Standards training: A current initiative to implement our state's newly adopted standards. Instructional coaches receive training with the state and redeliver to curriculum study groups for each academic area.

- Wireless classroom training: At present, this training is for sixth grade math teachers who are participating in a school-based action research program for one-to-one technology teaching.

- REAL math training: All math teachers, special education and regular education, are participating in this Research-based Engaged Authentic Learning class that was developed and is being taught by Dr. Vicki Rogers and her staff at Macon Educational Technology Training Center.

- Classroom management consultation: A school-based initiative in which a consultant, Cheryl Savage of Terry Alderman's Resources for Professionals, works with identified teachers to improve management and/or the classroom climate.

- All teachers at ULMS are members of curriculum study groups. Through these groups, teachers are given opportunities to collaborate with others, present and share new ideas and strategies, and have a voice in making curricular decisions.

To carry this one step further, literature and language teachers also meet to share student writing. Through guided questions, the teachers discuss and analyze student work as a means of improving their own practices.

A major component of in-house professional learning is led by the instructional coaching staff for each academic area. All teachers receive guidance from these facilitators of effective teaching. This highly effective component of our professional learning program is one of the most complimented and emulated initiatives at ULMS. It has been replicated in several schools in Georgia, and many other schools have requested our school-developed job description for this position. Originally, these coaches were hired to ensure implementation of all of the above-mentioned professional learning initiatives. Because there was a shift in teaching and how we did it, we felt that teachers needed more support and that we needed assurance that what we said was being done in our school improvement plan was actually occurring in the classroom. Along with administrators, instructional coaches conduct informal observations in and outside classrooms. These observations can range from 5–10 minutes to a full class period. The instructional coaches play key roles in supporting and implementing new strategies for effective teaching and are relied upon by all teachers.

ULMS instructional coaches are master teachers in their subject areas. Some may argue that the best teachers should be left in the classroom and that funding can only support a less experienced instructor for these positions. However, if a school needs a coach who can truly improve teaching, it needs someone the rest of the staff respects and knows has the ability to teach. By selecting the best of the best as instructional coaches, we ensure that every teacher in every academic level has the opportunity to improve teaching practices. Another benefit of master teachers as instructional coaches is their ability to interpret student reactions in the classroom and identify student learning needs that might not be readily apparent otherwise. In hiring a master teacher as an instructional coach, one very important characteristic of that person must be that the coach is capable of delivering constructive criticism to peers and doing the follow-through necessary to improve instructional techniques of individual teachers.

These instructional coaches also serve as my ear—not that they repeat every grumble they hear, but when they know an important undercurrent is developing, they inform me. There is a caveat: In the beginning, the relationship between the instructional coaches and teachers treaded on becoming a complaint desk situation. I had to let instructional coaches know early that although my leadership creates an open, team-oriented environment with all staff, students' needs come first. I welcome any problem-solving discussion that will improve our service to our students, but random complaints are not productive, and it is not the role of the instructional coach to hear or deliver them to the administration.

Another important professional development program is a unique use of planning time in which teachers meet twice weekly in grade-level meetings within each discipline, including the special education teacher assigned to that grade. These meetings are invaluable in coordinating teaching across teams. The groups prioritize curriculum objectives, establish time lines, and evaluate data, as well as collaboratively plan unit lessons. Because we teach from self-developed units instead of textbooks with a pre- and posttest for each unit, our teachers use this time to review the components of the prewritten unit they will need to meet the needs of their students.

They discuss strategies and conduct collaborative reviews of student work to inform their teaching. This is one of the strongest initiatives that we have found to integrate new teachers into our program or to improve all teaching. A beginning teacher can come on board and have the benefit of a master teacher's experience and knowledge twice each week in collaborative planning. Likewise, master teachers can learn new strategies from their peers. Teachers who resisted this collaboration in the beginning now tout it as one of the most helpful initiatives in our school. When we first implemented the program, I knew that the few who would be resistant were the ones who most needed collaboration. Therefore, with the instructional coaches, we developed a peer assessment tool—a one-to-five Likert scale—that each collaborative team member completes on his or her peers at the end of each month. This assessment tool covers participation level, promptness, and attendance. The assessments are reviewed by the instructional coach, who then deals with problems. I never see these assessments and have only heard once in the past two years of a situation that required my involvement.

Curriculum Design and Instructional Practices

Our students are offered a comprehensive basic curriculum to meet their individual needs as well as an opportunity for exploring special interests both within the curriculum and in student activities. Each student takes language, literature, math, social studies, and science. The average class size in these academic classes is 25. Science and social studies classes are heterogeneously grouped. An Extended Learning Time of 30 minutes is offered each day for all students. Selected students who did not pass their previous state tests are scheduled for math and/or reading remediation and acceleration during this time. Other opportunities for student remediation/acceleration outside of the regular school day include two programs offered and staffed by certified math and reading teachers, an after-school tutoring program, and a summer school program. Special needs students who qualify are given services in a collaborative setting in literature, language, math, science, and social studies. Resources classes are provided for our special-needs students.

Teaching strategies increasingly transfer responsibility for learning and goal-setting onto the student, and students are taught the principles of Bloom's Taxonomy and brain-based learning. Every sixth grade student takes a multiple intelligence inventory that is then shared with instructors and the student from year to year. Rubrics are known to and produced by students and employed in our classrooms. Reading and writing exercises engage students in critical-thinking skills by focusing on student responses to student-selected literature. Classroom dialogue encourages students to take positions on story-related issues and justify the reasons for those positions. Essay writing across the curriculum further develops students' critical-thinking skills. Project-based learning and performance tasks occur in all subject areas. These include, but are not limited to, an annual student-authored cookbook featuring recipes students gather during interviews with senior citizen family members and friends, and a required project and research paper for the annual science fair.

Reading and Language Arts

In terms of evaluating and improving student performance, we first looked at reading and writing scores, both key foundations of learning. With an estimated 25 percent community adult illiteracy rate, student achievement in literacy is a challenging goal in

Upson County. In 2000, Georgia's eighth-graders took the reformed Middle Georgia Writing Assessment (MGWA) with disappointing results. At ULMS, 75 percent of the regular education and 21 percent of special needs students passed the test, compared with 76 percent and 26 percent statewide. ULMS student scores in every subsequent MGWA testing cycle are a testament to the ability of leadership and staff to identify and implement successful educational solutions. In 2004, 95 percent of ULMS regular education and 74 percent of special needs students passed, outpacing statewide passing scores of 85 percent and 41 percent.

Reading and language scores are rising:

- From sixth to eighth grade, Accelerated Reader logs show students annually move upward an average of two reading zones.

- During 2000–02, students increased Criterion-Referenced Competency Tests (CRCT) reading scores from 73 percent passing as sixth-graders to 83 percent as eighth-graders. During 2001–03, students increased these scores from 70 percent passing as sixth-graders to 83 percent passing as eighth-graders. Special needs students achieved an 18 percent gain in reading scores from 2002 as sixth-graders (33% passing) to 2004 as eighth-graders (51% passing). The gender subgroups (male/female) scored in reading 74 percent and 87 percent, respectively, as sixth-graders and 84 percent and 88 percent as eighth-graders. The black/white subgroups scored 68 percent and 90 percent in 2002 as sixth-graders and 76 percent and 92 percent as eighth-graders.

- During 2002–04, sixth-graders increased CRCT language scores from 72 percent passing to 84 percent as eighth-graders, and special needs students achieved an 18 percent gain in language scores from 2002 as sixth-graders (27% passing) to 2004 as eighth-graders (45% passing). The gender subgroups (male/female) scored in language 63 percent and 81 percent, respectively, as sixth-graders and 80 percent and 89 percent as eighth-graders. The black/white subgroups scored in language respectively 62 percent and 79 percent in 2002 as sixth-graders and 74 percent and 90 percent as eighth-graders.

- In the past eight years, our media center has increased circulation from 25 books per day to approximately 450 books per day.

Literacy strategies that work at ULMS include the following:

- Benchmark testing in writing for all students establishes the same testing environment as the state test. Essays are sent to the state's testing agency. All students receive annotated writing results with comments used by teachers to facilitate student assessment. These results become part of their language portfolios. Benchmark testing is also used in reading.

- To ensure consistent instruction, modified when necessary, student-and-teacher-selected writings are placed in portfolios, which follow students year to year. Last year, we worked with the elementary school to begin this portfolio in the first grade and with the high school to continue it through the students' senior year.

- All students perform intense repetitive drills in power writing to increase and refine composition skills.

- Eighth grade students write 15 graded essays per year aligned with the state scoring rubric.

- Students compare their work with examples of high-quality work through the use of document cameras and ACTIVboards.

- Instructional coaches in writing, reading, and language provide support and curriculum guidance to teachers.

- Separate reading and language arts classes allow highly qualified teachers to provide a longer block of teaching time —110 minutes. Language and reading teachers plan cooperatively twice weekly within grade levels to coordinate instruction. Students engage in paired and buddy reading, choral reading, echo reading, and so on. Round robin reading is strongly discouraged.

- ULMS has shifted from teacher-selected to student-selected literature for practicing reading strategies outside the classroom.

- Instruction includes using Project Insight novels to stress critical thinking and incorporate the five strands of language arts.

- We support reading skills in all areas by using *Nine Good Habits for All Readers*. We have shifted from an emphasis solely on literature to a combination of reading skills and literature. Reading strategies are explicitly taught and modeled not only in the literature classrooms, but across the curriculum.

- Vocabulary instruction includes Greek and Latin roots, affixes, and cognates. A master list is divided into a three-year progression, so that students will have studied the entire list by the end of the third year.

- Our Career Education Institute lab—a reading lab for nonreaders and ELLs—and assistive technology lab are helpful with instruction of our students with disabilities, who make up 18 percent of our student body.

- Writing across the curriculum is implemented with students writing at least two writing assignments each month in all five subject areas. In each subject area, the teacher and student select two of these writings per semester to be included in the writing portfolio that is passed from grade to grade.

Mathematics/Science/Social Studies

One of our initial goals in the first school improvement plan was for students to demonstrate effective problem-solving skills in math. We now have an overall math performance goal. Our strategies have included the following:

- Formed curriculum study groups.

- Wrote learning-focused units.

- Used software, including Smart Math, Brainchild, CCC, Geometers sketchpad, and Zap-a-Graph.

- Administered CRCT practice tests.

- Correlated curriculum and instruction to National Council of Teachers of Mathematics standards.

- Purchased and used high-level-thinking skills workbooks.

- Worked in collaborative pairs.

- Offered after-school tutoring.

- Served special-needs students in collaborative classes.

- Formed math extension classes.

- Used writing across the curriculum.

- Developed authentic assessments.

- Incorporated mnemonic devices, graphic organizers, classifying, and so on.

- Used AIMS (Activities Integrating Math and Science).

- Incorporated performance tasks into each unit.

- Added an instructional math coach.

- Designed programs for remediation/acceleration for identified learners.

- Employed focused staff development.

We used various data and instruments to assess the effectiveness of the math strategies. Using the CRCT, our overall math scores improved from 61 percent of sixth-graders passing in 2000 to 66 percent of eighth-graders passing in 2002. CRCT eighth grade scores for regular education students went from 47 percent passing in 2000 to 69 percent passing in 2004, while the state math scores went from 57 percent passing in 2000 to 73 passing in 2004. Our eighth grade students with disabilities achieved a 22 percent gain in CRCT math performance from 2000 to 2004.

Math remains our greatest need area and is receiving an intense focus; we have adopted the Learning Focused Strategies Model using Robert Marzano's *What Works in Schools* and *Classroom Instruction that Works*. Our current involvement in the REAL training mentioned above will train our math teachers to deliver concept-based instruction with more skill and knowledge of the content and the learner.

Math and science instructional programs at ULMS are designed to engage the student in concept development, acquisition and application of skills, analysis, and evaluation. Our recent needs assessment indicated a need for more authentic learning activities and simulations in these areas. All students at ULMS complete a science fair project either in a small group or individually as an interdisciplinary project. We begin teaching the scientific process in the sixth grade, where all projects are completed in groups at school, in a teacher-facilitated process. In seventh and eighth grades, the students complete science fair projects according to state science fair guidelines. Our students do well at regional and state fairs. Furthermore, science students participate annually in the JASON Project, a year-long online program that connects students to a team of scientists and an expedition. This year the study is about Mars; last year, we studied the disappearing wetlands. Our science teachers are becoming more adept with small-group labs, such as the current sixth grade simulation lab on Katrina and the flooding of New Orleans. In earth science, students use Pasco's Probeware and the Explorer GLX sensors for measurement and graphing—hydrolysis, pH, water quality, rain, heat of water versus land, and so on. Our life science classes are using live specimens to study the behavior of organisms.

In another effort to foster 21st century learning, our science and social studies classes use trips outside the school to enhance learning. A project in life science last year resulted in a group of students working on the Flint River to assess water quality and organisms living in the river. Our sixth-graders recently completed a tour of the local wastewater plant, where they learned how wastewater is filtrated into usable water. In 2004, the seventh grade science classes attended the DNA exhibit at Fernbank Science Museum and an African artifacts exhibit at the High Museum. During a study of the Civil War, our eighth grade students visit Andersonville State Park, where captured

Yankee soldiers were held. Our Western Europe study will begin with a bagpipe group coming into the school to perform for the students.

Connections/Supplementary Programs

In addition to academic classes, our students complete rotations in PE and connections programs. A semester of the PE/health curriculum is required for all students. In an effort to encourage physical fitness, we have added the President's Physical Fitness Program to our PE curriculum. Our connections classes are a semester in length. They include a foreign culture program consisting of French, German, Japanese, and Spanish; four vocational classes consisting of agricultural science, family and consumer science, keyboarding and word processing, and a technology lab; and a fine arts program consisting of art, band, chorus, and general music. Other connections classes include geography, two academic extension classes in math reading for skill development, and a leadership/service class for the eighth grade peer helpers.

In our pursuit of high achievement for all students, in 2001–02 ULMS incorporated a reading connections class and a math connections class into the curriculum to provide opportunities during the regular school day to remediate and accelerate students who need improvement in those areas. Using Title I funding, we added a math teacher, who works only with identified students in SmartMath, and a reading teacher, who teaches reading strategies. Performance data on these students have proven these programs to be effective and have shown us that even when a student who has previously failed the CRCT passes strongly as a result of the intervention, another year of support in at least an acceleration program is needed. Another opportunity during the regular school day to provide remediation and acceleration for these students is ELT, a 30-minute class called Extended Learning Time. During the first nine weeks of school, we use this time to teach all students units on brain research and thinking processes, study skills, how to succeed in middle school, and motivation theory. Teachers and instructional coaches developed these research-based units, which are taught by all academic teachers. During the second and third nine weeks, we assign students to math and reading ELT classes based on the student data analysis of performance, mainly on the state assessment. These classes have a low student-teacher ratio and provide skill-based remediation with a preview of upcoming material. The remaining students attend ELT in language, science, and social studies on a three-week rotation. This time can be used for extension of the required classroom learning. We offer an after-school program that focuses mainly on helping with current assignments and concepts. In an effort to catch students before they fail, some teams are piloting a study hall initiative to catch the students who are failing two or more subjects at mid-term of each grading period. Each teacher on a five-member team gives up one planning period each week for four weeks to work with the identified students to help with the acquisition of concepts; the student gives up his or her connections class for that time. All of these programs have proven beneficial as we continue to close achievement gaps and raise the performance levels of all subgroups. Our students talk to visitors about the support that teachers give them in the learning process; they explain how they are encouraged to redo assignments to achieve mastery and how they can always find teachers who are willing to help them.

As evidenced in the language and reading curriculum outline, some of our most impressive gains in student performance have been made with our students with disabilities, who comprise approximately 18 percent of our student population. Our special education program has been restructured and has become an integrated part of our plan for excellence:

- In 1997, expectations for students with disabilities were much lower than those for regular education students, and special education students were not receiving all instruction in grade level curriculum and were seldom issued books. Now we deliver grade level curriculum to every student and set high expectations for all students, regardless of disability. They receive textbooks just as regular education students do. This was a major paradigm shift for the student, teacher, and special education program. I met some resistance but stuck to the belief that "whatever is best for the student" would determine our direction. I must note that the resistance came not from a lack of caring for the student, but from a long-standing belief that instruction for students with disabilities should meet the grade level performance of the student. How could we ask a student with a disability to do the same work as a child who did not have a disability? Part of the shift had to be in our belief that all children can learn when they are given opportunities. Although we were a step ahead in beginning to change this practice with the support of our local special education director, our state's education reform act and No Child Left Behind (NCLB) requirements have given this and other special education reform initiatives credence and urgency.

- Scheduled times for resource classes were not necessarily aligned with the grade level master schedule, which meant that students with disabilities were often in the halls for 5–10 minutes waiting for class change or had to enter a class as it ended. Not only did this create an opportunity for misbehavior, it identified the student to his or her peers as a student with disabilities and caused self-esteem issues. As we all know, no adolescent wants to appear different unless it is his or her choice. We devised a master schedule that allowed as much flexibility as possible for instructional blocks of time and aligned the resource class times with the teams at that grade level. No longer do you see special education students waiting in the hall for class changes. Their time is as valuable as every other student's time.

- When students with disabilities were placed in regular academic classes, there was no structured plan to ensure that the regular education teacher knew what modifications to use, or that the teacher actually used any modifications at all. We established documentation procedures and tools for regular education teachers, along with instructions as to how to make the modifications. We also had all teachers begin to document modifications in their lesson plans; these plans are turned in for review on a three-week rotation. We have improved significantly our level of modification implementation.

- Students with disabilities were receiving math, reading, and language instruction in the resource classroom; yet, for the most part, our strongest content-based teachers were in the regular classroom. This was not necessarily the fault of the special education teacher, because college preparation for teachers of students with disabilities is not content based. To facilitate the teachers' growth in content and instructional strategies, we began to offer in-house professional learning and encourage college-level classes in their content area. This approach is now a component of NCLB. We also determined to not only offer training but to change our inclusion program so that special education teachers could collaboratively teach with master teachers in their content areas. Not only did this significantly improve the instruction received by the student, it allowed us to train special education teachers in delivering content and their knowledge base. Now some of these teachers, who began as weak-content special education teachers, are placed in classrooms with beginning regular education teachers—they have become the master teachers providing training.

Moving from a resource classroom model to a majority of collaborative classes does create a need for more special education teachers and thus requires the support of the system special education department and the system administration.

Summary

When we began the school improvement process, we had no mentor or guide. We simply began by looking at where we were, where we wanted to be, and how to get there. Going into this, I knew that it would not be enough just to be good. I wanted us to be an example of what a middle school, when done right, could be for students, teachers, and parents. ULMS is now a great place to work and learn, and all stakeholders— staff, students, parents, board of education, central office personnel, and community supporters—should be commended for their part in supporting and encouraging success for all students.

In its summary report, the Lighthouse site visit team said, "[T]here is a central focus on academic achievement, [yet] this school overtly and intentionally supports the other developmental needs of students. Upson-Lee will serve as a strong model of not only what a middle school should be, but also what any school can be."

The current controversy over the correct structure for schooling the adolescent concerns me deeply. First of all, fostering the middle school concept is not all there is to an effective middle school. Effective middle schools must push for whatever reform initiatives are necessary to ensure exemplary education for all their students. I believe the educational system we are implementing and growing here at Upson-Lee Middle School is an educational setting that should be in every school on every level, from pre-K through college and adult education. All learners need to be nurtured and given responsibility. All educators should focus on "what is best for the student" and provide the support students need to reach their potential.

Q&A with the Principal
Patsy Dean
Upson-Lee Middle School

Q: *What has ULMS done to challenge advanced learners?*

A: Differentiated instruction provides opportunities for advanced learners to expand their learning in all subjects. Each subject routinely assigns out-of-class projects that are assessed with rubrics that allow the students to choose the level of performance. Students who excel in math and literature in the seventh and eighth grades are placed in advanced math and literature classes. We have an academic bowl competition team and participate in Mathcounts, a competition developed by engineers. Engineers Teaching Algebra is part of our program for algebra students; it involves an engineer presenting an authentic problem (e.g., the timing of traffic lights at multiple-lane intersections). We have a challenge program for gifted literature in all grades. Our reading incentive program encourages students to voluntarily read within a range of their independent/instructional level. We have a schoolwide study of Greek and Latin derivatives. We have a schoolwide emphasis on critical and creative thinking skills, brain-based learning, and metacognition. We offer Junior Beta Club for higher achieving academic students.

Q: *What do you see as the benefits of student-led conferences? Whom do they help most?*

A: Our first experience with student-led conferences occurred just a month ago. The response from parents may have been the most positive I have ever received. One parent said that he felt more involved than he had ever felt before in a conference. We believe that the foundation of parent involvement is a connection to what the student is learning. This kind of conference opens communication and allows for a focused discussion on learning between parent and child. In the training process, students are taught the presentation strategy and how to review their work and discuss the results. Because they must set up portfolios to prepare for the conference, students develop ownership of their work and set goals. Students are responsible for assessing their own weaknesses and strengths and reflect on their study habits and progress. Some of the most touching moments involved watching students who previously were unsure of themselves and uncomfortable in conference settings gain confidence as they presented their work to their parents.

Q: *You say that "parents are expected to be active partners in the day-to-day education of their children." In what specific ways have you fostered this involvement, and what have been the results?*

A: Our parents are expected to involve themselves in the day-to-day learning of the students. I always tell parents that the needed parent involvement is simply asking "What did you learn today?" "How did you do that?" "What's going on at school?" Not only does the parent stay in touch with what is being taught, a value for education is transferred. Parents are offered multiple volunteer and leadership opportunities. We begin the year with a parent information session during orientation, which establishes the expectations for parental involvement at Upson-Lee Middle School. This year, we invited parents of sixth-graders to participate in a Shadow Time, attending class with their children. We use our assignment books keep parents in touch with daily assignments, completion of assignments, and behavior. Parent Connect is a Web-based grade and behavior notification program; at grade-level orientations, we teach parents to access the program periodically. Parents, students, teachers, and administrators use e-mail frequently as one communication tool. Our school sign, local paper columns, and quarterly school newsletter help to keep parents informed of school events. Deanne Hopkins, parent involvement coordinator, schedules a variety of parent-centered workshops to help our parents understand their child and their child's learning.

Q: *Can you provide a specific example of how a teacher's learning to share materials and ideas had a profound impact on either the teacher or the class?*

A: At Upson-Lee Middle School, we use focused common planning to share ideas, create lessons together, and put them in teacher folders on the server, where everyone has access to them. We have found that sharing ensures quality education for all. Using ideas gleaned from working on advanced degrees, teachers are able to share innovative strategies with colleagues during the common planning time. Younger teachers, who are more familiar with new technology, are able to give helpful hints and suggestions for integrating technology to the less technologically proficient.

For example, our gifted teacher compiled 60 Greek and Latin vocabulary lists and shared them with the grade-level literature teachers; now each grade level teaches 20 lists. In another example, Debbie Martinez joined our faculty to teach eighth grade language arts. She had previously taught fourth grade and was worried that her students would suffer from having a new teacher; but because of the curriculum study groups and collaborative planning in our school, the change was almost seamless.

Sharing materials has included our teachers of special needs students as part of the learning community at our school. Teachers get wonderful ideas and advice from each other, and classes benefit because teachers can use tried and proven lessons and activities. Students with disabilities are able to work on the same materials as their regular education peers and on the same time line. These students feel proud when they see work on display in the hall and realize that they have just completed the same work. They feel better about themselves knowing that they can do the same work as other students.

Q: *Can you provide a specific example of how "thinking is valued" at ULMS, or how that sentiment manifests itself on a daily basis? How do you, as the principal, encourage this systematically?*

A: Higher order thinking is incorporated in all our lessons and units, along with authentic learning activities and assessments. Multiple intelligences are considered in our units, and every sixth-grader completes a formal multiple intelligence inventory. In order to equip our students with the information they need for effective learning, we teach them what we know about metacognition, brain research, and motivation theory. Every classroom has a chart of Bloom's Taxonomy on the wall, and students are taught to assess levels of thinking in activities. Essential questions and warm-ups are geared to make students think at a higher level. Fight free and drug free programs teach children how to think before they act. The ULMS creed is emphasized daily to impress upon the students the importance of their choices. The students are encouraged to ask questions, lead discussions, and creatively express themselves. Use of brainstorming as a prewriting, prereading, and preplanning strategy helps students. For projects and presentations, students evaluate, make judgments, and create rubrics.

Q: *You say that ULMS uses technology to challenge students in higher order thinking skills and to engage students as active learners. How do you, as the principal, measure the increase in higher order thinking skills and active learning?*

A: Higher order thinking skills are measured a bit on standardized tests, but they are more apparent in the caliber of work produced by the students. Students are given many opportunities to create authentic examples of what they have learned; they use higher order thinking skills to finalize these valuable activities. The higher order skills that are used by our students include, but are not limited to, extension, evaluation, compare and contrast, and analysis. As administrators, we measure the increase in student learning by observation and levels of student engagement in the classroom.

Leading a Text-Based Discussion on This Profile (see protocol in Appendix 4)

- Which practices would you like to see implemented in our school? What do we need to do to make that happen?

- The author indicates that teachers had to give up some autonomy to improve the school. In what areas did teachers give up autonomy? Are the outcomes compelling enough to encourage teachers to consider that here?

- What made the sixth grade classes "advanced" for everyone? Is that a practice worth pursuing at our school?

- Upson-Lee created homework guidelines and standard weighted grading charts for each academic area to encourage consistency in evaluation. What are the pros and cons of this practice?

- What would be the benefits of collaborating regularly to review student work?

- If money were no object, what would be the dream school that you would create?

- What did you like about this profile?

- What didn't you like about this profile?

Moving Forward

The Upson Lee school profile offers suggestions to help you lead your school in the area of personalizing the school environment and the focus of the next chapter: how to build relationships between students and ideas. How can you help students to want to learn? Chapter 4 offers practical tips to make that connection in the areas of curriculum, instruction, and assessment.

4 Making Learning Personal: Curriculum, Instruction, and Assessment

Designing lessons for understanding begins with what we want students to be able to do and proceeds to the evidence we will accept that they have learned it. Only then does it turn to how they will learn it. Along the way, we must be clear about what we want the students to understand and what we mean by understanding.

—*Ron Brandt, Introduction to* Understanding by Design
(quoted from Educational Alliance's Teaching to Each Student *p. 84)*

The challenge for schools is to align curriculum, instruction, and assessment so that students know what standards they need to meet and are then given the support to become engaged in achieving those standards. What does that support look like? In the preceding chapter, we discussed the critical importance of building personal relationships to open the door to, and generate excitement about, learning. In this chapter, we begin to address the *relationships between students and ideas*—how the student interacts and directs his or her own learning with the oversight, coaching, and motivational strategies associated with student-centered curriculum, instruction, and assessment. The relationship formed between students and ideas, also referred to as "personalized learning," lies at the heart of each of the Breaking Ranks in the Middle recommendations in this chapter. How can you create personalized learning in your school?

The Education Alliance at Brown University lists three components of personalized learning:

1. Self-awareness: What the student learns about his or her own values, ambitions, talents, knowledge, and special skills.

2. Explorations: What the student learns from classes and field experiences about the world.

3. Confirmation: What the student learns about defining pathways available to the future she or he has begun to imagine. (*Changing Systems to Personalize Learning*, p. 47)

Without structural changes and changes in classroom practice that promote student self-awareness and exploration, personalized learning cannot flourish. To more fully engage students in their own learning, we encourage each school to consider these Breaking Ranks in the Middle recommendations:

- Identify a set of essential learnings in which students must demonstrate achievement.

- Present alternatives to tracking and ability grouping.

- Foster the use of teacher teams and ample common planning time to integrate the school's curriculum.

- Connect the curriculum to real-life applications of knowledge and skills.

- Promote service programs and student activities.

- Engage students.

- Use a variety of strategies and settings that identify and accommodate each student's readiness, interest, and learning profile (gender, culture, learning style, and intelligence preference).

- Ensure that each teacher has a broad base of academic knowledge, with depth in at least one subject area.

- Encourage teachers to become adept at acting as coaches and facilitators.

- Integrate assessment into instruction.

- Reach out to elementary and high schools to better serve the articulation of student learning.

- Make technology integral to curriculum, instruction, and assessment, accommodating different learning profiles and helping teachers differentiate and improve the learning.

At the end of this chapter, these recommendations are described in greater detail and are accompanied by strategies, benefits, challenges, and measures of progress.

Figure 4.1
Purposes of Personalized Learning

Increase student motivation.	Banish anonymity from school life.
Help students imagine their future.	Assess progress toward standards.
Connect families to student learning.	Connect academic and applied learning.
Celebrate student achievement.	Encourage college aspirations.
Connect each student with a caring adult.	Promote reflection and reevaluation.
Relate student work to standards.	Assess basic skills (speaking and writing).
Explore noncurricular options.	Explore career choices.
Support identity formation.	Demonstrate personal talents.
Initiate lifelong learning.	Extend range of academic choice.
Increase self-awareness.	Evaluate content acquisition.
Emphasize applications of knowledge.	Recognize nonschool achievements.

Source: Adapted from Changing Systems to Personalize Learning, *p. 27.*

> Active participation in learning is a major determinant of performance on tests and in grades.
>
> *Source: p. 9 Changing Systems to Personalize Learning, Brown (Lee, et al., 1995; Newmann, et al., 1992; Stigler & Hiebert, 1999)*

Leading Curriculum Discussions

This chapter is not about designing curriculum. After all, that is not the responsibility of most principals. Some curriculum issues are simply beyond your control. However, as outlined in Cornerstone Strategy #1 and Breaking Ranks in the Middle recommendation #19, your role and involvement in creating your school's essential learnings is critical. Unfortunately, many schools believe that because the district and state have set standards, they do not need to engage in the conversation about essential learnings. However, schools need to put those standards through the local filter. As *Turning Points 2000* emphasizes

> For many schools, the idea of selecting academic standards may seem nonsensical. Schools do not select standards—standards are imposed by the state education department or the local district. Clearly, nearly all American schools will need to address mandated state and/or local standards…. Yet a school runs a grave risk in merely accepting such standards as the revealed wisdom of some all-knowing higher authority! Instead, each middle grades school, as a distinct learning community, must analyze its state and local standards to determine if they provide an adequate, high-quality basis for developing a coherent, engaging curriculum. Where the standards do not measure up…a school will need to adapt and augment state and local standards to do well on assessments and, more important, are truly able to use their minds well…. Almost inevitably, educators will need to supplement and modify standards to encompass what a particular school community believes its students should know and be able to do. (*Turning Points 2000*, p. 34)

Once you have developed essential learnings, your team will need to take a closer look at your existing curriculum, instruction, and assessment practices to determine specifically what must be learned and understood. You will need to use the collaborative process outlined in chapter 2 to help you determine what qualifies as understanding

---

Indicators of Personalized Learning

- Personalized learning begins with individual interests, so that each student becomes engaged in learning.
- The achievement of standards for all students is promoted.
- Teachers get to know each student's strengths, weaknesses, and interests.
- Adults in the school model and benefit from stronger professional and student relationships.
- Students learn to set goals and measure success for themselves against common standards.
- Reaching all students depends on reaching each one.

Source: DiMartino, 2001, p. 19.

---

well enough and what rubrics and assessments will be used. What instructional strategies will support learning and understanding for each student? How can your school go beyond what the state standards require? Those questions fall to you in your role as the instructional leader in the school. You will be judged by your ability to guide these conversations and by how well you are able to create an environment for personalized learning.

None of the indicators of personalized learning will occur without the principal and the leadership team creating the proper conditions. For example, integrating the curriculum may not happen unless teachers have common planning time. Similarly, working across the disciplines may require scheduling changes or schedule flexibility that the principal, ultimately, must be willing to shepherd into existence. The principal and the leadership team provide a structure and a vision in which interdisciplinary teaching, teaming, and other practices detailed at the end of this chapter can unfold.

[S]chools, as learning organizations, likely learn the way individuals do: "[L]earners use their current knowledge to construct new knowledge and…what they know and believe at the moment affects how they interpret new information. Sometimes learners' current knowledge supports new learning, sometimes it hampers learning…."

—Bransford et al., 1999, p. 141.

If we want to improve teaching and learning in schools, reformers must start with where schools are, just as teachers must discover what their students understand, and misunderstand, in order to target curriculum, instruction, and assessment appropriately.

—Turning Points 2000, p. 48.

Engaging Students in Learning

Successfully implementing a rigorous curriculum relies on engaged students who are willing to be challenged and to challenge themselves. When you look to establish a rigorous curriculum, consider these guidelines from the Breaking Ranks in the Middle training. The curriculum should be

1. Authentic

    - Product-oriented
    - Quality standards set in advance
    - Requires application of skills
    - Open-ended and problem-based

2. Thoughtful and reflective

    - Requires analysis, synthesis, evaluation
    - Has multiple outcomes
    - Requires new ways of thinking
    - Judged on quality criteria and evidence

3. Creates dissonance in learner

   ■ Uses real-world problems

   ■ No clear answer; only high-quality ones

   ■ Requires new behavior, skills, and learning

   ■ Entertains the possibility of failure

4. Individualized

   ■ Permits student to pursue interests

   ■ Is differentiated

   ■ Provides support

   ■ Requires self-evaluation

Are New Instructional Practices Necessary to Engage *All* Students?

Making
Learning Personal

If you are like most people, you're probably not anxious to try something new unless your current practices are in need of change. At the beginning of this field guide, we asked you 15 questions about how well you serve each student in your school. If you have read this far, there's a good chance you weren't completely satisfied with your responses to those questions. However, you still may be hesitant to try something new—especially if that something new touches on the hot-button issues of ability grouping, tracking, or differentiation. But these are issues you must address if you want to serve each student well. In the following essay, differentiation guru Carol Ann Tomlinson captures the latest thoughts to help guide you. Her essay may provide a focal point for faculty discussions.

Expert Essay

Revisiting Ability Grouping: In Search of a Viable Alternative

by Carol Ann Tomlinson, University of Virginia

The issue of ability grouping or tracking is an old one, but one in which research findings have generally been steady over the years. Ability grouping is a common approach to dealing with student variance in learning. In general, findings suggest that such an approach to dealing with student differences is disadvantageous to students who struggle in school (see, e.g., Carbonaro & Gamoran, 2002; Gamoran et al., 1995) and advantageous to advanced learners (see, e.g., Kulick & Kulick, 1992; Rogers, 1991).

It would likely be to our benefit in educational decision making to go a step beyond the findings to consider *why* the results are as they are. That understanding should open the way to developing instructional approaches designed to maximize the growth of each student rather than repeating the now highly predictable patterns of the past. While schools and classrooms are complex and defy easy analysis, at least one root cause for the disparity of instruction in low and high track classes is evident.

Impact of Teacher Expectations on Opportunity to Learn

When teachers work with a class largely or fully populated by students who have not done well in school, teacher expectations fall. That is likely not so much an intentional response as one triggered by below-the-surface reactions. In such instances, teachers draw the conclusion that the students will need tighter discipline, a slower pace of learning, less student-to-student interaction, a focus on fundamental or basic skills, easier materials, and so on. The nature of low-track or low-ability classes thus typically reflects what one author called a "pedagogy of poverty"—that is, a class in which emphasis is on compliance, memorizing and repeating information, doing drill and practice, checking work, stressing compliance, and so on (Haberman, 1991). Lowered expectations result in curriculum and instruction that not only reflect the economic poverty of students who are overrepresented in low-level classes but are also likely to prepare students for a future of poverty.

In contrast, when a teacher is faced with a class of learners designated as advanced or highly able, the teacher's expectations predictably rise. In these instances, teachers believe they should move at a more rapid pace, use more advanced materials, prepare students to be increasingly independent as learners, and focus on high-level thinking. The nature of high-track classes typically reflects what an author referred to as a "pedagogy of plenty"—that is, one that is focused on making meaning, dialogue, complexity of ideas and thought, authentic tasks, and varied social configurations (Hodges, 2001).

In conversations about findings related to ability grouping or tracking, we often overlook two key elements in the research. First, research suggests that students who are often assigned to low-track classes learn as much or more than their high-track counterparts when they have the opportunity to engage with the sort of curriculum and instruction typical of good high-track classes (Educational Research Service, 1992). Second, research that supports tracking advanced learners suggests that when curriculum is appropriately differentiated for these students, their achievement in heterogeneous classes is more positive than when all students in a class are taught exactly alike (Kulik & Kulik, 1992). There is very little research in the tracking literature that examines the impact on student achievement (as well as attitude, attendance, community, and so on) of classes in which high-quality differentiation is a persistent reality. Thus, our conversations continue to look at "solutions" in which we either do nothing to deal with student learning variance (one-size-fits-all hetero-geneity) or in which we put students into different learning settings that typically provide very uneven learning opportunities.

An Alternative Way to Address Learner Variance

If we accept what appears to be a demographic reality that students in the decades ahead will have a wide range of academic needs and simultaneously accept the premise that schools should help each student develop the kinds of understandings, skills, and attitudes that will prepare him or her for life in a complex and rapidly changing world in which all students will need to be creators of knowledge (Marx, 2000), it seems like educational malpractice to determine that some students should be assigned to low-level, often remedial, expectations that seldom result in robust academic gains (Tomlinson, 2004), while others receive opportunities to flourish. On the other hand, it also seems like educational malpractice to deprive students who are ready to move ahead with vigor and enthusiasm the opportunity to do so.

The concept of differentiation suggests that there is a third alternative to effective teaching of academically diverse student populations. Moving beyond a pedagogy that sorts students and a pedagogy that ignores their essential differences and needs, we would look at classrooms in which all students work with high-level, engaging, meaning-making curriculum in a flexible classroom environment. In such settings, teachers would routinely provide support for students who need additional scaffolding to succeed with meaningful curriculum and for students who need to work at a more complex level. In other words, such classrooms would raise both the floors of expecta-tions and the ceilings of possibility (Tomlinson, 2003).

In an era when academic diversity is a defining element in schools, and when eco-nomic viability demands a level of preparation for virtually all students that we once reserved for only a few, neither sorting nor teaching to the middle makes sense. We are likely at a point in educational history when educators have to work as teams of gener-alists and specialists to deliver higher quality curriculum in a range of ways in order to ensure both equity and excellence to each learner whom we serve (Marx, 2000).

In such classrooms, there is no need to sacrifice the advanced learner for the stu-dent who struggles (or vice versa) or to sacrifice the student who, for example, is both very able and speaks English as a second language or has a learning disability. The pres-ence of clear and meaningful learning goals, continual use of assessment data to under-stand student growth in meeting those goals, and flexible teaching routines allows for attention to a variety of needs—not just to the needs of one group of students. Key to developing defensibly differentiated classrooms is developing teachers who "teach to the top," simultaneously scaffolding the growth of students for whom academic excellence is already a reality and those for whom it is a new reality (Cone, 1992, 1993; Tomlinson & Allan, 2000).

As educators, most of us are not yet greatly skilled in developing and guiding such classes (Tomlinson et al., 2003). There are enough examples of them, however, to help us understand how they might operate and what their benefits might be for the full spectrum of students. The question is whether we have the will to move beyond paradigms that seem seriously flawed to those that seem more promising for far more students.

What Is a Principal's Role in "Teaching to the Top"?

Tomlinson makes a compelling case for raising expectations for all students. But how can you, as principal, support that effort? To help answer that question, read the following letter from one of your teachers.

Dear Principal:

Earlier this year, our school district identified "responsive education" as a key element in its strategic plan. The plan specified differentiated instruction as a best practice model to create classrooms that are responsive to the needs of every learner. As a teacher who has seen the positive effect of differentiation on student success in my own classroom and who has worked with other teachers in developing differentiated strategies, I am pleased and excited that our district has made this a high priority for all classrooms. However, mandating a good thing—from the district office or the principal's office—does not make it happen. Much more than a mandate is needed. Based on my own classroom practice and my work with other teachers in their efforts to differentiate, I offer my top 10 list of critical differentiation issues from the "school of hard knocks."

1. **Motivation**—strong moral purpose to meet the learning needs of every student.

   Mandates are generally weak motivators for change. For effective differentiated instruction to be successfully offered across the school, the motivation must be the belief of each staff member that the purpose of the school and his or her personal mission are to meet the academic, social, and developmental needs of each student.

2. **Collegial culture and positive attitudes**—Differentiation is difficult to accomplish, so hold hands and stick together.

   Engaging in a difficult task together requires that everyone in the school community plan together, practice and perform strategies in front of one another, foster reflection, give feedback, and support renewed attempts at professional growth. Mutual trust among staff members is a key factor in establishing a culture in which this operating procedure is standard.

3. **Principal and teacher leadership**—toward understanding and effective differentiated practice.

   Like the district mandate, a mandate from you as principal will not ensure that teachers have the understanding and skill to plan and deliver instruction that addresses the learning needs of every student. You must demonstrate a sound understanding of effective instruction. You must also share the responsibility for developing understanding and skill across the staff with the aid of teacher leaders who have the expertise and have been given the necessary time and authority to involve other teachers in extending their capacity for differentiation.

4. **Professional development**—ensuring each teacher's expertise in content and in strategies that support differentiation.

   Differentiated instruction is not possible unless the teacher possesses a high degree of knowledge, understanding, and skill in his or her subject area. On this content foundation, teachers most effectively develop skill in using instructional strategies that meet the varied learning needs of students when the professional development models differentiation to meet the varied learning needs of teachers.

5. **Time to plan and collaborate**—There is never enough time. We will never have more than we currently do; thus, we must decide how to use our time wisely.

School leaders cannot expect each teacher to make the decisions that will provide the structured time required for routine collaboration and planning among and across teams. The vision of the school is evident in the master schedule. Schedules that provide time for professional development as well as routine planning and collaboration among and across teams for differentiation are essential. After a busy school day and at the end of a hectic week in a middle school are not the optimal times for engaging in professional development opportunities or collaborative efforts.

6. **Resources**—Differentiation is impossible without adequate resources.

Providing multiple avenues to learning is the foundation of a differentiated classroom. Those avenues require varied and respectful formats. A beginning teacher has few resources and a limited repertoire. To expect a differentiated classroom without supporting this teacher by providing such resources as leveled texts, computer access, or collaboration experiences to develop meaningful learner opportunities is to doom the differentiation effort to failure.

7. **Assessment to inform instruction**—going beyond standards-driven assessment to learner challenge.

Teachers must embrace standards to design instruction that prepare students to pass benchmarks and state-mandated assessments. Further assessment of a student's interests, learning style, cultural background, experience, and current level of knowledge and skills is necessary to inform the teacher's attempts to differentiate the learning and provide appropriate challenge for that student. Teachers must develop skill in administering preassessments and using the data generated by these to guide instruction.

8. **Challenge and rigor**—the goal and guide in all differentiated practice.

While teachers must embrace standards, these too frequently imply a minimum benchmark. Teachers must accept the responsibility for incorporating appropriate challenge and rigor for all students to develop higher level critical thinking, problem-solving skills, and adaptive learning that will meet their needs in a rapidly changing world.

9. **Involving the school community**—parent awareness and student understanding of the purpose in differentiating instruction.

Experience and perceptions affect the success of a differentiated classroom. Parents must be aware of and have some understanding of the purpose, goals, and process of the differentiation model of instruction as it relates to the success of their children. Students must develop a high degree of comfort with how the differentiated classroom works and how it supports their learning success. They must also perceive the process to be fair and respectful to them and their classmates.

10. **Across the curriculum**—Differentiation is relevant to and enhances instruction in all subject areas.

Standards frequently do not address assessment of some subjects in the curriculum. This is not a rationale to ignore the importance of differentiated instruction in these areas. Students with interests and talents in areas not included in mandated assessments deserve opportunities to develop their gifts to the maximum potential.

So, my principal, it is a bit like what a sometimes less-than-gentle pediatric specialist told me after we had frantically pursued an effective treatment for our sick child by visiting numerous doctors and trying many different remedies, some of which seemed to make him sicker. This doctor said, "There is no magic pill. You must do this… and that… to heal the child and to strengthen his fragile body. It will be hard work, but he will get well if you follow through." We were surprised at his blunt response, but we faced the reality of his challenge. There was no quick fix; there was no magic pill to heal, to strengthen, and to make our baby well. Similarly, there is no magic pill to create the "classrooms of plenty" that Carol Tomlinson has cited as essential to meet the needs of each student. The leadership of a principal collaborating with an instructional team that specializes in instructional diagnoses and practices that include differentiation will help heal the malady of the "classrooms of poverty" in our school and help us ensure that each student meets his or her full learning potential. It will be hard work as we define the critical "this and that" and the essential "follow through" for each student in our school to be well.

Be well,
Your teacher

Are Structural Changes Enough?

In NASSP's *Leadership for Highly Successful Middle Level Schools: A National Study of Leadership in Middle Level Schools,* Valentine and others identified 98 highly successful middle level schools. Schools selected were, among other things, implementing middle level programs representative of the current research and literature about effective middle level schools (criteria were developed from recommendations in *Turning Points: Preparing Youth for the 21st Century and Turning Points 2000: Educating Adolescents in the 21st Century*). The evidence of structural changes outlined by Valentine and others was significant. (See figure 4.2.)

Figure 4.2
Instructionally Responsive Programmatic Practices

Practice	Very Important		Somewhat Important	
	Highly Successful	National Sample	Highly Successful	National Sample
Interdisciplinary teams of 2–5 teachers sharing common students, common planning time, housed in close proximity.	96	77	3	14
Exploratory course offerings that provide required (not elective) curricular opportunities for all students.	78	72	14	20
Adviser-advisee program regularly scheduled for 15 minutes or more during each classroom day.	61	48	34	31
Co-curricular program separate from regular graded courses but occurring during the school day, designed to provide students with the opportunity to pursue leadership roles, special interests, and socialization.	56	42	32	41
Intramural activities offered for all students during or immediately after the regular classroom day.	60	48	32	34

Source: Valentine et al., 2004, p. 28

While *Leadership for Highly Successful Middle Level Schools* reports that there have been widespread structural changes (e.g., increasing numbers of schools adopting interdisciplinary teaming and exploratory programs), teaching and learning have been relatively unaffected. To support this contention, the report quotes several authorities.

Structural changes in middle grades education—how students and teachers are organized for learning—have been fairly widespread and have produced good results. Research indicates that the adoption of middle grade structures has improved relationships within schools and that students are experiencing a greater sense of well-being. However, our observations suggest that relatively little has changed at the core of most students' school experience: curriculum, assessment, and instruction. (Midgley and Edelin, 1998, p. 195)

[In spite of the fact that middle level schools are] warmer, happier, and more peaceful places for students and adults…. [most schools] have not yet moved off this plateau and taken the critical next step to develop students who perform well academically with the intellectual wherewithal to improve their life conditions. (Lipsitz, Mizell, Jackson, and Austin, 1997, p. 535)

In *Through the Looking Glass,* Williamson and Johnston review some of the pitfalls of an inflexible adherence to middle level orthodoxy:

The advantages of teaming include improved student achievement and school climate, heightened teacher efficacy, and reduced student misbehavior. Such advantages led many middle level schools to include teaming in their program. They studied the literature on teaming and assumed that implementation alone yields the reported results. Their quest was to determine the "correct" team characteristics—size, subjects, and planning time.

Once teaming was implemented, however, schools found that little had changed. Teachers continued to teach their subjects in self-contained classrooms. Planning time was used to deal primarily with student issues. Few links were established among curricular areas. Many teams existed in name only….

Responsive middle level schools focus their energy and resources on developing effective learning communities—groups of students and teachers who work collaboratively to address the instructional and curricular program. The creation of learning communities requires a commitment to the construction of a personalized learning environment for all students. The magic is not in the size of the team, the amount of planning time, or the nature of the schedule. It lies in the commitment of the adults and the students to collaborative work that is focused on clear and meaningful tasks and is responsive to the varied needs of the students.

Learning communities require a conscious and deliberate faculty member commitment to work differently with students. They require examination of current practices and demand revitalization and recommitment to maintain their vitality.

Responsive middle level schools move from the implementation of standard interdisciplinary teams to creating learning communities that make substantive changes in the relationships of adults to students. Such schools reflect sensitivity and responsiveness to the diverse needs and interests of middle level learners as well as a genuine concern for supporting and challenging their academic pursuits. (pp. 1–2).

While great strides have been made in adopting systems to support the strategies to increase student engagement, those strategies within the classroom are lacking in many instances.

How Can You Tell Whether Instruction Is Effective and Engaging?

As the principal or a member of the leadership team, you are responsible for gathering and analyzing information about the instructional practices in your school and their overall effectiveness. Is it feasible to develop a schoolwide picture of student learning that can serve as the basis for faculty reflection, instructional change, and school improvement? More specifically,

- How do you collect data that will be accepted by faculty as a fair and accurate representation of student learning throughout the school?

- How do you depict those data in a simple, meaningful format for analysis?

- How do you engage all faculty members in study and reflection about the data that will lead to improved instructional practices throughout the school?

- How do you use the data to document enhanced learning experiences for all students?

These critical questions formed the basis for the development of the Instructional Practices Inventory (IPI) in 1996 and the continued refinement of the IPI in 2002 and 2005 (Valentine, 2005).

The IPI is a process and rubric for observing and categorizing engaged student learning and, thus, the nature of instruction across the entire school (see figure 4.3). Using the rubric as a categorical data-coding system, observers move from class to class, systematically recording student learning for one or more days. The observations are entered into a spreadsheet, and profiles are created for all classes and for core and non-core classes. The profile is analyzed by the faculty and forms the basis for the deep, reflective conversations and planning that are essential to improve and maintain high levels of instruction/learning throughout the school. Details about the IPI rubric, process, and workshops for observer validity and reliability are available at the website of the Middle Level Leadership Center (www.mllc.org).

As you review the recommendations on pages 195–218 regarding curriculum, instruction, and assessment, look at each through the prism of student engagement. Structural changes are all for naught if they do not translate into changes in classroom practices that entice each student to interact and direct his or her own learning. Developing a relationship between students and ideas is critical to the long-term success of your initiatives and the lifelong learning opportunities for your students. A love of lifelong learning must be fostered in the middle grades so that students aren't refused opportunities in the future. As Tom Rudin of the College Board reminds us in the following Q&A, the middle grades are a critical time to begin discussions about future learning. Students must take challenging coursework in the middle grades so they are not cut off from postsecondary opportunities.

Figure 4.3
Instructional Practices Inventory

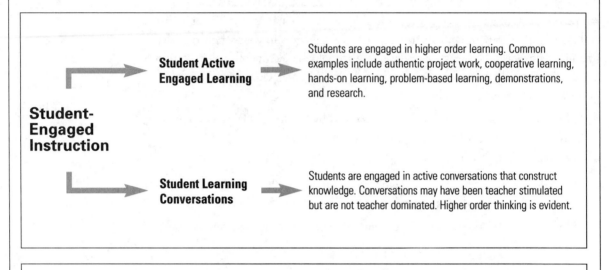

Student-Engaged Instruction

Student Active Engaged Learning → Students are engaged in higher order learning. Common examples include authentic project work, cooperative learning, hands-on learning, problem-based learning, demonstrations, and research.

Student Learning Conversations → Students are engaged in active conversations that construct knowledge. Conversations may have been teacher stimulated but are not teacher dominated. Higher order thinking is evident.

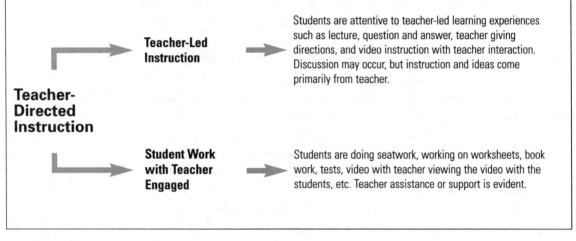

Teacher-Directed Instruction

Teacher-Led Instruction → Students are attentive to teacher-led learning experiences such as lecture, question and answer, teacher giving directions, and video instruction with teacher interaction. Discussion may occur, but instruction and ideas come primarily from teacher.

Student Work with Teacher Engaged → Students are doing seatwork, working on worksheets, book work, tests, video with teacher viewing the video with the students, etc. Teacher assistance or support is evident.

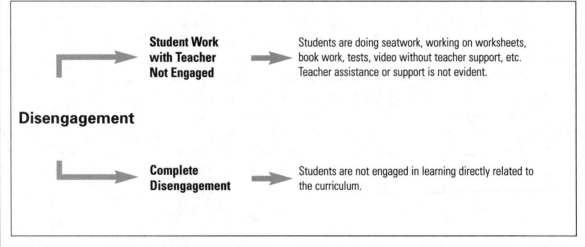

Student Work with Teacher Not Engaged → Students are doing seatwork, working on worksheets, book work, tests, video without teacher support, etc. Teacher assistance or support is not evident.

Disengagement

Complete Disengagement → Students are not engaged in learning directly related to the curriculum.

Source: The IPI was developed by Bryan Painter and Jerry Valentine in 1996, and revised by Valentine in 2002 and 2005. The IPI was designed to profile schoolwide student engagement with learning and was not designed for personnel evaluation. Valentine, J. (2005). Instructional Practices Inventory: Profiling Student Engagement for School Improvement. *Columbia, MO: Middle Level Leadership Center, University of Missouri. Jerry Valentine Middle Level Leadership Center (www.MLLC.org). Reprint only by written permission.*

Ask the Expert

Q&A with Tom Rudin
Vice President of Government Relations and Development,
The College Board

Q: *Why is it so important to introduce the concept of college to young adolescents?*

A: The College Board believes that *all* adolescents should complete a rigorous academic program in grades 6–12 that prepares them to enroll and succeed in college. Too often, for many reasons, college is not an option for every child. Some students are discouraged by peers or even parents from taking the kinds of rigorous courses essential for enrollment and success in college. In other cases, students are discouraged by teachers and counselors from considering the college-prep path. Students may pick up signals (both overt and subtle) that they are not suited for rigorous coursework.

Research suggests that while the current generation of adolescents has high ambitions, many are unaware of the steps they can take to achieve those ambitions. The College Board's goal is to help educators find ways to provide the kind of experiences and information that will open the door to college for all young people. A two- or four-year college degree is becoming increasingly important for unlocking the doors to economic and educational opportunity in America. Getting a college education requires a considerable investment of money, time, effort, and planning by parents and students, but it provides the knowledge, experience, and skills students will use for the rest of their lives to help them succeed in whatever they undertake. The benefits of college include the following:

- **Getting (and keeping) a better job.** Because the world is changing rapidly, and many jobs rely on new technology, more and more jobs require education beyond high school. With a two- or four-year college education, students will have more jobs from which to choose and will be better equipped to adapt to changes in the workplace throughout their lives.

  Earning more money. On average, a person who goes to college earns more than a person who does not. Someone with a two-year associate degree earns more than a high school graduate. In 2003, a man with a bachelor's degree earned about 40 percent more than a man with only a high school diploma, and a woman with a bachelor's degree earned 69 percent more than a woman with only a high school diploma.[1] By the age of 33, the typical college graduate has earned enough to compensate for both the cost of attending a four-year public college and earnings forgone during college years.

  Get a good start in life. A college education helps people acquire a wide range of knowledge in many subjects, as well as advanced knowledge in the specific subjects in which they are most interested. College also trains students to express thoughts clearly in speech and in writing, make informed decisions,

[1]Education Pays Update 2005. The College Board, New York, NY, 2005.

use technology, and acquire new skills and information when necessary—all useful skills both on and off the job.

Q: *Is it more than just the* concept *of college that should be introduced?*

A: Yes. Parents and students need to think about long-term educational goals at a relatively early age, when students still have strong *aspirations* to attend college, even though they may not have sufficient *information* about college. In one study, the Massachusetts Higher Education Information Center's Statewide Youth Awareness Program[2] (1991) provided access to college readiness materials to eighth-graders in four urban schools and found that not only were college aspirations higher in those four schools than in four control schools (measured at the end of the 8th grade and again at the end of the 12th grade), but graduation and college enrollment rates were much higher for the students from the four participating schools. More students who participated in early educational awareness programs planned to enroll in college-prep programs than students who did not participate in awareness programs. Students in the early awareness programs believed that their teachers had high expectations for their achievement. The benefits were highest for Latino students.

Grades seven and eight are especially pivotal times for students and their families on the path to college, as the courses students take in grades seven through nine are critically important factors in determining whether they will be ready for college enrollment after high school. Students who take algebra and geometry by the end of 9th and 10th grades are much more likely to go on to college than those who do not. Nationally, only 26 percent of low-income students who did not take geometry by 10th grade went to college, but 71 percent of low-income students who took geometry did.[3]

It is important, therefore, for students to take the right courses in middle school. Parents and counselors should guide all students into courses that prepare them for challenging academic experiences in high school. Grades seven and eight are not too early for students to take the following courses:

Algebra and geometry or equivalent challenging math courses that require the mastery of those subject areas. Algebra and geometry form the foundation for the advanced math and science courses that colleges look for (such as trigonometry and precalculus) and give students the skills they need to succeed on the Scholastic Aptitude Test (SAT), in math classes, and in their future careers.

English, science, and history or geography. Together with math, these courses make up the core—the basic academic classes that all students should take each year of middle school and high school. In these subject areas, students should be encouraged to develop their writing skills, which are critical for success in college.

Foreign language. Many colleges require students to study a foreign language for at least two years, and some prefer three or four years of one language. Foreign language skills also demonstrate that a potential employee is prepared to compete in the global economy.

Computer science. Basic computer skills are now essential for many jobs.

[2]Anne Wheelock. *Crossing the Tracks,* The New Press, New York, 1992.

[3]*Getting Ready for College Early.* U.S. Department of Education, 1998.

Arts. Many colleges view participation in the arts, including music, as a valuable experience that broadens students' understanding and appreciation of the world around them and contributes significantly to their intellectual development.

Q: *What steps can a middle school reasonably take to introduce the concept of college?*

A: Principals and other school leaders can take the initiative to make college awareness an important part of a school's culture in the following ways:

- **Setting the vision.** Principals can create a school "ethos" for college preparation for all students, primarily by fostering a shared vision of college planning and preparation, setting a rigorous curriculum, and placing high expectations on instructional personnel to commit to academic excellence and success for every child.

- **Providing instructional leadership.** Important to establishing a culture in which high expectations for all students is the norm is the distribution of leadership within the school (including counselors and teachers) so that all personnel own the commitment to high standards. A major commitment should be made to providing teachers with access—through ongoing professional development—to coaching and instructional strategies that enhance learning, and to aligning standards, curriculum, and assessment throughout the K–12 pipeline. The importance of professional development cannot be overemphasized.

Ask the Expert:
Tom Rudin

- **Removing barriers to learning.** Principals can offer safety nets for students who need extra support and enrichment, and can establish family and community support systems that enhance student learning. One way is to offer nonremedial after-school and Saturday programs for students and their parents, as enrichment experiences that enhance regular classroom activities.

- **Empowering parents as advocates for their children's academic development.** Many parents, especially those who have not been to college, lack an understanding of what it takes to prepare their children for college and never take steps to build their children's college aspirations. Schools need to reach out to parents with information about college preparation, admissions, and financing.

- **Using community resources as support systems for students.** Establish relationships with local colleges, universities, community colleges, and businesses with the aim of offering extra enrichment and support to students— and as a tool to build college aspirations. For students who do not have college graduates in their immediate family, student mentoring across grade levels or the opportunity to hear a recent graduate speak about success in college can be a motivating experience.

Q: *Can you recommend a specific resource (book, article, website) for the middle level students themselves?*

A: The College Board's middle level and high school college readiness curriculum, CollegeEd, builds students' college aspirations and informs them of the steps necessary to prepare for college enrollment and success. Through the lessons included in College Ed, students can do the following:

- Develop a strong interest in attending college.
- Learn that high school choices matter.
- Explore potential careers.
- Develop an academic plan for their high school career.
- Take practical steps to chart college and career paths.

Information about CollegeEd can be found at www.collegeboard.com/collegeed/collegeed/index.html.

Q: *What are the benefits of programs such as AP and IB at the middle level?*

A: AP and IB can be powerful tools for increasing academic rigor, improving teacher quality, and creating a culture of excellence for all students in high schools, but the path to success in AP and IB starts in the middle school.

Students who take AP courses in high school assume the intellectual responsibility of thinking for themselves and learn how to engage the world critically and analytically—both inside and outside the classroom. This is an important experience for students as they prepare for college or work. Schools in which AP is widely offered—and accessible to all students—almost always experience the diffusion of higher standards throughout the entire school curriculum. Superintendents and principals increasingly recognize the value of AP as leverage to increase opportunity and achievement for all students.

Through the implementation of vertical teams (whereby teachers align their curricula and pedagogy with the high standards students will be expected to reach by grades 11 and 12), the influence of AP extends into the middle level schools, raising standards and expectations among students and teachers in grades five through nine. Thus, the AP program has a substantial impact on the quality of teaching and learning in all grade levels in a school and school district. Because most AP teachers also teach several sections of non-AP courses, they bring their high-quality instructional skills to a wide range of students, not just those who take AP courses.

Q: *How would you respond to critics who charge that these programs promote tracking and ability grouping at a very young age?*

A: We strongly discourage the use of AP or IB as a means of sorting/selecting students, and we work with schools and districts across the country to use AP as an anchor for encouraging all students to prepare for college. The College Board has developed the following statement to assist districts and schools in developing an open enrollment policy that expands access to AP for all students:

> The College Board and the AP Program encourage teachers, AP coordinators and school administrators to make equitable access a guiding principle for their AP programs. The College Board is committed to the principle that all students deserve an opportunity to participate in rigorous and academically challenging courses and programs. All students who are willing to accept the

challenge of a rigorous academic curriculum should be given consideration for admission to AP courses. The Board encourages the elimination of barriers that restrict access to AP courses for students from ethnic, racial, and socio-economic groups that have been traditionally underrepresented in the AP program. Schools should make every effort to ensure that their AP classes reflect the diversity of their student population.

A College Board publication for both middle level and high school principals, *Opening Classroom Doors,* highlights strategies used by schools all over the country to expand access to AP and draw a more diverse group of students into challenging classes. The publication is targeted to administrators and teachers who want to learn about schools in situations similar to their own and who are looking for best practices for expanding access to AP. It can be accessed at http://apcentral.collegeboard.com/repository/ap04_openingdoors_35609.pdf.

Ask the Expert:
Tom Rudin

Breaking Ranks in the Middle Recommendations

Related to Curriculum, Instruction, and Assessment

RECOMMENDATION 19: Each school will identify a set of **essential learnings**—in literature and language, writing, mathematics, social studies, science, and the arts—in which students must demonstrate achievement in order to advance to the next level.

Strategies

- Establish habits and standards of learning through extended conversations about the purpose of the school, so the school can develop rigorous standards against which student achievement can be assessed in multiple ways (e.g., testing, portfolios, projects).

- Integrate discipline-specific staff into team structures to foster interdisciplinary planning and teaching that allows for the essential learnings to be taught across disciplines and through interdisciplinary projects.

- Align coursework and standards with state and national standards.

- Work with elementary schools and high schools to establish a logical continuum of essential learnings (vertical alignment from kindergarten through high school graduation).

- Establish student-led conferences.

- Define learning goals. Set clear expectations. Assess and revise goals as needed.

- Provide professional development to help staff create and articulate essential learnings and measure achievement against those learnings.

Benefits

- Establishes a focus for student learning and allows students to see their own progress on a path with a logically designed destination and clear expectations.

- Aligns coursework and practices vertically, as well as with state and national standards.

- Increases student achievement in core subjects and establishes a strong foundation in literacy skills.

- Creates the framework for a richer, more meaningful learning experience.

- Emphasis on skills to address and cover content is important to students with special needs.

Challenges

- Getting away from course-based instruction and expectations.

- Determining the proper level of understanding for a student to move to the next level.

- Aligning a school's essential learnings with state and district standards.

- Getting student and teacher buy-in.

- Addressing language barriers faced by ELL students.

- Providing challenges for students who are ready to move to the next level.

Progress Measures

- Conduct frequent reviews of student transcripts/permanent records to ensure that every student has access to high-quality learning experiences.

- Identify essential learnings before teaching each course or unit; devise and implement a method by which students can demonstrate the essential learnings in a concrete fashion.

- Gather evidence that coursework is aligned vertically and with state and national standards.

The following process for essential learnings development is offered in *Providing Focus and Direction Through Essential Learnings* (Westerberg & Webb, 1997):

1. Cultivate staff commitment and ownership.

   - Teachers should lead this process, and the rationale for the process must be centered in benefits to students.

   - It must be clear how essential learnings development will help teachers do their job more efficiently and effectively.

   - Discussions should focus on how essential learnings will help staff members hold students and one another accountable for learning; how essential learnings can help staff members decide what to teach and what to leave out; how essential learnings can help clarify and demystify the curriculum for students and teachers; how working together toward common targets for student learning will bring synergy to the staff's efforts; and how having a common vision for the school will help guide decision making.

2. Commission a broad-based essential learnings steering committee.

   - A steering committee composed of students, teachers, parents, and community members can oversee the process outlined in the following steps.

3. Use community focus groups to identify essential learnings.

   - The steering committee should focus on helping others understand the concept of essential learnings, not prepackaging and selling a set of essential learnings.

   - The community "…should identify learnings only as essential if they are fundamental to further learning and absolutely necessary and indispensable to [matriculation]." (p. 4)

   - Help others understand the difference between the conceptually broader essential learnings and the more specific content and behavioral standards that flesh out the essential learnings.

4. Develop content standards, performance standards, and assessments.

   - The steering committee establishes committees of teachers to develop standards for each of the essential learnings defined by the community, which tell us what students should know and be able to do (content), how well students must do these things (performance), and which instructional techniques or recommended activities (curriculum) should be used to assist students in accomplishing the "what" and the "how." [Editor's note: Current thinking would dictate that we add "understand" to the definition of content standards, so the standards would tell us what students know, *understand,* and are able to do. This would appear to be consistent with Westerberg and Webb.[1]]

5. Implement standards-based education.

   - Move from seat time to matriculation requirements centered around identified essential learnings and performance.

6. Restructure your school.

   ▪ Restructuring your school and its practices will be dictated by the essential learnings and how you propose to help students accomplish them. Implementing the changes (interdisciplinary learning, cooperative learning, block development, etc.) without aligning the practices with the student outcomes may lead to an incoherent overall strategy.

7. Conduct community forums.

   ▪ Assess the community's level of support for the drafts of the essential learnings, the content and performance standards, and the restructuring recommendations. One option for the forums is to divide the community into specific interest groups (e.g., the business community, parents, students, senior citizens) to determine patterns, trends, or perceptions about the essential learnings specific to each group (Schlechty, 1990).

8. Design performance tasks.

   ▪ Teachers design [differentiated] tasks for students.

9. Develop a final implementation plan and a time line.

   ▪ The preceding eight steps are part of the implementation plan. At this stage, the steering committee should develop a final implementation plan and time line and propose it to the administration and the board of education. The plan should include proposed staff development activities and the budget implications of the proposed changes, released time, stipends, consultants, and so on.

Recommendation 19 in Practice

Casey Middle School
At Casey, expectations are clear:

▪ Teachers supply students with exemplars of high-quality work that meets the performance standard. Students revise their work based on feedback until they meet or exceed the performance standard.

▪ Family conferences focus on standards.

▪ Students have led parent/teacher conferences.

▪ Teachers connect assignments to standards, provide rubrics and exemplars, model processes, and meet with students individually and in groups to improve their work.

▪ Peers review work.

▪ Content area teachers meet weekly to plan rigorous and nonrepetitive curriculum; student work is often reviewed to determine student needs and growth patterns.

▪ All students have planners, which allows them to share all assignments with their families.

▪ Common assignments for content areas are used to clarify what students throughout the school know and are able to do in that content, so that curriculum and instruction can be modified.

- Content standards for each content area are displayed in all classrooms and shared with families at Back to School Night; syllabi with the standards are sent home during the second week of school.

- Folders/portfolios are available in each class for student use in collecting work and monitoring progress.

The curriculum emphasizes deep understanding of important concepts, development of essential skills, and the ability to apply what one has learned to real-world problems. By making connections across the disciplines, the curriculum helps reinforce important concepts. Learning goals push students toward making connections, solving problems, and thinking critically.

- Grade-level teams plan integrated units of study: Mythology and Ancient Civilizations projects (sixth grade); Science Fair (seventh grade); U.S. Society Research Project (eighth grade); Leadership Community Service projects (all grades).

- Students write general quarterly goals and daily goals in their language arts classes.

- Teachers are trained in pre-AP strategies, which push students to think critically.

Culver City Middle School

All textbooks are aligned with the state content standards and provide a continuum of learning from one grade level to another. Criterion-referenced tests as well as alternative assessments are used in each class. Rubrics are used in all curricular areas, resulting in more uniform grading and in students who know what is expected of them. Every classroom has the appropriate content standards posted daily, many in "student-friendly" wording.

Hopkins West Junior High School

Essential learnings are established in each curricular area. High expectations exist for all students to meet or exceed standards for quality work by engaging in exploratory learning that is challenging, relevant, dynamic, and designed for success. Highlights include the following:

- A schoolwide literacy plan is in place that addresses students with identified needs, literacy for all, a culture of literacy, and professional development.

- Annual summer data retreats identify reading/writing/mathematics skills for each student and appropriate intervention strategies required to ensure mastery and success on state tests.

- A systemic assessment in reading/writing/mathematics is conducted for students new to the school to ensure appropriate placement for support services.

- Tutoring is provided to students in the bottom quartile in reading, writing, and mathematics.

- Reading/writing and mathematics intervention courses are available to support students.

Strategies

- Use heterogeneous grouping at the school, grade, and class levels that includes ELL and special education populations.
- Consider looping of students and teachers.
- Consider use of multiage classes.
- Create interdisciplinary teams.
- Provide time for remediation, enrichment, and support.
- Create a mechanism to combat parent misperceptions.

Benefits

- Ensures equity for all students.
- Provides opportunity for peer-to-peer mentoring, character development, and decreased isolation from other students.
- Offers rich curricula available to all students.
- Creates the opportunity for all students to learn with a diverse group of peers.
- Emphasizes tolerance and sensitivity to diversity.
- Increases expectations for ELL and students with special needs.
- Helps to reduce achievement gaps between classes and races.

Challenges

- Providing substantial professional development on differentiated instruction.
- Keeping more advanced students engaged and motivated.
- Addressing parent perceptions about heterogeneous grouping.
- Keeping the academic challenge for ALL students on an even playing field
- Engaging diverse students in high-level activities.

Progress Measures

- Examine longitudinal data for evidence of increased achievement in assessments across all student groups.
- Review grouping and scheduling practices to ensure diversity of economic, ethnic, and achievement groups in all classes.
- Document all remediation and enrichment activities provided: students served, time allotted, and topics.

Breaking Ranks in the Middle
Recommendations

Recommendation 20 in Practice

Saunders Middle School

The sixth and seventh grades are organized into teams, and each team is given the opportunity to use its block of time as best suits the needs of its students. Currently, the sixth grade has four academic classes of 65 minutes each. The seventh grade is divided: One team is replicating the sixth grade plan, while the other two teams hold to the traditional 55-minute period day for academics, with two periods in language arts. Teams have developed very specific identities, and their spaces in the building are labeled and adorned according to the team name. Special education students are part of a team and participate in all team field trips and celebrations. Gifted students are scheduled onto teams in an equitable manner, so that classes are truly heterogeneous.

Medea Creek Middle School

Students are exposed to a rigorous curriculum with open-ended assignments that are appropriate for all needs. To ensure that all students meet high standards, classes offer differentiated instruction. A continuum of opportunities exists, including gifted clusters, special education clusters, team teaching for combined regular and special education, and specialized pull-out classes. ELLs are provided support within classrooms by an ELL aide and through specialized reading programs such as the Rosetta Stone. High expectations for achievement of standards are present in all classes, and students are given exemplars upon which to model their work. Standards are posted in a variety of ways: in rooms, on teacher web pages, on weekly schedules, and on assignments.

Additionally, rubrics are provided to students so that expectations of high standards are clearly defined. High standards dictate that curriculum, instruction, and assessment be aligned successfully, and provide a coherent vision for what students should know and be able to achieve. There is K–12 consensus on key standards in curriculum serving as the foundation for curriculum planning. The goal of academic excellence for everyone is evident in the school year's structure of quarters (which allows new starts for students) and in every aspect of the school day. The fluidity of the master schedule's design, the variety of club offerings, the challenging enrichment opportunities (Math Counts, NASA competitions), the philosophy of open access and participation by all (intramurals), and support programs (Homework Club, Reading and Math Academies) produce a well-rounded and responsive program. Students are heterogeneously grouped, with special education, ELL, and gifted and talented students clustered in their academics. Math students are programmed according to need, not grade level, with some seventh-graders in algebra and some eighth-graders in geometry and algebra II. A rich elective program provides breadth and depth of experience, especially in the areas of music, visual and performing arts, technology, and leadership. For students who have an extended illness or desire a flexible program beyond the school's door, the school offers Home Hospital and Home Independent Study.

Hopkins West Junior High School

The school is attempting to increase the challenge for all students through programs such as these:

- Students identified through traditional and nontraditional ways are invited to participate in the Autonomous Learner Model, a gifted and talented program that serves students by helping them explore their talents in seminar-type sessions. The program has been expanded to include students of color who would not traditionally be selected to participate but have the potential to benefit from such a program, which will prepare them to take AP courses at Hopkins High School.

- The Hopkins School Success Program is designed to serve low-income students and students of color who will be the first in their families to attend college. The curriculum helps students and their parents explore ways to ensure that college is in their future.

- Summer Zoom (sixth grade into seventh grade), Step Up (seventh into eighth), and Boost (eighth into ninth) provide an extended-year program geared to serve underachieving students who need a literacy program and relationship-based experience to better prepare them for the next grade level.

RECOMMENDATION 21: The school will reorganize the traditional department structure and foster the use of teacher teams provided with ample common planning time to **integrate the school's curriculum** to the extent possible and emphasize depth over breadth of coverage.

Strategies

- Use interdisciplinary teaming. Create team-based integrated units.
- Promote the integration of literacy across content areas.
- Examine skills that are necessary across content areas and determine common benchmarks and strategies to use across the disciplines.
- Create student teams and keep them together all day.

Benefits

- Encourages students to form relationships with team teachers.
- Allows students to see the connections among disciplines.
- Creates teams of teachers that take ownership of a specific group of students.
- Encourages collaboration and opportunities for teams of teachers to look at student work and talk about individual students who need help.
- Allows students to go deeply into subjects rather than skim for breadth.

Challenges

- Overcoming the tradition of departments and department chairs.
- Aligning with district curriculum and pacing guides.
- Providing funding to support new structures.
- Soliciting buy-in from teachers and dealing with union issues.
- Seeking agreement on what the units should address.
- Ensuring teacher and material continuity.
- Providing specific, targeted, job-embedded professional development.
- Ensuring that curriculum integration is authentic to the natures of the various disciplines.

Progress Measures

- Examine team configuration to ensure that all teachers and students are placed on interdisciplinary teams based on integrated units, with students kept together throughout the day.
- Monitor the process, procedures, and structures created by each team to ensure that literacy, basic skills, common benchmarks, and strategies are taught or used across content areas.

Recommendation 21 in Practice

Alvarado Intermediate School

Alvarado maintains a school-within-a-school model of interdisciplinary teaming. This student-centered structure creates the vehicle for critical dialogue during a common preparation period. The English and social studies departments often coordinate thematic units to incorporate textual reading comprehension and writing across the curriculum while tying historical concepts to current real-world problems. Every department course has developed strategies to support schoolwide targets in writing, reading, and mathematics. Collaborative lesson planning allows all classes to support academic core standards and is aligned with California's *Taking Center Stage: A Commitment to Standards-Based Education for California's Middle Grades Students* (TCS) and its key element: holding all stakeholders accountable for high academic performance. Interdisciplinary teams encourage common and consistent expectations for student behavior and use classroom management strategies, both of which have provided a positive environment and kept discipline issues to a minimum.

Crabapple Middle School

Teachers are organized into teams composed of two to four academic core teachers. Most teams also include a special education collaboration/inclusion teacher. One team is a looping team, moving with the same students from sixth to seventh grade. Approximately 80 percent of the academic teachers hold a middle grades certificate; if new teachers do not hold this certificate, they enroll in the Nature and Needs of the Middle

Grades Child course. The block schedule reduces the number of students a teacher on a four-member team interacts with from 120–140 a day to 80–96. This allows for more interaction and the use of a variety of teaching strategies.

Hopkins West Junior High School

Interdisciplinary teams exist at each grade level to establish close relationships with students, develop common skills across core curricular areas, and form connections in students' learning. Teams hold regular meetings to address individual needs of students. Scheduled team collaboration time was lost this school year because of budget cuts; however, informal collaboration occurs during common preparation time for core teachers on each team. A proposal is in place to establish team/grade-level department collaboration time focusing on student data to improve instruction across the school district for the 2006–07 school year. The following are other items of note:

- A reading/writing intervention in seventh and eighth grades places 15 students in a daily 88-minute block with a reading teacher and an English teacher; students are looped with the same teachers for two years.

- An English (writing) teacher teams with special education teachers, the ELL teacher, and Area Learning Center (alternative program) teachers to ensure that the same writing skills are learned by all students.

- Each team has a counselor/social worker and a special educator to work with the teachers and their students to support academic, social, and other developmental needs.

Port Chester Middle School

English language arts (ELA) is the curriculum's keystone. The school has identified and mapped 24 essential skills that are "webbed" to all core subjects. These skills (aligned with the state's eighth grade ELA assessment, state performance standards, and the National Reading Panel recommendations) are "bundled" into a scope and sequence in each ELA class. Skills and reading strategies—deemed essential for reading comprehension, writing, and critical thinking—are embedded in all grade six through eight lessons in a curriculum that is spiraled, accelerated, and enriched with authentic literature. Instruction is data-driven and guided by ongoing assessment and differentiated instruction.

Rachel Carson Middle School

Teachers participate in two types of learning communities: interdisciplinary grade-level teams and subject-specific departmental teams. Each teacher is given one period a day in addition to his or her planning period to work with the teams. This time is used to conduct weekly focused technology workshops run by the school-based technology specialist, to hold weekly meetings of grade-level teams to share content updates and instructional strategies, or to plan for collaborative lessons and activities. At least once a week, each team meets with a member of the clinical support staff and the grade-level administrator to discuss student-specific issues.

In addition to these department-focused planning activities, teachers meet at least once a week with several other members of their department to work on self-determined projects related to their curriculum. This emphasis on self-reflection and intentional decision making is also seen in the activities held during the opening week of school.

Staff in-service days are designed to model ways that each member of the school community can translate the school philosophy into data-driven practices that will result in a nurturing environment to promote academic and personal excellence for our students.

Professional learning communities (grade-level department members) meet weekly to plan common assessments, map curriculum, and solve problems. Teams meet at least twice weekly for curriculum, activity, and student planning. Departments meet monthly to discuss programming and share initiatives. During the opening staff work week, we revisit and recommit to our vision-in-progress and our core values. The leadership team—made up of department chairs, team leaders, and other teacher leaders—meets monthly to discuss goals and big picture items, and to share information and feedback.

RECOMMENDATION 22: The content of the curriculum, where practical, will connect to **real-life applications** of knowledge and skills, and will extend beyond the school campus to help students link their education to the future and to the community.

Strategies

- Use a variety of methods—such as integrated coursework, project-based learning, guest speakers, service learning, exhibitions to the community, student-led conferences, and field trips—to make real-life connections between school and the larger world for students.

- Get to know the students so you will know their histories and where the gaps are, and can build on student knowledge and experiences.

- Use authentic learning activities; for example, write a letter to the editor and have it published rather than doing a writing "exercise"; run a mock business; plan a family vacation or day trip.

Benefits

- Provides authentic learning and developmentally appropriate activities for young adolescents to try out adult roles.

- Demonstrates the connection between the "real world" and what is taught/learned in the classroom.

- Engages students in learning, which leads to increased achievement.

- Increases attendance and engagement, which leads to a decrease in disciplinary issues.

Challenges

- Allocating time and resources to planning and implementation.

- Providing a rigorous academic focus to experiential learning activities.

- Aligning learning projects with state curriculum.

Progress Measures

- Document each quarter through the use of highly specific rubrics and student portfolios, the completion of assignments, quality work, a variety of real-world projects.

- Show the results and impact of learning as it is applied to school or community issues through team and student presentations.

Recommendation 22 in Practice

Casey Middle School

The school provides students with opportunities to develop citizenship skills, uses the community as a classroom, and engages the community in providing resources and support. Students study their community; learn its history; and study its problems. Students take on projects to improve the community.

- Eighth-graders study the history of Boulder and take field trips around the community.

- Art classes designed a bus stop mosaic bench with the supervision of an artist-in-residence.

- Students created a quilt for the firefighters across the street in honor of their service every day, but especially on September 11.

- Saturday ski trips for community members, students, and parents attract about 90 people a week.

Cordova Middle School

- On Student Leadership Day students apply for jobs at the school: principal, teacher, secretary, teacher assistant, librarian, nurse, and so on. Those who get the positions work with the staff member for a day, learning the intricacies of the job. The goal is to increase interest in future employment in education.

- The GEAR-UP program between Alhambra High School and Cordova Middle School in inner-city Phoenix has not only provided a vision of postsecondary education but has provided students with real-life college experiences through the summer enrichment program sponsored by Northern Arizona University. The program offers valuable mentoring experiences for middle school students and paying jobs for high school students.

Rachel Carson Middle School

The school is organized into teams, with teachers working together to provide a cohesive and coordinated curriculum. The Parallel Curriculum Model (PCM) allows teams to develop meaningful learning experiences that reflect the required standards and helps students make necessary connections within and across content areas. This model also gives students the opportunity to develop and apply their knowledge in meaningful ways and to discover and demonstrate their competence, much as a practitioner of that field might do. The model guides the students in understanding and reflecting on how new knowledge applies to their own lives.

Several teams use the PCM with emphasis on different skill areas. One team has developed the year-long theme "Soaring to New Heights" as it celebrates the 100th year of flight through each content area. This important historical milestone is approached through quarterly themes that build on one another. Foundations, Relationships, Variables, and Change are the four quarterly themes. Each teacher frames the curriculum within these themes, where important concepts and skill sets are reinforced.

Another team is building a sense of community and connection through Art Costa's "Habits of Intelligent Minds." The teachers work together to incorporate the 16 habits into various lessons throughout the year. These habits help students become more active critical thinkers. The basic idea is to get students to understand how to approach problems and situations they might encounter in both their academic and personal lives. Time is spent talking about each habit and how to combine them. For instance, a pamphlet entitled "How to Get Good Grades" is being used to reinforce these habits of mind.

Medea Creek Middle School

Students, who are familiar with their strengths in learning, choose myriad products to demonstrate new learning and real-life applications. Examples of projects that involve critical thinking and cross-curriculum work are the math calculations used in physical education classes, seventh grade Science Fair projects, and the Exploring Your World class (foreign language/art and culture). Real-world applications abound with our weather station; experiential science through sixth grade Outdoor Education, seventh grade Catalina Marine Biology, and eighth grade Astrocamp; and after-school enrichment such as the NASA class, the development of a rainforest, computer classes with student-centered projects, and math/technology projects such as "Spend, Spend, Spend."

RECOMMENDATION 23: The school will promote **service programs** and **student activities** as integral to an education, providing opportunities for all students that support and extend academic learning.

Strategies

■ Form partnerships with local community groups.

■ Ensure that activities and service programs are tied to the courses and goals of the school.

■ Define educational objectives and determine criteria for assessment.

■ Evaluate activities, including sports, in terms of the support they provide for your school's broader learning objectives.

Benefits

■ Increases opportunities for learning and allows students to become engaged in the community, which may lead to fewer discipline problems and increased student achievement.

■ Provides a potential "hook" to interest and involve students in school through co-curricular and/or sports programs. Once hooked, students are likely to become more involved in other learning opportunities.

■ Encourages students to see the connections among service programs, student activities, and classwork.

Challenges

■ Providing time, resources, coordination of activities, and transportation/safety for students.

■ Developing contacts in the community. Coordinating with independent operating groups (e.g., club sports teams in schools that have budget for sports).

■ Aligning student activities with the curriculum.

Progress Measures

■ Determine the number/percentage of students engaged in student activities; consider increasing the target each year.

■ Review data on individual students involved in student activities to look for decreases in discipline problems and increases in student achievement in that group.

■ Administer a questionnaire for specific feedback from those participating in "service learning" regarding the quality and quantity of the service received.

Recommendation 23 in Practice

Bowman Middle School

The Leadership Club was established to encourage all students to get involved in school programs—especially students who are not normally involved. The school's peer mediation program involves students from all levels and trains them to help other students resolve conflicts. The Bowman/Memorial Tutorial program allows students to volunteer to go to one of our feeder elementary schools in the morning to tutor kindergarten and first grade students. The BMS Intramural Soccer Program has been in existence for a number of years; it involves many students who are not normally involved in the student activities program (168 students were involved in the 2004–05 school year). Because the school found home finances limited the involvement of students, BMS offers scholarships to cover any costs associated with our student activities programs. (Funds are obtained through grants or donations.)

Crabapple Middle School

The board of education has continued to support the middle school philosophy by maintaining funding and allocations for a complete complement of Connections classes. Crabapple students have the opportunity to choose participation in year-long performing classes, such as band, chorus, and orchestra, along with one additional course in art, drama, general music, diversified technology, computer literacy, or foreign language for sixth grade students. All students who are not participating in a year-long performing class take four of the listed courses. All students also receive instruction in health and physical education during the school day. In addition to these offerings, the school sponsors 10 clubs, an intramural and extramural program, a student radio station, and a weekly closed-circuit television news program. Students have an opportunity to represent the school as members of the Junior Academic Bowl team, Math Counts team, or Future Problem Solvers of America and at spelling bees, the national geography bee, district technology fair, and local, district, and state science fairs.

Rachel Carson Middle School

The school is fortunate to have late buses on two afternoons a week, which allows students to explore areas such as art, aviation, chess, guitar, journalism, photography, stepping, ecology, and theatre. The school has several student publications that meet after school—throughout the year, students work on creating a literary magazine, yearbook, and quarterly newspaper. The goal is for these publications to be student-led, -created, and -produced. Students are responsible for providing editorial leadership, leading meetings, and organizing staff. This experience allows students to explore interests that they could pursue in the future.

The Science Olympiad is another activity that allows students to explore interests that could shape future education and career choices. The number of events and spaces is limited, but any student may complete an application to participate. The science department as a whole selects the members of the team. The support of the staff is apparent—all of the science teachers participate by coaching at least one event. With the number of events increasing to 20, the pool of coaches has expanded to include three math teachers, a civics teacher, and several parents. The events range from building bridges, rockets, and planes to solving problems in various areas, such as meteorology, water quality, map reading, astronomy, experimental design, and estimation.

In the Career Café Program, a career booth is set up at lunch time once a month; it features presenters (parent volunteers, business and community representatives) from a variety of career fields. This monthly program culminates with Career Day, which is a chance for the seventh-graders to learn about various career and job opportunities. A keynote speaker and four small group sessions expose the students to a wide variety of career choices. This is another opportunity for the students to feel a sense of community and belonging, and to take time for personal reflection on their goals and aspirations.

RECOMMENDATION 24: Teachers will design high-quality work and teach in ways that engage students, cause them to persist, and, when the work is successfully completed, result in student satisfaction and acquisition of knowledge, critical-thinking and problem-solving skills, and other abilities.

Strategies

- Use existing programs and materials designed to engage students; give teachers release time to develop new programs or adapt existing ones.

- Provide development for teachers in engaging instructional practices. Teachers' understanding of the concepts of engagement and their commitment to using these concepts are critical.

- Encourage teamwork among teachers.

- Use real-life community problems and issues to construct hands-on activities that articulate and demonstrate state/national standards while engaging students in the discovery process.

- Adopt cooperative learning activities, peer-to-peer mentoring, project-based learning, use of rubrics, weekly work, and plans.

- Develop curriculum units that begin with personal meaning for and experiences of students and end with a celebration and a sense of possibilities for what students can do with this learning.

- Establish nonnegotiable scope and sequence. Provide staff development for all teachers on language development and on cultural and disability issues.

- Provide opportunities for students with special needs to demonstrate mastery in a variety of ways, depending on their readiness, interest, and learning profiles.

Benefits

- Increases student engagement, which leads to increased achievement.

- Increases teacher satisfaction, which leads to greater retention.

- Emphasizes the shift from teaching to learning, from the teacher doing the work to students involved in a process.

- Encourages increased ownership of learning by students as they see meaning in the learning.

Challenges

- Addressing a climate of low expectations, particularly for minority and special needs students in some schools.

- Providing the necessary professional development.

- Identifying and paying for high-quality programs.

- Getting teacher buy-in for new strategies.

- Maintaining a qualified workforce (many teachers in urban schools have emergency certification).

Progress Measures

- Conduct classroom observations of student engagement, time on task, and task persistence.

- Review student work for evidence of critical-thinking and problem-solving skills.

- Provide evidence of increased student engagement (observation); a decrease in disciplinary issues (review of disciplinary data); increased teacher satisfaction (climate survey); and retention (chart teacher retention information during the school year and annually).

RECOMMENDATION 25: Teachers will know and be able to use a variety of strategies and settings that identify and accommodate **individual learning needs** and engage students.

Strategies

■ Provide in-depth and ongoing professional development on accommodating different learning needs.

■ Hire master teachers to work with staff on new skills.

■ Team teachers to support differentiated instruction.

■ Provide time and support for peer observation and feedback so teachers can learn from each other.

■ Provide opportunities for students and teachers to assess what learning modalities best suit each learner.

■ Provide time for reflection and for integration of ELL, IEP, and GT services.

■ Use special education, ELL, and gifted education teachers and specialists to model instructional practices and as resources/mentors for mainstream teachers.

Benefits

■ Encourages use of a variety of strategies to engage students in learning, which leads to increased achievement and decreased disciplinary problems.

■ Provides versatile learning modalities.

■ Provides critically needed support for students with special needs in inclusive general education classrooms.

Challenges

■ Budgeting for professional development and finding appropriate professional development providers.

■ Creating a variety of assessments, providing planning time, developing appropriate materials, and so on.

■ Helping teachers break from old patterns and broaden their ideas about how to teach and provide for individual differences.

Progress Measures

■ Collect and analyze student engagement data (observation) to document the degree of student involvement/engagement and compare individual increases in engagement with documented individual student achievement increases (student assessment analysis) and disciplinary referral decreases (discipline analysis).

■ Document increased teacher use of learning style inventories, multiple intelligence strategies, and responsive teaching strategies (Teacher Observation Form).

■ Verify teacher use of alternative assessments, such as student portfolio reviews and exhibitions.

Recommendations 24 and 25 in Practice

Alvarado Intermediate School

To reach all students, scaffolded lessons, role-playing units, cross-curricular activities, and varied technology are part of each teacher's repertoire. Hands-on activities such as creating short stories, magazines, historical newspapers, and brochures; science projects and experiments; models and diagrams; radio plays; journaling; and computer-generated interactive lessons are integrated with the curriculum to make it more interesting to students and increase participation. To encourage responsibility and organization techniques, teachers also require students to use daily planners and notebooks.

The collaboration among the English Learners Department, Special Education Department, and mainstream teachers creates schoolwide advocates for students with special needs. Special education and inclusion students have instructional aides to support them; English learner and special education students receive a modified curriculum and accommodations. Support programs include the following:

■ After-school tutoring.

■ English Learners Club.

■ Academic Academies to target specific gaps identified by standardized tests.

■ Phonics Club to promote literacy for the lowest-performing students.

- Advancement Via Individual Determination (AVID) classes prepare students from families without a college background for the rigors of college. Students learn about college requirements and interact with career and college speakers.

- Advanced learner support is offered, such as differentiated instruction throughout the day, after-school enrichment programs, and the Alvarado Baccalaureate Certificate (ABC) program, which prepares students to make the transition into high school AP, International IB, or honors courses.

Bowman Middle School

Teachers have been trained on learning styles and the cultural needs of students using Ruby Payne's *A Framework for Understanding Poverty*. Instructional strategies are created and modifications are made through Power Reading, Special Education, and ESOL classes. The Campus Assessment Team works with teachers to identify strategies to help students be successful. The Closing the Gap Cohort has been studying Robert Marzano's *Classroom Instruction That Works* and shares these strategies with the grade-level teachers. The Bowman Academy math classes are double-blocked, providing more time for focused math instruction. The Academy is designed to match the school's most capable teachers with students who are having the most difficulty. This team consists of six teachers who have a common planning time as well as an individual conference period. During the team planning time, the teachers meet daily with each other and every two weeks with an administrator, counselor, the academic specialist, and the behavior specialist to discuss successes, challenges, and strategies for improvement with the students.

Rachel Carson Middle School

The school places great emphasis on understanding mathematics. For students who have significant difficulties in math, the school uses a math specialist to deliver unique assistance. The teacher works with the same group of students for two years. In addition to building relationships with these students, the teacher provides additional support, modeling, and guided practice.

Another beneficial support system is the Pathways to Success Saturday School Program offered to eighth-graders who need specialized remediation in all core curriculum areas to prepare them for the state tests. Noticeable gains in standardized test scores have resulted from this program.

Meanwhile, a large number of students take part in high school credit courses in the eighth grade, and sometimes even in seventh grade. Algebra I, geometry, and several high school foreign language courses are offered. Two online courses are available: algebra II and precalculus. In addition, a Japanese immersion program is offered. If students complete this program successfully, they can move into the equivalent of high school Japanese Level 3.

Culver City Middle School

The instructional program is informed by current research; specifically, strategies for differentiating instruction based on the work of Robert Marzano and Carol Ann Tomlinson, and the reform document *Taking Center Stage*. Differentiated instruction has been the focus of staff development for the past two years. The development of effective differentiated strategies has been a topic at every faculty meeting, as teachers share ways to address standards through best practices. Last year, every teacher read *Classroom Instruction That Works* (Marzano). Grade-level teams presented a section at faculty meetings. This year, the staff is reading *The Differentiated Classroom* (Tomlinson). Teachers are bringing student work to staff meetings to generate discussions.

The school uses multiple assessments to measure and improve student achievement based on the California State content standards. At the classroom level, various assessments are used to measure progress and appeal to different learning styles. Oral and written assessments are used to accurately measure comprehension, vocabulary development, application of higher level thinking skills, and proficiency in the areas of writing and speaking as applied to related content standards. At the grade level, departments have developed formative and summative evaluations to determine and build on background knowledge. As a culminating schoolwide assessment, all eighth grade students prepare a portfolio to showcase their work in all subject areas. Students are required to reflect on, write about, and discuss their work during the process.

Hopkins West Junior High School

The building site improvement plan is composed of mission, objectives, and tactics to ensure that all students are meeting or exceeding Hopkins standards. The two tactics, literacy and equity, have action steps in place to ensure that teachers are equipped to evaluate individual learning styles and the cultural needs of students by tailoring instructional strategies and using multiple assessments. Highlights include the following:

- Professional development is designed to go a "mile deep rather than a mile wide" by focusing on literacy and equity.

- A critical mass of teachers representing all teams are participating in the National Urban Alliance literacy initiative, in which literacy strategies and David Hjerle's thinking maps are used. The maps have been particularly successful in engaging students of color, but they appeal to all learners, from the underachieving to the gifted. A common language among teachers and students has evolved around the thinking maps, which also serve as a quick assessment tool.

- Project-based assessments allow students to demonstrate their learning in all curricular areas.

- Preassessments in reading/writing/mathematics allow instructors, students, and parents to determine in-school support for students as well as at-home strategies to increase skills in these content areas.

- Initial training and support for teachers during the 2005–06 school year in the implementation of the pre-AP curriculum and instructional strategies will help increase students' critical-thinking skills and better prepare more students for AP courses at Hopkins High School.

RECOMMENDATION 26: Each teacher will have a broad base of **academic knowledge,** with depth in at least one subject area.

Strategies

- Hire only qualified and certified teachers.

- Encourage teachers to stretch their current knowledge in an area of interest in their discipline and pursue advanced degrees and certification in different subject areas.

- Provide ongoing, job-embedded professional development for content area teachers.

- Encourage active participation in professional discipline–specific associations.

Benefits

- Ensures higher quality instruction for students.

- Supports the imperative that at least one person on each academic team has depth in each academic field. In addition, if teachers have broad academic knowledge, they will have the ability to support general student learning to a higher degree.

- Encourages teachers to work with colleagues to integrate the curriculum.

Challenges

- Confronting the serious teacher shortage, especially where emergency certification is the norm, and the competition from other schools (public, private, and charter) for the best teacher candidates.

- Addressing the reality that highly qualified teachers demand higher salaries.

- Scheduling that too often assigns teachers to classes in more than one subject area.

- Certification standards that differ from state to state.

- Asking teachers to become proficient in another area and teach beyond what they already know.

Progress Measures

- Document a decrease in the percentage of teachers teaching "out of field" each year.

- Require a Personal Learning Plan from each teacher by October 1 each year, including documentation of newly researched areas in his or her field as evidence of ongoing personal professional development.

- Administer an end-of-year survey to teachers that includes specific items related to teacher satisfaction, such as teaching in a field of expertise. Correlate results to satisfaction (morale) issues. Compare with actual teacher turnover and substantiate by conducting an exit interview with the same questions.

RECOMMENDATION 27: Teachers will be adept at acting as coaches and facilitators to promote more **active involvement of students** in their own learning.

Strategies

- Provide teachers with training in facilitation and coaching.

- Use integrated coursework, project-based learning (with student choice of projects), and service learning to engage students.

- Require student portfolios and student-led conferences and exhibitions to the community.

- Adopt existing programs, such as the College Board's SpringBoard program, that are designed to promote active learning.

- Train teachers to be guides rather than lecturers.

- Use student team approaches similar to those in science labs.

- Provide students with choices in studies and assessments, and develop curriculum based on those choices.

Benefits

- Increases student engagement, satisfaction, and achievement; decreases discipline problems.

- Improves teacher satisfaction when all students can demonstrate individual and group comprehension of a topic/lesson.

- Promotes independence for students with special needs while at the same time fostering collaboration.

Challenges

- Providing money/resources and release time for training.

- Getting teachers to move away from lecture-driven teaching styles.

- Redesigning curriculum to promote active learning.

- Understanding how to determine and address each student's readiness, interest, and learning profile.

- Addressing the "everyday challenges": behavioral problems, absences, and so on.

Progress Measures

- Conduct classroom observations to measure the amount of class time spent in active learning as opposed to lecture or nonactive learning activities.

- Survey students and teachers to assess the success and impact of programs.

- Review sample teacher-administered assessments to ensure that they are geared toward specific modalities.

RECOMMENDATION 28: Teachers will **integrate assessment into instruction** so that assessment is accomplished using a variety of methods that do not merely measure students but become part of the learning process.

Strategies

- Use preassessment and formative assessment to guide instructional planning.

- Use assessment as a further opportunity to teach.

- Shift perceptions and practices of assessment from judging to supporting and advancing learning.

- Use student portfolios and conduct periodic evaluations of them with the student.

- Create small-scale diagnostic assessments to evaluate student learning and weaknesses, and modify instruction accordingly.

- Use programs that contain supplementary materials to focus on identified student weaknesses.

- Provide extra staff development in the use of assessment as a diagnostic tool.

- Include interactive "student centers" and evaluate students based on their individual skills and abilities.

- Align classroom assessment rubrics with state assessment rubrics.

- Encourage students to generate questions using their familiarity with rubrics and state standards.

- Use backward planning in designing units.

Benefits

- Encourages the use of diagnostic assessments that allow teachers to adjust instruction to meet student needs in identified areas.

- Changes the dynamic of assessment so that students begin to see tests and other assessments as a means of helping them learn.

- Provides an opportunity for students to become familiar with the format and, to a certain extent, the content of state and national assessments.

- Allows all students to be assessed and instructional strategies to be designed to focus on individual learning abilities and intelligences.

Challenges

- Providing time and resources for professional development on alternative assessments.

- Handling teacher resistance to new practices.

- Developing diagnostic assessments.

- Helping students see assessment as helpful to their growth rather than something to be feared.

- Addressing the time-consuming nature of student participation in multiple assessments as the lesson progresses. Some teachers will see this as an intrusion on limited instructional time rather than as an opportunity for learning.

Progress Measures

- Include self-evaluation and journal reflection by students as part of student portfolio reviews.

- Have classroom teachers consistently demonstrate articulation of goals, objectives, and benchmarks for courses and units, as well as teaching strategies and assessments.

Breaking Ranks in the Middle Recommendations

Recommendations 26–28 in Practice

Alvarado Intermediate

Expectations are clear and content standards are posted in every classroom and referenced throughout each lesson. Performance objectives are clearly delineated for students in the classroom, and teachers supply exemplars of high-quality work such as anchor papers, professional models, and scholarly products. Students receive timely feedback from teachers and are expected to edit and revise assignments to reach proficiency standards. Students also have the opportunity to retake tests after the re-teaching of difficult concepts. Alvarado gathers classroom and local assessment data to determine instructional practices. Teachers use a variety of methods to assess student performance: district benchmark tests, exams, oral presentations, and projects. In addition to teacher "read-arounds" of writing projects from other teachers' classes, students regularly assess and edit their own work as well as that of their peers. The school recently instituted the Alvarado Baccalaureate Certificate, which is an attempt to meet the needs of accelerated students. It is designed to offer a transition to high school AP, IB, or honors classes.

Casey Middle School

Teachers use a variety of methods to assess student performance (e.g., exhibitions, projects, performance tasks) and maintain a collection of student work. Students learn how to assess their own and others' work against the performance standards. Students can explain their work and have various opportunities to demonstrate their learning. They write, give talks, perform their works, and debate each other.

- Portfolios are maintained in language arts, reading, and math classes. The seventh grade team maintains a grade-level portfolio on each student.

- Students have a variety of opportunities to explain their work during classes and at the end of units in front of parents.

- Students are beginning to learn how to participate in Socratic seminars.

Teachers are knowledgeable about learning styles and intelligences, and incorporate the visual and performing arts, computer technology, and creative activities to make learning successful for all students. In addition, teachers incorporate the following:

- Varied presentation of materials and instructional styles.

- Models to differentiate instruction and assessment.

- Pre-AP strategies to support incorporating the arts, technology, and high-level questioning.

Rachel Carson Middle School

Teachers encourage the use of many tools and employ strategies and techniques to promote a deep understanding of the knowledge concepts and skills required to be successful. Interactive notebooks are one example. In English, science, and social studies classes, students have the opportunity to record factual information while also synthesizing and making personal reflections on the material at hand. Students make sense of content by having the freedom to create pictures, analytical writings, and personal notes. Students never feel passive in their learning and many have told the teachers that the notebook provides a structure for important facts but also allows space for creative input that is lacking in other note-taking systems.

The use of portfolios is another opportunity for students to reflect on their progress. Currently, several English teachers use portfolios to help students become reflective writers and to connect the classroom to the home. Each quarter, the students are given the opportunity to choose pieces of writing that show their growth as writers. Students write a short reflection that focuses on this growth over the past nine weeks and pinpoints areas for future growth. Parents become involved in this process when students share their portfolio choices and reflections. The English Department is developing a schoolwide portfolio system in which students will begin eighth grade with their portfolio from the previous year.

RECOMMENDATION 29: Recognizing that schooling is a continuum, educators must understand what is required of students at every stage and **ensure a smooth transition** academically and socially for each student from grade to grade and from level to level.

Strategies

- Communicate regularly with elementary schools, high schools, and institutions of higher education.

- Participate in vertical teaming strategies, and include principals in this communication.

- Reach out to parents while children are still in elementary school.

Benefits

- Mitigates students' fear and confusion about what is expected at each level.

- Improves parents' understanding of expectations.

- Provides specific information about student attainment around which teachers can plan instruction to ensure that students are where they need to be at the end of the year.

- Decreases time needed to diagnose incoming students, leading to more efficient use of the school year.

- Allows students to spend more time learning and less time transitioning.

Challenges

- Providing staff time and funding.

- Trying to find common planning time for teachers in different buildings and at different grade levels.

- Coming to consensus about appropriate expectations for the level of mastery students must have before and after the middle level years.

- Setting up a vertical system and operating it smoothly may take a number of years to achieve.

Progress Measures

- Provide evidence of systematic planning and communication between and among all school units at both the program and individual student levels—for example, orientation program agendas; memos; minutes of curriculum, instruction, and administrative articulation meetings; and transition plans.

- Solicit narrative descriptions from students and family members on transition issues encountered when moving from one division to another.

- Enlist content specialists who are not serving on vertical teams to review and make suggestions to the team regarding articulation plans.

Recommendation 29 in Practice

Casey Middle School

Students from the feeder elementary schools shadow students to prepare for the transition, and there is vertical teaming with the high school and the elementary schools. Open Enrollment Nights are held. To support the academic transition, content area teachers are offered pre-AP instruction and critical-thinking strategies are promoted in every classroom.

Culver City Middle School

Because the middle school is part of an educational complex that incorporates the high school, there is a natural articulation between the two schools. Preparation for high school is infused throughout the middle school instructional program. Vertical teaming with the high school is central to the standards-based instructional program. Middle school and high school teachers collaborate with academic departments several times throughout the year during district staff development. Over the past two years, faculty meetings also have been used as an opportunity for high school and middle school teachers to collaborate on developing standards. Teachers for the high school AP program worked with middle school teachers during a staff development day to build standards-based lessons that are differentiated and promote higher level thinking throughout content areas. Preparing for the California High School Exit Examination has been a joint effort between high school and middle school staff members, and the schools sponsored a parent night to provide information about the CAHSEE to both middle and high school parents. High school counselors visit eighth grade classes every spring to discuss ninth grade class offerings. High school and middle school administrators meet monthly at the district for secondary administration meetings to address the instructional needs of both schools, including standards, assessment, and secondary articulation. The middle school counselors work with the high school counselors to gain an understanding of how to best prepare students for a successful transition to high school.

Hopkins West Junior High School

The following are highlights of the school's grade-to-grade and school-to-school transition planning:

- Annual summer data retreats across three levels (elementary, middle, high school) assist in the alignment of curriculum and instruction as well as identify strands to be emphasized in reading/writing/mathematics.

- The summer "Zoom" program for underachieving students entering seventh grade focuses on academic, social, and personal needs during the transition from elementary school.

- Although the ninth grade is housed in the middle school, it is considered part of Hopkins High School in terms of credits, standards, and grade point averages, which helps students make the transition to the high school level.

- Vertical teaming by departments is in place to develop essential learnings in each curricular area K–12.

- During fall 2005, vertical teams implemented pre-AP curriculum and instruction for all students in grades 7–9 (English, science, social studies, and math), with plans to incorporate teams in grades 6–12.

- Vertical teaming by department develops scope and sequence for content area vocabulary development.

Saunders Middle School

The staff meets late each summer to vertically align the curriculum in each of the content areas to guarantee that all standards are thoroughly taught and that there is a clear progression through logically sequenced objectives. Provisions are in place for student learning to be reinforced and extended for those who have attained mastery. There are many opportunities for students not only to attain standards but also to recognize their own potential. The success of the school is evident, but along with that success is an increased self-esteem and respect that the students develop for themselves and their accomplishments.

Sixth, seventh, and eighth grade teachers in each content area meet as a group before the school year begins to analyze the scores on the state assessments. First they look for the highest scores by objective, then they identify the lowest scores. Next, they brainstorm how, during the previous year, instruction differed in the strongest areas compared with the weakest areas. At this session, the teachers look at the curriculum vertically to determine areas of overlap. Having everyone "own" the outcome at the eighth grade level enhances their involvement with delivering effective instruction at each grade level. They mutually agree to stress some objectives at each grade level, so the overall plan ensures that the various objectives are taught and reviewed.

There is a hidden benefit when the teachers meet in this format. Teachers of the younger students are familiar with the pace of learning that worked for those students the previous year and can share this information in planning for the coming year. Areas of strength and weakness can be identified, and the lesson designs can address this information. The class as a whole displays a certain level of maturity, as well as social and emotional developmental characteristics that play a critical role in how the students absorb instruction and master material.

Once this vertical piece is in place, the teachers break into grade-level meetings. Subject area teachers and special education teachers meet by grade level to develop the implementation plan for the outcomes of the vertical meeting. They analyze additional data, using local grade-level assessments, break the data down to the objective level, and make adjustments to the amount of time needed to increase learning in areas that show less desirable outcomes. Ongoing assessments are also built into the map and constitute the formative evaluation. Curriculum maps are posted in the main corridor of the building. This provides parents and teachers with a scope and sequence in each of the content areas and a specific time frame for learning. The maps can also be used to identify areas for cross-curricular planning and instruction.

Teachers at each grade level, including special education teachers, have common planning time during the year, and it is an ongoing expectation that they will monitor progress and the need to adjust the time line during quarterly meetings held at the end of each grading period. Also at these times, teachers can adjust and pace instruction to meet the needs of individual classes. Each group of students is different in how it approaches learning and masters material. Therefore, each year needs to be laid out differently. Collaboration and planning are the key to successful instruction.

Articulation meetings with both the elementary and high schools in the feeder pattern also provide meaningful information. A midyear breakfast with administrators and guidance counselors at each of these levels provides a venue for discussion of trends and needs of the students they represent. Scheduling is discussed from each of these perspectives, so that staff can identify what will be best for each student. The high school personnel lay out their freshman curriculum and describe the type of student who would be best suited for each class. At the elementary meeting, administrators and counselors outline clear criteria so that students in transition will have a good experience from the beginning of their middle school program on.

All curriculum areas follow the map they design as a group, and all aspects of student learning are reflected in the design and flow of instruction. As the school year progresses, reflections on the unit maps are noted, so that the overall plan for covering the curriculum in a timely manner relies on experience as the basis for change.

The curriculum is developed centrally and is aligned with the state standards of learning. It is a rare occurrence when a Saunders staff member is not a part of at least one committee. Staff participate in all aspects of curriculum and assessment development and implementation. Often, it is the Saunders direction that is followed, as the staff members are recognized in the district as being innovative and sensitive to students' developmental needs. Just as adolescents are in constant flux, so must be the program that aims to educate them.

RECOMMENDATION 30: Schools will develop a strategic plan to make **technology** integral to curriculum, instruction, and assessment, accommodating different learning needs and helping teachers individualize and improve the learning process.

Strategies

- Develop partnerships with businesses to provide technology support.

- Provide ongoing training for teachers to integrate technology into the curriculum.

- Encourage teachers to use available technologies as they develop lesson plans.

- Write grant proposals to various companies (e.g., Microsoft and Apple) to fund technology initiatives.

- Create a technology team and develop a technology plan; participate in programs based on computer technology.

Benefits

- Enables the use of a more diverse set of educational programs and products.

- Allows all students to be engaged while teachers are working with smaller groups.

- Teaches students skills that will be required throughout their lifetimes.

- Helps to individualize learning for all students, including those with special needs.

Challenges

- Ensuring that comprehensive technology programs in schools have the capacity to evolve as technology changes (anticipating the impact of changes can be difficult).

- Finding the time, money, training, and resources for ongoing support.

- Finding room for workstations that require nontraditional classroom setups.

- Motivating teachers to become tech-savvy.

Progress Measures

- Document schoolwide adoption of a technology plan with clear standards of use, assessments of effectiveness, plans for periodic updates of hardware and software, and a sound program to protect students from inappropriate material (plan-distributed, as appropriate, and available for review in the school).

- Evidence of teacher participation in an ongoing professional development program in the area of technology (record of activities, teacher participation and mastery of objectives).

- Evidence of technology integration, as appropriate, in teachers' daily lessons (observation).

- Measurements of the increase in the use of technology by students in their academic work.

- Evidence that the development of partnerships and location of grants to support technology initiatives has been undertaken by the technology team (e.g., meeting minutes, letters, e-mails, proposals, phone log, reports, narrative description of activities).

Recommendation 30 in Practice

See Upson-Lee Middle School profile (p. 153)

See Upson-Lee Middle School profile (p. 153)

In Their Own Words...

The following is the final of four school profiles. Each profile has been written from the personal perspective of the principal. The profiles are designed to show the comprehensive and interdependent nature of the reforms your school is being called upon to undertake. Although not all the changes each school has instituted will be appropriate for your school, the perspective of your colleagues should nevertheless be valuable and may form the basis of a discussion for your team. At the end of this profile, you will find a Q&A with the principal as well as several questions to help lead your faculty or team through a discussion. For a protocol to help lead the text-based discussion, see Appendix 4.

Doing Whatever It Takes to Close the Achievement Gap

by Clara Sale-Davis, Principal
Dedicated to Jeremy, whose memory reminds
us of the importance and power of relationships

School Profile 4
Freeport Intermediate School

School Profile 4
Freeport Intermediate School
Freeport, TX
639 students
Grade span 7–8
4 percent limited English proficient
75 percent economically disadvantaged
16 percent special education
For statistics, contacts, and other information about the school, go to www.principals.org/brim.

Practices to look for include:
collaborative leadership, teacher leadership, teaming, flexible schedules, mentoring, interdisciplinary/integrated instruction, and community partnerships.

It was like walking into a scene in a movie, with Guns and Roses playing "Welcome to the Jungle." As I walked through the blue front door on my first day as principal, I saw a courtyard full of children. On the right side of the courtyard was a sea of blue bandanas, and on the left, children waving red bandanas. I grew up on a ranch in East Texas, but I quickly realized that the purpose of these bandanas was not to protect anyone from the dust of a cattle roundup. This confrontation of red versus blue was a direct result of a local tragedy. Just before the start of school, our community had been thrown into turmoil by a drive-by shooting at a local hangout that left a child dead. Three of our students had been charged with capital murder, and the brother of the dead child was entering Freeport Intermediate School.

Parental and community involvement (which had been virtually nonexistent) reached an all-time high in the weeks following the shooting. Everyone gathered at night on the streets for candlelight vigils. At one of those vigils, a parent spotted me in the crowd. He shouted, "You're the principal! Say something to our kids!" I was holding my two-year-old daughter in my arms, but the urgency in his voice impelled me to speak. I stood before the angry crowd and spoke from my heart. I don't remember what I said, but I do remember that afterward there were lots of tears and hugs, and the crowd slowly dispersed. I thanked God for both the courage and the words, but mostly for the fact that no one else was shot by the retaliating gang.

The bandana standoff was the welcome I received on my first day as principal at Freeport Intermediate School more than a decade ago. Just minutes before entering the "Blue Door to Hell," I had been saying the Pledge of Allegiance with my elementary students. I had been offered this assignment as a last hope—Freeport had gone through five principals in six years. Because I did not want to give up my elementary principal-ship, I became principal of both O. A. Fleming Elementary and Freeport Intermediate School. The schools sat side by side, and the configuration had changed as the fifth and sixth grades had been given their own "center."

Ten years later, Freeport Intermediate School is a success story, something very few people would have thought possible. The school was considered a combat zone and was designated "low performing" according to our state standardized tests. As in many high-poverty schools, our economically disadvantaged students scored far below state averages, and children of color scored far below their white counterparts. Now, the school has risen to the top, and the students and their academic success are living proof that validates Freeport's motto, "The Place Where Great Things Happen"; our vision statement, "Success for All"; and our mission statement, "Whatever It Takes." Posted throughout the school, the sentiment "Whatever It Takes" serves as a constant reminder of the incredible journey from being a low-performing, scholastically challenged school with no esprit de corps to becoming one of four schools in the nation chosen by the National Forum to Accelerate Middle Grades Reform as a "National School to Watch" and a "National Blue Ribbon School." These awards reaffirm the staff's belief that all students can be successful when they are educated in a supportive environment that promotes academic excellence, social equity, and a rigorous curriculum with programs that are developmentally responsive to young adolescents and their unique needs.

In the Beginning: Establishing Professional Learning Communities

When spider webs unite, they can tie up a lion.

—Ethiopian proverb

I am often asked "Where does the journey begin?" "Where do you start?" And the most common question: "How do you get teacher buy-in?"

Where does the journey begin? In schools, there is usually a sense of urgency about *something*. That "something" could be school safety, low test scores, parental involvement, working in isolation, creating more rigor and relevance, differentiated instruction, or inclusion. These issues are all important, so where do you start?

First, the principal must demonstrate an unwavering resolve to do what must be done. At Freeport Intermediate, in the first year of our journey we focused on creating a safe and orderly school environment. Gang problems, an inexperienced staff, and threats to personal safety took precedence over rigor and relevance of curriculum. We first had to create collaborative groups to ensure a safe and orderly school environment. From my perspective, "organizing the troops to fight the battles" was nonnegotiable. Our "professional learning communities" included the Freeport Police Department and outside gang consultants. While other schools in the district were involved in curriculum mapping and learning styles, we were creating crisis plans for bomb threats, armed intruders, and drive-by shootings.

In addition to crisis management, ever present in our minds were the low test scores on the state standardized tests, which also showed large achievement gaps

Figure 4.4
The Deming Model of Total Quality Management

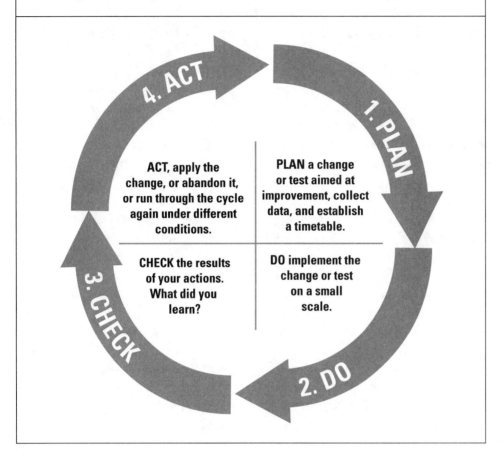

ACT, apply the change, or abandon it, or run through the cycle again under different conditions.

PLAN a change or test aimed at improvement, collect data, and establish a timetable.

CHECK the results of your actions. What did you learn?

DO implement the change or test on a small scale.

4. ACT

1. PLAN

3. CHECK

2. DO

between student groups. We were labeled "low performing" and required to create plans for improvement. The systems or organizational structures had to be created in order to focus on what was to be done. To involve all stakeholders in the campus improvement process, we organized cadres to ensure a plan-do-check-act (PDCA) model, based on the Deming model of total quality management and the work of John Goodlad (see figure 4.4). These cadres were designed to deal with issues that cut across all areas of school improvement and to drive the school improvement plan for the campus. Now, every staff member is required to be on a cadre—the custodians and lunchroom personnel are just now coming on board. The leaders and co-leaders of each cadre comprise the Campus Advisory Team (CAT), and this team serves as an advisory council in five areas:

- Curriculum and instruction—focusing on teaching and learning of all students (research and data-based).

- Staff development—focusing on quality, relevance, certification requirements, and innovative staff development throughout the year.

- Planning—focusing on student and faculty attendance and special projects to promote relevance, rigor, and fun.

- Communication—focusing on effective communication between home and school, intraschool, and school and community.

- School climate—focusing on student and staff morale, and schoolwide discipline; developing plans based on student, staff, parent, and community surveys.

The cadres have the autonomy to set up their own meeting times, but the goals established in the Campus Improvement Plan (CIP) are the driving force of their agendas. The leaders and co-leaders of each cadre work as a school leadership team to set the school budget and monitor the CIP. The leaders and co-leaders are chosen by cadre consensus and work collaboratively with the principal to ensure that goals are being met. The Campus Advisory Team meets during a summer retreat to study schoolwide data in order to set the goals outlined in the CIP. When school in-services begin, it is the responsibility of the leaders to report back to their cadres the information shared at the retreat. At that time, new goals are presented and discussed, and each cadre begins its individual action plan.

These organizational structures create "focused cells" for continuous improvement in almost every critical issue. The key to the success of these cadres is providing leadership training and drawing on the strengths that everyone brings to the table. As demonstrated when I was out on maternity leave and again when I was absent for a month for health reasons, we have succeeded in ensuring that these systems are not "principal co-dependent" and can be sustained when the principal is not around.

Transformational changes began to emerge as we started working not only in cadres but also as interdisciplinary teams and departments. The culture of working in isolation began to dissolve as the culture of teamwork emerged. As a direct result of this transformation, students began to benefit from more creative lessons and from seeing their teachers actually enjoy teaching! Cooperative teaching created cooperative learning, and cooperative learning created lots of risk-taking. Students were enjoying the lessons so much that they frequently forgot their gang affiliation.

Our collaborative work allowed us to begin to examine and reflect on what needed to be accomplished. Once our mission became clear, we created a laserlike focus on preparing students to use the state test as a tool to help them think more deeply about why and how they learn. We are often criticized for "teaching the test," but our goal actually is to teach the standards that are clearly outlined and to work collectively to improve student achievement. Our state tests became a means of creating unity of purpose. The test challenged us to reflect intensely on how we taught. We discovered that we often used common practices instead of common sense. Among other things, this reflection prompted us to move away from clustering English language learners and special education students in pull-outs, a practice that delivered dismal results, and to move toward an inclusive model that has created a culture of serving *all* students, resulting in higher performance and lower failure rates.

Collective Capacity to Support Student Learning

We can achieve our fundamental purpose of high levels of learning for all students only if we work together. We cultivate this collaborative culture through the development of high-performing teams.

—Rick DuFour

One of the most powerful opportunities afforded Freeport teachers is the time to learn from one another. At every faculty meeting one of our "expert" teacher leaders shares an area of instructional focus. In addition, block scheduling has allowed us to provide substantial vertical team alignment time and other opportunities for collaboration in our master schedule. Interdisciplinary teams meet on "A" days for 90 minutes, while departments of vertical teams meet on "B" days. Interdisciplinary teams and departments meet at least once a week, and agendas are submitted to the principal that reflect the use of meeting management tools. These regularly scheduled collaborative times reaffirm the staff's belief that power is gained from within by drawing on the strengths and expertise of others. Expertise is promulgated through sharing and collaboration, supported by the team-building atmosphere and culture. Students witness teachers sharing and learning from one another and understand that they, the students, are the ones who ultimately benefit.

By consciously setting aside time for planning, we have enabled interdisciplinary teams to integrate themes across the curriculum. In every classroom, students are encouraged to understand the connections among disciplines and to make real-world applications. This year, the CAT decided to help students understand the need to creatively solve unexpected problems. The math vertical teams, who meet on "B" days, took this project to heart and created an instructional video series focused on applying math skills to real-world scenarios. Teachers and staff ran obstacle courses, had eating contests, raced bumper boats and cars, played volleyball, and completed other "stunts" so that our students could assess their skills in real-world problem solving via the television broadcast. (After spending a day doing this film shoot, we decided that we truly live up to our mission: Whatever it takes!) Projects such as these are motivational enough to inspire and instructional enough to move students toward proficiency in the subject areas. Other examples of how interdisciplinary activities extend beyond the core classes include the following. Various clubs and organizations advertise dances and sponsored events using the "Hand" summary, an instrument in the language classes that is used to tell who, what, when, where, and why. Mrs. Livingston, a physical education teacher, uses a T-chart, a prewriting instrument that outlines advantages and disadvantages of a situation, to encourage students to join the track team. Our band director, Mrs. Crummel, researched and presented Eric Jensen's *Music With the Brain in Mind* to boost teaching, learning, and creativity, and the music department follows up by providing a collection of CDs for every teacher to use in his or her classroom.

One of the biggest challenges to establishing professional learning communities is finding the money to fund the projects, the staff development requests, materials for students, summer retreats, and other innovative strategies. We always seem to do it, "some how, some way." If it means working in concession stands or selling pickles and popcorn after school, that's what we do. One year, the CAT partnered with a school from Louisiana to provide their teachers with a staff development day. In return, we were given hotel rooms and a meal. They were surprised that we could fit 20 people in four rooms! That collaboration is ongoing, as we continue to learn from each other and share best practices. This past year we worked concession stands and had garage sales to pay for our retreat in Las Vegas. We divided what money we had earned collectively and used personal funds to pay for the trip. We spent two days and one late evening in a conference room, studying data and research from the Model Schools Conference, planning the upcoming school year, and refining the campus improvement plan.

How do you get teachers to buy in to these systems?

One-third of a teaching staff will embrace this kind of accountability and will want to be a part of the "think tanks" and problem-solving groups. Another third will not be sure about the changes. Target this group! Use research to support the need for continuous improvement and change. This group needs proof; they will be cautious in the beginning, until you and other members of your team convince them to come on board. The last third will *not* buy in. Don't stress over it—focus your energies on the second group. However, you will need to have some uncomfortable conversations with members of the third group. Perhaps they need additional information or more time to think about the process of change. Or perhaps they need to be counseled into another school or even another profession. If these naysayers are allowed to permeate your professional learning community, the result will be low morale and negativity. In his book *Good to Great,* Jim Collins offers what I call the "bus theory." First, get the right people on the bus, the wrong people off the bus, and the right people in the right seats, Collins says, then figure out where to drive it!

Improving Academic Achievement: It's All About Relationships

If relationships are wrong between teachers and students, for whatever reasons, you can restructure until the cows come home, but transformation won't take place.

—Maguire in Rothman (1992)

This quote is often recited by veteran teachers as they mentor new teachers. Relationships between teachers and students must be cultivated, promoted, nourished, and maintained. At Freeport Intermediate School, the relationships manifest themselves in learner-centered hallways full of student work, staff participation at sports events, faculty/student basketball games, yearbook parties, music concerts, lock-ins, drama events, school dances, and academic pep rallies, which take place every six weeks to recognize and encourage academic excellence.

We stretch the limits to fill in the gaps in students' lives so their essential needs are met and they can focus on learning. Everyone takes on the role of being a social worker, addressing fundamental issues such as food, shelter, clothing, medicine, and personal hygiene. In addition, the district employs one social worker for all the schools; fortunately, her home base is Freeport Intermediate. Our social worker and our school nurse help numerous families in the community to navigate social service agencies, health insurance companies, and medical offices. Coaches and staff supervise the locker rooms in the morning so students who are unable to wash at home can shower before classes. Students who need clean clothes can find them at school, along with a washer and dryer for their dirty clothes. We understand the hard reality of children living in poverty and, with a sense of urgency, we are teaching them that a good education is their ticket to success—a way to break certain cycles. By filling in the gaps related to personal needs, we have filled in the academic gaps: eliminating disparities in achievement among student groups, improving attendance, and dramatically decreasing discipline referrals.

Another way we are looking to break cycles and create opportunities is by starting conversations about completing high school and going on to college—something that has never been a vision for many of our students. We also solicit volunteers from our business partners—BASF and Dow Chemical Company—to join our staff in mentoring and after-school enrichment programs. For the past two years, Dow Chemical has sponsored the Comeback Kid Award, which honors a student who has overcome tremendous adversity to become academically successful. Other ways in which our community has helped provide opportunities for students include these: Dow has funded participation in state and national academic competitions for our students; Liquid Natural Gas Company has created a partnership with a Houston school to provide field trips and networking for students; and the Veterans of Foreign Wars help students compete in essay competitions and provide recognition and monetary prizes.

Welcome to the Tribe!

Community partnerships, addressing social issues, and planting the seed for high school and college have been critical to our success. But the core of our effort to create a personalized environment that supports each student's intellectual, ethical, social, and physical development is our tightly knit structure of tribes. The structure allows teachers to regularly discuss their students' academic and emotional needs and ensures that each student is known by several faculty members. The school operates a school within a school by dividing the students into four academic teams: two seventh grade tribes and two eighth grade tribes. Each tribe has a name, colors, and a chant. All teachers in the tribe feel a sense of responsibility and desire for each student's success. Elective teachers and support staff attach themselves to a tribe (or are adopted!). Students assigned to the tribe are grouped heterogeneously, including English language learners, special education students, and migrant students. Gifted and talented students are grouped for core classes so that a differentiated gifted curriculum can be delivered. All others are mainstreamed and are a part of the inclusion team. Special teachers and paraprofessionals travel to various classes to help provide modifications. Severely mentally challenged students receive instruction in a loving life skills classroom and are included in the mainstream as much as possible.

Tribes improve student self-esteem by providing a sense of "home" to students and a sense of safety, security, and belonging. Cultural differences are set aside, and students and teachers form a lasting bond. The tribal sense of family is so strong that the (retired) director of the Brazoria County Youth Home, Ann Huey, says our tribe system is one of the reasons students who are removed from their homes adjust so quickly in the youth home. The tribe teachers attempt to extend this sense of family to the actual families of each of their students. Often, when parents are unable to come to a tribe meeting because of work schedules, the tribe accommodates the parents by making a home visit after school. If it is impossible to meet, the tribe schedules a conference call and takes written minutes of the conversation. For our team, meeting outside contractual hours is not a problem if that's what it takes to make the contact. We understand that our blue-collar environment often does not allow parents to take time away from work.

Counselors also play a vital role in assisting tribes when students have special issues, providing far more than academic counseling. They work closely with Behavior Management Team members in developing and implementing behavior management interventions, and they work collaboratively with teachers, staff, and students to offer bullying mitigation, drug education, and conflict resolution programs. Often, counselors become the liaison between home and school and between student and teacher. Counselors also seek additional support for students and parents by making referrals to the appropriate agencies, such as Mental Health and Mental Retardation, Youth and Family Counseling, the Council on Alcohol and Substance Abuse, Alcoholics Anonymous, and Al-Anon. The counselors and assistant principals loop with each grade level and, on occasion, offer assistance to students in high school in filling out college applications.

The tribe structure creates strong bonds. The tribe concept has become part of our culture, with great rewards and a tiny downside: Parents call me in the summer requesting a certain tribe for their child. Before school started this year I received this message on my voicemail: "I was a Mayan when I was in school, my oldest daughter was a Mayan, and now I want my son to be a Mayan…make that happen for me!"

Can you sing? Can you dance?
Hiring teachers is a shared responsibility for each tribe. Rarely do I hire teachers without having other members of the tribe take part in the interview process. Recently, I was at a conference, and two teachers took my place at a job fair to hire their teammate. We have the standard interview questions, and then we add the Freeport "Questioning Norms." The first question goes like this:

> *A student in your class continually comes to your class without supplies. You have reminded this student on several occasions to please remember to bring his or her supplies to class, and the reminders have not changed the behavior. What is your next step?*

Acceptable answers vary, but we like to hear themes that support the sentiment that this is not a battle; or that are similar to the solution of one of our teachers, who created a spot in the classroom for the student to keep supplies, or that echo the words of one of our staff members, "Just give the kid a pencil and git 'er done!"

Other questions for the prospective teacher might be to describe his or her philosophy of homework. We believe that "homework" has a different meaning when you have no home. We believe that quality, not quantity, is the goal. We also believe in no homework on game nights, since we will be out late. Copying on the bus with a flashlight defeats the purpose.

We wait until the very end of the interview to ask our favorite questions: Can you sing? Can you dance? Will you try? At Freeport, teachers and staff routinely dress up in costumes and perform skits for the students. Tribes chant songs and inspirational rhymes at our famous academic pep rallies. We dress up in thematic clothing to celebrate our state tests. Our students think we are crazy, and visitors look on in awe (or disgust) as we dance with Shrek at the Swamp Karaoke Party. We refrain from complaining about the unmotivated, uncaring youth of today, and we do not blame hormones for shortcomings of middle school children. We simply do whatever it takes to "drill and thrill" our students. We pride ourselves in knowing that we are being developmentally responsive to young adolescents. We revel in our students' distinctive energy and spirit. As assistant principal Kristi Traylor said, "We're not afraid to make fools of ourselves to show them that we're human, too."

The team interview process can be a challenge, especially when members of the team try to seek out clones rather than valuing diversity in teaching styles. We put a lot of effort into matching the right person to the rest of the personalities on the tribe. In fact, we often use the *True Colors* program to reflect on our personality styles and to seek new members who have different colors (strengths) that will complement those of the tribe. We quickly detect and eliminate applicants who put down our community, think of it as a "tour of duty," or believe minority and poor children can't learn. My staff makes it miserable for anyone who just wants to draw a paycheck. If they are dead weight, they get the message that they don't belong here, and they get the heck out.

Academic Excellence: Rigor and Relevance in High-Stakes Accountability

Effective schools, which benefit all children, exist primarily for the purpose of teaching and learning. They have identified a core body of knowledge or set [of] skills which are to be taught to and mastered by all students. They have staffs willing to be held accountable for teaching these essential skills.

—Larry Lezotte and Ron Edmonds

The Texas Assessment of Knowledge and Skills (TAKS) is the driving force that creates for each teacher, student, and parent a pervasive sense of personal accountability for student learning and success. Academic success for each student is the foremost goal at Freeport, and the TAKS, which is the key to promotion and graduation, underlines the need for schools to focus on instruction. Freeport has embraced accountability when it comes to students passing the state standardized test, but test results are not the only measure of success. The staff takes the written curriculum—Texas Essential Knowledge and Skills (TEKS)—to a much higher level by incorporating creative methodology that enhances the delivery of instruction and keeps students on the edge of their seats as they experience real-world connections. Students are not only armed with tools for passing the test but are also gaining confidence for the transition to high school.

At Freeport, data drives what instruction is provided, to whom, when, and how. We analyze the results from the state tests to look for weaknesses, to make sure the required curriculum is covered, and to tailor future instructional time so that the proper amount of time is spent in each area. To evaluate how well the curriculum is being addressed, teachers conduct ongoing student assessments and share the results with colleagues. Often these assessments allow teams to see who has been particularly effective in teaching a skill, which in turn may prompt the team as a whole to adopt or replicate that practice.

To provide additional time to students who need tutorials and enrichment/extensions for those who have mastered the core curriculum as measured by the regular assessments, we have created a Team Time hour in the master schedule. The academic tribes group and regroup students according to individual needs and assessment results. These Team Time groups are ever-changing, so students benefit from receiving instruction from a variety of "voices" with varied areas of expertise.

Students who are still unable to demonstrate mastery are offered a "pyramid of interventions." During the spring semester, we offer an Extended Day Program for all students who are in danger of failing or who still need additional time for mastery. Rather than penalizing a student for doing poorly during the school year by requiring him or her to attend summer school, this proactive approach is used to help students before they fail. As a check on progress, tribe teachers, assisted by the counselors, track students who are not demonstrating success. They determine whether the problems are academic or social/emotional. Working collaboratively has proven to be successful in creating high performance on TAKS and has caused a dramatic decrease in failure rates. On average, only two students have been retained each year over the past five years, and the retentions have usually been attributed to truancy or failure to attend summer school. Summer school is offered for students who fail two or more core courses; enrollment has declined as a result of the successful intervention offered by the Extended Day Program. In summer 2000, we served 65 students; in 2001, 39 students; and in 2005, 16 students, of whom all but two successfully completed the summer school program. Another measure of our success is that enrollment in high school math prep classes has dropped from 10 to 2.

Over the summer, our Data Divas (Jeanne and Michelle, our math department leaders) carefully analyzed every item to determine the direction we need to take in creating the instructional calendars. We have mourned the fact that scores in math have dropped below the 90th percentile. Our challenge will be closing the gap for one of our student groups that showed a decline in math. In this student group, we found a direct correlation between low performance and students being sent to an alternative setting (Boot Camp) after committing a felony. Now we must decide where to build the pyramid of intervention in order to close the gap once again. We have started conversations about serving students in those alternative settings—we're not letting go, even though they are not being served in our building.

Another challenge will be the performance of special education students who have been in feeder school pull-out programs and are now merging into the mainstream. Meeting the AYP (annual yearly progress or, as one person calls it, "are you praying?") is always a priority. We hold firm to the idea that state standardized tests are not "one size fits all," and we are grateful that our state acknowledges that fact by allowing us to give a State Developed Alternative Assessment (SDAA) that measures whether or not we have met the expectations outlined in Individual Education Plans (IEPs). While we believe that all students can learn, we also believe that students with disabilities should not be measured with an inappropriate "standardized" assessment, which is the reasoning behind *Individual* Education Plans. In addition to focusing on special education performance, we will begin conversations about helping our gifted and talented (G/T) students reach "commended performance"—a recognition that should boost their confidence enough to enter more advanced classes in high school. (Our counselors also meet with individual G/T students in the spring of their eighth grade year to help them make choices for high school.)

"Celebrate Good Times! Come On!"

—Lyrics from "Celebration," by Kool and the Gang

Every six weeks, the excitement stirs as students and staff prepare for a communitywide celebration. Thundering sticks and the beat of drums grow louder and louder as students, clad in tribal shirts, parade through the doors of victory in the Freeport Performance Gym. Parents are seated and standing and the high school students are sneaking in through the back door, hoping they don't get caught by the assistant principals. What's at stake is not a winning team's sports event. Academics are the force driving the Freeport Intermediate Rowdy Redskins into a frenzy. Each tribe sits in its designated place, awaiting the arrival of its leader.

This is when I feel like a rock star getting ready to go onstage: the roar of the crowd, the anticipation, the enthusiasm. Sometimes I appear on a horse, riding in like George Strait at the Houston Rodeo. Other times, I appear in a rocket ship, with smoke concealing my presence, or I ride in on the back of a Harley-Davidson, relishing the sound of the revved-up motorcycle as it jumps off the ramp. At other times, I enter on a Roman chariot, with someone fanning me with a palm leaf. This may be the closest thing to greatness that I will ever experience in a school setting!

It may be hard to understand the feelings I have at these celebrations. Tears stream down my face each and every time, tears that are always wiped clean before I hit the stage. I look over a sea of children who do well despite the obstacles in their lives. We celebrate individual accomplishments and the achievements of teams who have had fun as they compete to outdo each other for highly coveted honors: a trophy for the best tribe attendance, a trophy for the tribe with the fewest number of discipline referrals, a trophy for the tribe having the most Accelerated Reading Team members, and a trophy for the tribe with the "Most Spirit." Every year, there is more and more to celebrate as the school continues to receive accolades. Visitors from around the country stand amazed at the camaraderie that is demonstrated as individual awards are received. Students cheer for the parents and community members who have joined them for this momentous celebration, a recognition that "it takes a whole village to become exemplary."

My welcoming speech is brief but filled with love. I tell the students that they are the best students in the nation and praise the staff for being the best teachers in the world. And they know I mean it. There is never a question in anyone's mind that the principal and the staff of Freeport Intermediate, although perhaps a little crazy, are on the students' team and are there to cheer them on.

(I never "caught" you sneaking in, Jeremy. I figured you probably needed to be there. I know now that your spirit will always be there to affirm that relationships really matter.)

Staff Development: If You Don't Go, You Won't Grow

When I die, I hope it will be during an inservice. That way, it will be such a subtle transition between life and death.

—A bored teacher (NOT at Freeport)

Sometimes staff development offerings make me think of the seagulls that fly around our school. Experts and consultants fly over, drop the poop, and leave. You are sometimes left with great ideas, but they are in the handout that you put somewhere on your desk...or is it still in the car? For the past two years, Freeport Intermediate has sought to alter this pattern of fly-by staff development by collaboratively planning meaningful workshops that fall into three categories: reflective staff development, sharing best practices, and motivation.

Reflective staff development. We closely examine the goals outlined in our improvement plan, and the Staff Development Cadre brainstorms ways to accomplish those goals and measure whether they have been met. This process is ongoing and is revisited at every staff meeting, every cadre meeting, every department meeting, and every team meeting. Our most powerful experts are our very own teachers. Teachers know that one of their responsibilities is to share best practices and effective teaching strategies. To meet their unique professional needs, each teacher must have a personal plan for professional development. These plans are discussed at length with the teachers during their summative conferences. Teachers who are new to the profession and veteran teachers who are new to our school begin by attending the Teacher Induction Program (TIP) sponsored by the district, in which master teachers help new teachers adopt basic classroom management techniques and strategies that will ensure high levels of success for all students. The TIP motto is "If you dare to teach, then you must dare to learn." At Freeport, the TIP is continued through the school year in the form of bimonthly meetings (Rowdy Redskin Rookie Camp) in which we immerse new staff members in the Freeport belief system, philosophy, policies, and procedures. First-year teachers are provided with a mentor after both mentor and mentee have received formal training in the mentoring process. Our Curriculum and Instruction Cadre is creating a teacher handbook for new personnel and, together with the Staff Development Cadre, we will take turns working with new teachers and meeting bimonthly to discuss the needs of our new teachers.

Sharing best practices. We believe that all ideas are stolen, modified to look like they are not stolen, and shared among thieves. Teachers are encouraged to attend content-specific conferences and workshops, and to share what they learn, especially if it correlates with our campus goals:

■ Each teacher is encouraged to obtain 30 contact hours toward GT certification. We want every core teacher to be highly qualified to meet the needs of gifted learners. This is a population that cannot be overlooked; yet, so often, mobility, poverty, or language barriers cause children to miss out in elementary school when the identification process takes place.

■ Each teacher should attend training to help meet the needs of our special populations as we continue to use inclusion methodology in our classrooms.

■ Teachers should integrate instructional technology into every aspect of teaching. We know that we cannot prepare our students for the 21st century one worksheet at a time. Students are ready for the technology, but are we? To ensure that we are meeting the technological needs of the future, our staff attends technology conferences each year. This year we are sending tech reps and teachers from each discipline in order to stay on the cutting edge of integrating technology in the classroom.

Motivation. To motivate students, the staff needs motivational direction. My Staff Development Cadre expressed weariness with book studies and research-based lectures. The cadre challenged me to think outside the box and promised to assist with any innovative idea that I chose to implement. Let the fun begin.... Instructions were mailed to staff members' homes. They were to dress casually and bring a lawn/lounge chair and a pillow. Our secretaries and assistant principals had transformed our gymnasium into a movie theater, complete with a concession stand and movie posters in the hallway. The staff was given a laminated rose as their "ticket." As they entered the "theater" they smelled popcorn and got to choose between Mike and Ikes and Milk Duds. We watched the movie "Seabiscuit." After the movie, we broke into cooperative learning groups to do an activity using numerous quotes from the movie. Each group gave its own interpretation of a quote and how that quote could be applied to our school and our children. At the close of the in-service, we taped our laminated roses around the horse's neck made for the occasion and made a commitment that we would strive to put every student at Freeport in the Winner's Circle. Sometimes movies say more than I can ever interpret from the research. For example, what better way to illustrate inclusion than the movie "Radio" or to illustrate teambuilding than "Miracle" or "Remember the Titans"? These opportunities motivated the unmotivated. The evaluations were glorious! Of course, the director of staff development called the next day to say that a movie was not considered a research-based in-service activity and was not considered quality staff development. I remembered a quote from "Seabiscuit": "He is fast in every direction. He is so screwed up and running in circles. He just needs to learn how to be a horse again." Sometimes it's healthy to get off the track and run free, even if we stir up a little dirt. Whatever it takes!

Parental Involvement: "In Loco Parentis"

My momma can't be at the game tonight, so you need to be there to watch me...and you need to be on time!

—Freeport student

We are constantly seeking innovative ways to increase parental involvement, especially for the hard-to-reach parent. I have to say up front that, for Freeport, this mission is a work in progress. The largest parent turnouts happen when children perform (e.g., sports events and band concerts), so I make it a point to be there and/or to schedule PTA meetings before the concerts begin. The majority of our parents work, many doing shiftwork in our plants on the "chemical coast." The stay-at-home mom is very rare in our area, and many of our children are raised by single parents or grandparents, or live in the Brazoria County Youth Home. Rather than using the lack of substantial parental volunteering and involvement as an excuse for low student performance, we build on the strengths of our PTA and the community patrons.

This year, I was able to replace our switchboard operator/receptionist with a bilingual staff member, and last year I hired a bilingual counselor. These two staff members have opened many doors and made connections with our Spanish-speaking parents and community members. We have had the following successes in encouraging parental participation: our sign-in logs indicate that we have had more parental participation in special education meetings than ever before and our Academic Pep Rallies, held every six weeks, attract more than 80 parents for each rally. During the summer we let everyone know the dates so parents can try to attend.

Our communications to parents include these:

- *TEE PEE TALK,* our school newsletter, which is created and disseminated by the Communication Cadre, mailed to all PTA members, posted on the website, and given to each student to take home. It includes a letter from the Princi-PAL, news from each tribe, a schedule of upcoming events, and a school lunch menu.

- Welcoming brochures that each tribe sends out at the beginning of the school year. The brochures contain a picture of the tribe members and important information (supply list, bell schedule, tribe conference times, e-mail addresses, and phone numbers).

- "Positive" postcards and e-mails that each teacher sends home on a regular basis to let parents hear good news from school. In this way, we begin to build a level of trust, and parents get a charge out of hearing something positive about their children.

I work closely with our PTA Executive Board to ensure that I hear the voices of our customers and share with them our mission and vision. The PTA offers parenting programs as part of many general meetings, and teachers often send requests for volunteers to complement the core team of volunteers that assists our teachers with copying, field trips, and hall monitoring during testing week. We are so grateful when a parent offers to help us. Thank you notes are sent, and morale is lifted.

Parents trust teachers at Freeport. They know that in a crisis we will be there to assist or to determine what needs to be done. Many parents have our cell phone numbers, and they call and leave messages during the day. Even after students leave to go to high school, I often stay connected to their parents. As a working parent with two school-age children, I can understand the difficulty of being visible in my children's schools. Like all parents, I know that I am sending the schools the best that I have: my precious children. I expect them to be taught creatively; to feel a sense of love, belonging, and security; and to be treated as though they are special—which they are. When I examine my expectations for my own children, I realize that we must create that same environment for all children. After all, they are "our" kids!

Smooth Transitions: Paving the Way for Student Success

At Freeport, numerous activities are in place to ensure the successful transition of students entering our school from feeder schools, transfer students, and eighth-graders preparing to enter high school.

- This year I will be working with two new principals: our fifth-sixth grade center principal and our new high school principal. We have committed to examining innovative ways to enhance what we have in place; our CATs are already working together to make this happen. One of our elementary campuses, Velasco Elementary, has organized a field trip for its fourth-graders to visit our school. The principal, Sam Williams, wants his students to have a vision so they can mentally prepare for middle school before they leave their elementary campus.

- To facilitate the transition from the middle school (5–6) to the intermediate school (7–8), Freeport's counselors go to our feeder campuses to give presentations to the students. At this meeting, schedule choices, dress code, lockers, the culture of the campus, and other topics are discussed. Elective teachers (band, choir, and orchestra) also visit the campuses to promote electives. In the spring, we invite parents to tour the campus. One year we had a luau for our sixth-graders; we helped more than 300 parents and children complete schedules that night before they left the building! It was a large undertaking, as we separated parents from children and took them to different "ports of call" on the campus. The evening culminated with a Style Show to demonstrate "What's Hot! What's Not!" Students walked down the catwalk modeling appropriate attire, while staff members demonstrated overly baggy pants, too much bling-bling, and "fallout." I will never forget the look on parents' faces. One parent said, "You guys are nuts! But I get the point."

- We invite one of our smaller feeder schools to our last Academic Pep Rally of the year. The students are welcomed by our faculty and students and given a tour of the campus by Student Council and National Junior Honor Society members, so they'll know where to go when they enter in the fall.

- In the fall, we have separate transition meetings with seventh- and eighth-graders to address the unique needs of each.

- During the summer, each student is mailed a brochure from the tribe to which he or she has been assigned. Students also get a letter from the principal with an invitation to attend our famous Back-to-School Pow-Wow. At this event, parents and students meet the teachers, receive their schedules, and tour the school. Parents and students enter the building to music and report to the gym for the opening ceremonies. This meeting is held several days before school starts so that problems such as immunizations, birth certificates, and schedules can be worked out. We try very hard to smooth the way for a great first day.

- Students who enter Freeport from other schools during the year also receive special attention. If the student is a non-English-speaker, we immediately make a bilingual aide available to interpret and assist in the enrollment process. For all new students, we assign a buddy from the Student Council to shadow them to their classes and to eat lunch with them. At the end of the day, the buddy will show the student where to catch the bus. Our guidance secretary makes it a point to let me know when new students have arrived for enrollment. I try to meet every new parent and child and welcome them to our school.

- As our students leave us to attend high school, the high school counselors meet with each of them to discuss options concerning schedules. Our own counselors follow up with another meeting to ensure that everyone understands the track students will be taking.

- Last spring, our PTA afforded parents an opportunity to meet the high school counselor, and she offered a presentation about ninth grade expectations.

- Coaches, many of whom are already familiar to our students, meet separately with groups of boys and girls to recruit them for the sports program.

- Each year, the high school holds an elective fair in the spring to familiarize students with schedule options.

Each student has support systems to make smooth transitions, and I look forward to working in vertical teams to make these support systems even better in the future.

Personalization and the Cost of Doing Without It

One of the most priceless experiences for me is high school graduation. Each year, all the feeder school principals (elementary and middle school) are invited to serve as "panel" guests on the platform for graduation. The high school principal acknowledges each feeder school and has the graduates stand when their elementary and middle schools are announced. Many of our teachers are in the audience, cheering the students on.

Every year for the past nine years, I have been at graduation. Each year I know that there are some faces missing. Where are they? Why didn't they make it across the stage? I see some in Wal-Mart. Monica, who now has three kids. She got pregnant in the ninth grade and felt that she had no other option except to quit school. Marcus, a fine athlete who is now serving time in prison. De'Ondre, whose "godmother" died. I loved Godmother. She once told me that she wasn't really De'Ondre's kin, but that she took him in when he was a baby "because his momma just couldn't seem to get things straightened out."

School Profile 4
Freeport Intermediate School

…And then there was Jeremy, a Freeport success story, the student to whom this essay is dedicated.

Jeremy was the student who got on everyone's last nerve. He knew just what buttons to push, yet always refrained from pushing the very last button. His first year at Freeport gained him frequent flyer miles to the office. The next year, he was embraced by his tribe and offered a "mountain" of interventions. He came to every Extended Day offered—for all subjects. In the end, he scored a perfect 4 in writing on his state test and passed all sections.

True to his tribe's slogan ("Once a Cherokee, always a Cherokee"), he bragged to everyone on the last day at Freeport that he was going to wear his Cherokee tribe shirt on the first day of high school. And he did, as we discovered when he came back to visit us that day. He came back quite frequently after that, wanting to see his former teachers. Whenever I spotted him, I reminded him that high school students were not supposed to be on the intermediate school campus. He would beg me, and then I would look the other way, knowing full well that he was sneaking in the back door. I noticed that his eyes were not sparkling as they had in the past. His red hair looked scruffy, and he no longer carried his shoulders up high. The bounce seemed to be missing from his step. I remember my last words to him were, "Jeremy, you know I love you, but if you continue to come on the campus, I will have to call the police." Then I turned the other way, and he slowly walked down the hall. He didn't sneak that last time. I didn't see him for a while, and I assumed that my lecture had put a stop to his noncompliant behavior.

Several weeks later, I got a call from the high school. They needed to borrow our counselor because there had been a horrible car wreck. Several boys had decided to skip school that day…there were no survivors.

Telling the Cherokee Tribe that Jeremy was gone was one of the hardest things that I have had to do in my career. At Jeremy's memorial, the casket was closed, but beautiful roses covered it, with a Cherokee shirt in the center of the cascading arrangement. Several students were wearing their shirts, as if to recall a happy time in their lives, a time when they felt connected.

I share this story to emphasize the importance of having systems in which children can feel a sense of belonging. Schools need to be places in which people care whether students are doing well physically, emotionally, and academically. We must come together to ensure effective transitions as our students move from one system to another. The connections could truly mean life or death for our students. **We could make lists about the challenges of creating these systems, but the lists must be put aside as we "lose" children, even when they are sitting in the desks in front of us.**

Q&A with the Principal
Clara Sale-Davis, Freeport Intermediate School

Q: *For an average school that might not need the kind of dramatic turnaround that your team led, what significant strategies or lessons would you share that could be equally fruitful in any school?*

A: For an average school that might not need such a turnaround, I offer a few strategies or best practices that could work in any middle school. These strategies, of course, are supported by activities that we consider developmentally responsive to this age group. I often ask average school leaders, "What do your test scores reflect?" The usual response is that students cannot and should not use one test measurement to determine their goals. This is followed by "Students need numerous exploratory classes, and we should provide these types of experiences and not focus on standardized test scores." The philosophy is often that if the public perception of the school is acceptable, problems don't really exist. I agree to some extent; however, whether we like it or not, we are measured by test scores. My students, staff, and the community take great pride when our school receives a high rating. Real estate agents are some of the first people to pick up on school ratings, because they can list the rating on their house brochures.

I love the book *Good to Great* by Jim Collins—he says that good is the worst enemy of great. So I offer "average" schools a few strategies that I feel could move them from good to great, or from mediocre to model. All ideas are stolen, modified to look like they are not stolen, and shared among thieves. Here are a few ideas that we've borrowed from some great educators.

- From the works of John Goodlad and Richard DuFour, we lifted an idea that is key to our success: organizing the staff into **professional learning communities.** This idea is currently in vogue, but from the very beginning we have organized the troops to focus on learning (rather than teaching), to work collaboratively in teams, and to accept accountability for the results. Our learning communities consider the cliché "all students can learn" as a pledge to ensure the success of each student, and of all staff members, too, in their own professional growth. We involve all stakeholders and continue to make changes; we operate in a continuum of asking questions regarding how students can achieve at high levels, how we can better serve our special populations, and how we can commit more fully to a positive collaborative culture.

- We've transformed the emotion surrounding "test results day" into a passion for continuous improvement. We have become very **data-driven.** We look at test data, assessment data, benchmark data, attendance data, and discipline data. Each reporting period, we look at failure rates and success rates, and analyze the interventions we need to offer. In addition, we look at internal and external customer surveys. Most important, we look at what the students are saying about everything we do, as they are our most important customers. Decisions are based on what the data reflect, and our professional learning communities provide the process for making change happen.

- Students need to feel that they have a voice in decision making at school. We create avenues for students to have a voice, whether it is a "tribe" voice or an organizational voice such as the Student Council, Multicultural Club, Spanish Club, or the National Junior Honor Society. In addition to these decision-making, goal-driven organizations, every six weeks a student is selected for the **Walk-with-the-Principal Award.** Each tribe selects a boy and a girl to meet with the principal to walk to a local restaurant to discuss issues. There are two questions for discussion. The first is "What do you love about our school?" The answers are recorded on a chart. The second question is "If you had a magic wand, what changes would you make in our school?" I get amazing responses on both questions. The responses are disseminated to every staff member, including lunchroom and custodial staff. Many changes have been made as a result of the feedback I've received at these Walk-with-the-Principal meetings (e.g., more supervision in locker rooms, changing yearbook companies because of student dissatisfaction, avoiding "worksheet city" when they have substitute teachers). The kids feel that someone is listening and that what they say can make a difference. As a principal, listening to my "customers" is one of my most effective practices. I look forward to these meetings, and to the "duty-free" lunch!

- I heard someone suggest that we were "edu-tainers" instead of educators. On our journey, we have discovered that the traditional style of lecturing behind a podium does not always ensure the attention of learners. The goal is to make lessons exciting and present them enthusiastically, so students can make a real-world application. We offer a rigorous curriculum and present it in such a way that it becomes relevant to each and every learner. Schoolwide interdisciplinary units play a big part in providing rigor and relevance for our students. Recently, we decided to do a schoolwide Invention Convention. It started in the science classes and then expanded into the history classes. The language and math classes all joined in, and the culminating activity was a band concert. In lieu of the traditional concert, we incorporated drama, speech (language classes), and historical excerpts (history classes), and the band played relevant songs. The students were able to make connections throughout each discipline. In everything we do, we try to make these connections—to ensure relevance not only to real-world applications but to the future. If students can create a vision for future opportunities, they can take relevance to a higher level.

■ What happens when students don't learn? That question is often asked. It is a difficult one for me to answer, because our campus embraces the "failure is not an option" rule. We offer a pyramid of interventions for struggling learners. These interventions include before- or after-school tutorials, assigning an adult or student mentor, contacting parents to set up a contract, and staying after football practice with the coaches (who are dedicated to academics, as reflected in our "no pass, no play" rule). One of the most effective interventions we offer is our Extended Day Program. Students who have not demonstrated mastery of the curriculum (based on frequent assessments, benchmark tests, and the previous year's test scores) are "invited" to attend an after-school tutorial. Parents support this after-school tutorial, as they have our assurance that (1) it will not interfere with any student activity; (2) a snack is provided; (3) transportation is provided; and (4) grades will improve. Teachers are paid $20 an hour and these monies are provided by local district funds, Title I funds, and the Optional Extended Day grant. The keys to success for our Extended Day Program are (1) a small teacher-pupil ratio (no more that 12:1); (2) a relaxed environment with creative lessons (this is a challenge for an after-school program, but the creativity abounds!); and (3) the close teacher-student and student-student relationships that develop. The philosophy of the program is "We sink or swim together." The Extended Day Program is usually held in the spring, after the benchmark (practice) test has been administered. This year we decided to have a fall Extended Day Program to address deficiencies that were reflected in the assessments. Let me emphasize again: It has to be "drill and thrill" not "drill and kill" or "longer and louder" instruction. We are always cognizant of the developmentally responsive aspect, knowing that no teenagers are going to voluntarily stay after school for a tutorial unless they know it will be action-packed and fun (rigorous and relevant).

■ Let's talk about homework. Homework has a different meaning when you don't have a home to go to. In high-poverty schools, some students are homeless, living in hotels, bouncing from one dwelling to another, or living in a shelter. It is unrealistic to assign homework and expect high-quality work. This Extended Day Program can often be "extended" to assist students with homework. In this case, the teacher provides a quiet place to work and is there to help with concepts the student did not grasp in class. Rather than being based on homework, most of our grades are based on what the students do in class, with the exception of long-term projects. In this way, students are measured on a level playing field; additionally, we know we're observing what the students themselves can do, not what someone else did (or did not do) for them at home. We do assign homework, but we don't weigh homework grades heavily, because these grades can be arbitrary and capricious.

- Another strategy we use is the maintenance operation. Every student has a "maintenance booklet" for mathematics, reading, writing, and social studies. (Science maintenance is forthcoming.) These booklets stay in the classroom and are periodically passed out to students during a warm-up or as a cooperative group activity. The teacher assigns one or two problems covering skills the students have previously been taught. Individual students or teams present each problem and describe how it was solved. These presentations are focused on maintaining skills that have been previously taught. We believe that the maintenance operation is an integral part of mastering the material. The department chairs ensure that the maintenance materials are challenging and that the booklets are printed in the summer so they are ready to disseminate the first day of school. If a student moves, the booklet is recycled for a new student to use (mark out the name, write in the new name).

Q: *How did your efforts to improve the school climate translate into an improved academic program?*

A: I have a simple response to this question: Happy teachers make happy students. It truly is all about relationships. If the student likes his or her teacher, and knows that the teacher really cares about his or her life, that student will do "whatever it takes" to please the teacher. If a student does not like the teacher, the relationship may become a power struggle for the remainder of the year. Teachers are positive and passionate about what they do, and this "I can" (and if you can't, I'll help you) philosophy permeates the building. Our emphasis is always on learning and working collaboratively on matters related to learning. The teams use their collective ability to help all students meet curriculum (and sometimes behavioral) challenges. Our success is the result of an unrelenting focus on results. Our results are sometimes uncomfortable, but we confront the data on student achievement and work together to improve the results rather than making excuses for them. We have a culture of shared accountability. By working together and sharing ideas as collaborative teams, we can develop consistent calendars (scope and sequence), common assessments for each instructional unit, and common cumulative exams. This unity of purpose builds collegiality and camaraderie not only among the staff but also with our students. We hope to instill the same values of collaboration and camaraderie in our students. Team building is self-esteem building; high self-esteem results in greater confidence; and having the confidence to succeed results in improved performance. It is our culture to share ideas as well as heartaches, and to do whatever it takes to meet our goals.

Q: *What are indicators that your curriculum and its delivery are substantial?*

A: Our indicators reflect the following:

- Low failure rates.
- High performance on standardized tests.
- High performance on end-of-course exams.
- Students who are amply prepared for high school coursework, including transition and collaborative planning with the high school for special needs students.

Training and staff development place a heavy emphasis on relevancy. Students are actively engaged in "why" questions, and teachers strive to provide activities that require higher order thinking skills. This training has led to a more rigorous curriculum, which we feel is actually harder than what our state standardized test measures. With the exception of math, students comment that what we give them is much more challenging than our state test. We like those kind of comments!

Q: *What specific strategies did you employ to improve curriculum and instruction?*

A: Teachers work in collaborative teams for 90 minutes daily to clarify the essential outcomes of their grade levels and courses. This gives the interdisciplinary teams (which meet on "A" days) and the vertical teams (which meets on "B" days) an opportunity to align outcomes with state and national standards.

Frequent assessment results are studied by the teams, and colleagues quickly learn when a teammate has been effective in teaching a certain skill. That effective lesson is shared among the team and is replicated in all classrooms. The teams provide a systematic support system and help one another execute the lesson. At times, teachers will put the boys and girls in one large classroom and co-teach. One teacher presents and facilitates, while the other monitors and assists. Then they switch the role; the other teacher presents while the first monitors and assists. Instructional technology plays a large role in addressing the needs of our visual and auditory learners. PowerPoint presentations/notes and video clips enhance each concept. We purchase a license to have access to video clips that make the lessons more understandable and relevant. This requires effective planning. We know that working together is the key, capitalizing on the strengths of each teacher. Lessons are often burned on a disk and shared throughout the grade level, or they may be shown schoolwide during Team Time (tutorial/enrichment—the last hour of the day).

Q: *Freeport uses words like "tribe" and "redskin" as part of the teaming activities in spite of the national debate over such terms. How are the terms used and presented to students?*

A: Although the term "redskin" may be controversial to many, we do not use it in a derogatory manner. Our goal at FIS is not to inflame racial tension but to celebrate the culture of our Native Americans along with other cultures. Our community sees it as a tradition of pride and respect, reflecting a mighty warrior who can fight and survive. The Native Americans are an integral part of our history curriculum, and we have in-depth studies of their heritage. The tribes—Karankawas, Mayans, Cherokees, and Apaches—represent strong and powerful nations in North America. At FIS, we choose to accentuate the positive and present these cultures proudly as part of our history. Each tribe researches its namesake's history, identifies its strengths, and plans activities accordingly. The tribes represent "family" and have their own colors, banners, and T-shirts. The students take great pride in their tribe and strive to win tribal awards (Most Spirited, Best Attendance, Best Readers, Best Disciplined) to proudly display in the hallway. The tribes all agree that academic performance is the main goal; with regard to this goal, the kids will chant, "The tribe has spoken; it won't be broken!"

I have had numerous conversations with the mayor, City Council, Freeport League, and other community patrons regarding our mascot. Attempts to change the name of our mascot have been met with much resistance. Some groups still organize "Redskin Reunions."

Leading a Text-Based Discussion on this Profile (see protocol in Appendix 4)

- Why and how did the faculty develop and maintain such a deep commitment to success for all students?

- What kinds of organizational structures did the principal create to make changes in the school?

- How do the tribes help personalize the experience for students?

- What can we learn from the way transitional activities are used at Freeport?

- What did you like about the profile?

- What didn't you like about the profile?

School Profile 4
Freeport Intermediate School

Focus on Transition

You've heard it before: A good transition is critical for students. Some schools do not do much to aid in the transition, while others have elaborate plans. How many of those plans simply focus on the incoming students—rather than both incoming students and those moving to the next level? Are the students who have left your school no longer your concern? How many plans address personalizing the environment and making incoming students comfortable but forget about the need to personalize instruction and assessment practices? Too often, transition programs at schools end after making sure that incoming students can find their way to class and their lockers. Clearly developing that level of comfort in the school is critical for students, but it should not be the end. One way to view the transition is through the eyes of the students who experience it.

Breaking Ranks through the Eyes of an Aspiring Sixth-Grader

It is easy for those who don't work regularly with middle level students to forget that sixth-graders are only five or six years removed from their teddy bears; those who do work with middle level students sometimes forget that, by the time students leave "the middle," the rigors of college are only four short years away. What does your school look like to an incoming student? What *could* it look like? If you implement Breaking Ranks in the Middle, your incoming student might see something like what this aspiring student describes in the journal below.

Third Grade

September 1—My mom and dad just got information about what I am supposed to learn between now and the end of high school. It gave me an idea of what I have to do in each grade. They said it was nice to see how everything tied together, how they can help me in school and keep an eye on my progress. They said a lot of schools don't do things like that for their students. I guess that means I am lucky.

Fifth Grade

February 6—I hear that some teachers from the school I'll be going to next year are coming here this month. My friends are dreading it—we hear the teachers are mean and all they do is yell. Why is my teacher letting this happen? Isn't it bad enough we have to be with these teachers next year?

February 19—This week we had a team of teachers who teach sixth grade come to our school. They were not mean at all. While those teachers were at our school, one of my teachers went to their school to find out how her former students were doing in school and to teach a lesson to the older kids. One of my other teachers went to a conference during the week to learn more about making math fun. The week was pretty cool, because we had a different schedule so we could do an awesome science project yesterday, and then today we got to do historical reenactments based on the research we did about the Revolutionary War. Lots of the classes were about things we learned in other classes during the week and throughout the year—it really helped me make sense of things. I'm looking forward to next year when we do this all the time. The best part—I already know some of the teachers!

March 15—The parents group arranged a pizza party for fifth- and sixth-graders and their parents at the middle school. Parents had the chance to hang out together, and I got teamed up with a bunch of my friends and a bunch of guys from another elementary school I never met before. We also had two sixth grade "buddies."

April 4—The parents group sponsored an "open gym" day at my new school during spring break. They had all kinds of information available about different activities at the school, and a bunch of the advisers were there to answer questions. I met the soccer coach and the school newspaper adviser. We get to do this again after spring break, but then some sixth-graders will be there, too. I heard that the sixth grade teachers will be meeting with our teachers to talk about each of the fifth-graders and what our strengths are. We may even be able to lead some of these discussions. I think we should be able to, because if they're going to be talking about me, I should know something about what they're saying so I can speak up.

April 15—Our teachers for next year and the principal came to our school tonight to answer questions from parents and students about what we can expect next year—just five months away! They talked about a letter the principal had sent to all of our parents a few weeks ago—something about a vision for our future. [See letter on page 183.]

May 1—I met with a bunch of advisers and teachers I might have next year. Get this: One of them used to teach overseas, another used to read movie scripts, and one used to work with kids who don't have much of anything somewhere out East. It's pretty cool, because businesses and residents in the area started a paid job program for teachers in the summertime. That way, if teachers want to, they can have fun and work on interesting projects over the summer. One of the teachers had the chance to

(continued)

go to a NASA lab to learn some awesome science tricks. Then they helped teach presentation techniques to some of the scientists. So the teachers get to teach adults also! Other teachers got to go to the state legislature and then to Washington, D.C. For two weeks they had a chance to see how ideas really become laws. They also got to talk to real senators and members of Congress.

June 1—A bunch of sixth-graders came to our field day and broke up into teams with us. It was pretty cool. Most of the older guys aren't that much bigger than me—one was, though, and he helped us win the tug-of-war *and* the news quiz game.

June 25—I'm kinda nervous. The school sent out a class list, and my parents are inviting over some of my new classmates and their parents for a barbecue. I only know two of the people who are coming over….

July 15—Getting ready to go to a community service project. The team of students I'll be with in the fall has gotten together twice this summer to do our project. The parent organizations from each of the schools arranged several other events this summer, too: a camping trip, ropes course, and movie night. I'm kinda shy, so it was good to be forced to do these organized activities with a couple friends and also with some kids I'd never met before. Some guys were on vacation for some of it, but there were enough events that most people made it to at least two.

August 1— I'm starting to get nervous about going to the new school. I hear some of the seventh-graders will be pretty rough on us—just to show us who's in charge. I also heard that last year a few kids got lost during the first week of school—they found one of them crying in a hallway—he ended up on the wrong floor and missed his first class.

Sixth Grade

August 26—three days before school starts! Our new teachers and some of the coaches and advisers set up a scavenger hunt for us. We broke into teams—a couple of my friends were on my team, but I also got to hang out with a bunch of the new people I met over the summer. We had to find clues all over the new school, which was pretty fun. I even got a chance to grab a clue from under the principal's desk lamp.

September 20—I got my adviser today—Mr. NASA. I'm not very good at math, but I really want to learn about science and space—he thinks I can learn the math I'll need for science if I really try. He has lots of great books and computer programs to help me, and he's going to talk to my math teacher, too. Next week I will sit down with him and start developing my Personal Plan for Progress. My adviser says it will help me set goals based on what I like and what the school wants me to do, too. He gave me a sheet with lots of questions on it about my personal interests, friends, favorite subjects, hobbies and strengths, homework habits, and the school things that are hard for me to do. I'm supposed to work on it with my parents and then discuss it next week.

September 29—Today I sat down with my adviser to talk about ideas for a project that I'll work on for the next three years. I get to pick the project—so I know it will be cool—and he will guide me to make sure I'm challenging myself. I can make up my own project or pick one from a long list of ideas that the school developed. The project has to do a few things: (1) Involve one of my hobbies or interests. (2) Allow me to work on a subject or skill that is hard for me. (3) Be connected in some way to three or more subject areas I will study the next three years or in high school. (4) Help me look at careers that might use the skills I learn on the project. (5) Discover other skills

(continued)

that I would need to learn for that career. Luckily, Mr. NASA has lots of ideas about the last one! He said I may even be able to talk with a telescope designer and an astronomer he knows.

October 30—Just had my end-of-quarter review of my learning goals and my Personal Plan for Progress with my adviser. Now I get to talk to Mom and Dad about them, and then all of us meet next week.

Like all students who are changing schools or teachers, our fictional sixth-grader had some anxiety about the middle level years. Fortunately, the school had systems and practices in place to address many of the common issues before they could become anxieties. It is impossible to alleviate all anxiety for each student (and perhaps some anxiety and anticipation are beneficial); however, implementing some of the practices touched on in the journal will go a long way toward mitigating potential problems.

Transitions can be difficult for young adolescents, but they can present an opportunity for teachers and principals to increase the amount of information they have about their new students. During the transition period, schools also have the opportunity to invite parents of underserved populations into the school, to get to know the school as well as other parents and staff. The following list includes activities that principals and teachers can plan as part of the transition from the elementary to the middle level. While many of these activities apply to a transition from one school to another, some also apply to "in-house" transitions from grade to grade.

Activities to Facilitate Middle Level Transition

Principal Activities	Parent Activities	Counselor Activities	Student Activities	Staff Activities
Middle level principal visits classrooms of aspiring middle level students (e.g., fifth-graders) to 1. Introduce him- or herself. 2. Meet the students. 3. Take pictures of the students (to be used later during student visits to the middle school). 4. Gather information from the students, such as ■ their greatest fear about middle school (top three: lunchroom, getting lost, and lockers). ■ the thing they are most excited about. ■ what they know about the new school. ■ their favorite subject. ■ the last book they read. ■ the thing they are best at. Middle level principal meets with parents at the individual elementary schools, at parent coffees in homes, at community centers, in churches, or in all of these places. (The emphasis here must be on meeting parents where they are comfortable and where they will come for a meeting. This will vary from one community to another.) Middle level principal sends information to aspiring students' parents in the languages spoken in the community.	Parents (e.g., of fifth grade students) are invited to the middle school to observe classes and general daily activities. Middle level principal hosts special-interest meetings, such as Hispanic Parents Night, and provides a translator if needed. (A highly successful variation of this is to have the meeting hosted by a well-known member of the Hispanic community.)	Middle level teachers and counselors meet with parents of fifth-graders to explain classes and the registration process. Teachers should be involved in as many meetings as possible, so that both the parents and their children become familiar with many staff members from the middle level school.	Whole-class visits of fifth-graders to the middle level school should happen in late winter or early spring of the fifth grade year. For many students, this will be their first time in the middle level school. Students come to an activity at the middle school, such as a school play or concert or sports event, and have the opportunity to learn about activities they will be able to participate in when they are in sixth grade. This information can be disseminated through an activity fair or some other way, using current students to tell future students about activities. During the summer, rising fifth-graders are invited to summer orientation programs. These can take the form of general orientation to the school building and school procedures. (The number one thing elementary students report being worried about is manipulating their lockers.) These sessions should also include some academic activity, such as study skills lessons or an informational session about subjects that may be new to the students. These orientation programs also provide an ideal opportunity to survey students about their fears, hopes, preferences, and so on. The pictures that the principal took during visits to fifth grade classrooms should be prominently displayed in the school during these summer visits.	Staff members need to learn everything they can about new students. Starting in the spring with the principal's visits, middle school staff should build individual profiles of each entering student. The information gathered by the principal, counselors, and teachers should be centralized and recorded in a searchable database that can be accessed by administrators, counselors, and teachers. This database should become the basis for placing students on teams, scheduling students into classes, providing students with resources that ensure their success, and giving teachers a solid base of information about each child on their teams. Information such as the following should be included in the database: ■ Basic identification information. ■ Demographic information. ■ Student strengths and needs (academic, social, emotional). ■ Student's past performance in classes. ■ Teacher impressions of student work habits and abilities. ■ Past standardized test performance. ■ Any special considerations, such as ELL level, special education status, or gifted education identification. ■ Performance on measures for giftedness/upper level performance. ■ Talents in the arts. ■ Physical talents. ■ Parent report of student strengths and needs. ■ Any other information that will help the sixth grade teachers get to know the students.

Ask the Expert

What Do We Do While They're Here?
Once students have settled in, how can schools serving middle
level students ease the internal transitions from grade to grade
and provide the attention required to address student academic
needs? To get an answer, we asked an expert.

Q&A with Nancy Doda, Ph.D.,
Associate Professor, National-Louis University

Q: *What are the key attributes for successful articulation and vertical teaming*
(across schools and grades) as they relate to transition?

A: As middle grades students make the transition from one grade level to the next, it
is imperative that middle level schools pay close attention to articulation in terms
of quality relationships and quality learning. Research has made it very clear that
teachers are more effective when they know students well and can plan learning
experiences that reflect that knowledge. Some middle schools use "houses," or clusters, of grade-level teams (e.g., one house contains one each of sixth, seventh, and
eighth grade teams), ensuring that teams of students remain within the house to
enhance familiarity, continuity, guidance counselor stability, and team-to-team
sharing with regard to communication about students making the transition.

Other middle level schools have employed looping, whereby students move from
grade to grade with the same team of teachers. Looping greatly enhances articulation, as students and teams of teachers cross grade levels and years together. In its
absence, schools must work to bridge the grade-level gap by finding ways to ensure
that receiving teams or schools have in place the means to establish relationships
with students and families, as well as entry points that help teachers plan for
appropriate curriculum and instruction. Perhaps the greatest challenge is that of
renegotiating the kind of trusting relationships needed to support quality learning.

Many middle level schools use a powerful first-day approach to ease a smooth transition. This approach could be applied to many diverse settings. On the opening
day of school, every child spends that entire day in a small team-based advisory

group. This day's plan dedicates the first day to welcoming new and old students into a safe culture. Every team plans varied group process activities, as well as activities designed to help students prepare for the first day of classes and movement. Lockers, supply lists, maps, and a host of business items are addressed during the first day, along with experiences that encourage the establishment of good relationships between teachers and students and among students.

To support better articulation with the curriculum, middle level schools need to develop curriculum maps of major content/concepts and standards addressed at each grade level. Too often, the existing curricula have never been reexamined from a cross-grade-level perspective and thus are awkward and redundant. It behooves middle level schools to examine as well the big picture of curriculum for incoming and outgoing grade levels. This exercise offers teachers a rich perspective on their own curriculum and helps them know where students have been and where they are heading. It's so simple, yet it happens so rarely.

Portfolios of student work are one of the most effective tools to carry student learning growth from teacher to teacher and grade to grade. Nothing provides a better understanding of student performance than actual student work, collected and analyzed over time. While many schools have portfolios in place, few use portfolios to support student transition. The time available for such review is often limited.

It is, of course, a wonderful professional development experience to engage teachers at various grade levels the chance to review student work; this practice also can help teams predict areas of need in their incoming population.

There are many more examples of middle level schools working hard to ensure that young adolescents have the kind of supportive relationships they need to be successful. Above all, we must know the children we serve and work to sustain personalization within and across grade levels.

Preparing Students for the Future

Doda's point that "above all, we must know the children we serve" is critical to the message of Breaking Ranks in the Middle. Schools cannot effectively serve students well unless student strengths, weaknesses, talents, and aspirations are well known. Improved student performance is more likely to occur if teachers and principals know the students well. As a number of experts make clear in the next section, once students have settled into the middle level years, it is the responsibility of middle level educators to prepare them academically for the transition they will make into high school and beyond. Simply working with your high school counterparts to ensure that students sign up for classes is not enough. The journey to high school begins in sixth grade or even earlier.

Expert Essay

Never Too Soon to Prepare for Their Successful Departure

by Ronald Williamson, Associate Professor,
Eastern Michigan University

The most high-stakes transition for students is the one that occurs when students move from the middle level to high school. It is at this juncture that students often make the decision about continuing their education or dropping out of school. The stakes are high not just for students but also for educators in middle level and high schools, for parents, and for society. Schools can no longer fail to equip students and their parents with the tools to successfully navigate the divide between the two levels. The two levels too often function as isolated units separated by a vast ocean of differences in philosophy, instruction, organization, and climate.

The roots of the middle level movement lie in a commitment to provide for the individual needs of students, to offer students a solid educational experience in a caring and supportive environment. Indeed, responsiveness to student needs is the hallmark of the movement. Middle level educators must, however, recommit to even greater responsiveness by recognizing the need to intentionally and deliberately provide students with the knowledge, skills, and dispositions for success in high school. Similarly, high schools must recognize that they must work with their feeder middle level schools to ensure that students receive high levels of support, support that reduces anonymity and ensures academic success for every student. A dramatic transformation in the approach to the student transition is called for, a transformation characterized by greater emphasis on providing students with the academic skills and dispositions for success required in high school.

Solid and comprehensive transition programs are directly linked to student success. Mizelle and Irvin (2000) reported that "schools with extensive transition programs have significantly lower failure and dropout rates than schools that provided students few articulation activities" (p. 58).

Much has been written about transition activities, those special events that occur at the end of the eighth grade and the beginning of high school. Such events are important connectors for both students and parents. The events generally focus on organizational issues: picking courses, visiting the new school, and learning about school policies. Such activities are important and should be continued; however, by themselves they are insufficient to maximize student success. In too many schools, the transition program consists solely of these activities. Little attention is paid to the academic transitions students face or to the curricular links between middle level and high school.

Greater emphasis must be placed on the academic preparation of students. Cooney and Bottoms (2002) identified three experiences that are directly linked to success in high-level courses in ninth grade: studying "something called algebra" in the middle grades; reading at least 10 books a year; and expecting to graduate from college. Simple

Expert Essay
Ronald Williamson

in their description, these ideas are more complex in implementation. They require raising expectations for all middle level students—more reading and more math—and they demand setting high expectations for student success in high school and beyond.

The same study identified specific activities in middle level schools that contribute to greater student success in high school. These activities include expecting students to read more fiction and nonfiction books, helping students and their parents develop a plan for high school based on the expectation that they will attend college, and strengthening instruction to include more integrated learning and hands-on learning experiences.

Thus, a more comprehensive approach to transition is required in order to ensure the success of students in high school. This approach includes the following:

- Modifying the curriculum so that students are expected to read more books across all curricular areas.

- Changing the mathematics curriculum so that every student moves to high school having completed either pre-algebra or algebra.

- Talking with students and their families about high school and college, and helping them design a multiyear educational plan to ensure success in high school and built on the expectation that they will attend college.

- Identifying students who need additional support and ensuring that they get the curricular and instructional support they need for success.

- Challenging long-standing norms about teaching assignments and teacher placement; the best teachers must work with students with the greatest need.

- Modifying the allocation of time to ensure more instructional time in reading/language arts and mathematics.

- Focusing teaching teams and advisory programs on ensuring that every student is known by an adult and receives a challenging educational experience; the core work of teams is improving curriculum and instruction.

The evidence is clear: Middle level educators play a significant role in helping students be successful in high school. The challenge is equally clear: Act on the knowledge that middle level schools affect student success; make significant changes in curriculum and instruction; raise expectations for all students; and challenge long-standing norms so that every student moves to high school with a high probability of success.

Ask the Expert

Q&A with Deborah Merriam,
Academic Dean, Parker Charter Essential School

Q: *What specific practices are in place at Parker that help students make the transition from eighth to ninth grade?*

A: The following practices and structures help students make the transition:

- **Divisional structure.** Parker is structured by domain (fields of academic study) and division (peer cohorts/developmental groupings). Division One is roughly grades 7 and 8; Division Two is roughly grades 9 and 10. Teams of teachers specifically address the developmental needs of their students at the divisional level, so students are supported through transition issues at both the classroom academic level and the social/emotional level through advisory.

- **Gateways.** Our program is centered on performance-based promotion through portfolios and public exhibition, so students move from junior high to high school academic work after demonstrating that they are ready to tackle work at that level. If they have not demonstrated a readiness to move to the next level of academic work, they remain in Division One classes. Students "gateway" (move from one level or division to the next) separately in each academic area, so their progression through the arts and humanities, for example, is not tied to their progression through the math, science, and technology curriculum.

- **Advisory program.** Our advisory program is organized by division, so that students are generally grouped by chronological age rather than academic attainment. Thus, ninth grade students who are in Division One classes and are still working to master the academic expectations at that level are in Division Two advisories. They are supported by advisors and peers at a developmentally appropriate level.

- **Orientation/welcoming sessions.** In the spring, we offer an orientation program to Division One students who will be moving to Division Two in the fall. This session gives them a sense of what the expectations will be in Division Two as they move to a new academic level.

- **Two-year academic cycles and heterogeneous classes.** In our divisional academic structure, students are generally in classes spanning grades 9 and 10. This allows students to work with each other and guide each other through the expectations of the program. The older students serve as guides to the younger students; every other year, students are either the "new" students or the "returning" students. This system builds a continuity of culture and allows students to help support each other through transition issues.

- **Early gatewayers.** Students who demonstrate a readiness for challenge beyond the Division One curriculum in arts and humanities have the option to "gateway" in January, but they remain in their Division One classes. They are given increased challenges in those classes, receive feedback on their work from a Division Two perspective, and are expected to adopt a greater leadership role. This approach provides students with developmentally appropriate challenges without forcing them into an unfamiliar social setting. It also scaffolds them into the greater expectations of high school work.

- **Adult communication.** Adults in the building meet across divisions to discuss specific students and the developmental needs of all students. School structures make room for and prioritize these conversations. We also have a clear system of passing on information from one year's to the following year's teachers.

- **Program consistency.** When students get to "high school," they already know what it means to compile a portfolio, gateway, be in an advisory, and have a learning plan for each student (developed each year in advisory).

Q: *How do you use exhibitions and portfolios to make the transition from the middle grades to high school successful for each student?*

A: The student prepares for a public exhibition of learning, called a gateway presentation. This gateway process involves compiling a portfolio of work that demonstrates a student's ability to meet standards at the current divisional level and readiness to move to the next division. The gateway presentation is attended by the student's domain teacher, advisor, parents, and other invited guests, as well as classmates and friends. The Division One gateway is considered a celebration of work that a student has already completed successfully. Therefore, this gateway is focused on student presentation of work that showcases the student's learning and growth. When the gateway portfolio is accepted, the student is considered to have gatewayed, and the public exhibition is really to celebrate this transition. This is in contrast to the gateway presentations at Divisions Two and Three, in which greater demands are placed on students and they are held to higher stakes expectations (such as knowledge on demand or synthesis of new research findings), as is more appropriate for their developmental level.

Students attend gateways of other students before their own, so they will have a clear understanding of and expectations for the process. Each student's gateway is different, but at the Division One level they all celebrate a student's achievements and readiness to progress to the challenge of high school curriculum. Students gateway when they show readiness to do so (gateways are available in each domain twice a year, in January and June); thus, one of the ways students are supported through this transition is that they don't move on to Division Two work until they show that they are ready for it.

Q: *What does "transition" mean at a school like yours that doesn't have a transition from one school to another? What would you say to the principal of a 6–8 middle school who might say that transition is not an issue for a 7–12 or K–12 school?*

A: "Transition" means that students' developmental needs are recognized and met as they progress through our program; even though we have a consistent schoolwide program and we are all in one building, we recognize and support the developmental needs of students at different levels and alter our program as appropriate to meet the needs of students at their divisional level.

Transition is a real issue for us as a 7–12 school, but it is addressed through the familiar and established systems that we have in place to work with students effectively. We don't have to have "transition programs" per se; rather, we are compelled to recognize and address the developmental issues that our students bring with them as they transition and mature.

Q: *Of all of the transition practices your school has established, is there one that stands out as most valuable to ensure that each student makes the transition?*

A: The principle of knowing students well is expressed through small class sizes, student conferences, gateway practices and exhibitions, and in many other ways. That said, the program that most allows us to know students well is advisory. Through the advisory system, conversations with and about students are facilitated to support them, and all students know that they always have at least one adult in the school who will be there to support them and advocate for them as they progress through our school program and through their adolescence.

Activities to Facilitate Ninth-Grade Transition

The Center for Transition Studies at Slippery Rock University and Pensacola Junior College, codirected by Jay Hertzog and Lená Morgan, offer the following guidance to facilitating students' transition from eighth to ninth grade:

- Provide eighth grade students with guidance sessions led by ninth grade counselors during the spring and fall to discuss high school curriculum, registration, and scheduling. This is also a good time to discuss expectations and responsibilities. A booklet or pamphlet detailing the information is helpful.

- Hold a parent night at the high school to discuss curriculum, scheduling, and student activities. Once again, this is a good time to include parents by detailing expectations at the high school level and noting the responsibilities of the incoming freshman.

- Organize an eighth grade field trip to the new high school.

- Develop a transition team composed of middle level and high school teachers. They should meet each month to plan and conduct a transition schedule for the school year.

- Institute an advisor/advisee program in the high school.

- Coordinate ongoing pen pal relationships between middle and high school students.

- Organize a "teacher swap-a-day," in which high school teachers teach eighth grade students and middle level teachers teach ninth grade students.

- Develop a program in which students, faculty, and administrators can shadow someone for a day.

- Hold celebrations that signify the end of the middle level and the beginning of the high school experience.

- Plan an information fair to disseminate information related to the high school curriculum, academics, vocational offerings, electives, and course offerings.

(continued)

Ask the Expert:
Deborah Merriam

- Offer an eighth grade exploratory session that provides students with the opportunity to analyze the connections between academic subjects and careers.

- Allot time for high school department chairs or high school students to visit the middle schools to discuss the life of high school students.

- Encourage ninth grade subject area teachers to review eighth grade student portfolios.

- Arrange for high school faculty members, counselors, and parents to work together to develop a five-year plan for seventh-graders.

- Develop ninth grade teams to aid in the transition.

Source: Hertzog and Morgan, 1997.

Ask the Expert

Q&A with Vicki Petzko,
Professor, University of Tennessee at Chattanooga

Q: *What strategies can the middle school use to mitigate the impact of transition on its students, who are used to the personalized atmosphere of the middle school, when they matriculate to a big high school?*

A: Most of the research on middle level students addresses "early adolescents from 11 to 15 years old." Schools need to realize that ninth-graders are 15 years old, and that the best practices and strategies employed in highly effective middle schools are age-appropriate for ninth-graders. A ninth grade program that looks like an 11th or 12th grade program is destined for failure for too many students.

In addition, not enough can be said about the value of recent research on eighth or ninth grade transition. Transition teams are needed that include parents, teachers, administrators, and students at both the middle and high school level to develop collaborative plans that address the needs of all stakeholders. The research must be reviewed, and strategies implemented that best fit the culture and needs as described by the transition team.

At a minimum, the following need to occur:

- Transition activities must begin early in eighth grade.

- Transition is a process, not an event, and activities should occur about once a month.

- Transition activities should not end when the student enters high school but should be continued into the ninth grade year.

- Middle level principals and high school principals need to involve all stake-holders in the planning as well as the transition itself.

Q: *What can middle level principals do to help high schools prepare students for the transition?*

A: Professional development regarding the unique social, emotional, and intellectual development of 14- and 15-year-olds needs to occur for all teachers who work with ninth-graders. The ninth grade program should be specifically designed for 14- and 15-year-olds.

In school systems that do not use curriculum alignment and data analysis, teachers will undoubtedly fail. Even if the best teaching strategies are employed, the wrong entry points, inaccurate assumptions of prior knowledge, and inappropriate scaffolding of curriculum can significantly minimize student achievement.

The "Last" Word

Is this the end, or just the beginning?

Just as your graduating students come to realize that their middle level years are over and that it is time to start anew, so too must you realize that some things must end in order for other things to blossom. For some middle level students, graduation is a time for dreaming, planning, and great activity. For others it is a time of insecurity and inaction. Are you, as principal, prepared to leave some things behind, to graduate from good to great—to dream, plan, and do? Or are you happy to leave well enough alone? If you have made it to this point in the guide, chances are good that you are the former, willing to lead your school's transformation.

Breaking Ranks in the Middle is the beginning, not the end. The nine cornerstone strategies, 30 recommendations, and hundreds of tips are a starting point for your conversations with the teachers, students, parents, and community members about how your school can make that transformation. Clearly, not all of the tips will be appropriate for your school. But as your school becomes a model for others, we hope that a dog-eared and thoroughly worn copy of this guide sits on your desk, not neatly tucked away on your bookshelf because you "already read it." If it finds its way onto your bookshelf, then this becomes a story with a decidedly unhappy ending. With this guide as a tool, you can create a happy ending for your students, and maintain your energy for the ongoing work of school improvement.

And your efforts must go well beyond your school doors. To help appreciate the magnitude of what is beyond those doors, consider one of the most critical points in the history of the United States, one which every middle level or elementary student has studied:

> …The moment finally arrived when the two entities, which had been previously content to operate in two different spheres of influence, were compelled to join forces in order to advance their own interests, the interests of those they served, and the interests of the nation.

The moment was, of course, May 10, 1869—the great "Wedding of the Rails" when the Central Pacific and the Union Pacific Railroads met at Promontory Summit and joined rails with the "golden spike," thereby joining East and West and forever changing our nation.

Our sincere aspiration is for this language to apply as well to the middle level–high school relationship? For too long middle level schools and high schools have operated in separate spheres of influence with minimal *institutional* effort to collaborate to advance the interests of schools, of students, and of the nation. Some school leaders in some districts attempt to look at education as a continuum, while others are content to view the education of students as limited to the 2–6 years when students grace their halls. Still fewer view the continuum in the context of creating schools that are *simultaneously*, in the words of the National Forum to Accelerate Middle Grades Reform, academically rigorous, socially equitable, and developmentally appropriate.

The strategies in Breaking Ranks in the Middle are closely aligned with the strategies in Breaking Ranks II (the publication for high school principals) which will allow middle level schools and high schools to collaborate and begin to view education as a continuum and to align curriculum and personalization efforts. The long term benefits of doing so could be just as profound as the Wedding of the Rails.

Works Cited and Resources

General Resources on School Restructuring

Carnegie Council on Adolescent Development. (1989). *Turning points: Preparing American youth for the 21st century.* Washington, DC: Author.

Collins, J. (2001). *Good to great: Why some companies make the leap...and others don't.* New York: Harper Collins.

Fullan, M. (2001). *Leading in a culture of change.* San Francisco: Jossey-Bass.

Gainey, D. D., & Webb, L. D. (1998). *The education leader's role in change: How to proceed.* Reston, VA: NASSP.

Jackson, A., & Davies, G. (2000). *Turning points 2000: Educating adolescents in the 21st century.* New York: Teachers College Press.

Lambert, L. (2003). *Leadership capacity for lasting school improvement.* Alexandria: VA: Association for Supervision and Curriculum Development (ASCD).

Lounsbury, J. H. (1982). *This we believe.* Columbus, OH: National Middle School Association.

NASSP. (1985). *An agenda for excellence at the middle level.* Reston, VA: Author.

NASSP. (1987). *Developing a mission statement for the middle level school.* Reston, VA: Author.

NASSP. (1988). *Assessing excellence: A guide for studying the middle level school.* Reston, VA: Author.

NASSP. (1989). *Middle level education's responsibility for intellectual development.* Reston, VA: Author.

NASSP. (1993). *Achieving excellence through the middle level curriculum.* Reston, VA: Author.

NASSP. (1996). *Breaking ranks: Changing an American institution.* Reston, VA: Author.

NASSP. (2004). *Breaking ranks II: Strategies for leading high school reform.* Reston, VA: Author.

Quinn, D., Greunert, S., & Valentine, J. (1999). *Using data for school improvement.* Reston, VA: NASSP.

Valentine, J., Clark, D., Hackmann, D., & Petzko, V. (2002). *A national study of middle level leaders and school programs: A national study of leadership in middle level schools* (Vol. I). Reston, VA: National Association of Secondary School Principals (NASSP).

Valentine, J., Clark, D., Hackmann, D., & Petzko, V. (2004). *Leadership for highly successful middle level schools: A national study of leadership in middle level schools* (Vol. II). Reston, VA: NASSP.

Williamson, R. D., & Johnston, J. H. (1996). *Through the looking glass: The future of middle level education.* Reston, VA: NASSP.

Collaborative Leadership and Professional Learning Communities

1. **The principal will provide leadership in the school community by building and maintaining a vision, direction, and focus for student learning.**

Anfara, V.A., Brown, K. M., Mills, R., Hartman, K., Mahar, R. J. (2000). *Middle level leadership for the 21st century: Principals' views on essential skills and knowledge; Implications for successful preparation.* American Educational Research Association Annual Meeting, New Orleans, LA, April 24–28, 2000.

Blankstein, A. M. (2004). *Failure is not an option™: Six principles that guide student achievement in high-performing schools.* Thousand Oaks, CA: Corwin Press.

Brown, K. M., & Anfara, V. A. (2003, June). Paving the way for change: Visionary leadership in action at the middle level. *NASSP Bulletin, 87*(635), 16–34.

Clark, S. N., & Clark, D. C. (2002, November). Making leadership for learning the top priority. *Middle School Journal, 34*(2), 50–55.

Eaker, R., DuFour, R., & DuFour, R. (2002). *Getting started: Reculturing schools to become professional learning communities.* Bloomington, IN: National Educational Service.

Metropolitan Life survey of the teacher 2003: An examination of school leadership. (2003) New York: MetLife.

Usdan, M., McCloud, B., & Podomostko, M. (2000). *Leadership for student learning: Reinventing the principalship.* Washington, DC: Institute for Educational Leadership.

2. **Each school will establish a site council and accord other meaningful roles in decision making to students, parents, and members of the staff to promote student learning and an atmosphere of participation, responsibility, and ownership.**

Costa, A., & Kallick, B. (2004, September). Launching self-directed learners. *Educational Leadership, 62*(1), 51–55.

Hirsh, S., & Valentine, J. W. (1998). *Building effective middle level teams.* Reston, VA: NASSP.

Lyons, E. B., & Shelton, M. M. (1994, January). Don't get stuck in the middle: Implement site-based management. *Middle School Journal, 25*(3), 45–47.

Painter, B., Lucas, S., Wooderson, M., & Valentine, J. (2000). *The use of teams in school improvement processes.* Reston, VA: NASSP.

3. **Each school will regard itself as a community in which members of the staff collaborate to develop and implement the school's learning goals.**

Cook, W. J. (2004, September). At odds strategic planning: When the smoke clears. *Phi Delta Kappan, 86*(1), 73–75.

Duggin, I. (2004, February). Give a little, get a lot. *Principal Leadership, 4*(6), 27–31.

Joyce, B. (2004, September). At odds strategic planning: How are professional learning communities created? *Phi Delta Kappan, 86*(1), 76–83.

Kochanek, J. R. (2005). *Building trust for better schools: Research-based practices.* Thousand Oaks, CA: Corwin Press.

Schmoker, M. (2004, September). At odds strategic planning: Learning communities at the crossroads: Toward the best schools we've ever had. *Phi Delta Kappan, 86*(1), 84–88.

Schmoker. M. (2004, February). Tipping point: From feckless reform to substantive instructional improvement. *Phi Delta Kappan, 85*(6), 424–432.

Scribner, J. P., Cockrell, K. S., Cockrell, D. H., & Valentine, J. V. (1999, February). Creating professional communities in schools through organizational learning: An evaluation of a school improvement process. *Educational Administration Quarterly, 35*(1), 130–160.

Sergiovanni, T. J. (2004, September). Collaborative cultures & communities of practice. *Principal Leadership, 5*(1), 49–52.

4. **Teachers and teacher teams will provide the leadership essential to the success of reform and will collaborate with others in the educational community to redefine the role of the teacher and identify sources of support for that redefined role.**

Crispeels, J. H., Martin, K. J., Harari, I., Strait, C. C., & Rodarte, M. A. (1999, September). Role conflict and role ambiguity: The challenges of team leadership at the middle school. *Journal of School Leadership, 9*(5), 422–453.

Crowther, F., Kaagan, S. S., Ferguson, M., & Hann., L. (2002). *Developing teacher leaders: How teacher leadership enhances school success.* Thousand Oaks, CA: Corwin Press.

Painter, B., & Valentine, J. (1999). *Engaging teachers in the school improvement process.* Reston, VA: NASSP.

Thompson, S. C. (2004). *Developing teacher leaders: The principal's role.* Westerville, OH: National Middle School Association.

Usdan, M., McCloud, B., & Podomostko, M. (2001). *Leadership for student learning: Redefining the teacher as leader.* Washington, DC: Institute for Educational Leadership.

5. **Every school will be a learning community in which professional development for teachers and the principal is guided by a Personal Learning Plan that addresses the individual's own learning and professional development needs as they relate to the academic achievement and developmental needs of students at the middle level.**

Duck, L. (2000, May). The ongoing professional journey. *Educational Leadership, 57*(8), 42–45.

National Staff Development Council. (2001). *Standards for staff development.* Oxford, OH: Author.

Pedigo, M. (2003). *Differentiating professional development: The principal's role.* Westerville, OH: National Middle School Association.

Webb, L. D., & Berkbuegler, R. (1998). *Personal learning plans for educators.* Reston, VA: NASSP.

6. **The school community will promote policies and practices that recognize diversity in accord with the core values of a democratic and civil society and will offer substantive, ongoing professional development to help educators appreciate issues of diversity and expose students to a rich array of viewpoints, perspectives, and experiences.**

Gutierrez, R. (2005, April). Student solutions to racial conflict. *Principal Leadership, 5*(8), 16–20.

Hoffman, L. M. (2004, March). The real beneficiaries of an ESOL program. *Principal Leadership, 4*(7), 34–38.

Lindsey, R. B., Kikanza, N. R., & Terrell, R. D. (1999). *Cultural proficiency: A manual for school leaders.* Thousand Oaks, CA: Corwin Press.

Lindsey, R. B., Roberts, L., & Jones, F. C. (2004). *The culturally proficient school: An implementation guide for school leaders.* Thousand Oaks, CA: Corwin Press.

Obiakor, F. E. (2001). *It even happens in "GOOD" schools: Responding to cultural diversity in today's classrooms.* Thousand Oaks, CA: Corwin Press.

Smith, M. (2002). *Building community: Refocusing diversity by celebrating ours.* Albuquerque, NM: DifferenceMakers, Ltd..

Smith-Davis, J. (2004, March), The world of immigrant students. *Principal Leadership, 4*(7), 44–49.

Garcia, E. E. (2000, December). Meeting the challenges of cultural diversity. *Principal Leadership, 4*(1), 50–53.

7. **Schools will build partnerships with institutions of higher education to provide teachers and administrators at both levels with ideas and opportunities to enhance the education, performance, and evaluation of educators.**

Ambrose, T., Natale, D., Murphey, C., & Schumacher, D. (1999). Professional development school partnerships: Reflections and perspectives. *Peabody Journal of Education, 74*(3/4), 289–299.

Balach, C. A., & Szymanski, G. J. (2003). The growth of a professional learning community through collaborative action research. American Educational Research Association Annual Meeting, April 21–25, 2003.

Mebane, D. J., & Galassi, J. P. (2000, May-June). Responses to first-year participants in a middle school professional development school partnership. *Journal of Educational Research, 93*(5), 287–293.

Passman, R. (2002–04). Going public: Middle-level teachers build a learning community through reflective discussions. American Educational Research Association Annual Meeting, April 1–5, 2002.

8. **Schools will develop political and financial relationships with individuals, organizations, and businesses to support and supplement educational programs and policies.**

Clearinghouse on Educational Management. (2002). *Corporate involvement in school reform.* Eugene, OR: Author.

Council for Corporate and School Partnerships. (2002). *Guiding principles for business and school partnership.* Atlanta, GA: Author.

Council for Corporate and School Partnerships. (2004). *How-to guide for school-business partnerships.* Atlanta, GA: Author.

Cunningham. C. (April 2002). Engaging the community to support student achievement. *ERIC Digest.* Eugene, OR: Educational Resources Information Center (ERIC) Clearinghouse on Educational Management.

Hindman, J. L., Brown, W. M., & Rogers, C. S. (2005, April). Beyond the school: Getting community members involved. *Principal Leadership, 5*(8), 36–39.

Marazza, L. L. (2003). *The 5 essentials of organizational excellence: Maximizing schoolwide student achievement and performance.* Thousand Oaks, CA: Corwin Press.

9. **At least once every five years, each school will convene a broadly based external review panel to develop and deliver a public description of the school, a requirement that could be met in conjunction with the evaluations of state, regional, and other accrediting groups.**

Clinard, J., & Foster, L. (1998). Leadership in a fishbowl: A new accreditation process. *Educational Leadership, 55*(7), 53–56.

Council for Higher Education Accreditation. (2002). The fundamentals of accreditation: What do you need to know? Washington, DC: Author.

Mid-Continent Regional Educational Lab. (1998). *Current school and district accreditation procedures in the McREL region: A potential support of curriculum reform.* Aurora, CO: Author.

Sinisi, R. V. & Bellamy, G. T. (1997, Winter). Balancing school quality assurances: A three-legged stool. *NCA Quarterly, 71*(3), 435–439.

Personalization and the School Environment

10. Schools will create small units in which anonymity is banished.

Beck, M., & Malley, J. (1998, Fall). A pedagogy of belonging. *Reclaiming Children and Youth: Journal of Emotional and Behavioral Problems, 7*(3), 133–137.

McAndrews, T., & Anderson, W. (January 2002). *Schools within schools.* (ERIC Document Reproduction Service No. ED461915). ERIC Digest.

Blum, R. W. (2005, April). A case for school connectedness. *Educational Leadership, 62*(7), 6–19.

Chaney, J. L., & DeGennaro, A. (2005, November). Where everybody knows your name. *Principal Leadership, 6*(3), 22–26.

Oxley, D. (2005, November). Small learning communities: Extending and improving practice. *Principal Leadership, 6*(3), 44–48.

11. Each teacher involved in the instructional program on a full-time basis will be responsible for contact time with no more than 90 students, so that the teacher can give greater attention to the needs of every student.

Cole, R. (2001). *More strategies for educating everybody's children.* Alexandria, VA: ASCD.

Hoffman, D., & Levak, B. A. (2003, September). Personalizing schools. *Educational Leadership, 61*(1), 30–43.

Jenkins, J. M., & Keefe, J. W. (2002, February). Two schools: Two approaches to personalized learning. *Phi Delta Kappan, 83*(6), 449–456.

Keefe, J. W., & Jenkins, J. M. (2002, February). Personalized instruction. *Phi Delta Kappan, 83*(6), 440–448.

Krajewski, B., Bonthuis, D., Kluznik, C., & Miller, N. (1997, April). Personalizing student learning through better use of organization and time: Continuing the Minnesota tradition. *NASSP Bulletin, 81*(588), 28–37.

12. Each student will have a Personal Plan for Progress (PPP) that will be reviewed often to ensure that the school takes individual needs into consideration and to allow students, within reasonable parameters, to design their own methods for learning in an effort to meet high standards.

Faas, L. A., Lindsay, D., & Webb, L. D. (1997). *Personal Plans for Progress for secondary school students.* Reston, VA: NASSP.

Hackmann, D. G., & Valentine, J. W. (1998). *Promoting student involvement in the learning process: Three successful strategies.* Reston, VA: NASSP.

Osofsky, D., Sinner, G, & Wolk, D. (2003). *Changing systems to personalize learning: Discover the power of advisories.* Providence, RI: The Education Alliance/LAB at Brown University.

13. Each student will have a Personal Adult Advocate to help him or her personalize the educational experience.

Burkhardt, R. M. (1999, January). Advisory: Advocacy for every student; This we believe and now we must act. *Middle School Journal, 30*(3), 51–54.

Pope, N., Metha, A., & Webb, L. D. (1997). *The Personal Adult Advocate Program.* Reston, VA: NASSP.

14. Teachers and administrators will convey a sense of caring so that students know that teachers have a stake in student learning.

Alder, N. (2002, March). Interpretations of the meaning of care: Creating caring relationships in urban middle school classrooms. *Urban Education, 37*(2), 241–266.

Brown, K. M. (2004, January). Loving the middle level. *Principal Leadership, 4*(5), 30–36.

Hertzog, J. P. (1992, Fall). Middle level advisory programs: From the ground up. *Schools in the Middle, 2*(1), 23.

Jenkins, J. M. (1992). *Advisement programs: A new look at an old practice.* Reston, VA: NASSP.

Jenlink, P. M., & Kinnucan-Welsch, K. (1999, October). Learning ways of caring, learning ways of knowing through communities of professional development. *Journal for a Just and Caring Education, 5*(4), 367–385.

Noddings. N. (2005, June). Identifying and responding to needs in education. *Cambridge Journal of Education, 35*(2), 147–159.

15. Each school will develop flexible scheduling and student grouping patterns to meet the individual needs of students and to ensure academic success.

Caldwell, J. S., & Ford, M. P. (2002). *Where have all the bluebirds gone? How to soar with flexible grouping.* Portsmouth, NH: Heinemann.

Denney, B. (2002). *Master schedule design for middle level schools.* Blufton, IN: Middle School Consulting, Inc.

Kasak, D. (1998, May). Flexible organizational structures: This we believe and now we must act. *Middle School Journal, 29*(5), 56–59.

Mills, R. (1998, June). Grouping students for instruction in middle schools. *ERIC Digest.* Champaign, IL: ERIC Clearinghouse on Elementary and Early Childhood Education.

Nolan, F. (1998, May). Ability grouping plus heterogeneous grouping: Win-win schedules. *Middle School Journal, 29*(5), 14–19.

Tomlinson, C. A. (1995). *How to differentiate instruction in mixed-ability classrooms.* Alexandria, VA: ASCD.

Williamson, R. D. (1998). *Scheduling middle level schools: Tools for improved student achievement.* Reston, VA: NASSP.

16. The school will engage students' families as partners in the students' education.

Black. S. (2005, October). Rethinking parent conferences. *American School Board Journal, 192*(10), 46–48.

Constantino, S. M. (2002). *Making your school family friendly.* Reston, VA: NASSP.

Dominguez, C. (2003, December). Involving parents, motivating students. *Principal Leadership, 4*(4), 43–46.

Epstein, J. L., & Salinas, K. C. (2004, May). Partnering with families and communities. *Educational Leadership, 61*(8), 12–18.

Henderson, A., Jacob, B., Kerman-Schloss, A., & Raimondo, B. (2004, January). *The case for parent leadership.* Lexington, KY: Prichard Committee for Academic Excellence.

Kinney, P. (2005, October). Letting students take the lead. *Principal Leadership, 6*(2), 33–36.

Kyle, D. W., McIntyre, E., Miller, K. B., & Moore, G. H. (2002). *Reaching out: A K-8 resource for connecting families and schools.* Corwin Press, Thousand Oaks, CA.

NASSP. (2003). *Bridge builders: Establishing effective school-community relationships.* Reston, VA: Author.

Whitaker, T., & Fiore, D. J. (2001). *Dealing with difficult parents (and with parents in difficult situations).* Larchmont, NY: Eye on Education.

17. The school community, which cannot be values-neutral, will advocate and model a set of core values essential in a democratic and civil society.

Ferrero, D. J. (2005, February). Does "research-based" mean "value-neutral"? *Phi Delta Kappan, 86*(6) 424–432.

Ferrero, D. J. (2005, February). Pathways to reform: Start with values. *Educational Leadership, 62* (5) 8–14.

Soder, R., Goodlad, J. I., & McMannon, T. J. (2001). *Developing democratic character in the young.* Hoboken, NJ: Jossey-Bass.

18. Schools, in conjunction with agencies in the community, will help coordinate the delivery of physical and mental health as well as social services.

Blank, M., Mealaville, A., & Shah, B. (2003). *Making the difference: Research and practice in community schools.* Washington, DC: Coalition for Community Schools, Institute for Educational Leadership.

Colgan, C. (2003, December). Inviting the outside in. *Principal Leadership, 4*(4), 26–31.

Dryfoos, J. G., Quinn, J., & Barkin, C. (2005). *Community schools in action: Lessons from a decade of practice.* New York: Oxford University Press.

Dryfoos, J., & Maquire, S. (2002). *Inside full-service community schools.* Thousand Oaks, CA: Corwin Press.

Curriculum, Instruction, and Assessment

19. Each school will identify a set of essential learnings—in literature and language, writing, mathematics, social studies, science, and the arts—in which students must demonstrate achievement in order to advance to the next level.

Camblin, S. J. (2003–04). *The middle grades: Putting all students on track for college.* Honolulu: Pacific Resources for Education and Learning (PREL).

Grotzer, T. A. (2004, October). Putting everyday science within reach. *Principal Leadership, 5*(2), 17–21.

Joftus, S. (2002). *Every child a graduate: A framework for excellent education for all middle and high school students.* Washington, DC: Alliance for Excellent Education.

NASSP. (2005). *Creating a culture of literacy: A guide for middle and high school principals.* Reston, VA: Author.

National Research Council. (2002). *Learning and understanding: Improving advanced study of mathematics and science in U.S. high schools.* Washington, DC: National Academy Press.

Phillips, M. (2004, October). A community of writers. *Principal Leadership, 5*(2), 33–37.

Seeley, C. (2004, October). 21st century mathematics. *Principal Leadership, 5*(2), 22–26.

U.S. Department of Education. (1997). *Getting ready for college early: A handbook for parents of students in the middle and junior high school years.* Washington, DC: Author.

Westerberg, T., & Webb, L. D. (1997). *Providing focus and direction through essential learnings.* Reston, VA: NASSP.

20. Each school will present alternatives to tracking and ability grouping.

Burnett, G. (1995). Alternatives to ability grouping: Still unanswered questions. (ERIC Document Reproduction Service No. ED390947). ERIC/CUE Digest.

Burris, C. C., & Welner, K. G. (2005, April). Closing the achievement gap by detracking. *Phi Delta Kappan, 86*(8), 594–598.

DiMartino, J., & Miles, S. (2004, December). Equity in the classroom. *Principal Leadership, 5*(4), 44–48.

Mills, R., & Irvin, J. L. (1998, May). Tracking students: A "punctuated event" for young adolescents: What research says. *Middle School Journal, 29*(5), 71–73.

Wheelock, A., & Lynn, L. (1997, January/February). Making detracking work. *The Harvard Education Letter, 8*(1), 1–10.

21. **The school will reorganize the traditional department structure and foster the use of teacher teams provided with ample common planning time to integrate the school's curriculum to the extent possible and emphasize depth over breadth of coverage.**

Flowers, N., Mertens, S. B., & Mulhall, P. F. (2000, March). What makes inter-disciplinary teams effective? Research on middle school renewal. *Middle School Journal, 31*(4), 53–56.

Shank, M. J. (2005, May). Common space, common time, common work. *Educational Leadership, 62*(8), 16–19.

Warren, L. L., & Muth, K. D. (1995, Summer). The impact of common planning time on middle grades students and teachers. *Research in Middle Level Education Quarterly, 18*(3), 41–58.

Warren, L. L., & Payne, B. D. (1997, May/June). Impact of middle grades' organization on teacher efficacy and environmental perceptions. *Journal of Educational Research, 90*(5), 301–308.

22. **The content of the curriculum, where practical, will connect to real-life applications of knowledge and skills, and will extend beyond the school campus to help students link their education to the future and to the community.**

Bottoms, G., & Webb, D. L. (1998). *Connecting the curriculum to "real life."* Reston, VA: NASSP.

Conley, D. T. (2005, September). College knowledge: Getting in is only half the battle. *Principal Leadership, 6*(1), 17–21.

Gordon, R. (1998, January). Balancing real-world problems with real-world results. *Phi Delta Kappan, 79*(5), 390–393.

Southern Regional Education Board. (2002). *Opening doors to the future: Preparing low-achieving middle grades students to succeed in high school.* Atlanta, GA: Author.

Stein, M., Robinson, S., Haycock, K., Vitale, D., & Schmeiser, C. (2005, September). College prep 101. *Principal Leadership, 6*(1), 22–26.

23. **The school will promote service programs and student activities as integral to an education, providing opportunities for all students that support and extend academic learning.**

Battistoni, R. (2004, September). Student-powered solutions. *Principal Leadership, 5*(1), 23–26.

Berman, S. H. (2004, September). Teaching civics: A call to action. *Principal Leadership, 5*(1), 16–20.

Blaustein, A. I. (2003). *Making a difference: Your guide to volunteering and community service.* Hoboken, NJ: Jossey-Bass.

Bohnenberger, J. E., & Terry, A. W. (2002, September). Community problem solving works for middle level students. *Middle School Journal, 34*(1), 5–12.

Wren, D. J. (2004, September). Reaching out, reaching in. *Principal Leadership, 5*(1), 28–33.

24. **Teachers will design high-quality work and teach in ways that engage students, cause them to persist, and, when the work is successfully completed, result in student satisfaction and acquisition of knowledge, critical-thinking and problem-solving skills, and other abilities.**

Anderson, L. H., & Midgley, C. (1998). Motivation and middle school students. (ERIC Document Reproduction Service No. ED421281). ERIC Digest.

Intrator, S. M. (2004, September). The engaged classroom. *Educational Leadership, 62*(1), 20–24.

Meece, J. L. (2003, Spring). Applying learner-centered principles to middle school education. *Theory into Practice, 42*(2), 109–116.

Tomlinson, C. A., & Doubet, K. (2005, April). Reach them to teach them. *Educational Leadership, 62*(7), 8–15.

25. **Teachers will know and be able to use a variety of strategies and settings that identify and accommodate individual learning needs and engage students.**

Benjamin, A. (2002). *Differentiated instruction: A guide for middle and high school teachers.* Larchmont, NY: Eye on Education.

Cooke, G. (2000). *Alternatives to grade retention.* Reston, VA: NASSP

Gregory, G. H., & Chapman, C. (2002). *Differentiated instructional strategies: One size doesn't fit all.* Thousand Oaks, CA: Corwin Press.

Melton, L., & Pickett, W. (1997). *Using multiple intelligences in middle school reading* Fastback 411. Bloomington, IN: Phi Delta Kappa.

Morrison, G. R., Ross, S. M., & Kemp, J .E. (2004). *Designing effective instruction* (4th ed.). Indianapolis, IN: Jossey-Bass.

Smutny, J. F. (2003). *Differentiated instruction.* Fastback. Bloomington, IN: Phi Delta Kappa.

Tomlinson, C. A. (1999). *The differentiated classroom: Responding to the needs of all learners.* Alexandria, VA: ASCD.

26. **Each teacher will have a broad base of academic knowledge, with depth in at least one subject area.**

Goldhaber, D., & Anthony, E. (2003). Indicators of teacher quality. (ERIC Document Reproduction Service No. ED478408). ERIC Digest.

Kaplan, L. S., & Owings, W. A. (2002). *Enhancing teaching quality.* Fastback 499. Bloomington, IN: Phi Delta Kappa International.

Kaplan, L. S., & Owings, W. A. (2002, December). The politics of teacher quality: Implications for principals. *NASSP Bulletin, 86*(633), 22–41.

Noddings, N. (1998, Fall). Teacher and subject matter knowledge. *Teacher Education Quarterly, 25*(4), 86–89.

Rotherham, A. J., & Mead, S. (2003, June). Teacher quality: Beyond No Child Left Behind. A response to Kaplan and Owings. *NASSP Bulletin, 86*(635), 65–76.

Suh, T., & Fore, R. (2002). The National Council on Teacher Quality: Expanding the teacher quality discussion. (ERIC Document Reproduction Service No. ED477730).ERIC Digest.

27. Teachers will be adept at acting as coaches and facilitators to promote more active involvement of students in their own learning.

Bartholomew, S. K., Melendez-Delaney, G., Orta, A., & White, S. (2005, May). Untapped resources: Assistant principals as instructional leaders. *Principal Leadership, 5*(9), 22–26.

Makibbin, S. S., & Sprague, M. M. (1997, February). The instructional coach: New role in instructional improvement. *NASSP Bulletin, 81*(586), 94–100.

Guiney, E. (2001, June). Coaching isn't just for athletes: The role of teacher leaders. *Phi Delta Kappan, 82*(10), 740–743.

Roberts, T., & Trainor, A. (2004, March). Performing for yourself and others: The Paideia Coached Project. *Phi Delta Kappan, 85*(7), 513–519.

Knight, J. (2005, May). A primer on instructional coaches. *Principal Leadership, 5*(9), 16–21.

28. Teachers will integrate assessment into instruction so that assessment is accomplished using a variety of methods that do not merely measure students but become part of the learning process.

Davies, A. (2000). *Making classroom assessment work.* Courtenay, BC, Canada: Connections Publishing.

Marzano, R. (2003). *What works in schools: Translating research into action.* Alexandria, VA: ASCD.

Marzano, R., Pickering, J., & Pollock, D. (2001). *Classroom instruction that works: Research-based strategies for increasing student achievement.* Alexandria, VA: ASCD.

Stiggins, R. J., Webb, L. D., Lange, J, McGregor, S., & Cotton, S. (1997). *Multiple assessment of student progress.* Reston, VA: NASSP.

Stiggins, R., & Chappuis, S. (2005, October). Putting testing in perspective: It's for learning. *Principal Leadership, 6*(2), 16–20.

Knoll, M. K. (2002). Administrator's guide to student achievement & higher test scores. Indianapolis, IN: Jossey-Bass.

29. Recognizing that schooling is a continuum, educators must understand what is required of students at every stage and ensure a smooth transition academically and socially for each student from grade to grade and from level to level.

Hertzog, J. C., & Morgan, P. L. (1997). From middle school to high school: Ease the transition. Educational Resources Information Clearinghouse. *ERIC Digest,* (62)7.

Hertzog, J. C., & Morgan, P. L. (1998, April). Breaking the barriers between middle school and high school: Developing a transition team for student success. *NASSP Bulletin, 82*(597), 94–98.

Hertzog, J. C., & Morgan, P. L. (2001, March). Designing comprehensive transitions. *Principal Leadership, 1*(7), 10–18.

Lampert, J. (2005, April). Easing the transition to high school. *Educational Leadership, 62*(7), 61–63.

Mizelle, N. B. (2005, April). Moving out of the middle school. *Educational Leadership, 62*(7), 56–59.

Prickett, C. (2004, December). And college for all: Revisited. *Principal Leadership, 5*(4), 28–31.

30. Schools will develop a strategic plan to make technology integral to curriculum, instruction, and assessment, accommodating different learning needs and helping teachers individualize and improve the learning process.

Barnett, H. (2003). Technology professional development: Successful strategies for teacher change. (ERIC Document Reproduction Service No. ED477616). ERIC Digest.

Beaver, R., & Moore, J. (2004, September). Curriculum design and technology integration: A model to use technology in support of knowledge generation and higher order thinking skills. *Learning and Leading with Technology, 32*(1), 42–45.

Graham, C., Culatta, R., Pratt, M., & West, R. (2004, September). Redesigning the teacher education technology course to emphasize integration. *Computers in the Schools, 21*(1/2), 127–148.

Morehead, P., & LaBeau, B. (2004–05, December-January). Successful curriculum mapping: Fostering smooth technology integration. *Learning and Leading with Technology, 32*(4), 12–17.

Sanders, M. E. (1999, September). Technology education in the middle level school: Its role and purpose. *NASSP Bulletin, 83*(608), 34–44.

Tanner, B. M., Bottoms, G., Feagin, C., & Bearman, A. (2003). *Instructional strategies: How teachers teach matters.* Atlanta, GA: Southern Regional Education Board.

Waddoups, G. L., Wentworth, N., & Earle, R. (2004, September). Principles of technology integration and curriculum development: A faculty design team approach. *Computers in the Schools, 21*(1/2), 15–23.

References for the Carol Ann Tomlinson Essay on Ability Grouping

Carbonaro, W., & Gamoran, A. (2003). The production of achievement inequality in high school English. *American Educational Research Journal, 39*, 801–827.

Cone, J. (1992). Untracking advanced placement English: Creating opportunity is not enough. *Phi Delta Kappan, 74*, 712–717.

Cone, J. (1993). Learning to teach an untracked class. *College Board Review, 169*, 20–27, 31.

Educational Research Service. (1992). *Academic challenge for the children of poverty: The summary report* (ERS Item #171). Arlington, VA: Author.

Gamoran, A., Nystrand, M., Berends, M., & LePore, P. (1995). An organizational analysis of the effects of ability grouping. *American Educational Research Journal, 32*, 687–715.

Haberman, M. (1991). The pedagogy of poverty vs. good teaching. *Phi Delta Kappan, 73*, 290–294.

Hodges, H. (2001). Overcoming a pedagogy of poverty. In R. Cole (Ed.), *More strategies for educating everybody's children* (pp. 1–9). Alexandria, VA: Association for Supervision and Curriculum Development (ASCD).

Kulick, J., & Kulick, C. (1992). Meta-analytic findings on grouping programs. *Gifted Child Quarterly, 36*, 73–77.

Marx, G. (2000). *Ten trends: Educating children for a profoundly different future.* Arlington, VA: Educational Research Service.

Rogers, K. (1991). *The relationship of grouping practices to the education of the gifted and talented learners.* Storrs, CT: University of Connecticut, National Research Center on the Gifted and Talented.

Tomlinson, C. (2003). *Fulfilling the promise of the differentiated classroom: Strategies and tools for responsive teaching.* Alexandria, VA: ASCD.

Tomlinson, C. (2004). The Mobius effect: Addressing learner variance in schools. *Journal of Learning Disabilities, 37*, 516–524.

Tomlinson, C., & Allan, S. (2000). *Leadership for differentiating schools and classrooms.* Alexandria, VA: ASCD.

Tomlinson, C., Brighton, C., Hertberg, H., Callahan, C., Moon, T., Brimijoin, K., et al. (2003). Differentiating instruction in response to student readiness, interest, and learning profile in academically diverse classrooms: A review of literature. *Gifted Child Quarterly, 27*, 119–14.

References for the Ron Williamson Essay on Transition

Cooney, S., & Bottoms, G. (2002). *Middle grades to high school: Mending a weak link.* Atlanta, GA: Southern Regional Education Board.

Mizelle, N. B., & Irvin, J. L. (2000, May). What the research says: Transitions from middle school into high school. *Middle School Journal [issue number]*, 57-61.

Appendix 1:
Student Advisory Programs

Student advisory programs provide an opportunity for middle level schools to introduce an adult advocate into the life of every student in the school. Many young adolescents suffer from feelings of isolation and loneliness, and advisory activities allow them to connect with caring adults and other students to help them through the rough spots during the middle level years.

The Education Alliance at Brown University has published a comprehensive guide to creating an advisory program in secondary schools. *Changing Systems to Personalize Learning: Discover the Power of Advisories* offers five key dimensions of an effective advisory program:

KEY DIMENSION #1: Purpose. A clearly defined purpose supported by the community.

Which of the following purposes makes the most sense for your school?

- To advise students about academic decisions and monitor academic achievement
- To provide developmental guidance (both formal and informal)
- To foster communication between the home and the school and among members of the school community
- To encourage supportive peer relationships and practice conflict resolution
- To promote an awareness of diversity and tolerance
- To undertake community service both within and outside the school
- To facilitate community governance and conversations
- To prepare students for life transitions, including career exploration and considering postsecondary opportunities
- To promote character development and explore moral dilemmas
- To explore the process of group development and have fun

The following chart can be used to sort out the different types of advisory programs and the activities that might accompany them, along with some of the other organizational elements that would be necessary to achieve the purpose. It is used along with a card-sorting exercise to clarify program purpose (see *Discover the Purpose of Advisories*, pp. 85–92 for the full exercise).

A Typology of Advisory Emphases
(for use with the card-sorting exercise)

Type	Need	Time	Goals & Focus	Advisor Skills	Sample Activities
Advocacy	Affective	Substantial implementation time	Adult-student relationship	Personal qualities—interest and concern for students	Individual student conferences
Community	Affective	Substantial implementation time	Group identity	Personal qualities—group management	Group discussions, projects, intramurals
Skills	Affective and cognitive	Substantial "prep" and implementation time	Developmental guidance	Personal qualities—group management, group facilitation	Decision-making, stress management, race relations, values clarification
Invigoration	Affective	Minimal "prep" time	Relaxing, recharging	Personal qualities—enthusiasm	Intramurals and clubs, parties, informal "fun" activities
Academic	Cognitive	Substantial implementation time	Academic performance	Personal qualities—teaching	Study skills, silent reading, writing, tutoring
Administration	Administrative	Minimal "prep" and implementation time	General school business, "housekeeping"	Clerical, organizational	Announcements, distributing school materials, collecting money

KEY DIMENSION #2: Organization. Organized to fulfill the purpose and to ensure personalization.

The following are some guiding questions as you and your staff discuss how your advisory should be organized.

People and Size

- How many advisees will each advisor have?
- Which adults in the school building will serve as advisors? What characteristics should they possess?
- If some teachers do not serve as advisors, what supportive roles can they take on?
- Will any advisories be co-facilitated (e.g., first-year teacher with veteran teacher)?
- By what criteria will students be sorted into advisories (e.g., age, grade level, gender, race/ethnicity)?
- By what criteria will individual advisees be assigned to individual advisors (e.g., advise only students you teach, common interests, previous relationship, self-selection, random)?
- Will advisors and advisees be paired for one year or multiple years?
- What will be the specific roles and responsibilities of advisors and advisees?
- How will parents be involved in the advisory program?
- How will community members outside the school be involved in the advisory program?

Time and Space

- How often will advisories meet (e.g., daily, twice daily, twice weekly)?
- How long will advisory meetings last (e.g., brief check-ins, longer activity periods)?
- Will there be time for individual meetings as well as group meetings?
- How will this time fit into the master schedule?
- Where will advisories meet?
- How will advisories be able to personalize their space?
- Will each advisory have its own space?

Professional Development and Support

- How do we create regularly scheduled time for advisors to meet (e.g., time for training, curriculum development, sharing successes, having kid talk)?
- In what types of configurations can advisors meet for training and support (e.g., clusters, teams, full faculty, pairs)?
- How will we identify the types of training and support that advisors need (e.g., group process and development, how to communicate with parents, listening skills, knowing when to refer advisees to others, academic advising)?
- How will initial and ongoing training be conducted, and by whom?
- What resources do advisors need (e.g., a program coordinator, curriculum, parent volunteers, counselors, petty cash)?
- What additional support will be given to advisors who are new to advising?
- What additional support will be given to advisors who are struggling?
- How will advisors be observed and assessed?
- How will advisory responsibilities be dealt with in the master contract?
- What type of budget will be required for the program?

Student Ownership

- Will students take part in creating/overseeing the advisory program?
- How can advisories serve as a vehicle for empowering students (e.g., through school governance or student-led groups, by taking on a community responsibility)?
- How can students in upper grade advisories mentor students in lower grade advisories?

KEY DIMENSION #3: Advisory Program Content. Content should be based on the purposes to be achieved, on the nature of the school, and on individual advisors. Content may

- Be organized around essential questions, themes, or skills.
- Be consistent across advisories or vary depending on an advisor's knowledge of his or her advisees.
- Follow a common curriculum, be chosen from an advisory handbook, or be organized by advisors to personalize their own advisory experience.

It is critical to the success of your advisory program that the content you decide on aligns with the purpose you've chosen, and that you organize the program to support it.

KEY DIMENSION #4: Assessment. Assessment should be conducted at several levels:

- Individual students/advisees
- Individual advisors
- Advisory groups as a whole
- Overall advisory program
- School and program leadership

Assessments should be conducted periodically to determine whether the purposes of the program are being met and whether participants are meeting expectations. Assessments can help you to gauge the need to modify your advisory program over time to continue to meet the needs of students in an ever-changing world.

KEY DIMENSION #5: Leadership. Strong leadership by an individual or team charged with designing, implementing, overseeing, supporting, and assessing the program.

Essential leadership duties include creating buy-in among community members and ensuring that advisors have adequate training, resources, and support. Questions to be answered include these:

- Who will assume primary leadership of your advisory program?
- What specific barriers do you foresee in the planning, implementation, and maintenance of your program? How do you plan to avoid or overcome these barriers?
- What processes can be put in place to build support for your advisory program among all school community members, including consideration of the master contract? How will you ensure that consensus is achieved around the stated purposes?

NOTE: The Education Alliance publication *Changing Systems to Personalize Learning: Discover the Power of Advisories* contains materials that your school can use to create an advisory program. The publication can be downloaded at www.alliance.brown.edu/pubs/changing_systems.

Appendix 2: Differentiating Instruction in Mixed-Ability Classrooms

The following questionnaire is designed to gauge a teacher's perception of the level to which differentiation is used in his or her classroom. Simply by completing the questionnaire, a teacher will have the opportunity to reflect on classroom practices. The questionnaire could also be adapted by a principal for observation and review of the level of differentiated instruction being used in an individual classroom.

Teacher Questionnaire

Use of Practices for Differentiated Instruction in Mixed-Ability Classrooms
Read each statement below. Circle the response that most closely describes the extent to which you use this practice in your classroom. Use the following scale:

(1) not at all   (2) to some degree   (3) much of the time   (4) most of the time   (5) all the time   (6) unsure of terms or meaning of statement

1.	I pre-assess students to determine their level of understanding.	1	2	3	4	5	6
2.	I assess student interests.	1	2	3	4	5	6
3.	I identify students' learning profiles.	1	2	3	4	5	6
4.	My classroom is student centered.	1	2	3	4	5	6
5.	I consistently use flexible grouping.	1	2	3	4	5	6
6.	I vary the pace of learning for varying learner needs.	1	2	3	4	5	6
7.	I use active learning.	1	2	3	4	5	6
8.	I differentiate using major concepts and generalizations.	1	2	3	4	5	6
9.	I use a variety of materials other than the standard text.	1	2	3	4	5	6
10.	I make accommodations for the needs of various learners by using support mechanisms (e.g., reading buddies, graphic organizers, study guides).	1	2	3	4	5	6
11.	I provide activities that require students to do something with their knowledge (apply and extend major concepts and generalizations as opposed to just repeating it back).	1	2	3	4	5	6

12.	I use higher level tasks for all learners (e.g., application, elaboration, providing evidence, synthesis) to provide appropriate challenges.	1	2	3	4	5	6
13.	I use tiered activities.	1	2	3	4	5	6
14.	I use activities that involve all learners in both critical and creative thinking.	1	2	3	4	5	6
15.	I vary tasks by students' interests.	1	2	3	4	5	6
16.	I vary tasks by learner profile.	1	2	3	4	5	6
17.	I provide opportunities for student products to be based on solving real and relevant problems.	1	2	3	4	5	6
18.	I allow for a wide range of product alternatives (e.g., oral, kinesthetic, visual, musical, spatial, creative, practical).	1	2	3	4	5	6
19.	The assignments I give differ based on individual (or group) readiness, learning needs, and interests.	1	2	3	4	5	6
20.	I provide students a wide range of resources.	1	2	3	4	5	6
21.	I use compacting.	1	2	3	4	5	6
21.	I use student learning contracts.	1	2	3	4	5	6
22.	I allow for independent study.	1	2	3	4	5	6
23.	I use interest centers/groups.	1	2	3	4	5	6
24.	I use various instructional strategies to differentiate (e.g., organizers, cubing, etc.).	1	2	3	4	5	6
25.	I use high-level cooperative strategies (e.g., complex instruction, group investigation).	1	2	3	4	5	6

Adapted from Tomlinson, C. A. and Allan, S. D. (2000). Leadership for differentiating schools and classrooms. *Alexandria, VA: Association for Supervision and Curriculum Development. Reprinted by Permission. The Association for Supervision and Curriculum Development is a worldwide community of educators advocating sound policies and sharing best practices to achieve the success of each learner. To learn more, visit ASCD at www.ascd.org.*

Appendix 3:
Creating a Personal Learning Plan

Professional development is effective only to the extent that individual teachers do the following:

- Identify skills, instructional practices, and/or knowledge that they want to acquire or improve.

- Ensure that the skills, practices, and knowledge identified are consistent with the student performance goals of the school and with what is known about the specific social, psychological, physical, academic, and emotional development of middle school learners.

- Develop a plan of action that articulates how the targeted skills, practices, or content will be accessed (e.g., workshops/training sessions, professional reading, course work, collaboration with coach or mentor on individually developed activities).

- Include in the plan of action a process that allows for repeated practice of new skills.

- Build a portfolio consisting of artifacts that indicate progress toward the identified professional growth goals (e.g., agendas of workshops attended, lesson plans that include new knowledge or acquired skills, examples of student work, video or audio tapes of lessons or parts of lessons).

- Include in the plan a method for evaluating the implementation of new or improved instructional practice against the rubric of improved student performance.

A Personal Learning Plan should include answers to these questions:

- What skills and/or practices will you study and what knowledge will you work to acquire?

- How are these skills/practices aligned with the student improvement goals of our school?

- What activities will you participate in and/or what methods will you use to acquire/improve and then practice each listed skill in your classroom?

- What data will you collect to indicate progress toward each goal?

- What indicators will demonstrate that you have met your goal(s)?

Sample Personal Learning Plan

Teacher _____

_____Middle School

School Year:_____

Personal learning goal(s): Reflect on your instructional strengths and weakness. Identify one or more skills or practices you plan to improve or acquire that relate specifically to the act of improving your teaching (e.g., differentiation of instruction, student performance assessments, lesson pacing) and, by extension, the performance of your students. Consider ways that you can participate in workshops, tap into the expertise of colleagues, and/or locate relevant readings or reference materials. Identify each personal learning goal, and respond to the listed questions to complete your plan.

1. **Goal:**

A. How is this goal consistent with our school's student achievement objectives?

B. Identify activities you will participate in and/or methods you will use to acquire/improve the skill.

C. How will you build opportunities for repeated practice of the skill into your plan?

D. What methods will you use to get feedback on your performance (from other professionals and from students)?

E. What data will you collect to demonstrate your progress?

F. What indicators will demonstrate that you have achieved (or made progress toward) your goal?

Appendix 4: Breaking Ranks in the Middle Text-Based Discussion Guidelines

Purpose: The purpose of a text-based discussion is to "enlarge" understanding of the text, **not** the achievement of some particular understanding. Multiple perspectives create broader understanding and present possibilities for new insights and meaning.

Organization: Provide each participant with a copy of the text (be sure that page numbers appear on the copies) ahead of time so that all participants have time to thoroughly read the piece. Encourage them to highlight passages and jot down notes about what they're reading to share during group discussion. Very large groups should be organized into discussion groups of 8–12 participants to allow for deeper discussion than is generally possible in large groups. Each small group should appoint a recorder to capture the main points of its discussion for reporting out during a large-group debriefing session. Allow the small groups to discuss the text for a certain amount of time (for Breaking Ranks in the Middle texts, this could be 45 minutes to an hour, depending on the text). At the conclusion of small-group discussions, reconvene as a large group to discuss the points made in small groups. Use chart paper to record the major points made by each group. The facilitator/leader calls for small-group reporting in a rotation of one point per group at a time…sharing the larger understandings and remaining questions discussed by each group.

Here are several possible formats to assist faculty groups in processing the information they have read:

- **Jigsaw Reading.** Individuals are assigned different parts of a larger article or chapter and take notes or highlight important passages. Expert group members share that information with home team members so that each member of that team puts a piece of the "jigsaw" together, forming the basis of holistic understanding of a topic. Listeners may ask clarifying questions. A recorder takes notes for the group.

- **Popcorn.** Everyone reads the same passage. When reading is completed, individuals are given a prompting question (e.g., What new question or insight are you left with? What action are you considering taking after having read this text?) Participants "pop up" to share responses, sitting down as soon as they have completed their thought. Responses may be recorded on chart paper to be further processed or discussed.

- **Think-Pair-Share.** This is a cooperative learning strategy, which allows partici-pants to think about a question, idea, or issue independently, and share their thoughts with a partner before discussion in a small group. The strategy allows par-ticipants to share their thoughts in a nonthreatening situation and involves all members of a group rather than the more confident, articulate few. The opinions of all members of the group are valued. The focus is on short-term, purposeful talk.

Ground Rules:

- All comments should be based on specific quotes from the text. Use page and paragraph line numbers, and wait until everyone has found the quote. Then the speaker reads that quote out loud.

- Listen actively and ask questions. A good text-based discussion is an inquiry into meaning: What did the author mean? What does the text mean to you? What do you think the text might mean to others? What are the implications of this text for …?

- Emphasize clarification, amplification, and the implications of ideas. Ask each other questions about what you're reading. Don't be afraid to say what you don't understand in the text, or what you disagree with.

Adapted from © Thompson-Grove, G. (2001). Text-based seminar guidelines. Bloomington, IN: National School Reform Faculty. Used with permission.

Appendix 5:
J. F. Kennedy Middle School
Peer Observations

TEACHER _____DATE _____PERIOD_____

YES	NO	Classroom Environment/Classroom Control/Lesson Plan
		1. Teacher is at door as students enter the room?
		2. Students enter the room in an orderly manner?
		3. Students quickly report to their assigned seat and get materials out, ready for instruction before the tardy bell rings?
		4. Classroom routines are well-established and followed by students? (No blurting out responses, students wait to be called upon, students raise hand to respond, no talking while another student is talking or teacher is talking—respect is evident)
		5. The teacher identifies the learning objective of the lesson?
		6. All students are engaged in the lesson during direct instruction—students are focused on the teacher? There are no passive learners?
		7. The teacher assesses for student understanding before moving to independent/group work?
		8. The transition between direct instruction and independent/group work is smooth and quick, with students moving from one task to the next quickly and without socializing?
		9. The teacher walks the room during independent/group work to monitor student progress and provide assistance as needed?
		10. If students are having difficulty, the teacher stops the independent/group work and re-teaches the material?
		11. The teacher assesses student comprehension of content before the end of the lesson to determine the amount of learning that has occurred?

YES	NO	Teaching Strategies
		12. Relates the lesson to real life?
		13. Uses cooperative groupings?
		14. Summarizing and note-taking?
		15. Cues, questions, advanced organizers?
		16. Nonlinguistic representatives?
		17. Reinforcing effort?
		18. Use of praise?
		19. Compare and contrast?
		20. Providing feedback?
		21. Homework and practice?
		22. Identifying similarities/differences?
		23. Uses wait time?
		24. Uses of student error?
		25. Direct instruction?
		26. Whole-group instruction?
		27. Small-group instruction?
		28. Elicits engagement?
		29. Whole-class questions?
		30. Teacher models/demonstrates?

A. What are the students working on/doing?

_____

_____

B. What does the teacher expect them to know and be able to do by the end of this lesson?

_____

_____

C. Was this accomplished?

_____

_____

_____

Other suggestions/concerns:

_____

_____

Index

Q

R

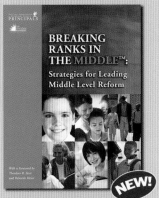